Berta

Unique in this century, Berta G............................ to hold
the posts of secretary to two of the world's greatest conductors – but
on very different sides of the cultural divide. The first was Wilhelm
Furtwängler, and the second was Sir Thomas Beecham.

Berta Geissmar came of an old Mannheim family which was
devoted to music with a passion typically German. In 1910, at the age
of eighteen, she went to read Philosophy at Heidelberg but was
eventually given her doctorate by Frankfurt. In 1921 she went with
Furtwängler as his secretary to Berlin when he was appointed conductor of the Berlin Philharmonic Orchestra, and she was ultimately given
the job of orchestra manager, a pioneering assignment for a woman in
those early years of the century. Dr Geissmar continued in this job until
1935 when, under pressure from the Nazis, she was forced to leave
Germany. But it was not long before she was able to work in a similar
capacity for Sir Thomas Beecham and the London Philharmonic. She
had a hand in the preparation of the brilliant seasons of opera at
Covent Garden given under Beecham's direction and during these
years her role in English musical life was a crucial one. With great
courage, and trepidation, she revisited Germany in connection with
the visits of the touring LPO and stayed in London at the orchestra's
right hand during the Blitz.

The narrative of *The Baton and the Jackboot* thus provides a highly
individual survey of music-making behind the scenes. Above all it
reveals how, in insidious, small ways, the Nazi dictatorship worked its
evil, contrasting it with the freer, democratic climate of Britain that
made Dr Geissmar's life a division between affection for the true spirit
of her native land and devotion to the land of her adoption.

The Lively Arts
General Editor: Robert Ottaway

Lively Arts Encore
(large format)

THE BATON
AND THE JACKBOOT

Recollections of Musical Life

*

BERTA GEISSMAR Ph.D.

FOREWORD BY
FELIX APRAHAMIAN

COLUMBUS BOOKS
LONDON

This trade paperback edition
published in Great Britain in 1988 by
Columbus Books Limited
19-23 Ludgate Hill
London, EC4M 7PD

First published in 1944 by Hamish Hamilton

British Library Cataloguing in Publication Data

Geissmar, Berta
The baton and the jackboot: recollections of
musical life.—(The Lively arts).
1. Music. Geissmar, Berta
I. Title II. Series ———
780'.92'4

ISBN 0–86287–925–6

Printed and bound by The Guernsey Press
Guernsey, CI

To
my friends
of the
London Philharmonic Orchestra

FOREWORD

Berta Geissmar's *The Baton and the Jackboot* is a unique document. Warmly welcomed when published in 1944, it provided an essential guide to the work and character of two great European conductors, but, equally, a fascinating glimpse of musical life in Germany and England in the period between the two world wars. Its remarkable author was in a privileged position, having served successively as the devoted private secretary of both Wilhelm Furtwängler and Thomas Beecham. The power she wielded as a musical *éminence grise* was considerable. When she completed her book in the spring of 1943, at the home of Sir Thomas Beecham's son and heir, her future was uncertain; she could not foresee that her work for Beecham would not be allowed to continue, for circumstances divided her from him, just as they divided him from the LPO which he had founded in 1932. But her own work was not yet over. This may be the place to record and commemorate it. As the Felix mentioned in the later chapters of this book, I shared an LPO office with Dr Geissmar, from the beginning of 1940 until I left the orchestra's employ in 1946. Correctly, as later events proved, she foretold that I would get on well with Sir Thomas. But that was in the future.

When, following a great Sibelius concert at the Queen's Hall on 4 April 1940, Sir Thomas at last left England to fulfil contractual obligations in Australia and America, the LPO, as her book describes, was already in control of its own destiny. So was Dr Geissmar. Without salary, she had attached herself to the orchestra, serving it with the same devotion that she had previously lavished on its conductor.

Alas, when Sir Thomas returned to England in 1944, there was a sad clash of loyalties. No absent king was ever treated with greater deference or respect than Beecham returning to his LPO. Thanks to the administrative genius of Thomas Russell, the orchestra had survived the war and its founder's absence. It had its own offices, house-journal and Arts Club. And, lest it be suggested that it had lost a few eminent players, one can recall some concerts of those days that were among its greatest.

The clash was not entirely due to Beecham's autocratic views about a self-governing orchestra, although he might have been rightly baffled as to how a mere viola-player could have set up so permanent an orchestral foundation – it still survives – something he himself had not previously achieved. Having, long before the days of CEMA, Arts Councils, state, civic and municipal subventions, spent his own fortune, and as much of his family's and friends' as he could, in providing England with its finest musical manifestations, Sir Thomas's actuarial mind saw clearly that his own future lay in the field of recordings. To that end, he found it necessary to create yet another orchestra, the destiny of which he could control himself, without reference to orchestral players.

When Beecham formed the RPO, Geissmar was shattered, for her loyalties were divided. There was an added difficulty. Sir Thomas had returned from America with a new consort. Lady Betty Humby Beecham was tolerant of me, as a relatively new boy; but, although relations were initially cordial, Geissmar, representing an *ancien régime*, became suspect. That and her fidelity to the LPO deprived her of access to Sir Thomas. For years she had been compiling a book of Beecham stories, signed by the contributor, and counter-signed by the victim, if there was one. (I remember Malcolm Sargent gladly signed all those relating to him.) But it was a wasted effort, for Sir Thomas barred Geissmar from publishing them, and she would not part with them. So, with renewed zeal, she bravely turned to providing the abandoned LPO with worthy visiting conductors, among them Victor de Sabata.

One of my last official LPO duties was going to Victoria Station with her and Adolph Borsdorf to welcome him to London. At his first rehearsal, he played right through *Le Carnaval Romain* without interruption; the only time I have witnessed an orchestra give a conductor a standing ovation after a run-through. Then he began to rehearse. Where Beecham beguiled, de Sabata, looking, according to one player, 'like a cross between Julius Caesar and Satan', terrified the orchestra. But they played for him like gods. Dr Geissmar had called a Roland for an Oliver. On Sunday afternoon, 21 April 1946, Toscanini's no less legendary successor at La Scala conducted his first public concert with the LPO at the Stoll Theatre. Lady Cunard and I were guests in her box. It was not until 15 September 1946 that Sir Thomas Beecham launched his new Royal Philharmonic Orchestra at the Davis Theatre, Croydon.

The previous month, knowing that I would be attending the Lucerne Festival, Dr Geissmar had armed me with letters of introduction to Richard Strauss and Wilhelm Furtwängler, still exiled in Switzerland, to Frau Beerli, the custodian of the Villa Triebschen, and to others. Berta was nothing if not thorough; and unswerving in, her loyalty to those whom she took under her wing. As Thomas Russell wrote in a footnote added to her obituary in *The Times* (7 November 1949): 'Dr Geissmar devoted the last ten years of her life to the undivided support of the London Philharmonic Orchestra. She attended the office every day until her final illness, took all LPO troubles and difficulties deeply to heart, and turned her affection and critical acumen upon its members. She was rewarded by the friendly response of the musicians, especially of those who had worked closely with her during the darkest days of the war.'

It was Berta Geissmar who, by putting me in touch with Tony Mayer, a *chargé de mission* at the French Embassy during the war years, was indirectly responsible for the series of more than a hundred Wigmore Hall *concerts de musique française* which I was able to organize for him, initially from the office of the LPO. They continued until well after the Liberation of Paris, and I have a happy recollection of a bravely cheerful Berta in her element at a dinner party given for Charles Münch at the Savoy Hotel, in June 1947, by the French *Conseiller Culturel*, when the guests also included Irène Joachim, Elizabeth Poston, Adrian Boult, William Walton, Petro Petrides, Eric Walter White, Edward Lockspeiser, William Montagu-Pollock and, of course, the Tony Mayers.

But, all too soon, a cruel stroke laid Berta low. It left her tearful and emotional when visitors reminded her of happier days. She knew that, exactly as she had predicted, I was seeing Beecham from time to time. Without my referring to her collection of Beecham stories, she volunteered: 'They are safely put away where Sir Thomas cannot reach them. I know that if I were to leave them to you, you are so devoted to him that he would persuade you to let him have them.' I protested that I would have been happy to carry out her wishes to the letter, but was happier not to have the responsibility. Sir Thomas was always firmly but quite wrongly convinced that I had them. It would appear that Berta had the last laugh.

Felix Aprahamian

PREFACE

This book, although touching on the musical life of seventy years ago, deals mainly with the last thirty years. Music, as every other part of cultural life, is, to a certain extent, connected with the social and economic conditions of the time. But never before the age of the dictators has it been seized and exploited for purposes of the 'Absolute State', in which Art has ceased to be independent.

Nothing is described in this book that has not actually happened. We see the problems arise out of the circumstances of the epoch, and we see the figures move according to their disposition and character. I would like the reader to look at them from this point of view and to read the book for what it is meant to be: an honest record of part of a period where tradition, evolution and freedom fought their battle against dictatorship; of music in Germany, fettered to Hitler's huge machine, and music in England, neglected perhaps, but free.

I owe a debt of gratitude to Sir Thomas Beecham who, though absent while this book was being written, has facilitated my work in every respect by kindly consenting to the publishing of papers and documents relating to his activities.

I welcome this opportunity of expressing my thanks to Mrs Tilly Barnett and Miss Elizabeth Needham for their help with my book in its early stages, to Mr Edwin Le Fèvre for his careful collaboration over a long period, and to Mr Alan Collingridge for much friendly advice.

I am also indebted to Mr Felix Aprahamian who, together with other members of the London Philharmonic Orchestra and its staff, gave information and enthusiastic assistance. My thanks are also due to many former members of the Covent Garden staff who have come forward with their personal reminiscences.

Last, but not least, my special thanks are due to Mrs Mona Andrade for her experienced guidance. Without her invaluable help I could not have achieved this book.

B.G.

The author in her office at the Royal Opera House,
Covent Garden.   (1938.)

(*Photo : Everard*)

Prelude

TOWNS OF character bequeath a sort of dowry to their children. My native town was Mannheim, and ever since the middle of the eighteenth century, when the art-loving Elector Karl Theodor reigned, it has tended to give to its descendants a love of music and of drama.

The great tradition of the town persisted through the years. The young Goethe admired its collections of art and literature; for Mozart, his visit to Mannheim meant a milestone in his artistic development. Charles Burney, Dr. Johnson's friend, wrote in 1773 in praise of Mannheim's Electoral band: ". . . indeed, there are more solo players and good composers in this, than perhaps any other orchestra in Europe; it is an army of generals, equally fit to plan a battle, as to fight it". Lessing very nearly became director of the theatre, and Richard Wagner's early career was influenced by his Mannheim friend, Emil Heckel, one of the first Wagner enthusiasts.

My mother came of one of the old patriarchal families which made its home in Mannheim about two hundred years ago. My father was a well-known lawyer, as was my paternal grandfather, whose junior partner he was. He was a brilliant speaker and had a large practice, but once at home no word of business was ever mentioned. He was extremely musical, and played the violin and viola in no amateur fashion. Once a week, during the whole of his life, his regular quartet assembled and played in our house. From early childhood I sat and listened, and so I got to know most chamber-music by heart.

In those days there were innumerable concert-societies all over Germany, nearly all run and supported by music loving amateurs, many of whom were far beyond the amateur standard. My father, with his enthusiasm for chamber-music, had also founded a concert-society. He, with some others, had guaranteed the money for giving four concerts during every winter, at which famous quartets played. All the business of running these concerts was done from

7

his office. Concert days of " our " Concert-Society were always very exciting. The artists, if they did not all stay with us, usually rehearsed in our house. There was no greater happiness imaginable for me than when I sat with my father at these concerts, following his score with him, while he pointed out to me what he loved, and told me how things ought to sound. After the concert, artists and friends foregathered with us. To be brought up in this way is a thing for which I can never be grateful enough ; it gives one for life that which makes one strong in oneself, a kind of armour against all mishap, something which no circumstances can ever take from one.

Many famous musicians and conductors stayed in our house during my youth, for the life of the family was inextricably bound up with music ; thus I learnt from childhood to love and respect the works of the great masters.

At the time when Brahms' compositions, especially his chamber-music works, became more widely known, Mannheim had its big Brahms community ; my family knew him personally. Whenever there was a new work of his performed in the neighbourhood, the Mannheimers flocked to hear it. Once my mother was taken to Karlsruhe for the first performance in that district of Brahms' Third Symphony, conducted by Felix Mottl, which had been first heard in December 1883, when it was conducted by Hans Richter in Vienna. Mottl is known to have been a champion of Wagner, a Bayreuth man, which in those days meant that he was a sworn enemy to Brahms. To us, who admire Wagner and Brahms impartially, the following incident appears almost incredible, but my mother vouches for its truth. After the concert Mottl burst into the artists' room, quite out of breath, exclaiming : " Thank God, we have made short work of that ! " (" *Gott sei Dank, die haben wir durchfallen lassen !* ") By falsifying Brahms' tempi he had spoilt the effect of the composition.

Brahms himself was not a good interpreter of his works. He played his concerto in B flat major in the historic *Rokokosaal* of the Mannheim theatre and his clumsy fingers often hit the wrong notes. However, the concert left a deep impression on the audience.

My family, although from the beginning ardent Brahms supporters, were at the same time not opposed to Wagner, and when my mother was seventeen, she was taken to Bayreuth, in those days a long and tiring journey. Bayreuth in 1889 was very different from the Bayreuth which I later knew. In those days, Hans Richter, Felix Mottl, and Herman Levi were the conductors. Mottl conducted *Tristan* with Alvary and Rosa Sucher, Richter conducted *Meistersinger*, and Levi conducted *Parsifal* with the incomparable van Dyck in the title rôle and with Amalie Materna and Therese Malten alternating as Kundry. People from all over the world, royalties and musicians, came to Bayreuth, and congregated after the performances in the restaurant, acclaiming the singers as they entered.

My father was such a passionate music lover that he even kept a violin in his office and played there at odd moments. He was also a connoisseur of string instruments, and his judgement was so respected that people came to consult him from all over Germany and even from abroad. His large correspondence about instruments was very interesting, and I myself was so involved in it that I gained a considerable knowledge of this subject. He always had a floating population of instruments in the house, and never failed to retain sufficient to make a quartet. In 1900 he realised the dream of the collectors' ideal : the " Vieuxtemps Stradivarius " was offered to him. My father consulted Joachim on this masterpiece of Antonio Stradivarius. He, of course, knew the famous instrument and sent him a post card saying : " *Diese Antonio ist nicht von Pappe* ". (" This Antonio is not a cardboard saint.") This was decisive, and father bought the " Vieuxtemps ". Several years later the Joachim Quartet played in Mannheim. Joachim asked to see the Strad, but remarked critically that there was some rosin under the bridge. My father started to clean it off with a silk handkerchief, but Joachim stopped him by saying : " I never do that, I spit on it ; that is the best method to preserve the varnish ", and in future we cleaned our instruments in the way advised by the great violinist.

Stradivarius made this violin in the year 1710, which is considered his best period. It is still in a fine state of preservation, having always been in careful hands. It is noted for its golden-orange colour which most Strads of this period share, and which reminds one of the golden hue of Rembrandt's best period. The instrument is known

9

as "The Vieuxtemps" because it had been owned by the famous virtuoso. The late Alfred Hill in London, the world-renowned connoisseur, told me, that, in his eyes, it ranks amongst the most handsome Stradivarius that exist.

From that time the collecting zeal of my father abated. The violin was the delight of his life, and he hardly ever parted from it. After his death we kept the instrument—it would have been the last thing with which my mother and I would have parted, in spite of all the tempting offers that were made to us. When I had to leave Hitler-Germany under circumstances to be described later, I tucked my Strad under my arm—export of such instruments being not yet forbidden. The Strad was the symbol to me of all I had loved and had to leave behind. I took it to London, and Messrs. Hill kept it for me while I was in America early in 1936. When I returned to England I had it with me for some time (it was occasionally played by the London Philharmonic leader in some concerts under Sir Thomas Beecham, who greatly admired its silvery tone, especially for Mozart), but since the war it has again been in the care of Messrs. Hill, who removed it from the danger zone during the "Blitz" to one mysterious place after another. "Don't you worry," said Mr. Hill, the venerable head of this famous Bond Street firm, "your fiddle is in the most illustrious company." He then told me of some other instruments removed to safety with my "Vieuxtemps", the names of which would make the heart of every violin lover beat more quickly were I allowed to disclose them. One strange coincidence I must, however, mention. For a certain time the "Vieuxtemps Strad" was sheltered with the "Vieuxtemps Guarnerius", the violin which Vieuxtemps used alternately with his Stradivarius.

There was a very perfect companionship between my father and myself. From him I have inherited my love of philosophy. He would perhaps have preferred me, as I grew up, to stick to music alone, and was not really in favour of a University career for me. However, in 1910 I went to Heidelberg to study philosophy; I was just eighteen then.

I was the only woman at the University taking philosophy as a principal subject. Heidelberg in those days was the most wonderful place for a young and ardent student. It was full of great scholars. My father, always concerned lest I should neglect my violin, carefully selected my courses, and I concentrated at first on Greek philosophy. My teacher, the famous Wilhelm Windelband, then already an old man, was greatly venerated. The celebrated scholars teaching at that time seemed almost god-like to the students ; we sat at their feet with that rapt feeling of discipleship which is so inspiring, and which remains a most beautiful memory in later years. Besides philosophy I studied psychology, the history of art, and archæology. I made lifelong friends, and have always remained deeply attached to the romantic old university town.

In the middle of my studies, I was sent to England. My parents wanted to avoid my becoming over-studious, as I seemed to concentrate too much on reading philosophy and on all concerned with it, and had no interest for the outside world whatever. So I was sent off to England from May to October 1911. I stayed as a paying-guest in a family in Harrow and from there explored the world. I adored England from the first ; that visit gave me something which has remained with me all my life. A German is never so free and unselfconscious as an Englishman. I was always shy and easily embarrassed, but much of this I lost in England. I learnt then what it means really to live in a free country. I went frequently to London and visited its museums ; I waited in the pit queues of the theatres ; I saw all the Shakespeare I could—and I especially remember a performance of *Henry VIII* at His Majesty's Theatre with Beerbohm Tree sweeping the stage pompously as Cardinal Wolsey. For the first time in my life I saw a ballet, and what a wonderful ballet it was ! It was the Pavlova Season at the Palace Theatre, that famous season during which Pavlova was dropped by her partner Mordkin in Glazunof's *Bachanale*, and slapped his face. Many, many years later, a member of the London Philharmonic Orchestra told me that this performance had been a climax of jealousies, as women had gone absolutely mad about Mordkin, and called for him after every number, to the irritation of Pavlova. When I sat there, thrilled by this new world, how could I have known that it was my future chief who was to be largely responsible for making London ballet-conscious by later bringing the Russian Ballet to England !

For the next three years my time was divided between my work at the University, and music ; but when war broke out in 1914 life was quickly put on a war basis. My mother was soon in charge of the feeding arrangements of one of the Military Hospitals, and I did my share of war work at the Emergency Hospital at the Heinrich Lanz Works, where I once nearly got into trouble by smuggling beer in for my Bavarian soldiers—huge men not content with what was accorded to them, and in whose enormous boots I used to hide the bottles.

Many of my university colleagues were called up at once. Many I never saw again. A small group remained, and though I could not go to Heidelberg much, I attended a course in philosophy held by Wilhelm Windelband in his private house. We were only eight in number, and in the first winter he read with us Kant's *Prolegomena*, and in the second winter his *Critique of Pure Reason*.

The last war was in no sense a total war, and during those four years cultural and artistic life was kept up in Germany. The authorities saw to it that those really indispensable for the maintenance of cultural life, of opera, drama, and concerts, were exempt from whole-time war work. One enjoyed, perhaps more than in normal times, seeing a good play or hearing an opera. People met frequently in a simple way ; more than ever did we play chambermusic at home. Although the news was sometimes good, sometimes bad, life was always stimulating.

When Bodanzky was appointed to the New York Metropolitan Opera after the first year of the war, the question of his successor as *Hofkapellmeister* in Mannheim was a serious one. A choice following the great musical tradition of the town was not easy, the less so as the war imposed limits. All questions concerning the Mannheim Theatre and Orchestra were dealt with by the so-called *Theater Commission*. A few candidates were selected, and a small committee, accompanied by Bodanzky, went to Lübeck to hear one of them. The young conductor was barely twenty-eight years of age. He conducted *Fidelio*—and while he himself was convinced that his performance had been far from what was expected from the future Mannheimer *Hofkapellmeister*, who was to be in charge of the whole opera and the traditional concerts, he had already been unanimously chosen. The *Theater Commission* had recognised his genius. He was Wilhelm Furtwängler.

Furtwängler took up his appointment in Mannheim in September 1915, as first conductor of the Opera and of the *Musikalische Akademien*, the concerts which had been in existence since 1779. The Mannheim public was in the habit of looking on its *Hofkapellmeister* as a kind of demi-god : he was general property, and all he said and did was the talk of the day. This was rather awkward for the young man, who was of an over-sensitive timidity, and therefore hid himself at first behind the broad back of Oskar Grohé, the intimate friend of the famous Lieder-composer Hugo Wolf, who, as a member of the *Theater Commission*, was well able to look after the newcomer.

Furtwängler's first performance was *Freischütz*, which he conducted in the presence of his predecessor, who sat with my mother in the centre box of the theatre. This first performance gave promise of what was to come, and his first concert, with Brahms' First Symphony, gave to the Mannheimers the satisfactory feeling that in spite of his youth the new man in charge of their musical life was well able to carry on the fame of their old tradition.

One afternoon our bell rang, and my mother called down to the maid, "I am not in". It was too late : a very tall young man in an enormous black hat and a *Loden* cape stood in the hall—it was Furtwängler. This was, however, not his first visit to my parents' house. His grandmother had lived in Mannheim, and our two families had known each other for many years. As a little boy, he used to spend his holidays with his grandmother. Even at an early age he had begun to compose, and my mother tells me that when he was a boy of fifteen my father and his friends played his first quartet. The parts were hardly readable, and he, with his head of golden curls, went from one music stand to the other to explain what he meant. Now the youth returned as a man, and the old friendship was renewed. My father took him under his wing, and soon he was at home with us, and found a sympathetic hearing for all the problems of his new life.

Furtwängler was tall, slim, and fair. The most arresting features of his fine artist's head were the high and noble forehead, and the

eyes. His were the eyes of a visionary, large, blue and expressive :
they were usually veiled and half closed when he conducted or played
the piano, but they were capable of widening and emitting a
tremendous vitality when he entered into an argument or a conversation which interested him, and they could grow tender and radiant
when he was in a softened and happy mood.

His character was an involved one. He had a logical and persistent mind, direct and forceful : at the same time he was shy to
the point of extreme sensitiveness. This latter characteristic was
more apparent in his youth : it seemed sometimes that he was only
completely at ease with his enormous dog "Lord", which followed
him everywhere, even occupying his room at the theatre during
rehearsals, with the result that nobody else could ever get in.

He was not then, nor did he ever become, an *homme du monde* ;
but he brought to bear on life not only his musical genius but much
other mental equipment. He had been carefully brought up by
parents both of whom came from scholarly and musical families.
From them he inherited, among other things, his love of beauty and
his appreciation of art. His mother was a gifted painter, who painted
charming portraits of her four children ; his father, the well-known
archæologist, Adolf Furtwängler, was a great authority on Greek
vases and coins, and was the Director of the Munich *Glyptothek* and
Professor at the Munich University, where he was adored almost
as much by his students as by his children, of whom Wilhelm
Furtwängler was the eldest. The journeys father and son took
together to Greece and Italy during Furtwängler's youth opened his
eyes to the world of ancient Greece and Rome, and to the Renaissance,
which meant so much to him during his whole life. Later on, when
we toured the world, his first excursion in any town was to its
museum. On our first visit to London we went to look at the Elgin
Marbles and the unique collection of Greek vases in the British
Museum, which represented for him the world in which he had
grown up.

One of his favourite pastimes derives from this love of art, and
he used to indulge in it as a relaxation from his strenuous and busy
life. A miscellanea of photographs of famous paintings would be
spread over a table ; one person was sent out of the room, and all
the reproductions were covered up except for some small piece of

detail. The victim would then be called upon to identify the work from the small portion of it which could still be seen. Furtwängler himself never went wrong : his uncanny knowledge in this respect was amazing.

Furtwängler's father was one of the first Germans to go in for ski-ing, and he took his sons when they were boys on tours in the Bavarian Alps. Furtwängler became so good at the sport as to attain almost professional skill, and he still tries to take a winter holiday where he can ski. Almost every sport appealed to him : he loved tennis, sailing, and swimming : the family's country house was on the beautiful Tegernsee, which was a paradise for children. He was a good horseman, but too dramatic a driver when he acquired a car. His passion for passing everything on the road occasionally landed him in serious trouble. Hardly had he obtained his driver's licence and a wonderful Daimler-Benz, when he offered to drive Richard Strauss to the Adlon Hotel, where he was staying. It was after a rehearsal at the State Opera, and the two famous musicians drove through the Linden in deep conversation, and ran straight into a brand new white car and entirely smashed it. Furtwängler and Strauss were unhurt, and got off with shock—but got into considerable trouble all the same.

His love of sport, and the training he received from his father has stood Furtwängler in good stead all his life. Without being in any way a faddist he is careful of his health, and no day is too busy to interrupt his routine of two walks a day and an " air-bath " before he goes to bed. It is probably to this that he owes the fact that he has hardly ever had a cold.

He maintains this same discipline over food. He is practically a vegetarian, never smokes and never drinks : before a concert his meal is always especially light—a couple of eggs, a little fruit, or some biscuits perhaps, though during the intervals of long operas, like *Götterdämmerung* he eats sandwiches, nuts, and fruit, and drinks quantities of fruit juice.

This, then, was the young man who came into my mother's hall in his long cape, and around whom my life was to centre for so many years : the genius compounded of intellectual directness and an almost excessive shyness : whose timidity made him efface himself in any gathering, but who had so great an attraction for women that, if they did not fall victim to his musical genius, were fascinated by his personality. It used to be said that there was something of the Parsifal about him, with his limpid blue gaze, and his voice that could be so caressing that the most ordinary sentence could sound like a passionate declaration of love.

Yet there never was anybody, not even the most beloved woman, who could ever deflect Furtwängler from his work. His music always came first with him. When he was going to be married he wrote to me—whom he knew as fully acknowledging this fact—a letter in which he expressed his anxiety as to whether his future wife, whom he dearly loved, would understand this.

In his work Furtwängler was a curious mixture of artistic instinct and intuition, and deliberating intellect ; these two main qualities can be traced all through his development, until they achieved a balance in his more mature years. He was always so obsessed by, and intent on his music that everything else was pushed into the background. Even when he was conductor of the Berlin Phil-harmonic he used to rush on to the platform for his rehearsal, raising his baton aloft, as if he could hardly wait to begin. I well remember how the famous Orchestra resented this at first, and came to me, complaining that he never even said "Good morning". When I cautiously tried to explain this to him he was completely taken by surprise and thrown into consternation ; but from that moment he always began his rehearsals with a friendly word.

This little incident, trivial in itself, is symbolic of the ever-varying and inexhaustible problem : the relation between conductor and orchestra. From the very beginning Furtwängler had the respect of the orchestras he conducted ; there could never be any doubt about his sincere and earnest musicianship ; but until the ideal stage of things was reached, until he knew his job not only musically but also psychologically, there were many phases in his relationship to orchestras which are perhaps typical for *any* conductor's relation to his orchestra, even if his authority is not supported by world-wide fame.

While Furtwängler was in the making he was often handicapped by conflicts between technique and vision. With his relentless self-criticism he was perfectly aware of his shortcomings, and tried to overcome them. During this phase he conducted in a restless and unbalanced way, and was not easy for the orchestra to follow. One thing, however, was all right from the beginning : the expressive and directing movements of his wonderful hands, which seemed to paint the music on an unseen screen or form it out of an unseen piece of clay. But apart from this, he gesticulated in all directions, shook his head constantly, walked about on his rostrum, made faces when something went wrong, stamped, sang, shouted, and even spat (so that a joke came into being that the first desks must be armed with umbrellas). Thus, occasional difficulties arose with the players, who complained that they could not understand his indications ; this worried him deeply.

However, he gradually mastered the situation. He realised that he had two different things to watch : his own technique and his relationship with the orchestra as an understanding medium and friend. He fully appreciated that there is nothing more delicate and sensitive, but at the same time nothing more relentless and clear-sighted than an orchestra, and that its handling requires the greatest skill, subtlety, human kindness—and an undisputed authority. In the course of time all these problems were solved. His orchestras worshipped him, though he often asked the impossible, and hardly ever praised them, hardly ever said a word of thanks ; but his players got to know that a nod given half in a trance during the performance was a greater acknowledgment from him than any spoken word of praise.

Furtwängler was an excellent pianist ; he had a velvety touch for which he was envied by many professionals, and to hear him play one of the great Beethoven sonatas, the "Moonlight", or the *Hammerklavier Sonata,* was a great experience. Even on the piano he had the gift of calling the music to life in a monumental and yet plastic way. He knew the whole repertoire of piano and chamber-music, and it was through him I got to know the true inwardness of the late Beethoven quartets, which he used to play in a wonderful way—at one and the same time volcanic and lucid. Never will I forget how he demonstrated to me for the first time the Choral Symphony—from beginning to end—giving me the true spirit and inner meaning of it.

When Furtwängler came to Mannheim in 1915 I was a young student. It was no wonder that I was fascinated by his personality,

17

that his music was a revelation, and that his sincerity and modesty made him sympathetic to me. I was so impressed by his wide knowledge on all subjects that it took me a long time to bridge the gulf which my respect for him created. This constraint was not due to Furtwängler himself. He was always simple and natural.

One day, however, this shyness of mine was overcome. We had met by chance at a party at a Heidelberg professor's house, and went home together. It was early summer, and when we came to the ancient bridge near the Neckar, facing the castle ruin, there sat a little shrivelled old woman selling the first cherries. Furtwängler bought a bagful, and said : " Now let's see who can spit the stones out farthest ". So we stood there spitting our stones into the Neckar ; it was great fun, and this playful moment sealed our lifelong friendship. As a matter of fact, I learned afterwards that spitting competitions were in great favour with the whole Furtwängler family, and that father and sons were all addicts. Furtwängler considered himself a champion, and for the sake of our future friendship it was perhaps just as well that he won that day on the Neckar bridge where we stood eating those early summer cherries as we leant on the parapet.

Furtwängler was at home in university circles, and when in the summer months I lived in Heidelberg he often came from Mannheim for a walk along the Neckar or on the Königstuhl, or we spent the evening with one of the professors, the *Geist von Heidelberg* as they were called. There was Ludwig Curtius, the fine archæologist and great scholar, who had been assistant to the elder Furtwängler, and had been tutor to the younger ; there were the philosophers, Rickert and Jaspers, the famous economist, Max Weber, and Friedrich Gundolf, the young romantic friend of the poet, Stefan George.

Soon we shared many interests. When Furtwängler came to dine with my parents, he usually came an hour earlier than the time fixed, and came up to my sitting-room. There we talked about my studies, about music, and about books. He began to tell me about his own work and troubles, and soon I was on the way to becoming a kind of confidential secretary.

In Mannheim, the Theatre became for me the centre of attraction. In the box which my family had occupied since the time of my greatgrandparents, I heard all the operas for the first time. I went to

Furtwängler's rehearsals whenever possible, and life, already rich, was enhanced by his friendship and our mutual interests.

Yet it was a grave time, and in spite of our full life the war weighed heavily on us. My private life was also shadowed : my father began to show signs of a serious illness, from which he was not to recover. He died in July 1918, before the tide of war had turned against Germany. My parents had been very happily married ; my own relations with my father had been closer than those of a daughter. My mother and I felt that life was over for us, and we retired to the seclusion of the Black Forest.

Furtwängler was on holiday when my father died. I knew he was my friend, but, of course, it seemed to me that all his interest was focused around the person of my father, and I did not know whether, with my father's death, our relationship might change. But one day he wrote to me ; he was back in Mannheim and wanted to discuss various things with me. Could I not come ? I went. We met in our house—our house, which seemed dead, and deprived of its real spirit. On that evening, Furtwängler put me on my feet. " I know," he said, " that you will face anything in life, and be brave." His confidence inspired me with courage, which I had entirely lost. He himself was preoccupied with many problems, and drew me closer into his life by discussing them with me. I felt that I was needed, and this emotion became the mainspring of my life.

Soon another problem was to arise. My father had been the soul of his own Concert Society ; who could take his place ? It was proposed that I should succeed him on the committee. I hesitated, naturally : in those days fewer women served on committees, but it was again Furtwängler who encouraged me. He declared that I was the only possible successor to my father, little guessing that the knowledge and experience that I was to gain from this would one day be to his own advantage.

Meanwhile the fateful month of November 1918 had come, and with it the Armistice. The relief was so tremendous that few realised the implications of the peace conditions.

When Furtwängler came to Mannheim there was no doubt that he was unusually talented, but he still lacked experience, and he himself realised this. Yet every single performance he gave was

19

already outstanding, and so it was no wonder that more and more invitations from other towns were extended to him. However, in contrast to so many other gifted young conductors I have known, he remained aloof from all these temptations; he had the self-control to wait, and was determined to continue to work towards the ripening of his own musical experience for as long as possible. However, during the two last years of his Mannheim contract, he found it difficult to adhere to this determination.

The first year after the war all rail travel was very complicated, and it seemed that Willem Mengelberg, then in charge of the Frankfurt Museum Concerts, in addition to his traditional *Concertgebouw* Concerts, would not be able to keep up his work in Frankfurt. Nothing could be more natural than that Furtwängler should be asked to combine the Frankfurt concerts with his work in Mannheim. However, although he occasionally went there as a guest conductor, he considered that his work in Mannheim excluded him from assuming further permanent responsibilities.

A similar decision with regard to Vienna was a far more difficult one. As an entirely unknown conductor he had gone there for a concert with the *Wiener Symphonie Orchester* in December 1918. The day after this concert, at which he performed Brahms' Third Symphony, the Viennese press and public acclaimed him as the greatest and most interesting conductor of the younger generation. From that moment, Vienna sought him whenever possible, the first invitation being for a cycle of concerts with the *Symphonie Orchester*— the so-called *Tonkünstlercyclus*, which he accepted from 1919 onwards. He, for his part, was fascinated by Vienna; he felt thrilled by the understanding of Vienna's musical public; he made friends who had known Bruckner, Brahms, and Mahler; he basked in the atmosphere of tradition and sympathy. With iron self-control, however, he kept to his decision of sticking to the Mannheim work as the necessary basis of preparation for his future activities. He went from time to time to Vienna, but the few visits he permitted himself seemed to become more and more difficult, and he wrote to me resignedly, during an unexpected breakdown on one of these journeys, that he was afraid he would not be able to keep them up.

Meanwhile, his career went its meteoric way. He had given some concerts in Berlin, and, like the Viennese, the Berliners took to him. When in 1920 Richard Strauss left the Berlin State Opera Concerts, Furtwängler was invited to conduct, as a possible successor. In the interval of the first rehearsal he was unanimously elected by the Orchestra, and appointed for the coming season (1920-21). Nothing stood in the way, his Mannheim contract expiring in June 1920, and the Berlin contract starting in October.

While Furtwängler was having his triumphant success with the Berlin *Staatskapelle* I submitted my thesis in philosophy : " Art and Science as Concepts of the Universe ". Rickert, successor of Windelband, the Dean of the Faculty of Philosophy at Heidelberg, with whom I was on very good terms, had known on what I was working, but as is the custom in philosophical work I had never discussed with him what I was writing, and had worked quite on my own. He rejected my thesis as being too independent, and proposed that I should re-edit it under his supervision for another year. I felt utterly defeated. I felt as if I would never be able to complete my Ph.D., so many obstacles always arose, and I sat on the banks of the Neckar and had a good cry.

However, I found my courage again and also a way out of my difficulties. In Germany there were many schools of philosophy, and therefore it was quite possible that what did not suit one philosopher might be quite welcome to another. I therefore went to Frankfurt, where my thesis was accepted, and I got my degree. This move to Frankfurt had another advantage as well. Furtwängler had decided to accept the Directorship of the Frankfurt Museum Concerts, besides the State Opera Concerts, and travelled regularly between Berlin, Frankfurt, and Vienna, where he had meanwhile also agreed to do some conducting. When he came to Frankfurt, which he did at regular intervals, we had always a great deal to discuss, and it was an advantage that I should be living in one of the towns in which he worked. I shared his general work as much as possible, and in January 1921 he wrote to me asking that I should consider coming to Berlin, the centre of Germany's musical life, and for Furtwängler the most exciting place of all. I went.

The political situation was perhaps desperate, but the town was full of life. Old friends were kind, and I quickly made new ones. I attended many concerts, and, of course, all the *Staatsoper* Concerts. These concerts, given on Thursdays, were, like the concerts of the

Vienna Philharmonic—purely the concern of the orchestra, which was the Opera Orchestra as well. This series had been in charge of noted conductors, the last of whom up to then had been Muck, Weingartner, and from 1908–20, Richard Strauss. In spite of the fact that there was hardly ever a seat to be had, I was lucky enough to get into one of the boxes above the orchestra where the famous Berlin painter, Max Liebermann, was regularly to be found making innumerable sketches of the orchestra and its conductor.

Yes, Berlin was exciting. There was a flood of concerts, to which everybody came, and there was an enormous competition between the various conductors, each concert being a new battle for maintaining a reputation. The political depression of the nation was said to be grave, but it is a significant fact, when one considers the cultural situation of pre-Hitler Germany, that whatever the *material* misery may have been, there was a free intellectual and spiritual life.

When one looks back on Germany's musical life in those years, one is amazed at how much went on in spite of the adverse times. In the spring of 1921 there was the first *Brahmsfest* after the Great War. It was held in Wiesbaden. These Brahms Festivals had been arranged by the *Deutsche Brahms Gesellschaft* since 1909. They had their own special community, which always assembled for these occasions, a community of real music lovers from all parts of Germany and from abroad. It was considered a great privilege for the artists to be invited to participate, and these occasions had become a traditional feature of German musical life. I remember at Wiesbaden in 1921 and at Hamburg in 1922 meeting old friends of the "Schumann-Brahms Kreis", Professor Julius Röntgen, born in 1855, and Fräulein Engelmann, both from Holland. Also Eugenie Schumann, born in 1851, daughter of Robert and Clara, and the nonagenarian Alwin von Beckerath, who had been an intimate friend of Brahms.

But the Brahms Festivals were not the only Music Festivals held after the Great War, for there were the famous *Schlesische Musikfeste*, there were the Handel Festivals, and there were the festivals of small groups of the I.S.C.M. (International Society of Contemporary Music). Somehow they all managed to get financial support from admirers and from the towns where they were held, and the festival spirit was always such as to make everybody temporarily forget that the outside world existed.

In the summer of 1921 my mother and I went to the Engadine again for the first time since the Great War. My parents and grandparents had gone there every summer. There they had met regularly the same group of friends, for many well-known people went to the Engadine to enjoy the clear air and the wonderful sun ; among them, in my mother's day and during the time of the Brahms controversy, Simrock, the famous Brahms publisher, and Hanslick, his great supporter and the enemy of Wagner—made immortal by Wagner as Beckmesser in the *Meistersinger*.

Furtwängler joined us this year. For once he gave himself a holiday of three weeks without work. We made many trips together, and he fell under the spell of the beautiful landscape. He was a marvellous mountaineer, trained to it from childhood by his father. He loved Nature, and soon knew every summit of the panorama ; he, with his long legs, liked to climb the mountains without making use of the better-known paths. We frequently took our food with us and spent the day on some mountain top. Often we made real climbs through snow and ice. A kind of ritual was observed on these occasions. We climbed in silence, almost grimly, till we had reached our objective—then we relaxed. Furtwängler threw off his coat and breathed deeply in the crystalline air, and here, sitting in solitude and peace, with the chain of snow-peaked mountains and glaciers facing us, much of our future work was discussed and planned. Many holidays from that time on were spent in the Engadine.

A few years later, in 1924, Furtwängler bought his own house there, situated on a lovely and lonely spot between St. Moritz and Pontresina. The house had every comfort. It had been a painter's chalet, and the studio made a wonderful music room. Later, Furtwängler's wife, with her Scandinavian hospitality, never counted the heads of those who sat down to meals, nor did she care how many slept, tucked away somehow in that house. Furtwängler was usually invisible and "not to be disturbed" while working, but at meals he always sat at the head of his table.

In the autumn of 1921, I made my move to Berlin. I looked after

Furtwängler and worked for the Artists' League. This was a kind of league for the protection of artist's interests, run on an honorary basis, which had been formed by the musicians themselves. Legal advice was given, and a concert department was attached which took less than the professional agency fee. This work gave me much valuable experience.

Furtwängler became more and more popular in Vienna during this time, and after a performance of the Brahms *Requiem*, which he conducted there, he was appointed in 1921 a Director of the *Gesellschaft der Musikfreunde* which had been founded in 1812. He travelled a lot, but in those days I did not always accompany him ; I sat in Berlin and held the fort.

During that winter, 1921–22, it was definitely necessary to hold the fort. There was a boom in musical life and a first-rate phalanx of conductors : Busch, Furtwängler, Klemperer, Strauss, Bruno Walter, Weingartner, and others. I went to every possible concert and reported daily to Furtwängler when he was absent.

Furtwängler, as I have said, was then director of the Berlin *Staatskapelle*, which was a magnificent orchestra and could look back on a splendid tradition. Yet an Opera House is not always suitable for concert purposes, and although Furtwängler highly appreciated the orchestra, he was often depressed after a concert because he had been unable to realise his artistic intentions ; the acoustics in the Opera House, with the orchestra sitting on the stage, damped the sound of a big heroic symphony. He considered this fact in the choice of his programmes but once could not resist including one of the big Bruckner symphonies. The performance left him unsatisfied, and I remember walking with him down the Linden afterwards and listening with helpless sympathy while he poured out his despair over the impossibility of achieving what he wanted.

While Furtwängler began to worry about the problem of the *Staatskapelle* Concerts, things moved unexpectedly to an exciting climax. On January 9, 1922, Arthur Nikisch conducted a Berlin Philharmonic Concert for the last time. He had been permanent conductor of these Concerts since 1895, and of the Hamburg Concerts with the Berlin Philharmonic since 1897. Since 1895 he had been in charge of the Leipzig *Gewandhaus* as well. On January 23, Max Fiedler conducted instead of Nikisch, who was ill with 'flu. At the

General Rehearsal on February 5, Nikisch was still advertised on the programme, but on February 6th Wilhelm Furtwängler conducted the concert : *In Memoriam Arthur Nikisch*. A great artist had passed away.

The Leipzig *Gewandhaus* was immediately offered to Furtwängler. It was alleged that this had been Nikisch's last wish ; the decision about the Berlin post was not taken immediately. Furtwängler fully realised that this was the opportunity of his life, and that only if, in addition to the Gewandhaus, he could obtain the direction of the Berlin Philharmonic Concerts with their acoustically perfect hall, could he live up to his artistic ideals.

Shortly afterwards, in spite of several competing conductors of rank, the Berlin Philharmonic Orchestra unanimously voted for Furtwängler, and thus he became successor to Nikisch in Leipzig and Berlin. His talent, the instinct of the Berlin Philharmonic Orchestra, and a kindly Fate, had made his dream come true.

Furtwängler was then thirty-six years old. Within a short time he had attained some of the highest musical positions that Europe had to offer.

At such a decisive turning-point in his career, it may perhaps interest the reader to know how Furtwängler works. In life, in his relation to the world, Furtwängler may seem to have a wavering and mutable attitude—but this is not so where music is concerned ; here he knows exactly what he wants. Even in the days when his name on a bill was sufficient to sell out the house at once, Furtwängler was always striving to improve his technique, and was keenly interested in that of other conductors. All his life, for instance, he has worked on his *beat*. Furtwängler's beat—as orchestras all over the world know— is an absolute nightmare to all players until they get used to it. A member of the London Philharmonic Orchestra once declared that it is " only after the thirteenth preliminary wiggle" that Furtwängler's baton descends. It has always been a riddle for the outsider how, with his particular beat, he gets results of exactitude as well as of richness in sound. He himself has never ceased to try to improve himself, and I remember him coming off the platform one evening, in some European capital, during the applause and saying to me that he had "just found out the beat" for a certain passage.

25

While he is preparing to conduct a work, he clearly and distinctly identifies himself with the piece he is going to perform : he absorbs it, and, deeply concentrated in it, he re-creates it as the composer intended. This he does again and again, even if he has performed the work a thousand times before. Nothing disturbs him while he works, that is, while he is walking up and down the room with time-beating movements and silently singing lips. He fixes the piece before his spiritual eye with intense concentration. The saying that genius is an infinite capacity for taking pains may have its limits, since all the pains in the world cannot of themselves produce a work of genius. None the less, an iron painstaking is always behind every performance that Furtwängler gives, and even in later years he has never taken advantage of his famous name to save himself trouble. He would never risk scamping the conscientious preparation of any concert, and in this may perhaps be found the clue to his artistic fascination. No unrest of the day ever touches him while he works ; nothing on earth is ever able to cause him to speed up his working time in order to be finished an hour earlier and thus to be free for something else. His whole organism is attuned to this exact conscientiousness, and he would never allow himself to be forced out of it by some exterior pressure. He needs time to live through a great masterpiece again and again in all tranquillity. Only in this way can he feel himself to be ready, and be sure of himself. When finally he arrives at a rehearsal his main work is already done, and he has only to transmit his intentions to the orchestra. When the concert begins, he seems to leave behind all earthly things : he is conscious neither of public nor of score. With half-closed eyes, he seems to mesmerise the orchestra, and owing to his deep musical feelings he re-lives the creative process of the composer, while the orchestra hang on his movements.

If the public leaves such a concert with a feeling of having lived through an extraordinary experience, it is because it has been made to feel the tension and the thrill of a truly visionary process of re-creation. Only if his vision of how a work should sound has been realised, does Furtwängler relax after the strain of the concert ; otherwise, he is nearly demented, and most difficult for those nearest to him, even if the public has acclaimed the performance with fanatical applause.

At the present time, when orchestras have to fight more than ever for their existence and their ideals, it may perhaps be of interest to survey the history of the Berlin Philharmonic Orchestra,[1] so popular everywhere in the pre-Hitler world. Since its foundation in the days of the monarchy, the Berlin Philharmonic has been a little republican island. It is the child of a spiritual revolution, a revolution in the presentation of musical masterpieces. This revolution is connected with a man with whom the history of the modern concert-life really begins : Hans von Bülow.

In January 1882 Bülow had come to Berlin with his *Meininger Hofkapelle*. He conducted in the *Sing-Akademie* Beethoven, Mendelssohn, and Brahms. At first Brahms himself played his Second Piano Concerto under Bülow's direction ; then Bülow played the First Concerto with Brahms conducting. Berlin was overwhelmed ; they did not recognise " their " Beethoven and Mendelssohn and for the first time realised the greatness of Brahms.

Twelve years after the foundation of the Reich, its young capital possessed neither a competent Symphony Orchestra nor an adequate concert hall. Among the different musical organisations, however, there had existed since 1868 the *Bilse'sche Orchester*, a collection of excellent musicians, especially of wind and strings, who gave concerts and made little tours under the worthy Benjamin Bilse, a former municipal musician from Liegnitz.

Early in 1882 there was a disagreement between the Orchestra and the patriarchal and despotic Bilse—and overnight the Orchestra of fifty-four members found that it was left to itself. Under the leadership of the second horn and a second violin, they constituted their own republic, and gave themselves their own constitution. From the beginning it was an independent creation of its own members, who held the shares of their limited company. Therefore, the conductor and new players were appointed by the popular vote of all members. By legal deed they pledged themselves to remain inviolably together. This first constitution has never been much changed, though it was enlarged in 1895.

By May 5, 1882, they played in a concert as an independent body,

[1] I am indebted to Dr. Alfred Einstein's brochure, 50 *Jahre Berliner Philharmonisches Orchester*, for much of the information about the Berlin Philharmonic's history. Though he quotes me as a source I could not have written what I have without his booklet, which he wrote on the occasion of the Orchestra's fiftieth anniversary in 1932.

and in the same summer gave concerts in Berlin and the provinces. Everywhere they had great success but little material profit. During this summer of 1882 this first self-governing orchestra in Germany got its name : The Berlin Philharmonic Orchestra.

In the same year an adequate hall was found for it. The old skating-rink, where till then roller-skating had been practised, was taken over to be devoted to music, and its name was changed to "*Philharmonie*"—the ugly, but acoustically perfect hall which is the home of the Berlin Philharmonic to this day.

The Orchestra began to give three or four popular concerts a week in its new hall. The great choirs gave concerts with them. Soloists began to engage them and eventually the great Berlin Philharmonic Concerts were started. They have always combined tradition and a progressive outlook, and were enlivened by the co-operation of famous soloists.

The first of the great Berlin Philharmonic Concerts took place on October 23, 1882. Several conductors officiated that first winter, amongst whom was Joseph Joachim.

Joseph Joachim was from the beginning the patron and friend of the Orchestra. He sent them his best pupils, and in 1883 he procured them some summer engagements, the first of which he conducted himself. He contrived their presence at official functions, and conducted six concerts of a series of twelve. When a financial crisis threatened, he found means of support given by the Mendelssohn and Siemens families. Joachim was also the first to plan the foundation of a Society of Friends of the Orchestra which would contribute to its maintenance, after both Berlin and the Reich had turned a deaf ear to the needs of the Orchestra bearing the name of the capital of the Reich. (It was exactly fifty years before the Berlin Philharmonic could count on a final settlement of the subsidy from city and state.)

The first five years of the Orchestra's activities had proved the necessity of its existence, but what it lacked was a leading personality. It was found in Hans von Bülow. Bülow, who had left Meiningen in 1882, had conducted one of the great Berlin Philharmonic Concerts once before (March 4, 1884). He had since conducted a series of concerts in Hamburg and Bremen, but this did not satisfy him. He came to the Berlin Philharmonic Orchestra and he, the first great trainer of a great orchestra whom the history of conducting knows, must be considered the real founder of the Berlin Philharmonic Orchestra, for it was he who had prepared the ground for its tradition.

Bülow was the initiator of the great age of conductors, which has now lasted for eighty years. It was through him that the technique and position of a conductor gained their importance and became independent and influential. It was only, in fact, from Bülow's day that the work of a conductor was taken seriously. He is the founder of modern orchestral culture, the first leader and master of the Orchestra.

The first of the ten Philharmonic Concerts planned under Bülow took place on October 21, 1887. By November, the idea of admitting the public to the final rehearsal was adopted. This was an important innovation, and the tradition then started has persisted to this day. In the season 1890-91 Bülow conducted the first concert for the newly-founded Pension Fund of the Orchestra. The Pension Fund concert, invariably with a classical programme, has also become a permanent institution. He conducted in all fifty-one concerts with the Berlin Philharmonic Orchestra. At the fiftieth concert, March 28, 1892, he made the famous speech after a performance of the *Eroica*, in which he dedicated the heroic symphony to Bismarck, the dismissed First Chancellor of the Reich. In his speech he called Bismarck " the Beethoven of German politics " ; the speech and the dedication were intended as a protest, Bismarck having just been given his congé by the young Kaiser.

In the winter of 1892-93, Bülow was already so ill that he could only conduct the last Philharmonic Concert of the season, at which he made a speech praising the artistry of the Orchestra. Hans Richter, Raphael Maszkowski, Felix Mottl, and Hermann Levi had conducted the previous concerts of that winter.

The winter of 1894-95 saw a memorable combination of conductors at the Philharmonic desk : Richard Strauss and Gustav Mahler, Strauss conducting the ten Berlin, Mahler the eight Hamburg concerts. But this winter could only be an interregnum. Strauss, the creative artist, could never submerge himself in the direction of an orchestra. Meanwhile, the right man was found : Arthur Nikisch.

29

There are some people who consider it wrong to identify the history of an orchestra with the history of its great conductors. My own opinion is that only the great leader-personality, combined with the artistry of his orchestra, can achieve the inspired creative performances which no orchestra, without his inspiration, can achieve alone.

There was no doubt that Arthur Nikisch was such a leader-personality, and the highlights of the enormous activity which the Orchestra now assumed were the ten Philharmonic Concerts under his direction. He was, in his art, the extreme opposite of Bülow; he gave the Orchestra, in addition to Bülow's discipline, what he himself as a conductor had to give: a great elasticity and a most sensitive adaptability. The Orchestra was increased to the number of ninety.

Until January 9, 1922—a full twenty-seven years—Nikisch uninterruptedly conducted the Berlin Philharmonic Concerts. They gave him an even greater prestige than the famous *Gewandhaus* concerts, which he conducted over the same period. He must have given about three hundred and fifty great concerts in Berlin. It would lead us too far afield to describe his programmes, the new works, and the constant succession of great soloists while he was in charge.

On January 9, 1922, Nikisch conducted the Berliners for the last time, and a new epoch began for them with their new chief, the young and idealistic Wilhelm Furtwängler.

At Furtwängler's first Philharmonic Concert in October 1922 I sat in a box with Marie von Bülow, the widow of the famous former conductor of these concerts. She had been his second wife—his first was Cosima Liszt—and the nine volumes of his letters and writings which she edited are a very interesting document of a great time in the history of music. She seemed very moved on this occasion, and said to me : " Not since Bülow's days has music been so conducted as to give me that thrill down the spine ".

The appointment of Furtwängler as the successor to Arthur Nikisch was also the turning-point in my own work. He had given up the State Opera Concerts and the direction of the Frankfurt Concerts, but he had to move about continuously between Berlin,

Leipzig, and Vienna. Each of the musical organisations of those towns had its own management, but the core of Furtwängler's whole work, the arrangement of his year's activity, the co-ordination of his concerts and programmes were worked out with me, and I found myself plunged into the most fascinating work a person of my interests could wish for. The amount of work Furtwängler had to cope with was considerable. Although it was only just after the last war, the Berlin Philharmonic and the *Gewandhaus* Concerts played an important part in European musical life. There was an endless number of soloists, composers, publishers, music agents, and other visitors from all over the world who had continually to be dealt with, and life was full to overflowing. The young successor to Nikisch was, of course, of interest to the international musical world, and so relations soon began to develop with concert institutions abroad.

The first venture of this kind was a visit to the *Concertgebouw* in Amsterdam. Connected with this first post-war engagement abroad is a story which was, in a way, decisive for my whole later career. The Berlin Philharmonic Concerts had been founded by Hermann Wolff, the director of the noted concert-agency, *Wolff und Sachs*. Wolff had not only been an impresario but also a friend of his artists and had been intimately connected with Hans von Bülow, Anton Rubinstein, and others. After his death his widow, Louise Wolff, well known to all internationally famous artists until Hitler's day, carried on the business, her daughters also working in the firm. Louise Wolff was a very capable woman and a terrific personality. She was a most popular figure in Berlin's social life, and was to be found in every salon, political or artistic. She was equally at home with *Reichspräsident* Ebert as with the Hohenzollerns, and every Embassy was open to her. There were innumerable tales of the strings she pulled, and the people with whom she had her regular telephone conversations in the early morning before she went to her office.

Yet in spite of all her cleverness she failed to see in which direction the tide was turning, and considered everything solely from the point of view of her firm, *Wolff und Sachs*. The firm and the family came first with her, and this view was gradually becoming incompatible with public interests. While an orchestra like the Berlin Philharmonic had to count on public support, it was in the long run impossible that seventy-five per cent. of the profit of the great concerts should go into the pocket of private enterprise.

Not only the Orchestra but also its new conductor had to face this situation of monopoly. Of course the Wolffs had had their say in Furtwängler's election as Nikisch's successor, but the Orchestra had cast their vote as well, and it was only natural that a young and promising musician had been chosen. Yet, in the beginning, Furtwängler was considered as a kind of private property of the Wolffs and was expected to do all his business through them. The first important outside offer however, these *Concertgebouw* Concerts, was brought to him by me in my capacity as executive of the Artists' League. Furtwängler expressed a doubt as to whether he would be free to sign the contract through the League. He had no " sole right " contract with Wolffs, but felt that it was in a way taken for granted. I, of course, objected to this. I had got the engagement, I wanted to sign it, and I declared that if things were going to be like that I did not care to work in Berlin at all. Furtwängler, probably secretly amused and possibly wishing to damp my ambitious ardour, said he was going to think it over, and next morning told me over the telephone that I was right in a way ; however, he did not sound wholly convinced. I, for my part, had also thought it over, so I said : " Please leave the matter to me and wait ".

Frau Wolff had always been extremely kind to me ; she frequently invited me to her at-homes and to her famous Sunday lunches. I telephoned to her at once, and she agreed to see me immediately. I remember that she produced the most marvellous Russian cherry brandy, an unheard-of thing in post-war Germany, sent to her by American friends. I sipped some of the lovely golden-red stuff and then went *in medias res*. " I want to ask you something, Frau Wolff," I said, and then proceeded to tell her the case as it was, but without mentioning names. " But there can be no question at all about this," she declared, " the person who made the offer must conclude the business." " That is just what I thought," I replied, and told her that the persons involved in the situation were herself, Furtwängler, and myself. At first her consternation was evident. But she was a superior woman, remarkable in many ways, and in that moment may have felt that she could not maintain her privileged policy for ever and that I represented a young generation and a new era. She put her arm round my shoulders and said : " You are a wonder ! I am going to tell Furtwängler the result of this conversation myself." This she did next day. Furtwängler never referred to the incident, but he casually instructed me to sign the *Concertgebouw* contract. Although my heart leapt, I behaved as if this was the most natural thing in the world, and from that moment until Hitler parted us, Furtwängler never used any intermediary other than myself when possible, and I was dubbed " Louise II " after Louise Wolff. It was, actually, an important step to break this monopoly, and I was instrumental at a later date in breaking the monopoly on the *Philharmonie* hall itself, which was shared by its proprietor Landecker and *Wolff und Sachs*, and excluded the Orchestra from direct transactions. However, when Hitler assumed power a new monopoly was to arise—that of the Third Reich.

On this first visit abroad, I accompanied Furtwängler, as I did on a subsequent tour in Switzerland with the *Gewandhaus* Orchestra, for which I also made the arrangments. He was to marry at the end of May, and I helped him to prepare his home. His future wife was Scandinavian and was only to arrive from Copenhagen on the day before the wedding, and so he took me along to buy the wedding rings. The salesman, naturally assuming that I was the chosen one, proceeded to try the ring on my hand, to the utter dismay of Furtwängler . . . !

I then left for Mannheim, and Furtwängler was married. Directly after the marriage, he had to attend a Congress of the *Allgemeine Deutsche Musik Verein* at Kassel. A few days later at 3 a.m. my telephone rang. It was Furtwängler, who had arrived in Mannheim from Kassel, and informed me that he was on his way to our house. He had to leave for Italy the next day to conduct there for the first time. I had always gone with him on important journeys, but this trip to Italy was a kind of honeymoon, and I certainly had not anticipated accompanying him. However, he took it for granted that I was not to break my rule on this occasion, so I had to get ready quickly. We left for Stuttgart, where we were joined by his wife.

This visit to Milan proved most interesting, and it was then that I first met Arturo Toscanini. Toscanini was then director at La Scala, and lived in Italy surrounded by the veneration and love of

the Italian people. His operatic performances were famous all over
the world, and people from everywhere, and especially musicians,
flocked to attend them. It was at La Scala that my visit to Toscanini
was arranged by his right-hand and secretary, Anita Colombo,
who herself later on became director of this famous Opera House.
While I waited for Toscanini, in Signorina Colombo's office, all
sorts of people went in and out, and I—still a greenhorn myself—
noted with envy the respect with which they talked to her and
wondered whether one day I would get as far as she.

Quick steps were heard outside, the door opened, and after
Colombo had introduced me: "La signorina, Maestro", I found
myself taken by the great Italian to the adjoining room. Nobody
who has talked to Toscanini can ever forget the extreme intensity
of expression in his strikingly handsome face. His brilliant, flashing
eyes are full of fire and temperamental intentness, of vitality mixed
with a strange obsessed wistfulness. Intent also is his way of speaking,
and he accompanies his words with quick and decisive gestures.
The conversation did not last long, and centred round musical
matters. Toscanini seemed interested to hear about the different
conductors working in Germany at the time—but he did not discuss
Furtwängler.

Toscanini's musical memory is famous : being half blind, he
conducts and rehearses independently of any score, relying entirely
on his knowledge of the piece. Apparently his memory for other
things is just as acute, because when I met him again at Bayreuth
during the great season of 1931, when he and Furtwängler both
conducted, the first thing he did was to remind me of what must
have been to him such a trivial incident as my visit to La Scala so
many years ago.

Toscanini, when not speaking Italian, generally spoke French ;
sometimes English, hardly ever German. That summer in Bayreuth
while rehearsing the orchestra, he used to convey his wishes by
gestures rather than by words, and when a passage was not yet as
he intended it to be, he used to make hypnotic movements with his
hands, accompanied by repeated exclamations of: "No ! . . .
No ! . . . No ! " The orchestra thenceforth called him "Tos-
canono."

From that time on, I have met him and his charming family on many occasions. In 1936, when I came to New York as a refugee, the first concert I heard was a Toscanini concert with the New York Philharmonic-Symphony ; I have never forgotten the kindness of Signora Toscanini when she asked me what had been happening to me. When I saw them next, he was conducting in London at the B.B.C., and I had landed at Covent Garden.

But this is jumping far ahead. These first concerts of Furtwängler in Italy formed the occasion for the initial meeting of the two conductors. During one of the innumerable rehearsals that Furtwängler, according to the Italian custom, now conducted, Toscanini who had been sitting unnoticed at the back, suddenly rushed forward and shook him warmly by the hand ; he and his family were extremely friendly to him during this whole visit. The year after, Furtwängler visited La Scala to attend some of Toscanini's own operatic productions.

During the season 1923–24, musical life in Berlin was very active, and many famous conductors could be heard. Three Opera Houses were busy all the time. During that winter, Furtwängler went to England for the first time. The English public took to him at once, and from 1924, when he first conducted for the Royal Philharmonic Society, he regularly went to England, until the growing gulf between Hitler-Germany and the rest of the world prevented him from doing so. Furtwängler had a great success in England, but Mr. Ernest Newman, the famous doyen of British musical criticism, wrote an unfavourable notice about him. The morning we left London, the First Secretary of the German Embassy, Herr Dufour-Feronce, a brother-in-law of Max Brockhaus, the noted Leipzig publisher, and chairman of the *Gewandhaus* went with us to the station and gave us a bundle of newspapers to read on the train. While Furtwängler talked to the diplomat, I glanced at the notices, and quickly and firmly sat on the *Sunday Times*. Furtwängler has always been amazingly touchy in respect of Press criticisms, and I wanted to avoid a stormy journey !

Times were difficult as far as finances were concerned, and the Berlin Philharmonic Orchestra did not know how they were going to get through that summer of 1924. " Let's try a tour," said Furtwängler, and we forthwith sent telegrams to several towns. They all accepted, and this was the beginning of the Berlin Philharmonic tours with Furtwängler. The first year we toured in Germany and in Switzerland only. Everywhere we went the Orchestra was asked to repeat its visit.

At the end of June, Furtwängler went with me to Mannheim. It had become his custom to conclude the season by combining a stay at my mother's house with some conducting in Mannheim. At the same time we used to deal with his remaining correspondence and with the scores sent to him for his approval. From there he used to proceed to his house in Switzerland. This year I was to go with him, and as we stepped out of the house to go to the station the postman handed me a letter. It was from Otto Müller, the chairman of the Berlin Philharmonic and a member since its foundation in May 1882. Müller, in his sprawling handwriting, wrote to me that the Orchestra had decided to confide the management of their tours to my " proven hands ", and hoped I would be willing to accept this task.

I cannot describe my pride on receiving this token of confidence. My activities could now be unified, as I was to work not only for Furtwängler but for the Orchestra as well. What a wonderful prelude to a holiday ! During that summer in the Engadine on our many tramps in the mountains Furtwängler and I made plans for the future, and they were all subsequently carried out.

For many years after this, there was uninterrupted activity. With our unique team we all served the cause with zest. Times were hard, but we were free to work as we liked and with whom we liked, and there were none of the darkening shadows later to be cast on the spirit by Hitlerdom. In those days orchestras had not started their extensive tours in Europe. They occasionally visited a neighbouring town, but there was no large-scale planning of tours at home or abroad. Never had I dreamed of organising anything of the sort, yet inspiration came to me and I sat down and thought it all out. It was only gradually that I developed my technique for an orchestral tour. It was like the invention of a new battle-strategy, and as the years went by I found more and more improvements which added to smooth running.

I always began work on a tour a year ahead. First I made sure which towns were to be visited. Then the sequence was planned. After that the first draft of programmes—often for thirty to fifty concerts—had to be made by Furtwängler. He could not always play what he alone wanted, because the towns had their own wishes and local taste had to be considered. The compilation of the programmes was always a very complicated task, because although an orchestra on tour has little time for rehearsing, Furtwängler disliked repeating the same items too often. I began to keep a programme book for reference in 1924. This book, my personal property, was the cause of one of my main disputes with the Nazis, who retained it after I left Germany and only returned it after I started to work for Sir Thomas Beecham.

Beside the business and musical sides of the tours many things had to be considered. The itinerary had to be planned in detail. I was hopeless at looking up trains, but Lorenz Höber, normally a viola player, and one of the executives, was a genius with a time-table. I had been the inventing and organising spirit of these tours in the beginning, but without Höber I could not have been successful. Linked to the question of trains was the transport of the instrument-and-luggage-van. The luggage of the Orchestra received the closest attention. They had well-designed instrument cases and specially constructed huge wardrobe-trunks containing the numbered dress-suits of the players. Before a concert each individual found his clothes with his instrument. There were seventy-seven cases and detailed lists of their contents were forwarded to the relevant customs authorities with an indication as to when we should pass their frontier. The instruments had often to be sent in advance at night immediately after a concert, in case they could not be coupled to the express on which the personnel travelled. The responsibility for the luggage rested upon two members of the Orchestra assisted by Franz Jastrau, the attendant. The latter, the prototype of the cockney, had a very strenuous job and made friends everywhere even if he occasionally did not understand the language.

There were fairly good halls all over the Continent, but the different size, and especially the varying acoustics, required different seating arrangements for the orchestra. It was the rule that a short " seating rehearsal " be held two hours before a concert. One of the players who had a special talent for this kind of thing undertook

37

to make a platform-plan of every hall we played in, putting on record the experience gained. Thus, when the Orchestra returned another year, the matter of the seating was quickly settled.

The billeting of the Orchestra in each town was at first also a complicated problem, but here, as usual, experience led to efficiency. For instance, snorers and non-snorers had to be well separated. It was important to get the players quickly settled when they arrived. I remember that when we came to London for the first time, the astonishment was great when the men disappeared into their hotel rooms within five minutes. The explanation of this was simple ; they had already been given the room-numbers on the boat.

But it was not I alone who did all the organising. The Orchestra themselves became very ingenious. Often they had to travel for weeks in railway carriages, and so they started to organise a *placement* to which each member had to submit. There were the smokers and the non-smokers, there were the *skat* players and there was the Rummy Club, there were the readers, and there were the talkers. They were all placed according to their various interests. Occasionally I was invited by a particular group. This I have always considered an honour equal only to that of sharing the compartment of the conductor on these long and often tiring journeys.

The organisation and building up of these tours was for me a wonderful combination of friendship and of work. I knew to what Furtwängler aspired, and I knew the Orchestra's ambitions. The relation between the Orchestra and their conductor, in whom they had absolute faith, was the basis of my own position with them. From the moment that they had confided to me the management of their tours they gave me their complete confidence. This perfect relationship between Furtwängler, the Orchestra, and myself lasted until I had to leave them all and they were forbidden to have any more to do with me—when under Hitler I became *persona non grata.*

When I first took over, the Orchestra had no offices. The three executive members divided their different duties amongst themselves, and dealt with them at their respective homes. Otto Müller, the chairman, always carried everything in his wallet, in which he fumbled as soon as a question arose. I had no office either, I had merely a bed-sitting-room and a typewriter. Soon I was given a typist on three afternoons a week, and this was the beginning of the Berlin Philharmonic Orchestra's Office.

Step by step the Orchestra organisation was built up, and one of the first milestones of its future road to power was a special agreement made between Furtwängler and the Orchestra that before taking an engagement with anybody else, they would always give him the first option on their time, while he pledged himself reciprocally. This " marriage " of Orchestra and Principal Conductor was for many years the core of the Orchestra's life, and around this they grouped their engagements under other conductors, and with soloists, and their popular concerts.

Meanwhile, there had been several invitations to Furtwängler to visit America. Tied up between Berlin, Leipzig, and Vienna, he had little time to spare, yet finally it was agreed that he should go for four weeks as a guest conductor of the New York Philharmonic Orchestra at the end of December 1924. We went on a Hamburg-Amerika liner, and nothing was left undone in Furtwängler's honour.

Germany was poor in those days, while America was flourishing. The hospitality of the Americans need not be described. From the moment we landed, and an unknown person packed us into a magnificent car to sweep us away to our hotel, until we left, and could hardly enter our cabins for presents, this first American visit was a unique experience. How interesting it was to hear the magnificent American orchestras—the Boston and Philadelphia Orchestras, as well as the New York Philharmonic ; or to sit in the Golden Horseshoe of the Metropolitan and hear the performances of that famous Opera House.

Furtwängler was conducting exclusively for the New York Philharmonic. His first appearance was one of the great successes which are milestones in an artist's life, and after it there was not a single ticket to be had for his forthcoming New York concerts. The Orchestra took to him, and so did the public. Furtwängler was immediately offered the directorship for the whole season of the following year, but on account of his European commitments he could not accept more than two months' activities in America. Many of the great international artists were in America at that time, and we saw them frequently. At the house of Frederick Steinway, the venerated chief of the famous firm, such a galaxy of musical genius and brilliance used to assemble as I have never seen elsewhere. I remember a dinner where Casals, Furtwängler, Gabrilowitsch, Landowska, Kreisler, Rachmaninoff, Stokowsky, and other famous people were present. Mr. Steinway's hock was memorable too ! Our stay in New York was exciting and strenuous but rushed past us like a dream, and on a quiet and peaceful English boat, where we were treated as " ordinary folk ", we slept our way back to Europe.

For the next two years Furtwängler worked intensely hard. There was an annual visit to America, and the Berlin Philharmonic made several successful tours on which I accompanied them.

Then in the winter of 1927 the Berlin Philharmonic went for the first time to England. This tour came about in a curious way. The Orchestra and I frequently discussed our aspirations and desires, and once I suggested : " Why don't we go to England ? " They all laughed at me, and said that I might just as well propose a visit to the moon. This was enough to stiffen my determination, and in due course I fixed up the tour. We had two concerts in London, and between them went to Manchester. The enthusiasm of the English public was enormous ; there was no feeling against the orchestra of their former enemies. Long paragraphs appeared about the wonderful Berlin Philharmonic and great interest was shown for the organization of the tour. The second London concert, in the Albert Hall, was filled to the last seat. I think that apart from the Paris success one year later, this was the greatest triumph the Orchestra has ever had, and after this they went to England every year, their English tours becoming more and more extensive, until Hitler at last created a gulf between the Berlin Philharmonic Orchestra and its London public.

It is astonishing to me even now to look back and remember how rich was the musical life in cities like Berlin and Vienna in the post-war years after 1918, and how culture flourished in Germany and Austria. While in France and England the capitals alone are the centres of all cultural and social life, in Germany towns like Dresden, Leipzig, Munich, Hamburg, Cologne, and Breslau all have their own individual life. In the musical field there were everywhere men of outstanding merit, and there was ample opportunity for all of them.

While his activities were actually centred in Berlin and Leipzig, Furtwängler had for many years been a favourite in Vienna. The romantic Viennese worshipped the passionate young conductor, and the Vienna Philharmonic Orchestra always found a way to arrange an "extraordinary Philharmonic Concert" or "Furtwängler Concert" when he came to conduct his choral concerts with the *Gesellschaft der Musikfreunde*. He had conducted the Vienna Philharmonic for the first time in 1922. It was a Brahms Concert, on the occasion of the twenty-fifth anniversary of Brahms' death. This was the beginning of a life-long artistic relationship. In Berlin and Leipzig he was the successor to Arthur Nikisch. Now Vienna, too, claimed him for the post of its first conductor. The Vienna Philharmonic knew that by offering Furtwängler the position of conductor of its concerts, founded in 1852, it fulfilled the ardent wish of the Viennese.

Furtwängler could not refuse what was the dream of every conductor on the Continent. The 1927–28 season therefore found him in charge of the Berlin Philharmonic, the Leipzig *Gewandhaus*, and the Vienna Philharmonic Orchestra, besides his other commitments.

Seen retrospectively the great success of Furtwängler in Vienna can only be appreciated if one has an idea of Vienna's musical life at that period. He had come there in 1919 at a moment when its musical life had reached a new climax. The Vienna Opera was in those days considered to be one of the most distinguished Opera Houses in Europe. After having been for years under the direction of Gustav Mahler, it was now under the joint direction of Richard Strauss and Franz Schalk. To listen to the playing of the Vienna Philharmonic, which was at the same time the Opera Orchestra, was a thrilling experience to any musician. Puccini had been moved to tears by hearing the Orchestra play on the occasion of the first *Tosca* performance in Vienna, November 20, 1907. The new great Strauss operas from *Rosenkavalier* to *Ariadne auf Naxos* had been first given as "festival performances" there during that period.

The Vienna Philharmonic, which, since Gustav Mahler had played under the batons of Nikisch, Mottl, Muck, and Schuch, had been for the last nineteen years under the direction of Felix Weingartner. Weingartner, a pupil of Liszt, who had conducted Brahms' Second

Symphony in the presence of the composer and had been kissed by
Brahms in his enthusiasm, gave to the Vienna Philharmonics that
great "everything" which only a classical conductor of his calibre
could. While having him as their permanent chief, they had played
under other conductors such as Furtwängler, Kleiber, Krauss, Mengelberg, Nikisch, Strauss, Schalk, and Bruno Walter.

No wonder that this Orchestra, with its outstanding artistry and
unique tradition, enthralled a young conductor like Furtwängler.
With enthusiasm he began his first Philharmonic Concert in the
autumn of 1927 with the *Freischütz Ouvertüre*, and he felt keenly
the historic atmosphere of the *Musikvereinssaal* where Brahms and
Bruckner had so often attended concerts in the traditional box of the
Committee.

This period, during which he occupied, besides his other commitments, two prominent positions in Vienna, was certainly a milestone
in his career, and has definitely influenced his musical development.

Furtwängler's activities in Vienna brought into being another
phase in my work with him. Of course the Vienna Philharmonic
had its own office and management; but there was a large correspondence with Furtwängler when he was in Berlin. There were
countless things to attend to, and a new world opened for me when
dealing with the famous Orchestra on his behalf.

The Rosé Quartet, consisting of prominent members of the
Orchestra, I had known in Mannheim, and they soon made a link
between me and the other players. I soon became devoted to the
chairman, the oboeist Wunderer, one of the most "Viennese"
and lovable musicians one could imagine.

Very frequently Furtwängler required me to accompany him to
Vienna, and I was always delighted to go. We usually had to leave
Berlin on the morning after a Philharmonic Concert. The train
left at 8 a.m. and was peculiar in that it had one old-fashioned
Austrian carriage containing a so-called half coupé, that is, a one-
sided compartment of three seats only. This compartment was
always coveted by Furtwängler. It was essential for him to work
on these journeys, and he had to be undisturbed. By a bureaucratic
decision this special compartment could not be reserved in advance,
and so I used to get up early in order to be on the platform when the
train drew in. I was nearly always successful in securing these seats.

Later on Furtwängler always went by aeroplane, but for years we used this train. The day of such a long journey—at that time one arrived in Vienna at 11 p.m.—was always methodically planned. First we had breakfast, then there was "silence". Furtwängler either read a new book, or studied his programme, taking advantage of the remoteness from the world for concentration. I remember that he read Spengler's *Decline of the West*, which had just been published and stirred intellectual circles, and that he learned Stravinsky's "*Sacre du Printemps*" on such a journey, while I—though a welcome guest in his compartment—was not allowed to break the spell of silence until he gave the sign. Lunch was always a happy interruption and we used to wait until we had passed the Czech frontier because the Czech diner gave such excellent fare. After lunch we relapsed again into silence until, towards evening, Furtwängler declared himself ready for talk.

The train was often late, but never too late for some enthusiastic friend who was invariably waiting for us on the station in Vienna ; and when all news had been discussed it was certainly past midnight. Departures from Vienna, on the other hand, were frequently subject to all sorts of surprises. Once we left Vienna for Paris, and I basked in the feeling of having at last got Furtwängler to myself for a bagful of work—when, at the last station at which the express stopped for many hours to come, the door opened, and with a radiant face a Viennese admirer entered, informing Furtwängler that he had decided to travel with him. For a secretary, this kind of enthusiasm is not very welcome, and I was often upset by similar demonstrations by the effusive Viennese, whom I otherwise loved dearly. The most trying experience of all I remember was that one of the Committee members of the *Gesellschaft* regularly appeared when Furtwängler was having his breakfast. Now, in Vienna Furtwängler used to breakfast in his hotel sitting-room, and took the opportunity to give me the instructions for the day for communications with Berlin and such-like matters. The telephone operator was always instructed to put no calls through ; the hall porter was always told that Furtwängler was still asleep. Nevertheless, to our surprise, Herr X entered every morning with the breakfast trolley, triumphantly and without fail. What was I to do ? I did some diligent detective work to discover how he knew when Furtwängler had his breakfast and found that by some mysterious means he got the information from the floor waiter. Needless to say I managed to get the waiter on my side !

Everybody who remembers this period will agree that Vienna had a unique magic of its own. The interest of the population in everything connected with their musical and theatrical life seems incredible to an outsider. The smallest detail of every performance was of the greatest importance to everybody, and the passion of the Viennese for everything concerned with their Opera House, their Stars, and their Orchestras cannot be described.

For many years Furtwängler went to Vienna for concerts only, but he was always on intimate terms with the *Staatsoper*, and frequently went in during the evening, if he was free, if only for an act or two.

Now Franz Schalk himself—who since Strauss' resignation in 1924 had been in sole charge of the Vienna State Opera—proposed that Furtwängler should be invited as guest-conductor. His first opera was *Rheingold*. This *Rheingold* was an outstanding performance, and was for days the sensation of the town. During a rehearsal I paid a visit to Schalk. With inscrutable face, he sat in his princely office with its unique atmosphere. Although he, the bearer of the classical tradition of Hans Richter and Gustav Mahler, had himself invited Furtwängler to conduct at the Vienna Opera, he was obviously jealous of his youthful fame, and did not appear at the rehearsals. " How are matters downstairs ? " he asked me cautiously. " Don't ask me," I replied. " I don't understand anything about it." (For once in my life I was trying to be diplomatic.) " No more do I," he answered.

But the season 1928–29 was to be the last with Franz Schalk as Director of the Vienna Opera and a new director had to be looked for. The intrigues growing out of such an occasion are indescribable, and the many official and semi-official people involved had the time of their lives. To cut a long story short—the direction of the Vienna State Opera was ultimately offered to Furtwängler. He was in Berlin at the moment. Effusive letters arrived from all his adherents, urging him to accept the offer and describing the situation, the attitude of the press, the public, the orchestra, the Ministry, the Opera personnel, and the singers. Finally he left to negotiate in Vienna. I remained in Berlin, but had promised to get into the next train and join him, should he want me. Hardly had he arrived when I received a telegram telling me to come at once. The executive of the Berlin Philharmonic, terrified that Furtwängler might accept the offer, saw me off. Arrived in Vienna I found him in the Imperial Hotel, absolutely inundated with telephone calls, confidential letters, and visitors who had " important things " to discuss with him alone, Nobody who has not been in Vienna during an Opera crisis can have the slightest idea what the Viennese can be like. I took over, to his great relief ; but I would not say that my protective energy added to my popularity in Vienna.

Perhaps the reader will find it hard to understand just why a decision of this kind should be so difficult, but for Furtwängler it *was* a difficult decision. Berlin had been the centre of his activities for so many years, he had had sole control over the magnificent Philharmonic, who were free to travel as much as he wanted them to, and he could conduct in all the Berlin Opera Houses as much as he liked. Vienna, on the other hand, had the unique fascination and charm that it has for every musician. Furtwängler was already director of the Vienna Philharmonic and was, as well, a Director of the *Wiener Gesellschaft der Musikfreunde* ; the Opera performances he had so far given had driven Vienna wild with enthusiasm. Vienna claimed him with equal rights, and laid siege to him with all available means.

The official negotiations were in the hands of Herr Schneiderhan, *Generaldirektor der Oesterreichischen Bundestheater*, who was a very skilled and sly diplomat of the old school. Furtwängler was pulled in two directions. In a way he longed to accept the position. Every artist sometimes needs a change, and what a unique opportunity this was ! On the other hand, he had grave doubts whether the Viennese post would not eat up all his energy ; in any case he cautiously decided that I was to accompany him to his first official interview.

Schneiderhan played variations on the whole scale of seduction and temptation. He even tried his best to tempt me. " You will come to our Opera House as Furtwängler's General Secretary, and you will be given Richard Strauss' former room," he told me. (All directorial offices were pompous and sumptuous and I loved the " air " of the inside of that famous Opera House.)

There had never been any question of Furtwängler giving up

the Berlin Philharmonic entirely, but there was no doubt that once Opera Director in Vienna, he would have very little time left for Berlin. Nevertheless Schneiderhan stressed that even I could easily go to Berlin for at least one week every month. More details were discussed, and finally Furtwängler and I left, having arranged that he was to decide by next morning at nine o'clock.

We spent our evening alone weighing all the pros and cons. Neither of us closed an eye that night, and every two hours Furtwängler came to another decision, each of which he fully justified. Although I myself make up my mind rather quickly, I appreciated that this was a decision that affected his whole life and understood that he had to consider the matter from all angles. When we finally set out next morning for the conference I had not the slightest idea what Furtwängler was going to say. Schneiderhan with diplomatic skill opened the conversation. Furtwängler replied, but with a kind of lethargic apathy—as if he expected that the decision would fall from the sky from some *Deus ex machina*. Suddenly Schneiderhan took Furtwängler's hand, which hung listlessly by his side and said : " I see that we are *d'accord*, so let us conclude our pact and sign the agreement ". Somehow I felt that there was something wrong. Furtwängler was so exhausted that he had no strength left at the moment, and I felt that he was being unfairly coerced. Certainly he was not ready for a decision of any kind. Like lightning I felt that I must protect him. Necessity gave me strength. I gave Schneiderhan's hands, which were holding Furtwängler's, a sharp slap—both men dropped their hands. Furtwängler immediately got to his feet and we got away. It was agreed that Furtwängler would be free to make his decision when he was back to Berlin.

One doesn't take an *Operndirektor* out of Vienna's grasp with impunity. That same evening at a concert, Dr. Dlabac, General Secretary of the *Gesellschaft der Musikfreunde*, informed me that everybody knew about my unpardonable behaviour and, as my friend, he advised me to avoid Vienna for some time to come !

Next morning we left for Berlin. The stationmaster personally conducted Furtwängler to his compartment. Was he not the future Opera chief ? The ticket controller confidentially addressed him as " Herr Director ". How tempting is this kind of intimate popularity ! Vienna seemed to have got him !

At the moment of departure Furtwängler was, in fact, quite inclined to decide in favour of Vienna. But the farther we moved away, the more the scale tipped, and when in the evening we arrived in Berlin, he knew that only under very special circumstances would he leave his work there—as it was clear that it would be out of the question to combine the work in the two towns.

Meanwhile the Berliners had not been asleep. All sorts of articles appeared in the papers, and one especially in the *Vossische Zeitung* : "*Geht Furtwängler nach Wien ?*" had the effect of a bombshell. The Berlin *Oberbürgermeister* was being attacked, Prussia and the Reich were being attacked—and it was unanimously declared that what Austria could do, Berlin should certainly be able to achieve.

This stirred things up with a vengeance. As soon as we got back, things began to move. I remember taking a most active part in all the manœuvres behind the scenes and having a telephone conversation as early as 7 A.M. with Berlin's Lord Mayor who was horrified by the idea that Berlin might lose Furtwängler during his régime. Meanwhile Schneiderhan, just as horrified at the idea that *he* might fail, arrived on the night train from Vienna in order to be on the spot.

At last things came to a head.

Furtwängler declared that if the Berlin Philharmonic Orchestra would get the necessary subsidy, promised for so long by the Prussian authorities, the Berlin municipality, and the Reich, and if he was enabled to issue the contracts of the players as was necessary for the standard of the Orchestra, he was willing to stay—otherwise he would accept the post in Vienna.

This ultimatum was accepted. Furtwängler remained in Berlin, and went to Vienna only as a guest-conductor. The Reich, Prussia, and Berlin undertook to guarantee the Orchestra's budget, and the *Reichsrundfunk* pledged itself to engage them for a certain number of broadcasts per annum, thus adding to their solvency. The guarantee required was modest, the Orchestra's income from the Berlin Philharmonic Concerts alone being considerable ; yet the feeling of security after nearly fifty years of struggle gave them a renewed zest for their work.

From that time on, the activities of each year were more or less regular. Furtwängler travelled between Berlin and Vienna, he went on tours with the Berlin Philharmonic and conducted some operas as a guest, among them the usual German Opera Season in spring in Paris. At the end of the 1927-28 season he had left the Leipzig *Gewandhaus*, as he felt that this institute needed a man who would be able to devote himself more fully to that particular task than was possible for him with all the growing demands on his time.

The next milestone in the history of the Berlin Philharmonic was their first visit to Paris in the spring of 1928. With their first London venture this Paris concert was one of the highlights of their whole career.

I had met M. Robert Brussel, the director of the *Association Française de l'Expansion et d'Echange Artistique*, the French cultural propaganda department, when in 1927 he visited the big exposition, " A Summer of Music ", at Frankfurt a/M. as representative of the French Government. With him I had arranged a visit of the Berlin Philharmonic to Paris for 1928 and he had soon afterwards invited the Orchestra to give their first Paris concert under the auspices of the *Association Française*, which was a department of the *Ministère des Affaires Étrangères et de l'Instruction Publique et des Beaux Arts*.

Nothing could have been more friendly than the French when I arrived for a preliminary talk with them about all the arrangements which had to be made. All our work was done within the Ministry at the Palais Royal, where I was able to admire the excellent apparatus of the cultural department with its very skilled staff. This was my first visit to Paris and it was an interesting task to prepare such an important concert on entirely new ground. It was then that I met the German Ambassador, von Hoesch, for the first time. He invited Furtwängler and myself to stay at his Embassy when we came to Paris for the concert. Hoesch was an ideal example of what was done by pre-Hitler Germany for an artistic enterprise. He supported us primarily because he was sincerely interested. Nothing was dictated, there was no "foreign propaganda", and there were no schemes and intrigues as there were later among the many political groups in Nazi times, all jealously controlling and watching each other, especially abroad.

We had naturally wanted this first Paris concert to take place in the *Opéra*, but M. Rouché, its director and patron, was a cautious man, and wanted to see what the Berlin Philharmonic was like before he gave us a date ; the concert had consequently to be given at the Salle Pleyel. His caution proved unnecessary, however. The enthusiasm of the French knew no limits, and M. Herriot, then *Ministre de l'Instruction Publique,* who had himself written a book on Beethoven and who loved music, was so enthusiastic that he rushed on to the platform and shook hands with Furtwängler. From that moment on there was never any difficulty when we wanted a date at the *Opéra.*

After this Paris concert I had the worst moment in all my work with Furtwängler and the Berlin Philharmonic—the worst, that is, until the advent of Hitler. Gala concerts in Paris begin at 9 p.m. in the evening, and they finish late. A big reception had been held after the concert at the Embassy. We had had only a few hours' rest, and had to leave by the morning train at eight o'clock for Strasbourg on our way to Freiburg, when the next concert was to take place. Furtwängler settled down to sleep in his reserved compartment, and I was dozing too, comfortably basking in the feeling one has after a great success, than which there is no greater tonic in life. We may have been travelling for about half an hour, when a member of the Orchestra committee came into the corridor outside our compartment, and with all the signs of despair beckoned to me to come out and speak to him. " What shall we do, Fräulein Doktor ? " the man exclaimed. " The instrument-van is not attached to the train ! " Now, I must leave to the reader's imagination what it means if an instrument-van with seventy-seven big cases, required for a concert on the same day, gets lost and separated from its owners, who have to manœuvre it across a frontier, where it was not unlikely that the officials would be less friendly than the Parisians had been. Never had such a thing occurred before. The Orchestra, thrilled and intoxicated with their success, had, of course, explored Paris night-life after the concert, and our worthy orchestra attendant, Jastrau, had not stayed at home either. He had packed his instruments into the van after the concert and then gone off and enjoyed himself, and after all who shall blame him !

There is no need to describe all we went through for the next half-hour, until we reached the next stop, from which we hoped to telegraph to Paris. At last the train drew into a station. We got out—Furtwängler still blissfully unconscious of the threatening tragedy—and while we were trying to explain our appalling dilemma to the stationmaster, a train arrived at the next platform. Attached to it was our van, which had been coupled to the wrong train. There are moments in life which one never forgets ; this was one of them !

During the first half of 1930 there was quite an unusual accumulation of touring orchestras on the Continent. The focus of interest was the New York Philharmonic which was to tour Europe under its Director, Toscanini. All the big continental towns wanted to have the Americans. As the traditional Berlin Philharmonic tour was taking place about the same time, Anita Colombo, Toscanini's former secretary, who was in charge of the American tour, and myself, had met at an early date at the Hotel Bristol in Vienna ; there we compared notes and arranged that our concerts should not clash. At the end of the tours the two orchestras met in Berlin. A reception was given for Toscanini at the Italian Embassy and a photo shows him surrounded by a number of his German confrères : Furtwängler, Kleiber, Klemperer, Walter.

During this same spring, before the tours of the Berlin and New York Philharmonic, the Vienna Philharmonic (to whom I was "graciously lent" by the Berliners to run their tour), went with Furtwängler via Germany to visit England. There was always a great Austria-loving public in London, and this visit of the Vienna Philharmonic to London had been planned for some time.

This tour showed what that famous orchestra and Furtwängler were able to achieve together. Yet he realised that to take on permanently the two Philharmonics would in the long run be unfair to both, and after careful consideration he gave up his position as Director of the Vienna Philharmonic shortly after this tour. However, he has never ceased to conduct for them as guest.

This giving up of his prominent position in Vienna marked an important point in Furtwängler's relations with Berlin. More and more did Berlin do everything to satisfy and honour the famous artist, who was by now in his forties. The Berlin Opera Houses opened their arms to him.

Work went on steadily for the next few years. The 1931 winter tour with the Berlin Philharmonic was especially successful. It was to embrace Germany, Belgium, England, and Holland, and a well-known photographer had offered to come with us.

When we left England after a happy and successful tour by the Hook of Holland train, the platform seemed unusually crowded. I said to myself : " Funny, this time the Orchestra seems to have picked up an unusual number of admirers ". (The admirers of the Orchestra were sometimes an unmitigated nuisance, especially in Paris, where almost every member used to approach me with the demand that some enigmatic female relation of his had, without fail, to be got into the concert—generally sold out long ago.)

In London it had never been quite so bad. Hence my astonishment about the crowded platform. But I was soon to be enlightened. Charlie Chaplin was in the same train and what were we in comparison to him ! Of course our photographer was excited, and at once proposed that Furtwängler and Chaplin should be photographed together getting on to the boat. I was despatched to arrange the matter with Chaplin's manager. When I got to the manager's compartment, he was by no means enthusiastic. Why should Chaplin be photographed with Furtwängler ? Who was Furtwängler, after all, in comparison with Chaplin ? Did he get four thousand love letters a day ? Did he have to employ three secretaries to deal with his fan mail ? Of course I felt quite small and insignificant in face of these overwhelming assets and retreated, beaten, from the battle-field. We went on the night-boat, and there was no sign of the great man, who, it was said, had retired to his cabin immediately on coming aboard. However, next morning, at the unearthly hour at which the boat gets in at the Hook, a message was sent that Mr. Chaplin would like to meet Dr. Furtwängler. So the two men met at dawn, and I at first could not believe that the charming and kind-looking man was the Charlie Chaplin we had seen in *The Gold Rush*. The photo was duly taken.

Chaplin left for Berlin, and we said good-bye to him, as our next destination was the Hague.

It was a time of crisis for the world and also for Germany—yet new tasks continued to arise. Siegfried Wagner had died on August 4, 1930, in the middle of the Bayreuth Festival Season. It was Toscanini's first season there. He conducted *Tristan* and the new production of the Paris version of *Tannhäuser*, with Siegfried Wagner as producer, and is said to have asked Siegfried on his death-bed for the privilege of conducting *Parsifal* the following season (1931).

After the Great War Bayreuth had had difficult times. Siegfried, assisted by his wife, Winifred, had done his utmost to carry on his father's legacy. Now the young widow was left alone to bring up her four minor children, and to bear the responsibility for the future of the *Festspielhügel*.

Bayreuth for many reasons had always been a centre of intrigue and jealousy, but it had also been a place of the highest artistic idealism and endeavour ; the greatest artists had always been proud to serve on the *Festspielhügel*.

However, after Siegfried Wagner's death, Karl Muck, the last " knight " of Richard Wagner, resigned from his co-operation with Bayreuth. Toscanini had promised to conduct in the summer of 1931, but a man with authority and knowledge who could be put in entire charge of the musical arrangements in Siegfried's place, and who was a good conductor as well, was badly needed.

In the December of 1930, Furtwängler to his utter surprise, received a letter from Frau Wagner, asking him whether Bayreuth might hope to have his services. This was no easy question for him to decide. Furtwängler had, since the Mannheim days, been known as a great Wagner conductor ; he had conducted Wagner's works in many big Opera Houses, but he had not been to Bayreuth, which was, naturally, the dream of every conductor. On the other hand, he needed rest badly, and so far had always managed to escape any summer commitments.

He took time to think the matter over, and it was all kept strictly secret. Then it was arranged that Frau Wagner should come to Berlin to discuss things with him. In order not to give vent to rumours they met at my home.

At first the real problem was not touched upon—everything was talked about but the main object—but finally they got down to brass tacks, and Furtwängler agreed to come to Bayreuth. Frau Wagner actually burst into tears of relief.

It was then arranged that for 1931 Furtwängler should take over *Tristan*, which otherwise Muck would have conducted, and that he was to be the Musical Director of the *Bayreuther Festspiele*. All musical questions were subject to his authority.

This was no small addition to his work, and for me it was another new and fascinating task. One of Furtwängler's main duties was the assembling of the *Bayreuther Festspielorchester*, which was always chosen out of orchestras from all over Germany. There was a special tradition among the players, and the old Bayreuthers knew all about every one of them. Many came year after year and considered it their greatest privilege to spend their summer holiday in playing at Bayreuth. To take one instance, the leader of the Bayreuth Orchestra, Professor Edgar Wollgandt, normally leader of the *Gewandhaus* Orchestra and Nikisch's son-in-law, could be found year after year at the first desk of the *Festspielhaus*.

The fact that Furtwängler, the great German conductor, was now in charge of Bayreuth resulted in an inundation of applications from orchestra players who wanted to join the *Festspielorchester* and there was a waiting list for every section. For the first time members of the Berlin Philharmonic applied to take part. They, of course, wanted to play opera under their own conductor. All sorts of young conductors and musicians asked for permission to attend the rehearsals. It fell mainly to me to deal with this correspondence and to report to Frau Wagner about it. Bayreuth had its inviolable tradition in this respect, and to deal with all this was a new experience for me.

During the Easter of 1931 Furtwängler had to go to Bayreuth for preliminary discussions with some of the collaborators and with Frau Wagner. He took me with him, and we stayed a few days as guests at Wahnfried, the famous Wagner home. Guests of the Wagner family were in those days usually lodged in the so-called Siegfried House—a low building tucked away in the garden, which had been Siegfried's home while Cosima Wagner was still reigning. Frau Wagner had rearranged it for her guests, and it was the most comfortable place imaginable—there were even English novels in the sitting-room.

In Wahnfried itself, Frau Wagner—in spite of the splendour surrounding her—was the most charming and hospitable hostess. One evening Cosima's daughters came to meet Furtwängler. Contessa Blandine Gravina, her second daughter by Hans von Bülow, lived for the most part in Florence ; Frau Isolde Beidler, her third daughter, had died in 1919, and so it was only her eldest daughter, Frau Daniela Thode, née von Bülow and Frau Eva Chamberlain who came to spend the evening on this occasion to inspect the new Musical Director. What this meeting meant for them, imbued as they were with a religious devotion to Wagner's and Cosima's heritage, I doubt whether the reader can fully appreciate.

I remembered Frau Thode from my first Heidelberg term when, as wife of the art-historian, Professor Henry Thode, she upheld the Wahnfried etiquette in a style that would not have been incongruous at Court. Outwardly there was little of her mother in her. She was slight and dark and her features were those of her father, Hans von Bülow. Her deep parti-coloured eyes had a fanatical expression, and fanatical she was in many ways. She was the most versatile and active of Cosima's daughters. She had had many years of close intimacy with her mother, and so possessed a minute and exact knowledge of Wagner's intentions up to the smallest details of his works; after the death of her brother, Siegfried, she was considered the last living source of the direct Wagner tradition. Never did she refer to him otherwise than as " der Meister ". Her fervent devotion to his cause and memory is one of the typical German qualities which—as long as it concerns a matter like this, and is exemplified by an exceptional person as was Frau Daniela—is only a source of strength. To what this tendency to hero worship can lead if unworthily directed we have seen in recent years.

Frau Thode was impressive in many ways; never did one forget that one was in the presence of a great lady. Like her mother, Cosima, she had regal manners, and sometimes even seemed to over-emphasise the outward forms of life. This occasionally led to the overrating of matters of secondary importance, as will be seen by the following incident. Frau Thode, while a great admirer of Furtwängler's Wagner interpretation, was much perturbed by his manner of conducting. As the reader will remember, the orchestra in Bayreuth is covered in, and the conductor cannot be seen by the audience. Furtwängler, though invisible, was conspicuous in other respects; the stamping with which he unconsciously used to accompany his conducting could be heard very distinctly. Shortly after he had begun his first season in Bayreuth Frau Thode actually came to discuss with me whether it would not be possible to put a mat under the feet of the wild man to muffle the noise, as his behaviour seemed to her incompatible with the noble tradition of the *Festspielhaus* !

But these are side issues ; in other ways she was a remarkable woman, whose deep and wide knowledge enabled her to write and edit many letters and documents connected with the Wagner family. In 1931 when Toscanini conducted *Parsifal* and *Tannhäuser* Frau Thode was in charge of the costumes, which she had designed after the beautiful illustrations of the *Manessesche Liederhandschrift*, the famous fourteenth century manuscript in the Heidelberg University Library, which is considered the most important collection of the twelfth to fourteenth century love songs (*Minnelieder*). Most of the famous illustrations are pictures of the minnesingers, Wolfram von Eschenbach among others, and these were used for the new Bayreuth production. Frau Thode also acted as producer, sitting on the stage with her notes throughout the rehearsals, thus serving the cause of Wagner, and of Toscanini, whom she worshipped.

With the advent of Hitler and the resignation of Toscanini, she retired more and more from the official life in Bayreuth, where she kept, however, a modest *pied à terre*.

It was in 1938 that I heard of her for the last time. I was shown a letter that she had written to an old and intimate friend of hers. This letter reveals what she was at the end of her life ; full of dignity and resignation, living in her memories which nobody could take from her—without bitterness, a model to all of us who are living in this chaotic age.

Her sister, Frau Eva Chamberlain, was born in 1867 ; she was the daughter of Cosima v. Bülow by Richard Wagner. She was the widow of Houston Stewart Chamberlain, whose book, *The Foundations of the 19th Century*, has had such a fatal influence on Hitler. Frau Chamberlain was tall and stately, and of a most imposing appearance ; her distinguished face bore the features of Cosima as well as those of Richard Wagner. Her reputation was that of a clever woman ; but she was rarely communicative, and on that evening when she came to meet Furtwängler, though obviously interested, she remained slightly aloof and condescending. After the death of her husband she continued to live in the old Chamberlain house, next door to Wahnfried—and yet, how far away. The wall over which she could look into her parental home and garden was in a way symbolic—it was an insurmountable wall between herself and the young generation.

Cosima's daughters have actually never bowed to the Nazi régime, which for them meant a new régime at Bayreuth in many respects—not only politically. While their brother Siegfried lived, they had more or less belonged to the reigning generation ; now they had to yield to the younger one, which went its own way, and could not always religiously adhere to the letter of the old laws.

It was this deep chasm between the two generations in the Wagner family that I felt acutely on that strange evening ; and a strange evening it was, spent in the unique atmosphere of Wahnfried, with the two old ladies, symbols of past splendour and greatness : Winifred, the young, energetic trustee and heir to it all, the mother of the coming generation, and Furtwängler, the fervent Wagner adherent, filled with holy determination to do his best and live up to his new task.

Finally all was well in hand for the summer. Frau Wagner had offered Furtwängler a romantic and secluded abode, an old farmhouse near a mill. The proprietors, the Feustel family, connected with Wahnfried for many years, were willing to move out for the summer and let Furtwängler have the house with its old-fashioned garden. A horse was put at his disposal—he was an enthusiastic rider then—and this horse was for him one of Bayreuth's greatest attractions.

It was arranged that I was to accompany him to Bayreuth and I was put up in a lovely house on the *Festspielhügel* belonging to the former *Festspielhaus-direktor*, Herr Schuler. Frau Schuler, an old friend of Cosima's, was my warm friend from the first.

The 1931 spring tour with the Berlin Philharmonic and other engagements had to be limited, as Furtwängler had to be in Bayreuth at the beginning of June.

The introduction of a new conductor at Bayreuth was always a great occasion—but Furtwängler's first appearance there was particularly sensational and most dramatic. In those days he had just began to appreciate flying, and a young airman with a private plane offered to fly him to Bayreuth. They had engine trouble and had to make a forced landing half-way. The machine turned over—and Furtwängler, always athletic, prepared coolly for the crash by doing a handspring. Only thus did he save his life. Bruised and still half dazed from the shock he arrived in Bayreuth by car at 7 A.M. on the very morning on which he was to begin rehearsing at 9 A.M. The beginning of the rehearsals at Bayreuth is almost a state ceremony. The orchestra sit in their places full of expectancy, the *musikalische Assistenz*, as all the young coaches and volunteers are called, sit in attendance, thrilled, with their scores in their hands. The Wagner family, especially the older generation, appears with all the solemn dignity they give to the cause of the " Meister ".

But something happened on this occasion, which had never happened before at Bayreuth : the principal figure, the new Musical Director was not punctually on the spot. This was a crime, in comparison to which the fact that he had nearly lost his life on his way to Bayreuth was insignificant.

The press, of course, recorded the incident of Furtwängler's entry to Bayreuth at full length. Soon I was accused of arranging press-stunts for Furtwängler, to the detriment of others. It was unfair, I was told, and I was advised not to do it again. I pointed out timidly that the public was, of course, more interested in incidents connected with Furtwängler than with the ordinary run of folk, but this was of no avail. I was in for trouble, and trouble of this kind never ceased for me that summer.

This first season without Siegfried Wagner was difficult for all who missed his friendly and welcoming smile at the *Festspielhügel*. Naturally the new management headed by the young widow had at first to find its way between the necessary innovations and the jealously guarded old tradition.

The first clash of the season was that Lauritz Melchior, the Tristan of Furtwängler's first performance in Bayreuth, declared that he would leave immediately and would never return again, the management apparently being the cause of the trouble. He finally consented to fulfil his contract for that summer, but since then the world's greatest Wagner tenor has never set foot in Bayreuth again.

There was also a Toscanini incident which was reported and distorted all over the world. The *Festspiel Direktion* had arranged a memorial concert for Siegfried Wagner on the anniversary of his death, August 4, 1931. This was a novelty in Bayreuth, concerts never having been held in the *Festspielhaus*. The conductors of that year, Elmendorff, Furtwängler, and Toscanini were to participate. In the general rehearsal in the morning the notorious incident occurred when Toscanini broke his baton and left the platform, a nonplussed orchestra and a nonplussed audience. (It later appeared that the maestro, who on account of the limited time available for rehearsing, had expected to rehearse undisturbed, was upset by finding the house full—admittance having been granted to all relations of members of the staff, singers, Orchestra, and Chorus by the management.) To cut a long story short, Toscanini, greatly upset, left the rehearsal, and said to Furtwängler, who rushed after him, that he would leave Bayreuth at once and would not conduct the memorial concert in the evening. He made straight for his car and left the *Festspielhügel*.

Furtwängler, as Musical Director, conducted the rehearsal to the end and meanwhile sent me to inform Frau Wagner of Toscanini's intention. She declared : " I don't think that Toscanini will do this to me, he would never desert me on such an occasion ". She sent me, however, straightaway in her car, with her nephew, Gil Gravina who, as he spoke Italian fluently, often acted as the maestro's interpreter, to Wahnfried, where Toscanini was then staying as her guest at the *Siegfried Haus*. The servants told me that Toscanini had just left for Marienbad with his chauffeur and his adored little dog. All his passionate love for pre-Hitler Bayreuth had not sufficed to alter his decision ; and so he left the widow of Siegfried Wagner on the anniversary of her husband's death. For Toscanini no compromise was ever possible once he had made up his mind. And so, although his personal relations with the Wagner family were not interrupted by this incident, the 1931 season was actually to be his last on the *Festspielhügel*. For this, however, there were several other reasons yet to come—last but not least, Adolf Hitler.

Furtwängler himself at this, his first Bayreuth Season, never felt quite at ease. He had his own definite ideas about how the legacy of Richard Wagner should be dealt with. Things came to such a pass that he wanted to resign even before his first performance. He wrote a long letter to Frau Wagner at this time—a document revealing how earnestly and seriously he takes all his responsibilities —explaining his ideas, and that he felt that they were incompatible with the way Bayreuth was now conducted. The incident was patched up, but it was the beginning of his later conflicts and he resigned from Bayreuth before the next season, explaining his views in an article published in June 1932 in the *Vossische Zeitung* : " *Um die Zukunft von Bayreuth* " (" The Future of Bayreuth ").

Yet for the international world he became more and more the acknowledged Wagner conductor and, besides Germany and Austria, he regularly conducted the Wagner Festivals in Paris and Wagner Operas at Covent Garden—until this activity was, like so many others, rendered impossible by Hitler.

After Furtwängler had resigned from Bayreuth Berlin became more and more the centre of his life and activity, though he regularly went to Vienna as guest-conductor. Naturally Berlin also became more of a home for me. The Berlin Philharmonic Orchestra received his closest attention, and was improved more and more in every respect. The international tours, now regularly undertaken twice a year in addition to the smaller tours within Germany itself, had become not only artistic but also financial successes. Although the political tide moved in a heavy ebb and flow, the artistic life was strong and independent ; and in Berlin, as in Vienna, much of the social life revolved around the Philharmonic Concerts and the Opera. The concerts were always sold out, and besides the great Philharmonic Concerts, many other cycles with prominent conductors, Bruno Walter, for instance, had become a regular institution. Foreign conductors were also invited, and a special cycle was arranged for them.

I took an eager part in all these activities ; the day was always too short for all that was to be done. Social life was brilliant, and there was a friendly relationship with many of the diplomats, who came regularly to the concerts. One of the most faithful visitors to the Berlin Philharmonic Concerts was the British Ambassador, Sir Horace Rumbold, with his wife and daughters, and only recently I came across a press cutting mentioning myself as representing the Berlin Philharmonic at a reception at the British Embassy given for Sir Thomas Beecham on the occasion of one of his concerts in Berlin. After that concert a photo of Sir Horace with Sir Thomas and Furtwängler was taken in the artists' room of the *Philharmonie*. I was present, and little did I then realise the turn events would take.

The Orchestra kept me very busy, but Furtwängler alone required most of my time. He used to work at the oddest hours. All clerical or organising matters he, of course, considered as of secondary importance, and so he fitted them in when it suited him. Very often he used to ring me up late at night, to ask whether I would come to his flat "for a moment", and it became more of a rule than an exception for me to get out of bed in order to work with him. He himself, having concentrated on music as late as midnight, never thought that ordinary mortals often go to bed before that hour. I nearly always travelled with the Orchestra, and I continued to accompany him whenever he travelled or to join him somewhere on his journeys. Our friendship and mutual work for the cause of music had forged a wonderful bond between us. It was a relation built on mutual reliance, strengthened by my belief in him as an artist and by his confidence in me as friend and collaborator.

The year 1932 began for me with a rush, for we were approaching the culmination of our activities. At the beginning of the year I went to Rome to make arrangements for the Philharmonic spring tour which was to be the first extensive visit to Italy. This visit to Rome was most interesting, and when I arrived I was told that Mussolini had expressed the wish to see the woman who was the touring manager of an orchestra. However, he was absent while I was there, and instead of him I was invited to tea with his former secretary and biographer, Marghuerita Sarfatti.

As soon as my task was completed I had to rush back to Berlin. Hardly arrived there, the necessity arose for me to dash over to London on account of the impending English tour, where some difficulty had arisen through the death of our manager, Lionel Powell. After two days in London I returned to Berlin, and left again with the Orchestra a fortnight later for Holland, Belgium, and England.

The financial difficulties of the Orchestra were then almost over-come. It was now a limited liability company. The Orchestra itself, the city of Berlin, Prussia, the Reich, and the Rundfunk were repre-sented on the board of seventeen directors. The chairman was Dr. Lange, the First Mayor of Berlin (First Mayor, that is, the Mayor directly in authority after the Lord Mayor). He devoted himself with energy and humour to the affairs of the Berlin Philharmonic Orchestra, and fought like a lion for its interests against the inevit-able intrigues in the meetings of the city councils. During concerts, he liked to sit in the Orchestra. He admired Furtwängler, towards whom he had adopted a protective fatherly attitude, gently steering him through the obstacles of bureaucracy.

To me he was the most understanding and kindly chief, always available to smooth away difficulties. He will always be connected with the fulfilment of what was then the dream of my life : a real office for the Orchestra, organised as I had planned it. I had found a flat, near Furtwängler's home and not far from the *Philharmonie,* big enough to have my own private apartment in it as well as the office. But the whole new arrangement had, of course, to be agreed to by the board of directors. For days before the meeting of the board I was distracted. I was quite sure of my supporters, but everybody who knows anything about committees will agree that one can never be sure beforehand of what will happen. Finally—late at night—Dr. Lange rang me up : " Go ahead and arrange your office ". How happy I was !

The office was charming. It did not look like a place of business at all except the one room used as the general office. I furnished it with my old furniture and pictures. There was a music room for auditions (which we later used for our chamber-music evenings as well). A wonderful Bechstein was given us for that purpose. My own office gradually assumed a delightful atmosphere, filled as it was by my books and my comfortable easy chairs—in which visitors from all over the world were soon sitting. A young East Prussian maid followed me from my former quarters and looked after me perfectly, and after the office as well. Soon she arranged to have lunch always ready for anybody who wanted to have a meal in the office. Her cooking was perfect. " Trudchen ", as she was called, was most popular with the Orchestra, and used to deal in a very efficient way with even the most illustrious telephone callers when I was out.

It was a full and active life, and when we started to make arrangements for the celebration of the fiftieth anniversary of the Berlin Philharmonic Orchestra we did so with the grateful feeling that the work and devotion for so many years of all those concerned had not been in vain, and that Furtwängler had been able to carry on the tradition started by Bülow and Nikisch.

The celebrations consisted of two festival concerts. At the first a new composition of Hindemith's named *Philharmonisches Konzert* was played which Hindemith had dedicated to the Orchestra and its conductor for this occasion. The celebrations were opened by an inaugural assembly at which all the persons of importance in Berlin's public life were present. Diplomatic representatives of all countries sat in the front rows with Berlin's Lord Mayor. Hindenburg sent as his deputy the Secretary of State of the Ministry of Interior, who made the speech and handed the *Goethe Medaille* to Furtwängler— a new decoration founded by the *Reichspräsident* for men of science and art.

The fateful year 1932 went by. We toured Europe. Furtwängler conducted many operas in Vienna and Paris. On his next birthday we gave a party in our office flat which was eminently suitable for such occasions. Members of the Orchestra and famous soloists performed Haydn's toy symphony, dressed as children. Hindemith, who in those days was learning the bassoon, had composed an additional bassoon part and practised it for weeks ahead, to the despair of his wife.

Spirited musical jokes were in those days a recognised entertainment. Hindemith had composed a parody on Wagner's *Fliegende Holländer* overture. It was played by some members of the Philharmonic dressed in dirty old-fashioned frock coats, with red handkerchiefs hanging out of their pockets. The joke of the parody was that the players were supposed to be village musicians playing that piece for the first time. They missed their cue, and quickly switched over to the safety of a Viennese waltz from which they, with great virtuosity, modulated back to the music expressing the ecstatic reunion of Senta and the Holländer in death.

Arthur Schnabel, who was one of those present, told me that

only a musician could appreciate the masterly way this parody was arranged.

It was the most perfect and harmonious evening, a gathering of a number of Germany's greatest artists and leading personalities. The Orchestra was to leave for England immediately afterwards. Nobody had an inkling how near was the thunderstorm—but when I recall those present on that evening, I find that hardly one of them has escaped a tragic change of existence. It was January 25, 1933.

[1 9 3 3]

Chapter 1

ON January 30, 1933, the Third Reich was proclaimed and Adolf Hitler became *Reichskanzler*. Whilst a transformation took place in Germany, the extent of which few people realised at the time, the Berlin Philharmonic Orchestra paid its annual visit to England, Holland and Belgium. We had given our last concert abroad at the Hague on February 22, and we were in the train to Bielefeld to give the first concert on German soil since Hitler's nomination to power.

One of the luncheon services on the train was reserved for members of the Orchestra, but there were a few strangers present, hardly noticed by us. A friend had joined us shortly after crossing the frontier, one of the many German music-lovers who managed to arrange their business journeys to fit in with the Orchestra's schedule.

Holland at that time was in the throes of a " Mengelberg crisis ", for Mengelberg had removed his domicile to Switzerland, it was alleged for the purpose of evading the increasingly high taxation in Holland. The Orchestra was in high spirits after a successful tour and chattered freely. I joined in the conversation and discussed the question of taxes with Furtwängler, who had owned a house in the Engadine since 1924, and I jokingly suggested that he should do the same as Mengelberg.

No sooner had we arrived at Bielefeld than our music-loving friend came to us in consternation and excitement. It appeared that among the strangers in the dining-car, a high S.S. leader had been sitting and listening to every word we spoke. He regarded us as "anti-National" criminals, threatened to order the boycott of the Bielefeld concert, to report us to Berlin, and so on. As I was the only woman travelling with the Orchestra, he had taken me for Frau Furtwängler, and was aghast to hear such views as I had expressed emanating from the wife of this prominent man. Actually, Frau

Furtwängler was Scandinavian and the prototype of Hitler's " Aryan "
ideal. Our friend did not want to allow suspicion to rest on this
innocent lady, but on the other hand thought it inadvisable to direct
the Nazis' attention to Furtwängler's secretary, since—as I was to
learn later—I had long been regarded with displeasure by the Nazi
Party and had been on their black list for some time. He therefore
explained that the lady concerned was merely a friend of the
Orchestra.

Argument waxed hot over this incident and dragged on throughout
the afternoon. Finally, the concert took place. The local Nazis,
apparently, did not want to risk interfering with Germany's famous
orchestra.

This was our return to Germany—now Hitler's Germany. Our
initiation into its new code of ideals had not been long delayed.
The Nazis were already swollen with their new importance—their
false ideology. What did it mean to them if the Berlin Philharmonic
had won honour, success, and fame all over the world ? What did
they know of real culture ? They were far too taken up with their
ridiculous and fortuitous distinctions as to what was or was not,
in accord with " national sentiment ", to respect the traditions of
art and science, let alone that of free speech or free opinion.

After our return this incident had a long sequel, and crystallised
finally into one of the then customary " denunciations ". Hitler
was handed a memorandum accusing Furtwängler, among other
things, of depositing abroad the large fees from his foreign engagements, assisted, of course, by his " Jewish " secretary, while the
Orchestra was left without salary for many months. Actually, the
exact opposite was true. Often during this unsettled period owing
to the political change, Furtwängler did not draw his own fees, so
as not to jeopardise the salary of the Orchestra. However, this
report to Hitler gave us an inkling of things to come.

I remember at that time a constant feeling of vague uneasiness.
How could it have been other than vague ? How could one foresee
what was to come ? My work had taken me across the world,
but, with many others I had made the mistake of not watching
political events at home. I had never read *Mein Kampf* and had
never taken the problem of Hitler seriously. Our activities were
not connected with propaganda and politics, their object was music,

music and nothing else. What could have been more in the interests of the real Germany than our work in the cause of music? How could one imagine that even matters of art and culture would henceforth be handled in a hypocritical and arbitrary way? Under the cover of national sentiment and the new concepts *tragbar* or *untragbar* (meaning admissible or inadmissible) the lust for power of mediocre minds was given free rein. No achievement was to be recognised unless it originated from the Nazis themselves and was acknowledged by their own propaganda. "Art" and "values" had no objective significance for them, except as means to an end.

Few realised then the ultimate aims of the Nazis. Their new laws were not yet in existence, but coming events cast their shadows before. Rumour spread with regard to "racial" discrimination, and it was soon whispered that the Jewish members of the Orchestra would shortly be no longer "admissible".

Furtwängler had at that time many interviews with various people. Yet he never thought for one moment that anybody would seriously interfere with his work or his responsibilities. He was an idealist, convinced that he need only explain things to put everything right. His faith in himself gave him courage to take a stand and to voice his demands again and again to the "Leaders" of the Reich.

Many posts in the new State were in the hands of unqualified and inexperienced people, Party members, quickly rewarded for their loyalty to Hitler by being given high positions. Knowing their incompetence, one expected, accordingly, to see them disappear again at an early date, and hoped that common sense would take the place of Party frenzy. It was obvious that it was mainly the "small fry" that clamoured for power and influence, at first, and who caused such confusion. One was hopelessly at their mercy, for the so-called "Leaders" were generally inaccessible, but the hope was generally nurtured that they would soon disappear into the background again.

Furtwängler was determined that he would not submit to arbitrary encroachment upon his sphere of work—the sensitive, artistic organisation of the Berlin Philharmonic Orchestra. He made no secret of his view, and so the Nazi authorities soon heard of his attitude. Perhaps they did not feel sure of themselves on this question, important as it was to foreign opinion. At any rate, for this or some other reason, the respect Furtwängler enjoyed prevented, for the time being, a Nazi-engineered catastrophe overtaking the Orchestra.

At this moment a new personality suddenly appeared on the scene, as sometimes happened in these days of upheaval, an aristocratic landowner, a flying officer with Goering in the Great War and a passionate music-lover. Although an early Party member with access to all authorities, he was apparently a man of understanding and of decent character. In the continual unauthorised interferences with individual liberties that now occurred, this type of person proved to be a temporary salvation for many institutions, because, being of the Party and yet possessing a cultural background, he was able to make a stand where ordinary people could not. He was introduced to Furtwängler and, by agreement with the authorities, was appointed *Kommissar* to the Berlin Philharmonic Orchestra. This gave the Orchestra a go-between without whom the growing mistrust of the Nazis would have made the continuation of work impossible.

In the meantime, I had grown more conscious of the strange times we were living in, but was still without the least realisation what it might mean for myself. I was of Jewish origin and Protestant upbringing. Most of the old, cultured Jewish families who had lived in Germany for centuries had assimilated themselves to the national life. " The Jewish problem," as it was to be created by Hitler, simply did not exist.

From the beginning of the Nazi régime, Furtwängler had declared me to be indispensable to him and his work. Through my efforts the Orchestra had in many respects been made independent. Their frequent tours were mostly due to my initiative. They were financially and artistically highly successful, and had become an essential part of the Orchestra's life.

One afternoon in March, a man who had been a member of the Orchestra Committee for many years, the new *Kommissar*, and myself were sitting in my office. After a few irrelevant remarks, this Orchestra member suddenly flourished a piece of paper :

" I have here," he said, " a letter from Professor Havemann (then head of the Fighting League for German Culture), concerning the Orchestra. He writes that the Jewish members of the Orchestra and, of course, Dr. Geissmar, are no longer *tragbar* in the New Germany."

At first I did not take this seriously. This particular man was always full of fun, and I thought this was one of his usual jokes. Eventually, however, he reluctantly handed me the letter, and when I found his words confirmed I felt as if I had been struck by lightning. An iron hand seemed to grip me, and a feeling came over me that I was not to lose for many years. . . . I began to understand.

Untragbar, amazing word ! Why should I be *untragbar* ? I had always served the Orchestra and its chief not only with integrity, but with the greatest fervour and passionate devotion. My position was such that the new Nazi legislation so far did not apply to me. But, of course, I did not then fathom the depth of cunning to which the Nazis descended in cases beyond their legal grasp.

Professor Havemann, the author of the ominous letter, was a very doubtful character. Long before Hitler came to power he had secretly been a Party member. He was a drunkard, no girl student was safe from him at the *Hochschule für Musik*, where he taught, and he was always in debt. His fellow Party members later discarded him and circulated among the authorities a bulky document enumerating all the accusations against him. This, however, was yet to come. For a long time, pompously officiating in Party uniform, he interfered unopposed and did a great deal of harm. Everyone was helpless against the methods of terrorism he applied under cover of Party authority. It was one of Havemann's habits to catch his victim on the telephone if anything annoyed him, and then to rave in an uncontrolled torrent of words. I did not know him personally, but one day he rang me up. Without any preliminaries he shouted at me : " Dr. Geissmar, I have just seen the programme for the Brahms Festival in Vienna. You can take it from me that this Festival will not take place as planned. Your Jewish influence is indubitably responsible for the choice of soloists." (They were Huberman, Casals, and Schnabel—the engagement of the latter instead of Backhaus, then the great favourite of Hitler, was particularly galling to the Nazis.) " We shall soon get rid of you, you may be sure," he roared. Before I could open my mouth he rang off.

The programme for the Brahms Centenary Festival to be held in May 1933 had been fixed by the Vienna committee in agreement with Furtwängler and the *Deutsche Brahms Gesellschaft*. As usual, since Furtwängler was chairman of the *Brahms Gesellschaft*, I had assisted in the preparations. Vienna still had a free hand in those days, and the power of the Nazis came to an end at Germany's frontiers. Needless to say, the Brahms Festival took place exactly as planned. Havemann's threat was without effect for the moment. The question of my dismissal, so categorically demanded by his letter, was temporarily dropped. The personnel of the Orchestra also remained unchanged.

Meanwhile, continuous changes and interferences in every institution throughout Germany went on, illegally and arbitrarily. The slogan "The voice of the people" was invoked to justify everything : envy, lust for power, and jobbery were rampant under the banner of the glorious "New Germany". Yet many people, so far not directly involved, did not realise what was at stake, and I remember a friend who, though on intimate terms with the Mendelssohn family and a close friend of the late Joseph Joachim, saying quite seriously to me : "We are approaching wonderful times". They were wonderful indeed !

On March 21st, the official inauguration of the Third Reich was to take place. It was a great day for the Nazis, enhanced by a brilliant, clear sky. I went for a walk through the Tiergarten, budding in the early spring. It swarmed with S.A. men and with couples of *Hitler-Jugend* who for the first time dared openly to display the brown uniform. I felt very depressed, but I still had no vision of the fateful course events were to take. On my solitary walk, my thoughts turned to the cause of the Berlin Philharmonic Orchestra to which Furtwängler and myself had devoted so much love, energy, and time. Germany owed an immense debt to Furtwängler. Undisturbed work was a basic requirement for conserving his nervous energy, and I fervently hoped that he would be allowed to remain free from interference.

A gala performance of *Die Meistersinger* at the State Opera with Furtwängler conducting, had been arranged to celebrate the great day of the nation. *Generalintendant* Tietjen, the head of the Prussian State Theatres, had inquired a few days before if Furtwängler would be available on that day as Hitler had expressed the wish that he should conduct. Hindenburg would be present. Attendance was

by invitation only. I was given a seat in my usual box. The fact
that I went shows how little I realised how matters really stood.

The *Staatsoper* was filled with unknown faces and uniforms.
Furtwängler conducted, ill as he was with incipient influenza.
During the interval he was commanded to the presence of the
Führer who sat in the middle of the circle. I was only a few yards
away, and so was able to see an ecstatic Hitler grasp the hands of
Furtwängler, who was as pale as death. In the interval all windows
were thrown open, and the sounds of fanatical youth marching in
a torchlight procession in honour of their Führer filled the Opera
House.

The rest of March 1933 was a hectic period of uncertainty and
harassment. Events preceding the first of April 1933 in Germany
were reminiscent of the Dark Ages. No atrocities reported in the
foreign press could equal in horror those which actually occurred.
The Nazis used the outcry abroad as an excuse for tightening the
screw at home. To this day I do not know who was the originator
of the idea of the unrestricted boycott of the Jews. Like a nightmare, it was suddenly there. The Nazis were always great gamblers,
and from the very beginning this fact should have been more realised
abroad. They seemed to be lucky whatever they staked. In spite
of the many "protests" by foreign powers they knew quite well
that many of these protests were only nominal, and the rest meant
merely condemnation without action. They took a chance on what
might happen to the millions of Germans abroad if they gradually
strangled the 500,000 Jews in Germany.

By the end of March a crisis was approaching. There appeared
one day without warning on the front pages of the newspapers,
in heavy type, a notice prohibiting Jewish employees from working.
It was not the "Civil Servants' Law", later to be promulgated;
in fact, it was no law at all. It caused an enormous panic, because
neither employers nor employees knew what to make of it. An
indescribable insecurity pervaded life, and rumours of the impending
boycott hung heavily over the people. They were torn by anguish
and uncertainty.

There were whispers of American intervention, of continuous
Government meetings, and then of a " deterioration of the situation "

due to (invented) incidents abroad. It was said that the Reich-leaders were not in agreement about the boycott, and that until the last minute Party officials were in conference with Goering, who, it was alleged, was against the boycott. Influential voices tried to advise a moderate course. Nobody really knew what would happen ; I believe the Government itself did not know until the last moment. Finally, on March 31st, it was announced that Goebbels was to speak on this subject on all radio stations at nine o'clock at night. Everybody listened with apprehension to the speech, which was a most cunning mixture of sadism, slyness, and empty rhetoric. After a climax, which led everybody to expect the worst, Goebbels announced that the boycott was to come into force on April 1st, and was to last until six p.m. on the same day. At the same time he uttered a threat—obviously intended for foreign consumption— to resume the boycott in the case of " bad behaviour "—presumably of the foreign press.

I had been advised to efface myself on the boycott day, because Furtwängler's attitude with regard to the dismissal of the Jewish members of the Orchestra and of myself made it appear likely that our office would be an object of the " people's fury ", staged, of course, by Goebbels. Accordingly, in the early morning of April 1st, I went to the Grunewald, outside Berlin, accompanied by the leader of the Orchestra, Goldberg, the first violinist, Back, and the two principal cellists, Schuster and Graudan and their wives. We picnicked there, strolled about, and returned late in the evening.

What had been going on in Berlin in the meantime ? It will never be forgotten by those who witnessed it.

Every artifice of demagogy had been used to whip up public opinion. It seemed unbelievable that such infamy was possible in a civilised age. Old and established Jewish-owned firms were assailed by groups of young Storm Troopers, wild with Party frenzy. The nameplates of physicians and lawyers whose ancestors had been long domiciled in Germany were covered with mud-coloured placards, notices with "*Jud*", "*Jüdisches Geschäft*", or the Star of David, symbol of Jewry, were daubed on the walls of houses known to be inhabited by Jews. Jewish-owned shops were guarded by Storm Troopers who prevented the shoppers from entering and kept watch at the entrance. All this was applied exclusively to German Jews. Jews of foreign nationality, many of whom had settled in Germany after the Great War and who had come from Eastern Europe, were left undisturbed.

Nothing happened to the Philharmonic Office. The Nazi ventriloquist knew exactly when to produce the " voice of the people ". Our day had not yet arrived !

All this organised hooliganism was infinitely upsetting, but almost as upsetting as the persecution was the sympathy one met. Many of the people were ashamed and said so. If only they had had the strength of mind to persist in this attitude !

A few other incidents of these days are still in my mind. The then French Ambassador in Berlin, M. François-Poncet, was very fond of music. He was very hospitable, and regularly arranged concerts at the Embassy at which I sometimes advised on the programmes. I was a frequent guest at the Embassy, and on friendly terms with some of the secretaries. The First Counsellor and his wife, who came from Alsace-Lorraine, were charming hosts and created a very stimulating atmosphere in their home. One day they invited me to a small luncheon-party at which the well-known American journalist, Knickerbocker, was present. He was late, and when he arrived he explained that he had been summoned to Goering because he had sent reports to America on the cruel treatment of the Jews—the whispered talk of Berlin at that time. The cable had, of course, been intercepted and reported to Goering, who immediately sent for the journalist and reproached him in what had apparently been a stormy interview.

On yet another occasion M. François-Poncet gave a luncheon-party at the French Embassy in honour of Cortot, who was the soloist at a Philharmonic concert. The day had not yet come when great international artists were to refuse to play in Berlin. The Philharmonic question was much in the limelight at this time, and there was wide speculation as to whether Furtwängler would be able to retain his Jewish musicians and myself as his secretary. At this luncheon I found myself placed at the Ambassador's right hand, with Cortot as my other neighbour. Opposite me sat the newly appointed musical critic of the *Völkische Beobachter*, the official Nazi organ. Since Hitler's seizure of power this gentleman had revealed himself as a member of the Party, and was never seen out of his S.A.

uniform. Being a good Nazi he had, of course, ignored me since Hitler's advent, though we constantly met. I knew him for an enemy and could not help being amused that he, invited to an Embassy for the first time, should find himself confronted with this " stain on German culture " occupying the place of honour at table.

The Ambassador, Cortot, and I naturally conversed in French. Few Nazis speak a foreign language. The " new people " in Germany were for the most part uncultivated and narrow, and laboured under a strong sense of inferiority. While people such as I were still invited to official functions they, while resenting us, had still to take us into account, and to compromise when they met us on the neutral ground of an Embassy. At this luncheon the Nazi critic displayed an overwhelming charm and tried his best to join in our conversation. When we left he and I parted " the best of friends " ; he actually took to greeting me again—when nobody else was about. !

Chapter 2

AS WAS usual in Spring the Berlin Philharmonic had then before it an extensive foreign tour, the first one during the Nazi régime. It was to take us first through several German towns, then to France, and finally to Switzerland, and it was to begin on April 22, 1933.

At the outset of the Hitler régime foreign travel had been banned for everyone. A special exit permit had to be affixed to the passport of anyone whom the Nazis allowed out of the country. When it was agreed, in principle, that the seven Jewish members would remain in the Orchestra, and that I was to retain my post, I assumed that there would be no obstacle to getting my passport visaed.

These matters were dealt with in Berlin by the Ministry of the Interior. I gave Furtwängler's passport and my own to an " intermediary ", one of those indispensable persons who were recognised by the Nazis but were not beyond helping non-Nazis. I asked him to attend to the matter because I knew he was friendly with the A.D.C. to the Minister, Dr. Frick. The A.D.C., an old civil servant, was rectitude personified. Both he and his wife were the most strait-laced people imaginable. The only thing incompatible with their virtuous attitude was their constant demand for free tickets for the opera, and the Philharmonic concerts. Requests for complimentary seats by ministerial officials and their friends were, it was alleged, prohibited by Hitler, but this practice went on worse than ever.

To this authority my man turned. He came back quickly, very embarrassed. "What is the matter?" I asked him, "any new trouble?" He would not say at first, but finally, with great reluctance, he came out with: "I do not know how to put it, but the Nazis want to know whether you and Furtwängler . . ." He was embarrassed, but I was not. With a good conscience I could reassure the Nazis. Our friend disappeared again, and soon returned with the passports visaed. My exit permit was due to his guarantee that I was not Furtwängler's mistress. The knowledge that work and friendship, and these alone, were the link between Furtwängler and myself frequently upheld me during this humiliating period.

The spirit of unrest brooding over the capital in these days was reflected and even exaggerated in the provinces. Every day reports came in of interference in every sphere of life by the new Party officials. Second-rate people, under some pretext or other, managed to insinuate themselves into every institution, and former chiefs were simply dismissed by the Nazi "cell" which now came into the open, but actually had long existed underground. What happened in the field of municipal government, banks, universities, and hospitals has been discussed elsewhere; absolute chaos reigned in the musical world. The field of music where, even in normal times, competition and exaggerated egotism played a big part, was now a network of intrigues.

Germany and Austria had always been alive with musical controversies, but how different had been the nature of the disputes in the old days! There was the Wagner-Brahms controversy in which the famous surgeon, Billroth, took part by fulminating against Wagner and strongly supporting Brahms. How bitter was the Wagner-Verdi controversy, how passionate the battles about composers like Bruckner, Reger, Mahler, or Strauss. How devotedly did the Bach and Handel societies work! With how much enthusiasm was chamber-music cultivated by amateurs! How really profound and earnest was the interest in music then! But this side of things did not matter to the Nazis. Under the cover of the "race-theory", objective discussion of differences of opinion vanished.

The innumerable concert-societies, some of which, like the Leipzig *Gewandhaus,* with a century-old tradition, found themselves suddenly threatened in their work. Their committees generally consisted of highly educated idealists who gave their services to the good cause. Now each committee member was scrutinised as to his ancestry—nothing else mattered.

Concert-agencies, too, were menaced unless they chose to forestall the compulsory "*gleichschaltung*" by liquidating themselves!

The authorities deemed it advisable to give out that conditions would be "legalised", that there was no intention of throttling free competition, and that the free work of concert-agencies would be regulated and protected. This, however, was obviously only said to gain time. As a matter of fact, the new intermediary controlling bodies resulted in such over-organisation that every concert programme and every intended engagement had to be submitted to the authorities. Free activity was stifled.

It was a great mistake not to realise immediately what all this meant. It could easily be seen that the racial point of view was often the merest pretext. At bottom all the reshuffling was principally due to the lust for power of the Party. The ambitions of those who were allegedly kept down in the past were cleverly used for political purposes.

The position of artists was naturally also unsettled. The status of those who were in State employment was soon to be defined through the new Civil Servants' Law. But what would happen to the prominent soloists, the conductors, the chamber-music associations, the composers, and foreign artists? Who would be permitted to perform? Who could be engaged? Most artists living in Germany were so deeply rooted there that they did not contemplate emigration at that time and preferred to wait for things to clarify.

To mention only one or two—Schnabel, for instance, being an Austrian and therefore out of reach of the law, stayed on at first; Adolf Busch, the great German violinist, who had a loving and enormous public, immediately cancelled all his engagements in Germany and left the country with his family and his quartet as a protest, and because the Fighting League for German Culture made extensive research into the ancestry of the second violin, and declared Rudolf Serkin, the famous pianist and Busch's collaborator for many years, to be *untragbar*. Bruno Walter had cancelled his last Berlin concert, and Richard Strauss had taken his place. It was alleged that Storm Troopers had threatened to create a disturbance in the *Philharmonie* if Walter conducted. If it suited the Nazis, they were capable of manufacturing public opinion, and this was what Walter had had to reckon with. Protection for his concert was asked for but was refused, and so he naturally preferred to cancel it. Events have proved him right. In Leipzig, where he was director of the *Gewandhaus,* at first nothing happened, but shortly after the inauguration of the Reich in March 1933 he arrived one day for his rehearsal and found the *Gewandhaus* closed to him—the *Gewandhaus Direktion* having been defeated in their fight against the authorities in Saxony, who were especially ferocious.

Germany, with her deeply rooted and traditionally evolved age-old musical life, was suddenly faced with the fact that she was not in a position to protect this precious part of her cultural life. Musical life, like so much else in Nazi Germany, was annexed by the Party, made to serve political ends and propaganda, and was rife with nepotism. Music, for its own sake, seemed at an end. In spite of the many great artists Germany possesses and the big funds allocated to orchestras and opera houses, artistic life had ceased to be untrammelled and spontaneous. Hitler himself admitted in a private talk that for him art was never " art for art's sake " but always had to serve a purpose.

Furtwängler saw with consternation and dismay what was happening, but he was firmly convinced that it could not last. He was on good terms with the Government ; he represented one of their few assets abroad. Although he was criticised by the Nazis for not immediately " aryanising " his Orchestra, he was treated with consideration and respect, and so was confirmed in his feeling of security. He risked opposition, was frank, and was no diplomat. He believed then that it would be easy for him to persuade those in power to mend their ways in time. He was in a strong position at this period, and had innumerable adherents in the Reich. Many hopes were concentrated in him.

As soon as the interferences with and encroachments on musical institutions began, he received masses of reports and desperate appeals for help. Everybody wrote to him about their troubles, and received replies promising the help he thought was his to give. Heads of concert associations arrived, artists begged for interviews and advice. Dismissed opera directors and broadcasting officials appeared to implore his aid. The files dealing with these cases form a most moving document of the early days of Nazi tyranny.

Furtwängler began to submit to the authorities individual cases that he deemed important. His requests were always most civilly received, but were passed on from one authority to another. If he spoke to a high Government official, he was always promised an immediate settlement of the case. The fulfilment of the promise, however, was either cynically ignored or sabotaged by some underling. One soon learned that even the Minister was helpless if the subordinate bodies disagreed. Nevertheless, Furtwängler was untiring in his efforts. Day after day was passed in the attempts to contact officials and their staffs. All this was nerve-wracking to a sensitive artist. Once, when a minister who had asked him to telephone at a certain hour was still unavailable at the fourth attempt, Furtwängler angrily banged his fist through a window and hurt his hand. I got off with a splinter in my face.

The distress of everybody affected by these conditions grew, and chaos and disruption became widespread. Furtwängler was tormented. He saw that something had to be done to stem the current. He knew, too, that the whole of intellectual Germany was behind him in his endeavours. For several days he shut himself up and wrote a statement on the neutrality of art and the freedom of achievement, which he issued in the form of an open letter to Dr. Goebbels (April 12, 1933). He took up the case of his Jewish colleagues and urged the right to choose artists with absolute freedom. He declared that the function of art and the artist was to unite and not to sever, and that there was only one ultimate line of demarcation, that between good art and bad. He added that " the contemporary world of music, already weakened by the world depression and the radio, can stand up to no more experiments ".

"When this fight is directed against the real artist, it is against the interests of culture as a whole," he said. His letter continued :

"It must, therefore, be said plainly that men like Walter, Klemperer, and Reinhardt must be enabled to have their say in Germany in the future. I say again : let our fight be against the reckless, disintegrating, shallow, destructive spirit, but not against the real artist, who in his own way, however his art may be appraised, is always creative and thus constructive.

"In this spirit I appeal to you in the name of German art lest things happen that can never be righted."

The press was then already muzzled by Goebbels. Without his consent nothing could be published. It was one of the cleverest manœuvres of the little Propaganda Minister that he accepted this letter of Furtwängler as being of topical interest, declaring that he would release it for publication. I think myself that he purposely published Furtwängler's letter in order to gain credit for a tolerance which would give him time for future action. Goebbels himself wrote a reply, and published it on the same page as Furtwängler's letter.

If one reads this reply carefully it will be seen how dishonest it is. Apart from the rash assertion that "politics, too, is an art, and what is more, the highest and most comprehensive art of all" and that, accordingly, those who take part in modern politics feel themselves to be artists—apart from this—he sets up the thesis that only art which is rooted in the people can be good. What he really means by "rooted in the people" he wisely leaves unsaid. His theories on art having to be responsible, "potent", and militant, are equally senseless.

"Real artists are rare," he continues, "and they have to be encouraged," but—he argues circuitously—"they have to be *real* artists." He promises that they will be heard in Germany, in the future, too, and that every real artist will have a field of "unhampered activity". This was all nonsense, of course. Goebbels knew all too well that as the valuation of an artist depended on his race (which was a main feature of the Nazi programme), there could be no question of "unhampered activity".

In spite of the artificiality of Goebbels' reply, the atmosphere was somewhat eased by this exchange of letters.

The effect of Furtwängler's article was enormous. It was printed in papers all over the world and Furtwängler was inundated by congratulations, telegrams, and letters.

Furtwängler was relieved that he had been able to say what he wished ; he had given expression to the opinion of the majority, and supported a principle that was of vital necessity both to himself and to the whole German nation. He hoped that things would gradually revert to normal and sound instincts prevail before too much had been destroyed.

Chapter 3

THE FIRST tour which Furtwängler undertook with the Berlin Philharmonic Orchestra since the beginning of the Nazi régime illustrated the turn musical life in Germany had taken and the problems which had to be faced.

As mentioned already, from the very beginning Furtwängler in his frequent interviews with Nazis of all types, had pointed out that the principle of achievement was the only principle applicable to cultural matters, and he had emphatically declared that racial discrimination, if inflicted on German musical life, would paralyse it. Quite apart from the great soloists and conductors, there were first-rate people of Jewish extraction among the orchestra musicians, especially among the string players. Furthermore, a large section of the music-loving public in Germany consisted of Jews, many of them lawyers, physicians, scholars, and bankers who were amateur performers and frequent supporters of music and musicians.

By the middle of April 1933, at the beginning of our first tour through Hitler-Germany, Nazi politics had had a most devastating effect on concert audiences. The Jews did not attend the concerts ; they were intimidated and perplexed, and their pride barred them from what the letter of law still conceded them. The Nazis, for the most part, did not go because the Orchestra had not been "aryanised" and did not conform to the "ethics" of the New Germany, and they were afraid to endanger their own reputations if they attended.

What was left was only a thin stratum of those inspired by Furtwängler's courage, and those enthusiasts whom nothing could daunt. However, they could not fill the concert halls, and this, the first Philharmonic tour since Hitler's advent, was also their first played to half-empty houses.

I had not accompanied the Orchestra for the first part of the journey, but met them in Mannheim, on the way to Paris. Long before the Hitler régime a joint concert of the Berlin Philharmonic and the Mannheim Orchestra had been arranged for this spring of 1933. It was the last concert within the regular Mannheim subscription series, and the profits were to be for the benefit of the Mannheim Orchestra.

In the course of his correspondence about this concert, Furt-wängler had informed the executive of the Mannheim Orchestra that the Berlin Philharmonic would come with its usual personnel, including the Jewish members. Since the Government had consented to the retention of the Jews in the Orchestra, the provincial authorities had to accept this fact, although they were then "more Catholic than the Pope". The Mannheim Orchestra committee wrote, however, that they could not agree that the Jew, Simon Goldberg, the Berlin leader, should be the leader of the joint Orchestras. Goldberg had been engaged by Furtwängler when nineteen years of age; he was universally considered one of the best Orchestra leaders in the world. The Mannheimers demanded that their own leader should occupy Goldberg's place. Furtwängler replied that if the placing of the musicians was not to remain as arranged by him, or that if any of *his* artists did not suit them, he would have to cancel the concert.

The Berlin Orchestra duly arrived in Mannheim. Furtwängler stayed with my mother, as he usually did when he visited Mannheim During the first rehearsal another attempt was made to remove the Berlin leader from his legitimate place, but Furtwängler was adamant on the point. Here, as elsewhere, when the Nazis pretended to be concerned over national sentiment, or disagreements with their *Weltanschauung*, the real issue was petty jealousy and personal ambition. The Mannheim leader was an inferior player; but he was a Nazi, and had immediately donned the swastika under the new régime. Now, he felt, his moment had come. What did it

matter if his Berlin colleague was a superior artist? This did not
count. What counted was the importance of political power. There
were few people in Germany who at that time would have dared
to resist the Nazis in this apparently trivial matter. Personal
courage such as Furtwängler had displayed since Hitler's advent
was rare then, and only the future was to reveal how dearly the
Germans would have to pay for this national lack of character.

At this concert, for the first time, Nazi uniforms were to be seen
in the front rows. Honest civic dignitaries, harmless enough in themselves, sat there in their brown shirts, decorated with the swastika.
The concert was sold out. After the performance a banquet was
to take place for both Orchestras, with the mayor and civic dignitaries present; only men were to attend.

After the concert, my mother and I were sitting quietly at dinner
when the door opened and Furtwängler, whom we had thought
to be upstairs, changing for the banquet, appeared, dressed in his
travelling clothes. I said to him: "Good gracious, what is the
matter? You can't go to the banquet like that!" "I'm not going,
I shall stay here", he replied, white as a sheet. He was very over-
wrought, and in a great state of agitation: only gradually could
we find out what had happened. After the performance which,
by the way, had financed their whole series, the executive members
of the Mannheim Orchestra had gone to see Furtwängler in the
artists' room and had reproached him for his lack of national sentiment. At this, Furtwängler, without replying, threw his score at
their feet and left them. Throughout the whole evening they sent
messages and telephoned to him, imploring him to attend the
banquet, but he was inflexible. He declared that notwithstanding
the honorary membership conferred upon him on the occasion of
the Orchestra's 150th anniversary, in 1929, and the freedom of
the city with which he had been invested, he would never conduct
the Mannheim Orchestra again or return to the city. He enforced
his words by an official letter to the Mannheim Orchestra.

I describe this Mannheim incident of 1933 in detail, as I do not
believe that anybody in years to come will be able to believe that
a political upheaval could have such extraordinary repercussions.
People whom one would never have suspected of lack of balance
seemed now to have lost all reason. As I have said before, national

sentiment was used as a cover for the basest envy and paltry ambition. Every provincial town was crowded with managing *Kommissars* and other Nazi Party officials. The Mannheim incident was, of course, a matter of tremendous importance to these new dignitaries. Furtwängler, the favourite of the Führer, and Germany's great conductor, had proved to be of doubtful allegiance to the Party. He had not only refused to adapt his Orchestra to the demands of the New Germany, but had been tactless enough to stay with his Jewish friends in Mannheim! Reports were sent to Berlin, and Mannheim Nazi officials immediately went to Karlsruhe, where a concert of the Berlin Philharmonic Orchestra with Furtwängler was due to take place two days later, to inform the provincial Nazi Government of this scandal. Accordingly, the Government seats were conspicuously empty at the Karlsruhe concert, as they were at Baden-Baden two days later—a symbol of the spirit of the New Germany.

Meanwhile I had gone straight on to Paris from Mannheim. Here, for the first time after many weeks of tension, sleeplessness, humiliation, and despair, I could breathe freely again. With all the energy left to me I concentrated on the preparations for the two concerts due to take place at the Opera. A Strasbourg concert preceding the Paris performances had had to be cancelled, because the management declared that they could not give any guarantee of safety to an Orchestra that came from a country where artists were debarred from appearance for other than artistic reasons. There was also strong opposition in Paris ; nevertheless the concerts were sold out.

It was now known all over the world that Furtwängler could not be considered a Nazi, and that the Berlin Philharmonic Orchestra had not been " aryanised ", but there were many people who blamed him for remaining in Germany under the changed conditions. In fact, from the very beginning of the Hitler régime Furtwängler had to defend himself against two attacks : within Germany against the Nazis who reproached him for his lack of national sentiment —in the outside world against those who resented his remaining in Nazi Germany.

Our local agent in Paris received all sorts of threatening letters. There was one group especially, very active and energetic, which informed him that they were planning disturbances at the concerts.

They called themselves, " The Union for combating Anti-semitism ". It was in vain that we explained that actually their activities in our case were rather misplaced ; that Jews were still in the Orchestra and nothing was changed. We tried to convince them that we were altogether the wrong target for their propaganda ; but all arguments proved useless. They declared that although Furtwängler and the Berlin Philharmonic Orchestra were not practising antisemitism, their Union was concerned with the principle of opposing any visitor from anti-semitic Nazi Germany and, therefore, the planned demonstration would have to take place.

In the end, a rather peculiar deal was made. They agreed to confine themselves to a silent dropping of leaflets, provided they were granted free entry to the concert. This was arranged, and at the beginning of the interval, in the presence of the whole French Government, and among the thunderous applause of a house filled to capacity, thousands of their leaflets were dropped from the gallery.

The concerts of the Berlin Philharmonic Orchestra in Paris had been gala performances ever since 1928, taking place amidst much splendour and enthusiasm, and they were the high lights of our tours. In 1933, with conditions at home so radically changed, we had become ultra-sensitive and we especially appreciated everything—at any rate so far as our public and our friends were concerned—that was still as it had been in pre-Hitler times.

During all our journeys, spread over many years, we had formed friendships in all the towns we visited, and we were always glad to see these friends again. In Paris we had our own community, in no small measure due to the efforts of the German Ambassador, von Hoesch.

M. Jacques Rouché, the director and patron of the Paris *Opéra*, who dominated opera and concert activities in France to a great extent, had been devoted to Furtwängler since his first visit to Paris, and he and his family formed a centre of friendly support.

Things worked fairly smoothly throughout the French tour, as the successful concerts indicated. Furtwängler's upright attitude in standing up for his Orchestra and its secretary, was known to the world. In France, as elsewhere, his letter to Goebbels had been reprinted. A theory gained currency that he only wrote it in view of the impending foreign tour, but I can vouch for the integrity and profound conviction which urged him to raise his voice.

Deputies appeared in every French town we passed, to honour Furtwängler for his attitude. In the newspaper *Le Marseillais* there appeared a very fine leader, entitled " *Une voix* " and emphasising the *one* humane voice of Furtwängler amidst all the distressful clamour caused by Hitler. The concert in Marseilles was received with terrific applause, and a truly southern demonstration of enthusiasm. The concert in Lyons was to have been cancelled owing to a threatened boycott by the populace, but took place after these reassuring events, and was very successful.

Afterwards France, Geneva, Zurich, and Basle were visited. Here, for the first time, one saw German refugees at the concerts. I avoid using the word " emigrant " to which Hitler has imparted a sinister flavour.

While the Orchestra, with Furtwängler, had a few more engagements in Germany, I left for Vienna to be present at the final preparations for the Brahms Festival (May 16–21, 1933).

Chapter 4

THE EIGHTH Brahms Festival coincided with the centenary of Brahms' birth. It was announced as : *Johannes Brahms-Fest, Wien, 100 Jahr-Feier, Mai* 1933. The *Deutsche Brahmsgesellschaft* had agreed with the Viennese *Gesellschaft der Musikfreunde*, whose honorary member Brahms had been, that the festival was to take place in Vienna. Both societies therefore collaborated in the preparations for this outstanding event.

At the Vienna festival the *Gesellschaft der Musikfreunde* had the predominating influence. The soloists had been chosen by mutual agreement. Furtwängler, an honorary member of the G.d.M., was to be the principal conductor. Huberman and Casals, both honorary members, were to play the Double Concerto. Schnabel was to play the B flat major concerto, and he, Huberman, and Hindemith were to take part in the chamber-music. A Dutch singer and Manowarda (later very pro-Nazi), were the soloists in the " Requiem ".

At that time Vienna's artistic life was in full bloom. Many authors and actors had gone there, hoping to begin a new life in this last German-speaking land where there was still some freedom left. Vienna has always been the home of German music, and music was actually flourishing more than ever. All the famous conductors, including Toscanini, were then at home in Vienna.

The Brahms Centenary was one of the last international occasions where the invisible barriers which were soon to arise between Germans and other people were not yet much in evidence. Visitors from all over the world came to Vienna for it. Once more, great artists from every country were united, later to be inexorably separated by Hitler.

At the opening of the Festival Furtwängler delivered the Brahms oration. Dollfuss, who was to have welcomed the participants on behalf of the Austrian Government, was unable to attend, and Schuschnigg spoke in his stead.

Those who remember the beauty and serenity of musical festivals of pre-Hitler times will agree that the atmosphere of this last international Brahms Festival was untarnished, and worthy of comparison with that of former occasions. For the last time the serene spirit of the wonderful music dominated everything ; free human contacts, soon to be lost, were enjoyed.

Furtwängler's time during the Festival Week was fully occupied, yet I remember that in his spare moments we discussed the problems which constantly preoccupied and worried him. He was still the rock on whom many built their faith, but the ways of artists were already beginning to diverge.

The evenings after the concerts were spent in the *Schwemme* (a kind of *brasserie*) of the Hotel Imperial, in the company of the various artists and their friends. We sat there till the early hours, and whatever we talked about we always came back to the same insoluble desperate problem which Hitler had created. In spite of many years of joint work which linked Furtwängler and the great soloists, I felt clearly and hopelessly on these evenings that their roads lay in different directions.

Only a fortnight elapsed between the end of the Brahms Festival and the beginning of the annual German opera performances in

Paris. This period we spent in Berlin; the days were filled with hectic activities, interviews with Ministers, correspondence with desperate people from all parts of the Reich, and in dealing with the problems that arose in connection with the Orchestra and the Berlin State Opera, where Furtwängler conducted some performances at that period.

It was a blessing to escape from this witches' cauldron and to go to Paris for some time. The Wagner Festival performances in Paris under Furtwängler, with prominent singers, had become quite a regular feature of the spring season. Paris, at this time, was delightful, and people from all over the world attended. Some of the singers used to return to Europe after the end of the New York Metropolitan Opera Season, and Paris and Covent Garden shared the great artists in May and June. Lauritz Melchior was a great favourite in Paris; we used to watch in silent amazement the amount of food he consumed at the Norwegian restaurant, Viking, where we frequently went after the Opera. The singers, among themselves, were like one great family, especially the cast of *Tristan*, at that time including Frieda Leider, Melchior, and Herbert Janssen. Whether the performance took place in Paris, Berlin, Bayreuth, or London, those three were generally engaged together, while *Brangäne* and *Marke* were apt to vary. There were two performances of *Tristan* and two of *Walküre*. In the latter *Wotan* and *Sieglinde* were sung by Friedrich Schorr and Lotte Lehmann, just back from New York. We all stayed together at the Villa Majestic. The Nazi troubles receded into the background, like a bad dream we wished to forget. The days were full of fun and gaiety, and we were all happy.

Naturally, undercurrents arising indirectly from the political situation could be sensed. The press was not always friendly. Paris was full of hostile elements of chauvinistic origin, and difficulties arose, too, from refugee quarters. However, not all refugees were hostile. Some of them came to see Furtwängler, and many to see me. Yet our relation with our exiled compatriots was becoming more and more strained. For those who had lost everything by leaving Germany it became almost impossible to have anything to do with those who remained. The refugees were torn between the love of their deeply-rooted traditions and life, and the recognition

that the new order in their country was incompatible with spiritual
liberty. Yet, some of the people who had fled to France later returned
to Germany, deceived by a short political lull. They were to regret
this bitterly. And those who remained in France became a prey
later on to the Gestapo, in the vicissitudes through which that country
has passed.

Between the Paris performances I took a short business trip to
London where the World Economic Conference was then being
held. London's parks were radiant in the spring sun. The Season
was in full swing. The conference was the principal topic, and
Dollfuss was the focus of interest because of the excellent and
courageous speech he had delivered on June 14th. Nobody who
heard him forgot his allusion to the " wicked neighbour "—Germany.
The text of his speech for the conference had presumably been already
prepared in Vienna. But while he was in London, the Press attaché
of the Austrian Legation in Berlin, Dr. Wasserbäck, was disavowed
as a reprisal for Austria's measures against the illegal activities of
Herr Theo Habicht, head of the Austrian Nazis. Before he was taken
into custody Wasserbäck had telephoned to Dollfuss in London,
and so Dollfuss added one sentence to the text of his speech in which
he referred to the incident. He quoted two lines of Schiller's
" Wilhelm Tell " :

> " Es kann der Frömmste nicht in Frieden bleiben,
> Wenn es dem bösen Nachbar nicht gefällt."

The Times reported his speech on June 15th, translating the quota-
tion as : " Even the best country cannot live in peace if its wicked
neighbour chooses not to allow it ".

Chapter 5

EVEN IN the early days of Nazidom one could already see the falsi-
fication of values. " Right " and " wrong ", " good " and " bad "
had lost their meaning. Neither the State nor the individual can
exist if the principle that right remains right and wrong remains

wrong is not upheld. The old Roman maxim, *Justitia est fundamentum regnorum* still holds, and always will.

If only the outside world had taken a firmer attitude from the beginning, things might not have come to such a pass, and the surprisingly few courageous men in Germany who disagreed openly with the Nazis would have been better supported in their effort to stem the tide. At the time of which I am writing Germany was still very dependent on foreign opinion, and everything connected with foreign countries was at first handled very gingerly by the Government. This was not, actually, due to timidity as far as the Nazis were concerned, but was part of the whole political manœuvre, a tactful camouflage for relentlessness.

Though Furtwängler was desperately disturbed by the course things were taking, he still did not think it irreparable. From his numerous interviews in which he tried to explain the fatal consequences of their racial and party policies on Germany's cultural life to Goebbels, Hitler, and lesser authorities he sometimes returned quite hopeful, because he underrated the tenacity and ruthlessness of the Nazis. He did not realise that they only pretended to agree with him in order to keep him quiet, and that they put him off with empty promises while in fact they did only what *they* wanted. Because he was respectfully treated and listened to, he imagined that he had authority, and therefore he continued to adhere to his belief that all could be righted and that musical life would, after all, be able to function free from the " Aryan clause ".

As mentioned above, many prominent musicians had fallen prey to the first " purifying " waves set in motion by the Nazis. This was in March and April, before any " law " in this connection had been passed. There was hardly a concert institute or opera house that had not given " indefinite leave " to a conductor, director, or manager, while others had simply retired of their own accord. The same thing applied to the universities and all similar institutions, of course. While a great number of people disappeared from public life, others profited by the vacancies. Corruption flourished, and it was not astonishing that actions against prominent people of Jewish descent sprang up like mushrooms and that new " stars ", hitherto allegedly " suppressed " by the Jews, made their appearance. Many soloists, composers, conductors, and teachers, who by pre-

Hitler standards had not been considered worthy of public notice, now rose in the glory of their Party membership and demanded their due. One day, for instance, it was intimated to Furtwängler that the Minister of Propaganda would like to see a certain musical work performed. It was a work that Furtwängler had declined to accept many years before. The composer was one of those nonentities who exist in the Jewish as well as in the " Aryan " world ; now his *opus* reappeared, dedicated to Goebbels, and the composer himself appeared as a fully-fledged member of the Party. However, the work remained banned from Furtwängler's programmes.

Gradually the outside world became aware of what was going on, and raised its voice in protest. Prominent artists such as Bodanzky, Gabrilowitsch, Kreisler, and others sent a joint telegram to Hitler supporting their colleagues. Toscanini cancelled his participation in the Bayreuth Festival. The fact that Hitler wrote a personal letter to him urging him to revoke his decision offended many Germans, because while Hitler was courting the Italian anti-Fascist, he was expelling many men of worth from Germany.

Personal interest in music and musicians has always been deep and strong in Germany and Austria. It was an essential part of life. No wonder that in all sections of the public there was a growing unrest about all that went on. Much of this unrest surged up to Furtwängler. He still clung to the belief that the upheaval in the musical life of Germany could not go on indefinitely, and felt it to be his sacred mission to use his prominent position in this cause, and to fight for the return to normal conditions. With special care, therefore, he attended to his programmes for the Season 1934.

Preparations for the Berlin Philharmonic Concerts always began a year ahead. Nobody was ever allowed to book the *Philharmonie* before the ten Sundays and Mondays for the Philharmonic General Rehearsals and Concerts had been fixed. As soon as this was settled, invitations were issued to the soloists. The same procedure was followed in 1933 as in preceding years. Everybody concerned was fully aware of the fact that the choice of the soloists for the Berlin Philharmonic Concerts in the first season under the Nazi régime would be a test case. Furtwängler, naturally, always chose his soloists to suit his programmes, and was determined to keep the programmes of these famous concerts free from interference.

In addition to that, he felt sure that if the great international "non-Aryan" artists played in Berlin, the provinces, like the Leipzig *Gewandhaus* and others, would be supported in their endeavours to uphold the tradition. He was also convinced that once prominent "non-Aryan" artists appeared again, the lesser ones would also have a chance to survive the crisis.

Furtwängler had discussed his ideas with an understanding and moderate authority who was closely connected with the Reich-chancellery. His suggestions had been agreed to, and Furtwängler personally wrote his invitations to Casals, Cortot, Josef Hofmann, Huberman, Kreisler, Menuhin, Piatigorsky (former principal cello of the Orchestra), Thibaud, and Arthur Schnabel.

The replies he received from these great artists were not only highly interesting, but also profoundly moving. Menuhin, who was then still a minor, immediately refused by cable and his father explained this refusal in a long letter. Kreisler, Piatigorsky, and Thibaud also declined. Casals, a man of strong character, wrote a wonderful letter of great dignity on the whole subject, in which he at the same time emphasised his strong, personal friendship for Furtwängler. He understood the desperate struggle in which Furt-wängler was engaged, but he said that he would not enter Germany until its musical life was normal again. Cortot refused on the spur of the moment, but later on changed his mind and accepted.

Furtwängler in his invitations argued that art and politics were separate things, but the soloists in their replies unanimously stressed the point that in spite of Furtwängler's personal efforts, politics had intruded into German musical life, and all of them—"Aryans" and others—refused to accept privileges solely on account of their prominence. They would not play in Germany as long as equal rights were not accorded to everyone.

They doubted that Furtwängler could win his battle. History has already proved them right.

Furtwängler had been particularly insistent in his correspondence with Bronislaw Huberman. They had known each other for many years of mutual work in Berlin and in Vienna. Huberman was extremely popular in Berlin and was one of the few who could fill the *Philharmonie* with a recital several times in a season. However, he flatly refused to return to Germany. Furtwängler then wrote him again a very detailed and friendly letter asking him to consider their correspondence and exchange of view-points as purely private. He further wrote that in his view the mission of art was to bridge all gulfs, and that he wished Huberman could see his way to help him to make a start in this sense.

Furtwängler had written to Huberman out of a strong and sincere conviction. Fighting a brave and lonely battle, he fervently hoped that he might overcome the unnatural measures threatening to strangle Germany's artistic life, if those who shared his feeling would side with him. He reasoned that in all their measures the Nazis always referred to the " Voice of the People ". He was convinced that the People would warmly welcome the artists whom they had applauded for many years. He hoped that the great soloists with whom he was linked by so many unforgettable memories would help him to convince the new régime of what the People really wished for. What he did not realise was that the new régime did not *want* to be convinced.

Huberman then replied to Furtwängler and simultaneously gave his reply to the press. This reply has a message for the whole civilised world and deserves to be quoted fully. Huberman, like Furtwängler, wrote with passionate conviction. Here is his letter :

VIENNA,
August 31, 1933.

DEAR FRIEND,—Permit me first of all to express my admiration for the fearlessness, determination, tenacity, and sense of responsibility with which you have conducted your campaign begun in April for rescuing the concert stage from threatening destruction by racial " purifiers ".

When I place your action—the only one, by the way, that has led to a positive result in the Germany of to-day—alongside that of Toscanini, Paderewski, and the Busch brothers, all of which sprang from the same feeling of solidarity and concern for the continuation of our culture, I am seized with a feeling of pride that I, too, may call myself a musician.

Precisely these models of a high sense of duty, however, must prevent all our colleagues from accepting any compromise that might endanger the final goal.

Although the Government's declarations, which owe their origin to you, may represent the maximum of what may presently be attained, yet, unfortunately, I cannot accept them as sufficient for my reparticipation in German concert life. My attitude is based on the following fundamental objective human and ethical considerations :

The Government deems it necessary to emphasise the selective principle of highest achievement as the decisive one for music, as for every other form of art. This underscoring of something that ought to be self-evident would be meaningless if it did not imply a determination to apply the principle of selection on a racial basis—a principle that it is impossible to understand—to all other realms of culture.

Moreover, there is a wide gap between the announcement of the principle of achievement arbitrarily limited to art and its practical application—a gap that simply cannot be bridged. For included in the general concept of the advancement of art are, first and foremost, the institutions of learning and art collections.

As far as the special realm of the furtherance of the art of music is concerned, municipal and State Opera houses are an essential factor ; yet no case has come to my attention of the intended reinstatement of those museum directors, orchestra conductors, and music teachers who were dismissed on account of their Jewish origin, their different political views, or even their lack of interest in politics.

In other words, the intention of " re-establishing the principle of achievement in art " by no means embraces art in general, or even the entire field of music. Merely the relatively narrow and special field of the concert or recital is to be restored to the free competition of those " real artists " who are to fill the concert hall.

And as every concert of importance is connected with extensive international publicity, while the research specialist or teacher can only on rare occasions appear before the public with the results of his work, it is quite conceivable that the few foreign or Jewish artists who have been asked to assist at such concerts might be used as arguments that everything is well culturally in Germany.

In reality, German thoroughness would continue to find ever-new definitions for racial purity and apply them to the still immature student of art in the schools, laboratories, and so forth.

I am confident, of course, that you, honoured friend, would regret such a result quite as much as would the majority of German concert-goers.

There is, however, also a human-ethical side to the problem.

I should like a definite rendering of music as a sort of artistic projection of the best and most valuable in man.

Can you expect this process of sublimation, which presupposes complete abandonment of one's self to one's art, of the musician who feels his human dignity trodden upon and who is officially degraded to the rank of a pariah ? Can you expect it of the musician to whom the guardians of German culture deny, because of his race, the ability to understand " pure German music " ?

At the same time they deliberately keep silent, on the one hand, concerning the half-Jewish origin of Richard Wagner, which has now been proved beyond peradventure of doubt, and on the other hand, concerning the historic rôle played by Mendelssohn, Anton Rubinstein, Herrmann Levi, Joseph Joachim, and so forth.

You try to convince me by writing, " Someone must make a beginning to break down the wall that keeps us apart ". Yes, if it were only a wall in the concert hall ! But the question of more or less than authoritative interpretation of a violin concerto is but one of numerous aspects—and, God knows, not the most important one—behind which the real problem is hidden.

In reality it is not a question of violin concertos nor even merely of the Jews ; the issue is the retention of those things that our fathers achieved by blood and sacrifice, of the elementary pre-conditions of our European culture, the freedom of personality and its unconditional self-responsibility unhampered by fetters of caste or race.

Whether these achievements shall again be recognised depends not upon the readiness of the individual who is " the first to break through the wall that separates ", but, as in the past, upon the urge of the conscience of artists collectively, which, once aroused, will crash through sources of resistance with the impulse of a force of nature, breaking them as it would a paper wall.

I cannot close this letter without expressing to you my deep regret at the conditions that have resulted in my being separated for the moment from Germany. I am especially grieved and pained in my relationship as a friend of my German friends and as an interpreter of German music who very much misses the echo awakened in his German hearers. And nothing could make me happier than to observe a change also outside the realm of concert life which would liberate me from the compulsion of conscience, striking at my very heartstrings, to renounce Germany. With warm greetings, Sincerely yours.—BRONISLAW HUBERMAN.

Huberman did not give up the struggle at this point, as is shown in the following letter to the *Manchester Guardian*, published on

March 7, 1936, on the Nuremberg legislation and the destruction of intellectual freedom :

SIR,—I shall be glad if you will print the following " open letter " which I have addressed to the German intellectuals :

Since the publication of the ordinances regulating the application of the Nuremberg legislation—this document of barbarism—I have been waiting to hear from you one word of consternation or to observe one act of liberation. Some few of you at least, certainly must have some comment to make upon what has happened, if your avowals of the past are to endure. But I have been waiting in vain. In the face of this silence I must no longer stand mute. It is two and a half years since my exchange of correspondence with Dr. Wilhelm Furtwängler, one of the most representative leaders of spiritual Germany. It will be recalled that Dr. Furtwängler endeavoured to prevent me from publishing my refusal of his invitation to play with his orchestra in Germany. His astonishing argument was that such a publication would close Germany to me, for many years, and perhaps for ever. My answer on August 31, 1933, stated among other things :

" . . . In spite of this I would perhaps have hesitated with this publication if the chasm between Germany and the cultural world had not been rendered even more impassable by recent events. Nothing discloses more dreadfully the brutalisation of large sections of the German population than the threats which have been published for weeks in the newspapers that German girls will be placed in the pillory if found in the company of Jews at coffee-houses or on excursions, or if they carry on love affairs with them. This kind of baiting could not fail to result in such bestialities of the darkest Middle Ages as described in *The Times.*"

The description referred to was in the London *Times* of August 23, 1933, and told the story of a gentle Aryan girl who in punishment of her alleged commerce with a Jew was dragged in a pillory through the principal streets of Nuremberg amid the howls of the mob. As a consequence she suffered a stroke of insanity and was put in the asylum of Erlangen.

Dr. Furtwängler was profoundly revolted not only at the Nuremberg incidents, which he assured me he and all " real Germans " condemned as indignantly as I, but also against me because of my reference to the brutalisation of large sections of the German population. He felt himself compelled to regard this as a " monstrous generalization which had nothing to do with reality ".

In the meantime two and a half years have passed. Countless people have been thrown into gaols and concentration camps, exiled, killed, and driven to suicide. Catholic and Protestant ministers, Jews, Democrats, Socialists, Communists, army generals became the victims of a like fate. I am not familiar with Dr. Furtwängler's attitude to these happenings, but he expressed clearly enough his own opinion of all "real Germans" concerning the shamefulness of the so-called race-ravishing pillories ; and I have not the slightest doubt of the genuineness of his consternation, and believe firmly that many, perhaps the majority of Germans, share his feelings.

Well then, what have you, the "real Germans", done to rid conscience and Germany and humanity of this ignominy since these make-believe Germans, born in the Argentine, in Bohemia, in Egypt, and in Latvia, have changed my alleged "monstrous generalisation" to legal reality ? Where are the German Zolas, Clemenceaus, Painlevés, Picquarts, in this monster Dreyfus case against an entire defenceless minority ; where are the Masaryks in this super-dimensional Polna case ? Where has the voice of blood, if not the voice of justice and common sense, been raised against the even more inhuman persecution of those born of mixed marriages between Aryans and Jews, and of pure Aryans who have the misfortune to be the spouses of Jews ?

Before the whole world I accuse you, German intellectuals, you non-Nazis, as those truly guilty of all these Nazi crimes, all this lamentable breakdown of a great people—a destruction which shames the whole white race. It is not the first time in history that the gutter has reached out for power, but it remained for the German intellectuals to assist the gutter to achieve success. It is a horrifying drama which an astonished world is invited to witness ; German spiritual leaders with world citizenship who until but yesterday represented German conscience and German genius, men called to lead their nation by their precept and example, seemed incapable from the beginning of any other reaction to this assault upon the most sacred possessions of mankind than to coquet, co-operate, and condone. And when, to cap it all, demagogical usurpation and ignorance rob them of their innermost conceptions from their own spiritual workshop, in order thereby to disguise the embodiment of terror, cowardice, immorality, falsfication of history in a mantle of freedom, heroism, ethics, German intellectuals reach the pinnacle of their treachery : they bow down and remain silent.

Must, then, the Catholic Church and the Protestant Church in

Germany battle alone in their truly heroic struggle for Germany's honour, tradition, and future ?

Germany, you people of poets and thinkers, the whole world —not only the world of your enemies, but the world of your friends—waits in amazed anxiety for your word of liberation. Yours, etc.—BRONISLAW HUBERMAN.

Chapter 6

THE REFUSAL of the soloists to play for the Berlin Philharmonic Concerts was a tragic enough symptom of the position, but worse was to come. The Orchestra's organisation itself, its freedom of unfettered activity were suddenly endangered, and the Orchestra found itself engaged in a desperate fight to preserve its prestige and artistic standards. This struggle which the Berlin Philharmonic Orchestra waged for its artistic and material existence was, in essence, the battle between Freedom and Dictatorship.

In March 1933 when the breaking down of the pre-Hitler and the building up of a new world were taking place simultaneously, the Orchestra did not know where it stood. However high the receipts might be, it was certain that without the guarantee of a balanced budget the Orchestra could not continue to exist, let alone keep up its artistic standard.

From the very first days of the Nazi régime there had been a re-shuffle in all administrative organisations, and the Orchestra found itself in consequence in a perilous position. It was suddenly dependent for its financial position upon fresh factors, and new holders of power who could withdraw their backing if the Orchestra did not toe the line. It was dependant upon the whims of persons, to the Party principles and theories of whom the conductor was unwilling to make concessions, particularly in so far as they concerned the personnel of the Orchestra.

At the time of Hitler's seizure of power, the Orchestra was a limited liability company. Dr. Lange, the " Aryan " and Social-Democratic First Mayor of Berlin was the chairman.

Many people coveted the rank of First Mayor, and so it happened that Dr. Lange was relieved of his post as early as March 1933. In any case, he would hardly have been able to protect the Orchestra much longer—having been a member of the Social-Democratic Party. The Berlin municipal government, until then rather more " red " than " brown ", suddenly seemed to be more Nazi than the Nazis. Those, especially, who managed to stick to the posts they had held in pre-Nazi times could not do enough to denounce their former colleagues and push them out of office.

The Orchestra had been built up by selection based on competence, every single aspirant, before being accepted, having to play before Furtwängler and all the members of the Orchestra. These auditions were held in a critically judicious spirit : often Furtwängler stopped an audition after only a few bars had been played, and in such a case nothing more could be done for the aspirant.

The Berlin Philharmonic in these early Nazi days was caught in the swirl of all the different undercurrents, political and social, that were seething just under the surface. Moreover, there was undoubtedly a certain amount of jealousy of Furtwängler himself, both on the part of disappointed musicians and the members of other orchestras. Musicians rejected at the Philharmonic auditions were bound to have friends in the Party and used them to make their new power felt. Soon accusations against Furtwängler, the Berlin Philharmonic Orchestra, and myself poured in to Ministries and Party offices.

The morale of the Orchestra itself was, generally speaking, very high. It was one of the few organisations which did not possess a Nazi " cell ". However, orchestral musicians are an odd lot, especially if they meddle in politics, and even this Orchestra was entangled in some political incidents. There was, for instance, a wind player, a not very intelligent personage, whose work had lately deteriorated, and whose supersession had even been considered. He, insignificant as he was, appeared one day in a S.A. uniform and tried to make trouble. He got short shrift.

Meanwhile the financial problems of the Orchestra continued unsolved. All payments on the part of the city of Berlin and Prussia had stopped, although, pending a new arrangement, the former board was still responsible. But as long as the superior authority was undefined, not only did our work suffer from interference from each former member of the late board of the Orchestra Company, but from every one of the new Nazi organisations.

While the Philharmonic question was not the concern of Prussia, Goering, then Prime Minister of Prussia, was very anxious to come to an agreement with Furtwängler, to whom he had offered the post of Director of the Berlin State Opera, thereby creating a double position for him. It is well known that Goering had asked Hitler for the privilege of having the State Opera under his sole authority, thus withdrawing it for all time from the grasp of Goebbels, who presently made himself the master of all theatres in the Reich. Goering took the office of chief of the State Opera very seriously. He attended the performances whenever possible, especially during the first year. And so it came about that during the initial stages of his Opera negotiations Furtwängler found that Goering lent him, if not actual help, at least a willing ear for his Philharmonic troubles.

As indicated, the question of the administration and budget of the Orchestra was one part of the problem, its "aryanisation" the other. If the Berlin municipal authorities alone had had the right to decide on this matter, all those musicians considered "inadmissible" as civil servants would have been dismissed on the spot. Indeed, an attempt was made to convene a Town Council meeting for this purpose. Berlin was legally entitled to that, since, owing to the delay, the Board of which it was a member still existed in its old form. Furt-wängler however, anticipating trouble, managed to get the meeting cancelled by the higher authority of the Reich and thus again averted disaster. Owing to the unsettled state of affairs no radical interference was yet possible, and Furtwängler was able to protect the Orchestra for the time being.

The whole Government had been present at the last Philharmonic Concert of the season 1932–33 before the Orchestra had left for the tour which I have already described. Dr. Goebbels then came into the artists' room and informed Furtwängler that in future the Orchestra would be under his authority. Goebbels can be charming, if he wishes, as many people can testify. Often enough he beguiled Furtwängler by his charm. On this occasion, too, he completely hoodwinked him. Furtwängler left for his tour reassured.

During the tour correspondence on Philharmonic matters went

on, but nothing was decided. In the middle of June, when we returned, there had not been the least progress towards a settlement. The Ministry of Propaganda was known to be the centre of doubtful elements. In no other Ministry was the craving for power of subordinate officials, jealousy, and envy of promotion so developed as there. It was, curiously enough, almost a crime in the Totalitarian State to deal direct with the Minister. This sounds grotesque, but it is a fact. Furtwängler had never dealt with bureaucracy, he had been spared all this in pre-Hitler times, and so he naturally thought that if he went to Goebbels direct everything could be settled. Was this not the Absolute State and had not the head of the Ministry only to press a button and the thing was done ? The contrary was actually the case, and became all the more so the more the Reich Ministers were overburdened with work and worried by increasing complications. If the minor officials were not sufficiently flattered by the petitioner even the Minister's word carried no weight. The whole state of the administration, especially at the Propaganda Ministry, shows how insincere and shallow all theories of the new Absolute State are. Far from simplification, one was faced with a greatly increased bureaucracy.

In spite of Goebbels' promise in early April no single payment by the Reich had been made by June 1933. The relevant official in the Ministry of Propaganda, a man of the old régime, explained that Goebbels should never have given a promise regarding the Orchestra before securing the necessary funds in his budget. The Prussian Minister of Finance simply stopped the budgeted amount due to the Orchestra from Prussia. The *Reichsrundfunk* declared their agreement null and void under the present altered circumstances. Goering, on behalf of Prussia, explained he could do nothing in the matter since, according to the German Official Gazette, Goebbels on behalf of the Reich, was responsible. It was a deadlock.

Tension due to the constant insecurity began to rise in the Orchestra, and the view gained ground, fostered by Party people, that unless the Jewish members and myself resigned, the Nazis would always find a pretext for avoiding a satisfactory solution of the problem.

This was certainly contrary to all the agreements with the Government, which, so far, had declared the Orchestra sacrosanct pending further decisions. However, these "terror methods" used parallel to, and independent of, ministerial promises, produced their results.

All this had its effect on the weaker spirits in the Orchestra who one day pronounced Höber, for many years member of the executive, dismissed, and expressed their intention of moving the office of the Orchestra to another address, thus separating it from my rooms. At this Furtwängler lost his patience—it was still possible then to lose patience with the Nazis. He forced Goebbels, who had persistently evaded him, to grant him a personal interview. This conversation, at least theoretically, straightened matters out. Goebbels reiterated that he was willing to take over the Orchestra provided Furtwängler became its leader in every respect. The board of seventeen directors were to renounce all their rights in favour of Furtwängler. Goebbels gave his assurance that he would honour his promise. Accordingly Furtwängler reinstituted the *status quo ante*, and issued a circular to the Orchestra explaining the situation.

He informed the Orchestra that all the rights of the board of directors had been invested in him. He alone would be responsible to the Government for everything concerning the Orchestra, and any attempt on the part of members to hold meetings or take political steps was arbitrarily prohibited. On the whole, the Orchestra was entirely on Furtwängler's side. This instruction was therefore only intended for the very few agitators among the members of the Orchestra who had to be held in check to meet the exigencies of the time.

I must enlighten those who believe such a "Leader-position" as was designed by Goebbels for Furtwängler to have been in fact possible. It was not only impossible, it was utterly inconceivable. Elsewhere, personality might count for something, but not under a Fascist régime where the so-called Leader is the slave of those he leads. Actually, this projected solution was nothing so far but a hollow farce. Furtwängler had only been reassured by empty words, and everything dragged on as before. Goebbels himself called a meeting of the former board of directors, but on the appointed day he simply disappeared on holiday without informing anybody concerned, which meant another adjournment for an indefinite time.

Furtwängler was, of course, very troublesome to the authorities;

with his constant demands he frayed the nerves of the leaders of the Reich. In spite of their admiration for him, officials avoided him as much as possible.

Hitler had, in principle, assured Furtwängler of any support he might need, and a discussion on concert and opera questions had been planned. However, he, too, vanished to Berchtesgaden and one was casually informed that the Führer would not return to Berlin for some time, but would go on to Bayreuth from Berchtesgaden to attend the Festival.

The Orchestra, therefore, in July 1933 was faced with complete bankruptcy. There was only one way to avoid disaster—a personal appeal to Hitler. It was therefore decided to send our Party member Kommissar to Bayreuth. Hitler, whom he knew from the early days of the Party, received him immediately. He expressed his great admiration for Furtwängler, and was most astonished and annoyed that the position of the Berlin Philharmonic Orchestra, which he believed to have been settled long ago, was still unsolved. He was furious when he heard that the Orchestra would have to declare itself bankrupt on the first of August, and stated emphatically that this scandal in connection with Germany's famous Orchestra must be avoided at all costs. He instantly sent for Goebbels, who was also in Bayreuth. Goebbels, for once, felt extremely uncomfortable. He found himself in much the same plight as an official who has sabotaged the intentions of his chief. Hitler asked him most indignantly how such an important matter could have been neglected. Goebbels squirmed in his embarrassment, especially as he could not prevent Hitler being told in his very presence that the Orchestra was faced with financial ruin. Hitler decreed that the matter would have to be tackled immediately and assured our envoy that the funds would be provided at once. He also sent word to Furtwängler to visit him as soon as possible to talk things over.

Furtwängler's visit to Obersalzberg took place at the beginning of August. He departed from Berlin armed with a huge memorandum concerning the Orchestra's problems and the reports on individual cases. He always prepared his notes most carefully for such occasions. One of the shortcomings of his sensitive and complex nature in connection with these political encounters was his inability to adapt himself to the crude and primitive mentality peculiar to the

Nazis. He for his part was quickly roused to anger, and thus he often failed to achieve all that he might have done had he used different tactics.

This particular meeting seems to have been very stormy. During their discussion of general and political matters, Hitler and Furtwängler shouted at each other for about two hours, and Furtwängler almost forgot the main subject—the Orchestra. He was so perturbed by the interview that he rang me up from Munich immediately after-wards, saying that he now understood what was at the bottom of Hitler's stubborn point of view. It was not the Jewish question alone, but his attitude inimical to *all* intellectual matters. This telephone conversation—as we soon discovered—was tapped by the Nazis.

Although the encounter with Hitler had occasioned fierce disputes, the future of the Orchestra now seemed finally assured—Hitler saw to that.

On October 26, 1933, the Orchestra was officially taken over by the Reich. The salaries and pensions of the musicians were guaranteed, the ominous " Aryan clause " was not to be applied to the Orchestra. The office for the time being was left untouched.

If it had really been the honest intention of leaving the Orchestra its autonomy without allowing new and inexperienced people to interfere in its affairs, one might have expected a safeguard for quiet and steady work.

The further development of events, however, shows that this point of view could not be held in the Third Reich.

Chapter 7

ALTHOUGH, later on, a new stratum of society came into being as another disappeared, it took some time (certainly till the beginning or middle of 1934) for the cleavage caused by the Nazi ideology to take effect in all classes of the people. It is true that, from the very beginning, encroachment on liberty took place resulting in immediate and irreparable losses. This was felt in every walk of life—in the universities, in the great hospitals, and in private clinics, as well as in banks and industry. In civic and government administrations, all officials—even if " Aryan "—who were unfortunate enough to displease some Nazi, were pushed out of their job. Scholars and professors of world fame were dismissed from the universities. All the people affected in this way were cut off from their former life ; they withdrew from normal social intercourse and eventually disappeared.

But for all this it would be wrong to assume that because of these drastic changes, life on the surface was already completely altered.

Social life—as distinct from political—in connection with musical activities, for instance, was not very much changed for the present. Almost every night concerts were held in the *Philharmonie* and in the *Beethovensaal*, as well as elsewhere. The social events revolving round the great Philharmonic Concerts continued. After the Sunday morning General Rehearsals there was usually an official luncheon, and after the Monday evening concerts a reception or a party. Very often friends came to my home.

The Berlin State Opera continued to be an interesting centre. Apart from the fine performances given there, it was a meeting-ground of many interests, and important matters were often settled during the intervals. The *Opernhaus unter den Linden,* as it was called, had always maintained a high standard, and continued to do so. It did justice to the most modern requirements, and was up-to-date not only with regard to technical stage devices but also in every other respect. So far it kept up its fine old tradition—there were no new Nazi functionaries working either on the stage or in the administration—it was still mostly run by old and tried officials. Thanks to Goering's influence, moderation still prevailed here !

How intimate and yet ceremonious were the attendants of the boxes, the genuine type of old officialdom ! I well recall the two attendants outside the boxes of the *Generalintendant.* They had held office since the Kaiser's time and their inimitable dignity left far behind any emulation by the Nazi Ministers who surrounded themselves with scores of S.A. or S.S. guards when visiting the Opera House. (The Berlin State Opera was hit in a British air attack on Berlin in the spring of 1941.)

There was always great interest in events at the State Opera. In March 1933 a new production of Richard Strauss' *Elektra* was given with Furtwängler, then only a guest-conductor. Strauss, who spent a great deal of time in Berlin at the beginning of the Nazi régime, was present. He nursed his relations to Opera Houses carefully, and was on especially good terms with the Berlin State Opera and its management. In the autumn of 1933 the Berlin première of his new opera, *Arabella*, took place, with Furtwängler conducting. Strauss was present throughout the rehearsals.

Once during a rehearsal he discovered me at the far end of the stalls and called out : " Ah ! There is Fräulein Geissmar. Please come out into the corridor ! " While we strolled about he asked me what I thought of his new opera and whether I did not agree that the wind instruments were too loud. " Couldn't you convey this to Furtwängler ? " he asked. What a situation ! The great Richard Strauss dared not tell the conductor of his own opera something about a purely technical matter regarding the interpretation of the music. He knew how sensitive Furtwängler was, and he wanted to keep him in a good temper. After this rehearsal I had lunch with Furtwängler and cautiously mentioned the troubles of the great composer. Furtwängler was so amused that Strauss had not dared to approach him directly that he calmly accepted the musical criticism.

There were old ties between Strauss and my family. While my father was still alive Strauss regularly called for a game of *Skat* with him whenever he came to Mannheim. Once when Strauss was dining at our house, my father said to my mother after dinner : " I think you had better go to bed now, dear, because we are going to play cards ". Strauss, the notoriously henpecked husband of Pauline, exclaimed in amazement : " How on earth do you manage to ask your wife to leave the room, and what is more, get her to do so ? " Yet, despite the old acquaintanceship with my family at the time when the German Government seemed to have nothing more important to do than to discuss how to free Furtwängler of his secretary, Strauss failed to take up the cudgels on my behalf.

Artists from the provinces came more frequently to Berlin than before those troubled days. Many came to see Furtwängler, who, by his courage, had assumed an almost mythical fame. They often brought news of what was happening underground as well as officially ;

much of it was distressing and much tragic. These visitors and the correspondence that followed with them caused me many sleepless nights.

At that time, Furtwängler was conductor of the Berlin Philharmonic Orchestra, director of the Berlin State Opera, vice-president of the *Reichsmusikkammer*, and from July 1933, also a Prussian *Staatsrat*. The world has often reproached Furtwängler for accepting this title. Actually, the whole Prussian State Council, at least as far as its functions were concerned, was one of the meaningless, pompous displays staged by Goering. It was, so to speak, a private affair of Goering's and has hardly met more than twice.

One Sunday morning while he was on holiday, Furtwängler, the director of Goering's Opera House, received a telegram : " Appoint you herewith Prussian Councillor of State. Hermann Goering." The story goes that Goering, on the point of leaving his office one Saturday suddenly said : " Quick, let's make Furtwängler a Councillor of State ". The nomination occurred at a moment when the struggle for the retention of standards was still at its height and was not considered a lost battle. It would have been completely wrong for Furtwängler to refuse this sign of confidence. On the contrary, it was hoped that he would gain in authority through the new appointment and would be able to enforce his views more easily. The hope was vain, but this naturally could not be foreseen.

In spite of all the growing difficulties there was a fine community spirit amongst the musicians in Berlin.

Perfect comradeship reigned among the section leaders of the Orchestra who had formed a chamber-music association. They frequently came to my home and played quartets. Furtwängler, who was a wonderful chamber-music player, occasionally joined us, and sometimes Hindemith came, delighting everybody with his glorious viola tone. I can never forget the occasion when we played Brahms' piano Quintet with Furtwängler at the piano, Goldberg, first violin, myself second, Hindemith the violist, and Graudan, principal cello of the Berlin Philharmonic.

From this period dates the following story, showing how little the " opinion of the people " was reflected by the Government's measures.

Since things had remained unchanged for the time being in the

Orchestra, Brahms' Double Concerto was put on the programmes of one of the weekly popular concerts with the much discussed first violin and first cello, Goldberg and Graudan, as soloists. Hundreds of people had to be turned away, jubilant applause ! The genuine *vox populi* was quite sound ! And as it was so, the Nazis had often to manufacture " providence " in order to impose their will. Unfortunately on one occasion " providence " and the " voice of the people " interrupted by mistake one of the Bach concerts given by Edwin Fischer—they had gone to the wrong hall ! What they had been supposed to do was to disturb a Jewish singer next door !

Foreign artists had always been among Berlin's regular visitors ; the type changed only gradually. The refusals I have already mentioned of the great international soloists to take part in the Berlin Philharmonic Concerts in 1933-34 were the first indications that international musical life was undergoing a radical change in its relation to Germany.

Italy was then by no means friendly to the Nazi régime. The comparison between Hitler and Mussolini was very unfavourable to the former in the eyes of the world in general and Italy in particular. However, Italian artists came in great numbers to Germany. Respighi arrived in the early autumn, Casella, Mainardi, Cassadó—more Spanish than Italian—and others, all saw no reason why they should not take advantage of the situation. The Nazi régime was more keen on the display of foreigners than any preceding German Government, and nothing was left undone to facilitate visits of artists from abroad.

The Japanese conductor, Viscount Konoye, brother of the Japanese Premier, arrived in Berlin in 1933 and conducted a concert with the Berlin Philharmonic Orchestra. He was quite a good musician, brought up on German music.

One can readily understand that the atmosphere at foreign Embassies was the last to degenerate. Here one sensed nothing of the sinister spirit that had crept into life.

The Italian Embassy, especially since Cerruti had become its Ambassador, was the liveliest. The Ambassadress, Donna Elisabetha Cerruti, was indefatigable. She was Hungarian, well educated, ambitious, and free from snobbishness. She worked as ceaselessly for the interests of the Embassy as if she were herself the Ambassador. She was a handsome and stately woman with a finely-poised head. In the circumstances, the Italian Embassy was the most important one for the Nazis to conciliate, and was in high favour with them. Whenever Hitler went out socially, it was the Italian Ambassadress who was placed beside him. Although it was occasionally whispered that she was Jewish, this did not interfere with their relationship in the least ; on the contrary, it was said that Hitler always enjoyed the presence of this clever and experienced *femme du monde*.

When an Italian artist came to Berlin, a function was always arranged for him at the Embassy. If for some time he happened to have no professional engagement, the Ambassadress saw to it that this was rectified. Nothing was too much trouble for her ; if I was unable to leave my office, she came and discussed her plans with me. She arranged a series of concerts in the great music hall of the Embassy at which mainly Italian works and Italian artists were heard. It may be assumed that the Embassy had a special grant for these purposes. These concerts, despite their length, were very popular, and one used to stay on at this hospitable house till late at night.

Other Embassies were also hospitable, but not to such a degree as the Italian. The French Embassy was always a centre of social events. The Ambassador, M. François-Poncet, with his Mephistophelian smile, was a very pleasant host. He had many children and was more in the limelight than his wife. Many *bons mots* are attributed to him, such as the substitution of "le Fureur" for "the Führer".

In the winter of 1933-34 there were At-Homes at the British as well as the French Embassy. At the latter there was always a great assembly of guests, and one could still meet people who had already withdrawn themselves from ordinary social life in the new era.

The British Embassy was always very exclusive, and one met there—if any—only very high Nazi officials. Sir Eric Phipps, then Ambassador to Berlin, was a typical representative of old-fashioned British diplomacy. Even his greatest enemy could not call him pro-Nazi. Hitler is reputed to have had a certain sympathy for him which expressed itself in his excellent imitations of Sir Eric.

The Dutch, and especially the Americans, were very reserved as regards National Socialists, and accordingly restrained their social activities. The other Embassies and Legations lived their routine life of duties which varied with the political sitation.

Amidst all these new developments the German Foreign Office still, and for some time to come, embodied the hopes of many, and was a kind of sheet anchor. The part the Foreign Office played at first was entirely concentrated on putting things right and undoing Nazi blunders, as it was at that time continually inundated with complaints. This was by no means pleasant for the disciplined officials who had at least as many grounds for complaints as the plaintiffs. All sorts of rumours were floating about on the subject. At one time it was said that the Foreign Office and the Army would together lead the country in the right direction. Another time, one heard rumours of combined efforts of the Foreign Office and the great banking concerns ; many other hares were started. While the old and the new powers were endeavouring to assert themselves against each other, the Nazis pursued their aims unfalteringly, if recklessly, untrammelled by any regard for traditions. The new elements of the Party, free from any burden of tradition and responsibility, " rushed in where angels feared to tread ", and this was part of their strength.

Every aspect of art in need of official support, such as the position of artists in foreign countries, exhibitions abroad, artistic activities in frontier districts—were all under the control of Department VII of the Foreign Office. In pre-Hitler times the officials dealing with this work had always been highly educated and cultured men carefully chosen for their duties. One could hardly imagine that the " New Germany " would dispense with their services.

The Berlin Philharmonic was generally independent of any diplomatic support, but when needed it came promptly and discreetly from Department VII. For as long as possible they assisted us—until one day they were found to have disappeared from the Wilhelmstrasse.

This Department of the German Foreign Office was considered immensely important by Goebbels, since one of his principal aims was to bring under his control all cultural activities within Germany and, as far as they concerned Germans, abroad. Of all bodies concerned with cultural questions, this Department was the plum, and so it was not astonishing that Goebbels, by Machiavellian policy, managed to transfer the precious Art Division to the authority of the Ministry of Propaganda.

Those officials of the Goebbels Ministry who now gradually ousted the former members of the Department and took over their duties, were an entirely different set of people. Uncouth, inefficient, knowing little or nothing of their subject, but full of the bullying assertiveness of the typical Nazi, they were a sorry contrast to those gentlemen of the old school who were so well versed in the subtle intricacies of the work. From now on one could only stand by regretfully and watch the gradual disintegration and decay of this carefully built-up edifice.

[1 9 3 4]

Chapter 8

THE END of 1933 passed in comparative quiet. Many people had left Germany for political reasons, while others still hesitated. A faint hope still persisted that the excesses of the Nazis might be stemmed ; but a shadow hung over everything, and we all felt at the mercy of the uncertain storms of fate.

Just as individuals struggled for positions and power in the New Germany, individual members of the Government did the same among themselves. Many matters hung on the question as to whether at a particular moment it was Goering, Goebbels, Hess, or Rosenberg who was in favour, and had the ear of the Führer. In its relation to foreign politics the *dritte Reich* was far from being consolidated.

In January 1934 the Berlin Philharmonic Orchestra, with Furt-wängler, set out for another tour, embracing Germany, England, Holland, and Belgium, and ending naturally in Germany again. I went direct to London, where I stayed with the German Ambassador, von Hoesch. Hoesch's attitude was exemplary. A man of integrity, as he was, was bound to resent the policy of the Nazis. He never revealed any sign of his opinion, however, but helped the cause of the true Germany as long as, and wherever, he could.

The Philharmonic Orchestra and Furtwängler followed me in due course. For the first time, feeling in England was divided with regard to the visit of the Berlin Philharmonic Orchestra. Many people declared that one could no longer attend their concerts, and we were warned of possible demonstrations. The Queen's Hall was given special police protection. Nevertheless the concert passed off without any trouble, amidst the great enthusiasm of the audience, and the London as well as provincial concerts were sold out. At that time Sir Thomas Beecham, who was a staunch friend of the Berlin Philharmonic, wrote an Open Letter supporting their visit.

The music-loving Austrian Minister, Baron Franckenstein, who attended every rehearsal, was photographed with Furtwängler. This photo was published in *The Times* and caused the political speculation that Furtwängler would leave Germany to accept the direction of the Vienna State Opera.

On the return journey a concert had been arranged at the Hague. We stayed with the German Minister, Count Zech, whose wife was *née* von Bethmann-Hollweg. They were charming survivals of the *ancien régime*. Count Zech was badly afflicted by the political changes. He was very fond of music, yet, being the German Minister he not only could not attend Bruno Walter's concerts, but even the recitals of his old friend, Adolf Busch, were out of bounds for him. He, like so many people, tried to do his best to help the true Germany over this period, and, just like Hoesch, he spared no efforts. Holland was then very hostile towards Nazi Germany. The Philharmonic Concert was obviously being boycotted. During our stay at the Hague we had already received news that although our concerts in Belgium were sold out, the political atmosphere was very hostile, and demonstrations might be expected. Our old friend, the former German Minister to Belgium, Count Lerchenfeld, had already been retired, and his post was vacant.

When we reached Brussels we had a rehearsal in the afternoon, before the concert in the *Palais des Beaux Arts*. In order to be protected against hostile demonstrations between this rehearsal and the beginning of the concert, Furtwängler and the Orchestra were not allowed to leave the hall, and our food was brought in to us. Mounted police surrounded the concert hall. The Belgian Government did all it could to prevent serious incidents. The counter propaganda was considerable. Before the concert began the Belgian General, Menin, who for many years had been on the board of the *Société Philharmonique de Bruxelles*, made a short speech from the platform. Then, and then only, Furtwängler appeared and was accorded thunderous applause. The concert was a great success ; the atmosphere in the streets, however, was tense.

The Antwerp concert was sold out, but the feeling there was even stronger than in Brussels. There were police cordons, mounted police demonstrations, and even Red Cross nurses were provided in the hall. A stink-bomb was thrown during the concert. Afterwards Furtwängler had to be escorted through a side exit by twelve policemen to his train for Brussels.

At the beginning of February 1934 we were back in Berlin. The only pleasant event at that time was the visit of Sir Thomas Beecham. His short stay was like a breath of fresh air to us all. There he sat in the hotel sampling the wonderful hocks, inviting all his old friends to see him without any racial discrimination whatever, kindness itself to everyone—and totally impervious to the shadows the Nazis were casting over everything.

Chapter 9

THE Berlin Philharmonic Orchestra, as mentioned before, had been legally taken over by the Reich on October 26, 1933. This, however, was only a decree, and carried with it no practical solution of the administrative problems of the Orchestra. To arrive at this solution, the Reich had sent towards the end of 1933 a State investigator who was to audit our books and go through our whole correspondence. One could not expect great understanding from such an official, and already while we were abroad hints had reached us leading us to suspect that this examination of our books and files had not been carried out in an unbiassed spirit. The investigator's report was unfavourable to the Orchestra. When Furtwängler read this bulky and grossly unfair document, he started to compile a counter-report, and attacked mercilessly all the people concerned, stressing the serious consequences of their threatened actions.

Again I must point out what were the immediate incentives to much that was happening in Germany at that time. It is possible that the Government would have liked to proceed carefully in the delicate matter of the Philharmonic. It is even possible that they would have liked to leave Furtwängler his independence—at least for some time. But what could they do in the face of the many petty officials concerned, in the face of their own Party, their own bureaucracy? Every insignificant civil servant in the Ministry of Propaganda was longing for the moment when the independent organisation of the Berlin Philharmonic Orchestra and its proud conductor would be caught in the Nazi net and subjugated to Nazi methods. The Germans, by allowing the stifling of all individual initiative, were systematically destroying themselves.

Added to this was the fact that the new Orchestra Company was a State Company, and thus every State authority assumed that they had the right to interfere. This happened only too soon. Hardly had the Reich taken over, when the Nazis not only wanted to find a post for an additional manager in the Orchestra office, but also ordered us to engage a man who was unemployed at the time. This was how they reduced the apparent number of unemployed! All this meant infinite complications for an organisation which— apart from its work inside Germany—was designed to maintain continuous international contacts, and every member of which had hitherto been an expert in his particular sphere.

However, the Reich paid the piper, and so it considered itself entitled to call the tune. After the reorganisation by the Nazis, with the additional staff they insisted upon, the actual cost of running the Berlin Philharmonic office proved to be higher even than our previous estimated budgets which had been rejected by the State investigator as being too expensive.

Furtwängler wielded a certain power by virtue of his outstanding achievements. Yet all this was of no avail. He was constantly attacked from all sides, and difficulties grew. He could not always attain a solution by reaching a Minister's ear. His prominent position, his far-reaching reputation—gained independently of the Nazis—his demands, contrary to all current usage, for maintaining unchanged his artistic organisation and the necessary staff, all made him irritating to and disliked by minor officials, and gradually also by the higher ones. His outspoken remarks were discussed and distorted.

I was constantly attacked without the chance of defence. Though my life on the surface might have seemed interesting, it was at bottom merely torture. The reader may ask me : " Why ? " I was free, I was not detained in a concentration camp. No, I was not, but in what mental misery one had to live—as if afflicted with an infectious disease—an outcast in one's own home. One had to get used to hiding like a leper. All the customary ideas and values with which one had been brought up changed rapidly. True, in personal contact with friends nothing of this was noticeable, but the psychological pressure made one always self-conscious. The natural relation to one's surroundings were insidiously undermined, and the mind was assailed as is the body when invaded by a bacillus. To live under such circumstances is a permanent torture, and it requires a good deal of self-control to conceal one's feelings. Furtwängler was always the same to me, and I carefully concealed my worries from him. In spite of it all, even while I had the freedom to decide, I would never voluntarily have left him after so many years of joint work. He fought a noble battle, and deserved better from me than desertion. Yet, while remaining at my post, I realised clearly the gravity of the situation.

The following incident is characteristic of the sinister suspension of all normal standards.

One day, an old friend of Furtwängler's came to see me. Like so many Germans he was always a bit pompous, and on that day he appeared with an extra important air, saying he had something to tell me. After many preliminaries he finally came out with the advice that I should avoid the *Philharmonie* in future, as my presence was harmful to Furtwängler. Though he knew better than any-one else how Furtwängler relied on me, and how I saved him time and nervous energy, he now had the effrontery to assert that I, who for twenty years had assisted Furtwängler, could suddenly harm him by attending his concerts ! Of course I was popular in the *Philharmonie*, which was a thorn in the side of the Nazis. If I walked about during the interval of a concert, they said that I was too conspicuous. If I remained seated, they complained that people gathered round to talk to me. Now it was hinted that I had better not go at all ! At the next Philharmonic Concert, accordingly, I stayed at home. As soon as the concert was over, Furtwängler rang me up to ask if I was ill. " No," I said, " but I have been told my going to the *Philharmonie* is doing you harm." Furtwängler was furious. " Who had the insolence to interfere ? " he asked. " Please don't take any notice of such nonsense ! " " All right," I replied, with a lump in my throat, " just as you like."

Life was growing more and more difficult. The Nazis groped their way forward, and experimented to see how far they could go before meeting with resistance. They used the same procedure in the reorganisation of the Orchestra. One day it seemed as if Furt-wängler, in spite of all promises, would not be able to keep any of his collaborators, let alone myself. He thereupon informed Dr. Funk, then Under-Secretary of State in Goebbels' Ministry (now Minister of Finance and successor of Schacht) whom he had accidentally met at a reception given by President Hindenburg, that if the Government had so little understanding of his merits as to allow these interferences to continue he would resign his positions, deeming it impossible to work under such circumstances.

This helped—at least for the moment. After endless negotiations, an agreement was reached. The final formalities for the change-over from the Berlin Philharmonic Orchestra Co. Ltd. to the Reich Company had to be effected by April 1, 1934. The whole staff was, for the time being, retained. A business manager, chosen by the Ministry of Propaganda, was added to it as well as the unemployed man.

Our joint office was left untouched. In Furtwängler's agreement a special grant was made for myself and my own secretary. The part of the office dealing with Furtwängler's concerts, foreign tours, and foreign negotiations was formed into a separate *Furtwängler Sekretariat*. A lump sum was allocated to him to finance this. My name was no longer allowed to occur in transactions with the Reich, nor was I permitted to have anything to do with the newly formed Reich Company, either in financial or other matters. I was not allowed to sign any letters except those concerning my own department.

I had my own letter heading printed differently from the Orchestra's paper. I moved from my room, which was in the middle of the offices, to another at the farthest end. Although from that time I strictly refrained from setting foot in the rest of the office, all the members of the Orchestra management met at my room as before and we discussed what was necessary.

I accepted this "solution", fully realising what it implied. Furt-wängler had exerted all his energy to keep the situation somewhat in control and he had to be supported. He was the only one who ceaselessly tried to stem the current. It was easy to criticise from outside, far more courage was necessary to oppose from within and to carry on.

Chapter 10

THERE IS no doubt that all the conflicts which dominated our lives played havoc with our nerves. Instead of being able to devote oneself to one's work, one had to cope with new troubles every day. It was very difficult to live in constant uncertainty about what would happen next, and to keep one's nervous system under control.

At the beginning of the spring tour I went ahead to Paris in order to be there a few days before the Orchestra arrived. By this time the difference between the atmosphere of Germany and that of foreign countries was felt as soon as one crossed the frontier. One sighed with relief as at a breath of fresh air.

Barthou was then French Foreign Minister. I had frequently met him before. He was a highly cultured man, with many interests, and owned a magnificent library. He loved music, and had written a preface to a book on Hector Berlioz, as well as a book on Wagner, of whom he was an enthusiastic admirer. He was a well-known figure at Bayreuth. Greatly interested in art and artists, he had, at a previous meeting, asked me many questions about my professional work. On that occasion he had told me to let him know immediately when I was next in Paris.

When I arrived in Paris, exhausted and depressed, I was longing for an understanding soul, and, although I had many good friends there, I felt it was Barthou whom I most wanted to see. I sent him a *petit bleu* to the Quai d'Orsay. Later, during the same morning, he rang me up and I immediately went to see him. He sat in his sumptuous room, the small man with a typical French face, the most arresting feature of which were his eyes, full of vivacity, humour, intelligence, and scintillating with kindness. He received me with great warmth and sympathy, and put many questions to me, among them some about my own present life. We talked about things in general, and I attempted to describe to him how Furtwängler was fighting to uphold the old tradition. He must have felt how deeply troubled I was, for he asked me: "*Est-ce qu'on vous persécute?*" Never shall I forget his tact and subtlety of feeling. He avoided saying anything hostile about Germany, just as I would never have openly complained; but in his question and the way it was put, there was real understanding of our problems. I was deeply moved. Barthou said that he had been the first to buy tickets for our concerts; he would attend, and he hoped we would meet again.

Meanwhile I followed my usual routine in Paris. The rift between those Germans who had emigrated and those who continued their life in the Reich was then already deep. The former saw in my work for Furtwängler and the Berlin Philharmonic some kind of "treason". After I had been in Paris for a few days, an article appeared in the *Pariser Tageblatt*, the refugee newspaper, labelling me a "Hitler Jewess". I was greatly upset. At home, we fought unending battles, and now we also had to fight adversaries abroad.

When I visited the German Ambassador, Dr. Köster, successor to Hoesch, who was known as non-Nazi and a decent man of the old school, I poured my heart out to him. Köster refused to be rattled. "First let us have tea," he proposed. He made the tea himself, got some English marmalade out of his cupboard, and then comforted me. "Don't be upset," he said, "you are in good company! Look at the back page of the paper!" I did so, and there was a fierce attack on the German Ambassador himself. I ventured to say that it was easier for an Ambassador to bear than it was for me, but I could not convince him.

The Paris concerts took place as usual. The President of the Republic was present and received Furtwängler during the interval.

We saw the French composers, Milhaud, Honegger, Roussel, our Bayreuth friend, Guy de Pourtalès, and many others.

Barthou, whom in the meantime I had met again, came to the first concert. He walked with me through the foyer of *L'Opéra*. It was on the eve of his departure for his memorable mission to Poland, and for the crowd of journalists, French and other nationalities, not the least for the German, his presence at this concert was a sensation. He went back stage to see Furtwängler, with whom he talked for a while. At the time, his journey to Poland was the focus of interest, and on this evening I was bombarded with questions from all sides. Had he said anything about his journey? I shook my head. How could I admit that he had declared he would pass through Berlin without seeing anybody? Actually he did not even show himself at the window of his carriage, and kept the blinds drawn while the train was stopped at the *Schlesische Bahnhof*. In spite of everything, the concerts ended with great demonstrative applause which overcame all political differences and was inspired solely by the wonderful performance. When Barthou said good-bye to me after it, he held both my hands and said : " *Êtes-vous heureuse ?* "

I saw him only once after that ; it was at the end of May 1934 at a Toscanini concert. On October 13, 1934, he was assassinated in Marseilles.

In the middle of February, when the next spring tour had long been settled, the Italian Ambassador in Berlin, Cerruti, rang me up just after midnight and said he had been urgently requested to invite the Philharmonic and Furtwängler to a tour in Italy for the coming April. I told him that his request came too late ; but he was so insistent that I finally promised to do my best, provided that the change of schedule could be arranged. At the time I stipulated that after upsetting our plans the least we could expect was for Mussolini to grant Furtwängler an audience in Rome. I did my work, Cerruti did his. The Italian tour was tacked on to the French one. In Paris I got a telegram indicating that *Il Capo del Governo* would expect Furtwängler at five p.m. on the free day between the two concerts in the Palazzo Venezia. This telegram almost cost me my head, but of this more presently.

While the Orchestra travelled south in stages, I went straight from Paris to Rome. Soon I discovered that—quite contrary to former times—the feeling in Italy towards the Berlin Philharmonic was definitely hostile. Advance booking was bad, everything was complicated, nothing was quite as it had been before. As soon as I arrived I received a message from Count Ciano asking me to call on him at the Palazzo Chigi. I went there straightaway, and after being led through innumerable resplendent anterooms by even more luxuriously attired footmen, I found myself in the presence of Il Duce's elegant son-in-law, who inquired into my wishes and placed his office at my disposal for anything I might need. He asked if I had time to spare for anything besides the tour, and when I naturally answered in the affirmative, he gave orders that I should be shown the handling of artistic matters in the " Fascio ".

Meanwhile, the Orchestra had arrived. A rehearsal took place in the *Augusteo*, at which most peculiar things occurred, which in retrospect furnish a demonstration of the inconsistencies of Fascist policy.

Austrian journalists, none of whom would have satisfied Hitler's racial desiderata, appeared at this rehearsal in great numbers and were most vociferous. The Austrians then felt very secure under the protection of Il Duce and greatly profited by Italian anti-Nazi feeling. It was 1934 and not yet 1938 !

Suddenly, during the rehearsal, the problem arose whether one had better be prepared to play the *Horst Wessel* song in case the *Giovinezza* had to be played. While the Nazi journalists sat passively about in the hall, an overzealous Austrian journalist offered to get us the score from the Party—as if he were on the most intimate terms with the Nazis.

All these paradoxical happenings were then still possible in Italy, because Italy had not yet become a vassal of Nazi-Germany.

No information had been given that any member of the Italian Government would attend the first concert, and Furtwängler, who, in any case, disliked to combine a purely artistic matter such as his concerts naturally were for him, with the playing of national anthems, especially when they were as musically atrocious as the *Horst Wessel* song, simply began by conducting his Haydn symphony. No sooner had the concert started—I was sitting on a drum behind the stage— when a member of the Fascist secret police pounced on me furiously, declaring that members of the Government were expected to attend and Furtwängler was to be interrupted to play the *Giovinezza*. The man was raving, and I instantly said to myself : " If I am not very careful in handling this matter we shall have a second Toscanini incident ". It is well known that Toscanini has never conducted in Italy since, on his refusing a request for the *Giovinezza* in the middle of a concert, the Fascists set about him bodily. Accordingly, I said guardedly : " Dr. Furtwängler has been explicitly informed that the national anthems are not required this evening. Don't you think the Duce, who is so musical, would disapprove of an interruption in the middle of a Haydn symphony ? " This had the desired effect. With the promise that he would see to it that we would be notified in time for the second concert, the man disappeared.

At the first concert the hall was half empty. The gallery, usually fully occupied by the clergy, showed rows of unoccupied seats instead of the customary elaborate and picturesque spectacle—obviously a protest by the Catholic church. There were only a few dress-circle boxes which were occupied. The artistic success of the concert was complete, but otherwise it was a situation such as the Orchestra had never experienced before. I telephoned Count Ciano the next day and asked him point blank : " What is the point of especially inviting our Orchestra to Rome at great cost, if the concert is boycotted ? " He replied cautiously with the information that Mussolini would attend the second concert. The day after the first concert Furt-wängler had an audience with Il Duce who slyly began the conversation with the words : " I am coming to your concert to-morrow ". Next he asked, " What do you think of Adolf Hitler ? " Here we had better leave the conversation unrecorded.

At that time Italy's attitude towards Hitler was still undefined and very critical. It was reported that Richard Strauss had tried in vain to be received by Mussolini during his visit to Rome early in the spring of 1934. His quick change of front towards National Socialism was scorned, while Furtwängler's attitude was then greatly admired. How really formidable anti-Nazi feeling was in Italy at that time was proved by this boycotting of our first concert in Rome, in spite of Italian admiration for Furtwängler.

The second concert was sold out. Mussolini and his daughter Edda occupied a box above the platform. Il Duce has always been said to be a great music-lover and there he sat with his favourite daughter, his energetic and brutal face turned fascinatedly towards the Orchestra. Long before the concert started the hall was filled with secret police, who very reluctantly permitted me to go back to the box-office once I had been in the hall.

Furtwängler was given an Italian decoration of such a high order that as an artist he could receive no greater honour. For the evening of our free day, Prince Ludovisi, then Governor of Rome, had put his box in the *Teatro Reale* at Furtwängler's disposal. We went with Curtius, the well-known archæologist and an old friend of Furtwängler and spent an interesting evening in Rome's famous Opera House, though we were only reluctantly admitted, as Furtwängler and Curtius, after a day of sightseeing, were dressed *en touriste*.

Those adherents of political movements who are situated farthest from the storm-centre are frequently the most extreme : this fact was borne out by the German Nazis in Rome. We heard later that Major Wirth, the district leader of the National Socialist Group in Rome, greatly disturbed by the fact that the Berlin Philharmonic had not been " aryanised ", had sent a report on the Italian tour to the Party headquarters, complaining about the " non-Aryan " members of the Orchestra. The extraordinary musical success he did not find worth mentioning. This was intended to inflame the Party executive against the Orchestra and its conductor. The German Ambassador, von Hassell, on the other hand, reported to the German Foreign Office emphasising the great success of the tour, particularly in view of the obviously hostile feeling of the Italians towards the Nazis. Herr von Hassell and his wife, who was a daughter of Admiral von Tirpitz, were extremely refined people of pre-Hitler days. Hassell, a diplomat of the old school, later was treated very badly. He was recalled at the time of the Austrian crisis.

In spite of the gravity of the time an amusing incident occurred in Rome which demonstrated the relativity of the Nazi *Weltanschauung* and—seen in the light of present events—also the deviations of Fascist principles. Furtwängler was suffering from severe toothache while in Rome, and was urged to consult a certain Dr. Gatto, whose skill was reported to be truly miraculous. He accordingly consulted Dr. Gatto and returned from his treatment, if still a little in pain, very charmed with the doctor and his pleasing nurse. Who was

Dr. Gatto ? He was in fact Dr. Katz, a German dentist who, having emigrated from Karlsruhe at the outset of the Hitler régime, had changed his name from the German to the Italian equivalent of " cat ". Where he has gone since Italy also discovered that people like him were *untragbar* one does not know.

While I was unsuspectingly performing my various duties in Rome darker thunderclouds were gathering in addition to the constant shadow that lay over me. One would have thought that the successful concerts and the great honours bestowed upon Furtwängler would have satisfied authorities at home. At any rate, the German Foreign Office counted the Rome concerts and Mussolini's attendance there as an asset. Not so the Nazis ! While still in Rome, I received a telephone call from Berlin in the middle of the night. I was told to behave as unobtrusively as possible in Rome ; the rest I was to hear on my return.

Only those who know what it means to be entirely dependent on the whims of creatures like the Nazis can appreciate the torment of suspense, often worse than the actuality itself, brought about by mysterious telephone calls, veiled hints, and whispered advice. I had to wait till I was back in Berlin to elucidate this mystery.

After Rome we went to Florence, where we gave two concerts. The old Contessa Gravina, Cosima's second daughter, lived there, and we spent an afternoon with her. Furtwängler had not returned to Bayreuth after 1931, but Cosima's daughters were always on friendly terms with him. Toscanini, the idol of the older Wagner generation, had also left Bayreuth in 1931, and, since the outset of the Nazi régime, he had refused every engagement in Germany. In spite of a personal invitation from Hitler, he declined to return to Bayreuth. As far as Bayreuth was concerned, therefore, Furt-wängler and Toscanini were in the same position, if for different reasons.

The " old ladies ", Contessa Gravina, Frau Thode, and Frau Eva Chamberlain, had for Toscanini a fanatical devotion, and followed him whenever it was possible to Salzburg and to Lucerne.

Mussolini, at that time, was still considered a pillar of support for many intellectuals who were persecuted by the Nazis, but in the conflict with Toscanini, he rocked on his pedestal. After the Bologna incident, Toscanini never conducted in Italy again. Mussolini never breached this gap, and thus a great Italian was lost to Italy. On that afternoon Contessa Gravina spoke of her ardent desire to bring about a conciliation between Toscanini and Mussolini, to re-establish the great musician in Italy and in its famous Opera House.

Who would have thought then that Mussolini would disappear overnight, and that the Italian people would seize the occasion immediately to renew their claim for Toscanini's return ; their love and veneration for him having been unimpaired by the long years of Mussolini's régime.

Ever since 1924, when they had first visited Switzerland, Furtwängler and the Berlin Philharmonic had had a following there. The Zurich concert, which followed the Florence concerts, was splendid, and the hall was more than full. Afterwards, the civic authorities gave a reception in honour of Furtwängler and Richard Strauss, who was then in Zurich for his opera performances. We stayed at the well-known and comfortable hotel *Baur au Lac*, and the reception was held there. For some reason on that evening the thought that I no longer belonged to that world was clearer than ever to me. Like poison, the conviction crept into me, and robbed me of ease. Although I had no inkling that this tour was to be my last with Furtwängler and the Berlin Philharmonic, I returned to Germany with a heavy heart.

Each return to Berlin was more disconcerting than the last, and I re-entered the capital full of apprehension about what was behind the mysterious message I had received in Rome. This is what I was told :

The fact that I had arranged the Furtwängler-Mussolini meeting merely with the help of the Italian Ambassador, and without the knowledge of the German Embassy or the Nazi authorities (who would gladly have boasted of this achievement) was a " crime " against the State ! Goebbels is said to have rushed to Hitler, enraged by my action, and to have demanded my immediate dismissal. It was, actually, a lost opportunity for the Nazis ! How proud would they have been had *they* arranged this meeting ! That I should have been the one to pull the strings was infuriating to them. What counted with them was not whether an idea was intrinsically good, but whether it was their own.

Hitler had promised Furtwängler that I would remain unmolested ; in other words, that I would officially and formally retain my post. What does such a promise mean to Nazis ? They have many ways of eliminating an undesirable person. While I was in Italy I had already been discarded in Berlin. This would have been final if Goering had not intervened. Tietjen, in his position as head of all the Prussian State Theatres, as usual had heard about the whole affair as soon as it happened. He knew exactly how to appraise a situation, often depending on the degree of favour enjoyed at any particular moment by each Nazi leader. He disapproved of Goebbels' action—especially as he was not entirely uninterested in the issue of the matter and feared its effect on the sensitive Furtwängler who was indispensable to the State Opera. He therefore immediately informed Goering, who was always ready to listen to him, of the matter. Goering, (most likely delighted to spoil Goebbels' game), went to see Hitler. God knows what he may have told him—but the Führer is said to have rung the Under-Secretary of State in the Goebbels Ministry, Dr. Funk, under whose control the Philharmonic affairs were at that period, and have given the order to stop the action against me. Thus, I was given a breathing space—but not for long.

The short time we now spent in Germany passed very quickly. There were a number of opera performances, lots of work and lots of trouble. My case was brought up again. Again Furtwängler battled with all the Ministers and with Hitler. Once more things were settled for the moment, and without any obstacles I proceeded to Paris where as usual the Summer Wagner Festivals (*Meistersinger* and *Tristan*) were to take place under Furtwängler's direction.

German " Aryan " artists so far were still free to appear in foreign countries. However, gradually, limitations were imposed. Soon the *Reichsmusikkammer* had to receive notice of, and sanction, every engagement abroad. Exit permits were granted in one case and refused in another. In this way the Nazis could launch their own people and suppress the work of others. Gradually control of performances abroad began, and German opera singers, entirely dependent for engagements on the German stage, grew shy of commitments abroad at which Jews and other *Untragbare* took part. For this reason many of them were afraid to go to places like

Salzburg, where before the *Anschluss* Toscanini and Bruno Walter conducted. Nazi Germany began to exert pressure on everything within its reach. This went so far that immediately after the *Anschluss* in 1938, the Italian Government was coerced into cancelling agreements with Bruno Walter and with the former stage director of the Vienna State Opera, Lothar Wallerstein, now at the Metropolitan, New York, who had been engaged for the *Maggio Musicale* in Florence. Even the "Aryan" Carl Ebert, the excellent producer, who had left Germany immediately after Hitler's advent, and who has furthered Glyndebourne so much, was informed that his previously coveted services were no longer required in Italy.

Italy was naturally the most fruitful ground for these machinations ; but wherever possible, in Holland, Belgium, and Switzerland this same influence was exerted.

The Nazi Stage Agency under the authority of the Ministry of Propaganda controlled all foreign engagements within their reach. If this department decided to place a singer on a foreign stage he was compelled to accept only part of his fee in foreign exchange and the remainder in German marks, which the Germans themselves supplied, thus lowering his "price" in the foreign market. All opera houses naturally welcome an easing of their finances, and so Nazi Germany was able to worm its way into many important events on the foreign stage.

Not all foreign institutions, however, were party to this practice of making bargains with the Nazi "art" organisations. Neither the Paris Opera nor Covent Garden agreed to their manœuvres. Sir Thomas Beecham whose sole object was to find the best singers for his international opera seasons engaged his cast to suit himself. He had no time for other considerations. If everyone in control of opera had acted likewise, the Nazis would not have been able to push their policy so far, and the interests of music would have been safeguarded.

When, later on, the cultural policy of the Nazis comes to be examined in a more distant perspective, we shall be in a better position to see how rarely, if ever, art for art's sake was for them the primary consideration. Not even for the sake of the Arts were they capable of disregarding the demands of their *Weltanschauung*. And while they gave their ideas of the world a wider and wider application, the "brown net" of Nazi organisation spread gradually further and further like a malignant growth until it covered even the most remote and insignificant activity.

From Paris I went to London on business. On that occasion I went to Covent Garden for the first time. My future chief, Sir Thomas Beecham, the soul of the famous opera house, and a living dynamo, was in the midst of his opera season. He invited me to a rehearsal and took me out to luncheon at Boulestin's. He also inquired solicitously how we were faring under Nazi rule—but as his questions were a combination of malice and wit, they did not evoke the fundamental despair that had overcome me during the conversation with Barthou on the same subject. Sir Thomas repeated what he had already said to me in Berlin. "If you ever have any trouble with Hitler, come to me." Perhaps he did not mean it altogether seriously, but how comforting it was ! He suggested that Furtwängler should conduct several German operas in Covent Garden in the summer of 1935, and so I went home, well loaded with new plans.

Chapter 11

I WAS back in Berlin on June 11th. Without being able to name it, I sensed something increasingly ominous in the air. By the old standards which valued continuity highly, everything had gone off extremely well ; the engagements of the Berlin Philharmonic and of Furtwängler for 1935 had been arranged abroad as usual. The Nazis—so far—had not curtailed my activities, and I had been able to complete all negotiations successfully.

On my return, however, I noticed that my successful arrangements were of no interest whatsoever to the Nazis. It is true that the new business manager of the Berlin Philharmonic installed in our office by the Ministry of Propaganda—allegedly to improve our book-keeping—said to me : " You must be proud of what you have achieved ", but at the same time he made a determined effort to insinuate himself into the management of our tours and I saw only too clearly where his efforts were leading.

Other dirty work was going on. The Music Department of the

Reichsmusikkammer had great ambitions. It was easy to see that it aimed at becoming the State Concert Agency controlling *all* engagements. By pressure and all sorts of blackmail, they attempted to control the bookings of all soloists.

Contact with emigrants, especially with German refugees in other countries, was now strictly forbidden in Nazi Germany, and innumerable people had got into trouble when it was discovered that they had had business connections with such people. Yet so corrupt was the Music Department, so cynical in its disregard for its own Nazi regulations, and so little used to any dealings abroad that they made frequent use of *emigré* concert agents to form foreign connections which they themselves did not possess.

If there had not been a constant clamour by the Nazis that they were able to do things "alone" without the former experts one would have had nothing to say about it. The hypocrisy was manifest when, on the one hand, the respective authorities in the *Musikkammer* relentlessly persecuted and excluded from musical life within Germany even the minor "non-Ayran" employee under the guise of national sentiment, whereas on the other hand, they made use of refugee Jews abroad. Despite their claims, they were unable to uphold the old standard of business relations, without assistance from outside, especially since Berlin quickly ceased to be a centre of the artists' exchange which it had been in the times of the much-abused Weimar Republic, and even before, in Imperial Germany.

I was perhaps one of the few people left in Germany who then had a thorough knowledge of international musical life. I had all the experience and connections which the Nazis lacked. No wonder, therefore, that I was odious to the *Reichsmusikkammer* as well as to the *emigrés* who were endeavouring to represent them abroad. Furtwängler, however, at that time, was still the great power. I still represented him everywhere, and dealt with all his concerts, and opera affairs as before.

About this time Furtwängler received the first request to conduct at the Nuremberg *Parteitag* (Party Rally) that was to take place in September under the slogan : *Triumpf des Willens* ("The triumph of will"). This invitation, as was customary, was accompanied by the intimation that it had been issued "by desire of the Führer".

Furtwängler was on the horns of a dilemma. If he were to conduct on purely political occasions, it would mean the end of his career as a free artist.

It was obvious that the minor Party officials were delighted with the idea of fettering Furtwängler, who was not a Party member, with Party restrictions, and they would have been only too pleased if Furtwängler's conducting at the Party Rally lost him prestige abroad. This prestige was a thorn in their side anyhow, and it can safely be stated that they regarded Furtwängler—even if unconsciously so— with the instinctive hostility of mediocrity towards a man of genius.

Furtwängler's desire to keep his artistic activities independent of political display was quite logical. But it was prevented to some degree from gaining strength by the spineless attitude of prominent foreigners who ignored events like the 30th of June and many other occurrences in Germany. As long as influential Englishmen, for instance, accepted invitations to Nuremberg and other Nazi celebrations, it was very difficult for right-thinking Germans to make a stand. It is well known how uncertain of themselves the Nazis were in those days. The attitude of many prominent foreigners actually took the wind out of the sails of those Germans who were putting up a fight for their honour. It was these foreigners who supplied the Nazis with the argument that the world was indifferent to those very events which a large section of Germany was ready to condemn.

At this time, things were more or less in a state of flux ; at any rate it was still possible to discuss matters of this sort. Furtwängler, accordingly, found means to convey his view-point to Hitler. Hitler thereupon emphatically declared that he had not known about the demand for Furtwängler's appearance at Nuremberg. He agreed with his attitude, and understood that he did not want his art to be used for political ends. The Führer found it advisable to say this at that time. So Furtwängler did not, after all, conduct at Nuremberg during the Party rally.

This was, however, by no means our only problem. The interest of everybody concerned was focused at that time on Hindemith's new opera, *Mathis der Maler*. The very beautiful and moving text had been written by Hindemith himself and dealt with the life of the great German painter, Matthias Grünewald. Furtwängler had studied the work ; he had judged it to be of a very high standard, and had decided to put it on the repertoire of the Berlin State Opera for the coming season. All the larger German opera houses as well as those abroad had applied for the opera after the Berlin world's première.

Hindemith was the young hope of German music. His book *Unterweisung im Tonsatz*, hailed by Sir Donald Francis Tovey as the most important contribution to musical theory for over a century, had made a great impression. A young, unaffected, and gifted man, he was the prototype of the best kind of musician, and never let himself be thrown off his balance. In spite of the attacks made on him by the Nazis, he remained the idol of the young musical generation. For many years he had been the mainspring of the great International Festivals for Contemporary Music as well as of many other festivals of modern music on the Continent. Besides being a composer and teacher, he was a wonderful viola player, a recognised soloist as well as quartet player. It will perhaps be remembered that it was Hindemith who played in the first performance in this country of William Walton's Viola Concerto.

Hitler, however, had a strong antipathy to Hindemith, fostered by his musical adviser and court jester, Hanfstängl. The only opera of Hindemith's which he had himself heard was *Neues vom Tage* in which a naked woman is seen on the stage sitting in her bath. This naked woman was Hitler's " King Charles' head " ; but as Hindemith was " pure Aryan "—as the Nazis would say—the Nazi code supplied no legal weapon against him.

When Furtwängler compiled his programme for the State Opera Season 1934-35, he was suddenly faced by the startling information that *Mathis der Maler* could not be performed before Goering, as " chief " of the Berlin State Opera, had obtained the Führer's consent. Pending Hitler's decision, the performance of the opera in the Reich would be in abeyance.

Furtwängler took a very serious view of this incident, which proved again that in the Nazi Reich artistic authority and expert knowledge meant nothing as against the brutal force of dictatorship. For him this was a test case. *He* was the Musical Director of the Berlin State Opera and no one else. When did the head of a State ever interfere with details of a theatre repertoire? It was as if Mr. Churchill suddenly sent a message to Covent Garden telling Sir Thomas Beecham what to do, or Mr. Roosevelt asked the Metropolitan to put on a certain opera while prohibiting another.

Furtwängler's application for the release of the opera remained ignored. As there was obviously no sufficient reason for its prohibition, the decision was simply evaded. On this decision a great drama hinged.

While this was all in a state of ferment, a great deal of grumbling against the Nazis was heard in Berlin on other scores. Much was at stake at home and abroad. Hitler went to Venice for his famous first meeting with Mussolini. He was accompanied by Herr v. Neurath, then Foreign Minister, and the Cerrutis, among others. The true facts about this journey were carefully suppressed, but the most incredible accounts of the meeting cropped up in the shape of rumours. By all accounts the two dictators were by no means blood-brothers. Mussolini, whose star was in the ascendant at that time, was not overwhelmed with admiration for his fellow-dictator, who bored and annoyed everybody by his ceaseless harangues. So much so that one heard Mussolini nearly broke off the Conference in disgust. The day after the Cerrutis returned I was having dinner with them alone at the Embassy, and told them all the stories I had heard. Naturally, an Ambassador cannot divulge anything in such a case, and the Cerrutis were far too loyal and discreet to make an exception in this instance. It appeared, however, that their task had been by no means an easy one. The Ambassadress confirmed to me, incidentally, the legend of Hitler's passionate interest in architecture, for during her trip with him on the Grand Canal he appeared to know the story of every Palazzo.

Meanwhile, the fatal midsummer of 1934 approached. The 30th of June 1934 has been frequently described. It was a Saturday. As usual, after office hours on Saturday, I went to lunch with a friend of mine who lived at the Tiergarten corner of the *Hohenzollernstrasse*. Strangely enough I found the *Tiergartenstrasse* roped off in the direction leading to the Brandenburger Tor. Röhm's house lay that way. The S.A. men were conspicuous by their absence. Only the so-called "green" Goering police, whom the

Berliners used to call *Schupos* (*Schutzpolizei*) were seen. Was this a *putsch* against Hitler? We quickly and hopefully drove with many detours to the *Wilhelmstrasse* to see what we could see. However, all was quiet and there was no reason to think that anything unusual was happening. We therefore returned to the *Hohenzollern-strasse*, and there heard on the radio at regular intervals the gruesome account of all that had taken place at *Wiessee* in the early morning. Already rumours were rife in Berlin, and the fate of many was discussed. We soon heard that the whole von Papen family was not allowed to leave its house, while Jung and Bose, Papen's secretaries, had already been shot. The fate of General von Schleicher and his family is known to the world. A document in which Schleicher's housekeeper describes exactly what happened when he was killed is now in England.

A great restlessness pervaded Berlin. In the evening, I felt that I could not stay quietly indoors. I walked along the *Lützowufer*, under the beautiful old chestnut trees, and there ran into Cerruti who, animated by the same restlessness as myself, was strolling in the dusk. He had no authentic information, but he had heard that in the house of the S.A. Leader, Röhm, who—by now—had been shot, a detailed plan had been found for the overthrow of the Hitler régime. The plan—it was said—provided exact instructions as to which of the Nazi leaders in such an eventuality was to be shot and which was only to be arrested. Who can tell whether such a document really existed? Whether it had really been found? All one knew was that the atmosphere was most sinister. Rumours sprung up like mushrooms. It was said that in *Grosslichterfelde* the screams of people who were being shot were heard all through the night. More and more people fled from the capital. " Our " Nazi in the office declared surprisingly enough : " This is the first nail in Hitler's coffin ! "

One might have thought so. But as in the case of all Nazi crimes one could only wonder at how much the world, and particularly Germany, would stand. Thousands of people of all classes were involved in the unspeakable horrors of June 30th. Despair reigned —especially after the cynical and perverse explanation which Hitler gave to the quickly summoned Reichstag a few days later—the explanation that he in a moment of danger for the nation had to usurp for this one day the power of the supreme judge of the Reich. But Germany, and the world, stood by and accepted it.

Unfortunately Hitler's reputation and power did not suffer decisively through this event. This would have been an occasion for the world to say : " We want no truck with such ruffians ! " The German people were sore, exhausted, and ready for revolt at that moment. A guiding hand might have saved Europe then.

Abroad, again—as usual—vain protests, but no action ! Nothing decisive happened. Again Hitler found how far he could venture. He gambled with ever rising stakes. He had got away with it again.

Chapter 12

THE HORRORS of June 30th overshadowed the days that followed. The State Opera closed down at the beginning of July. Furtwängler, exhausted by this turmoil, went to stay in Poland. The Nazis' lust for blood seemed to be still unsatiated and I was actually told that when another purge was due Furtwängler would be a victim.

Furtwängler, although he had decided to remain in Germany, was certainly no Nazi. He was an outspoken man and never chose his words when his anger was roused. He had a private telephone line to me which was not connected *via* the exchange. When he lifted the receiver on his desk my bell rang. We had understood it could not be tapped. Furtwängler would not have cared either way. Before going to bed, he used to chat with me over the telephone. Sometimes I told him amusing stories to cheer him up, sometimes he talked politics. One of the main threats the Nazis used against Furtwängler and myself later on was the assertion that they had recorded all these conversations. I should not have thought it possible ! Was there enough shellac ? If the Nazis really did this, their ears must certainly have burnt, and it was not surprising that Furtwängler was eventually put on their black list, let alone myself.

I went on holiday to Switzerland, where one heard many details about the 30th of June, hitherto unknown in Germany. Everybody was seething with indignation. Yet, of what avail was all this? Dollfuss was murdered!—Hindenburg died. Hitler became his successor, and the army backed his "election". The Nazis staged a great funeral ceremony at Tannenberg, at which Furtwängler was supposed to conduct the funeral music. He declined.

Despite the rumours rife in the Engadine all that summer, one breathed more freely. Many musicians lived around the lakes. Furtwängler had his house near St. Moritz. Bodanzky came there every year from New York. Bruno Walter and Edwin Fischer were there too. The pianist, Wladimir Horowitz, had taken a house at Sils Maria, and his future wife, Toscanini's daughter, Wanda, was his guest, as was also Gregor Piatigorsky.

Serafin, the Italian conductor, came to St. Moritz from Rome with Commendatore Passigli, the organiser of the *Maggio Musicale* of Florence. The latter was very anxious to present the *St. Matthew's Passion*, with the Kittel Choir and Furtwängler as conductor at the *Maggio Musicale*, and so we spent many hours sitting beside the beautiful Lake of St. Moritz working out the details of this ambitious undertaking.

The Salzburg Festivals which Toscanini conducted for the first time, were overshadowed by the events in Austria. Rouché from Paris, who had taken a large house near Salzburg and had invited me there, changed his plans after the railway bridge at Vöcklabrück near Salzburg had been blown up by the Nazis. One after the other of the Jewish section-leaders left the Berlin Philharmonic Orchestra. I had frequent telephone calls to the Engadine from our first cellist, Joseph Schuster, who had decided to go to America, though the parting was hard. Of course his decision was right.

At the end of August I was back in Berlin. Meanwhile the reorganisation of the Orchestra's office had been completed. I took courage. Bruno Kittel, the director of the Kittel choir, who later was one of the first to urge that Furtwängler should part with me, sat in my office for days on end beside himself with joy at the prospect of the Italian concerts. He told me he was in contact with the Party, with Hess, and others whom he knew well, and he constantly assured me that "everybody" was behind me and that I need take no notice of difficulties made by "petty minds". It was the later attitude of this excellent musician and collaborator

of long standing that hurt me deeply and seemed to me a sign of
the general decline in morale. When, later on, I went to Germany
with Sir Thomas, a humble friend said to me confidentially : " *Lieber
Gott !* Herr Kittel ! He shouts ' Heil Hitler ! '—even before he
has got into the room ! "

Meanwhile, the Hindemith case had come to a head. Hindemith,
calm and poised, and sunk in his work as a creative artist, remained
outside the controversy. For Furtwängler, however, the decision
as to whether he was to be allowed to produce Hindemith's opera
was not only an artistic matter, but a vote of confidence and prestige.
How could he, the director of Germany's leading Opera House,
reconcile with his sense of responsibility the docking of authority
which the Nazis were imposing upon him ? He declared with great
firmness that if this question of principle was not cleared up satisfactorily he would draw his own conclusions.

It will perhaps be astonishing for the English reader that an acute
crisis could arise in official life out of such an incident. But an
appointment like Furtwängler's as Director of the Berlin State Opera
was an official one, of a defined kind not known at all in the English
artistic world. These appointments to great musical positions both
in Germany and Austria were made for reasons the roots of which
lay deep in the German attitude to artistic matters. They were
positions of unquestioned authority, and were given precisely to
those personalities whose absolute authority in their own spheres it
was desired to confirm and reinforce by their official character.

While the decision on the release of the Hindemith opera was
pending, Furtwängler had written seriously and at length to Goering,
but so far Goering had not replied. Eventually, however, he answered,
advising Furtwängler not to take his responsibility as director of
the Berlin State Opera too seriously. This *responsibility*—so he wrote
—was borne only by the National State and its Leaders, and Furtwängler would be well advised not to make a *cause célèbre* out of
the Hindemith matter, irrespective of what the decision might
be. Shortly afterwards I received a telephone call from Goering's
office requesting me in the " simple " style of the Third Reich
to inform the *Herr Staatsrat* Furtwängler on behalf of the
Herr Ministerpräsident that the *Herr Reichskanzler* had prohibited
the presentation of the Hindemith opera. A cloak of official

pomposity was therefore thrown round the whole affair in true Nazi manner.

A vision of the shape of things to come rose before my eyes. At first I did not dare to convey the message to Furtwängler, and when, two days later, I did so, he immediately declared that if this decision were not revoked he would resign from the Berlin State Opera.

The atmosphere grew more and more tense. This was most noticeable in the Philharmonic office into which all kinds of news penetrated from the various Ministries. An ill wind blew over Germany. Furtwängler also felt it and was most depressed.

At the beginning of September very early one morning my door bell rang. It was a message from Furtwängler. I was to leave Berlin at once and go away to the South of Germany. I was to behave as unobtrusively as possible. On receipt of a prearranged coded message I was to set out for a still more remote hiding-place.

I left immediately without question. Would I ever come back again?

What had happened? I learned afterwards that while all the Government officials were out of reach at the Party Rally at Nuremberg, Furtwängler had heard of a denunciation against me, which had been sent to Hitler, Goering, and Goebbels requesting my immediate arrest.

This action was a Party matter without any "legal" basis, but all the more dangerous for this very reason; and what was "legal" in these days anyway?

These were the actual facts: Havemann, my old enemy, the leader of the *Reichsmusikerschaft*, had informed against me, in these words:

> "Dr. Geissmar is sabotaging the building of the National State through her connection with Jews and emigrants abroad, and through her negotiations with foreign countries. It is proposed therefore that she should be taken into protective custody."

In order to enforce his denunciation, he had enclosed a copy of a denunciatory letter from abroad to this effect, written on notepaper with the heading of a foreign firm of concert agents, which did not include their names, however. Actually, Havemann was suppressing the fact that this concert agency was run by refugee Germans abroad, who were trying to curry favour with the Party. These agents had spread the story abroad—where people were still badly informed on how these matters were dealt with in Germany—that only the Music Department of the *Reichsmusikkammer* had the right to engage artists for Germany, and that outside Germany all engagements had to be made through their organisation, which was the representative of the Music Department.

Furtwängler and I, when questioned abroad, had truthfully declared that such a monopoly did not exist, and that everybody could engage his soloists as he wanted. This had been immediately reported to their " Nazi partner " by the refugees in question, written on their new notepaper, and this document with the foreign letter-heading was sent to the Leaders of the Reich. How could they know that behind the foreign letter-heading were the very people whom they themselves had expelled ? The denunciation, very cleverly compiled and apparently from a blameless foreign source, could not but have the desired effect.

Not until many years later—when I was already in British service— was I shown the original document. What a perfidious and inglorious fraud !

Furtwängler was extremely upset, but he concealed—for the moment—all the details of this affair from me, to spare my feelings. I would have told him the only possible way to deal with it : to disclose the truth immediately, to disclose immediately in fact *who* maintained business connections with Jews abroad : namely, the management of the *Reichsmusikerschaft* itself. Then the fat would have been in the fire. The Ministry of Propaganda could not have afforded to have such a scandal laid bare, involving, as it did, a Department under its authority. Furtwängler did not see the implications clearly. After all, he was a musician, and I avoided, when I could, discussing controversial subjects with him. He was not well enough informed of the intricacies of the whole business to use the only possible weapon—the true facts, and I, the victim, at that moment had no idea what was at the bottom of it all.

Furtwängler behaved with integrity. He sent telegrams to Hitler, Goering, and Goebbels at Nuremberg, saying that he had been informed of the demand for my arrest. He declared himself responsible for all accusations against his secretary and requested an interview to clear the matter up.

Even before the interview took place, the incident was smoothed over. The authorities were inclined now to hush it up, all the more as evidence against the informer emanating from the Party itself was accumulating. Once more it seemed that I was to be reprieved, and Furtwängler soon asked me to return to Berlin. With many forebodings I did so.

Chapter 13

THE FOLLOWING weeks were not in point of fact too bad. My absence from Berlin, which in the summer was half empty, had not been noticed, especially as I habitually travelled so much. Although I felt degraded and humiliated, I had come to the conclusion that it was wrong to allow myself to be influenced by any accusation or defamation coming from the Nazis. The only right thing to do was to continue on one's way, whatever the imposed circumstances. It is not what happens to us that matters, but how we face it. What we are, rests with us alone. This, of course, is easier said than done. None the less it is true, and the knowledge of this has often sustained me in difficult times.

In October the German Ambassador to London, von Hoesch, came to Berlin. I visited him in the Hotel Esplanade. He was human as well as wise, and I sought his advice. For many years he had been interested in my work, and I imagine I was not the only one who now went to him depressed by the new conditions. It was easy to see how acutely he felt the circumstances, and I tried not to exaggerate my difficulties. I asked him point blank, however, whether I ought to give up my post in order to put an end to the exhausting struggle. His answer was an emphatic : " No ". Even a German Ambassador did not foresee the future !

During this time there were several fine performances at the Berlin State Opera. Pfitzner conducted his opera *Palestrina* and several concerts. Two cycles of the *Ring* in a new production were given, with Furtwängler conducting ; the scenery was by Preetorius, Germany's ace stage designer, who worked almost exclusively for the Berlin State Opera and Bayreuth. Tietjen was the producer.

Goering, the "chief" of the Opera House, followed the new production with passionate interest, and during a rehearsal of *Walküre* he rushed straight on to the stage to show *Wotan* (Bockelmann) how to wield a spear.

Generalintendant Tietjen was in one of the most difficult positions in Berlin. He had constantly to maintain the balance between the clashing political and artistic interests in the Opera House. However, he had his own technique for managing things. Furtwängler and Tietjen had begun their joint work with great enthusiasm, but their relations gradually became strained, through their different temperaments. My friendship with Tietjen greatly helped their collaboration. In all my troubles with the Nazis, he always encouraged me and recommended my "sticking to my job". However, I was more and more inclined to resign in order to spare Furtwängler and myself future strain. Hoesch, in his advice to me, may have been influenced by his foreign perspective; his counsel was not sufficient for me in Germany itself. I sought other aid. A confidential friend of Goering's approached him privately with my troubles. Goering—so I was told—replied that I was not to worry, as Furtwängler needed me; this was to decide the issue for the time. Goering, it was said, always maintained: "It is for me to decide who is a Jew". This may have been his opinion then. But it must not be forgotten that in the Totalitarian State the Leaders control the development of events far less than some of the small party agitators.

The development of matters followed a certain rhythmic ebb and flow. There were times when the storm seemed to blow up, then again calm reigned for a while. In 1934 attacks were made not only against those outside the Party, but within the Party itself there was considerable tension. Officials of all kinds rose to power and fell again, and many suddenly and surprisingly installed in high office in March 1933 had already sunk into oblivion. However, the Nazis never dropped a person entirely if it was at all avoidable. If anyone was dismissed from his post he was sure to reappear in some other guise in another place. It rarely happened that they released anybody entirely from their clutches.

In the Government departments in charge of musical activities everything was in flux. The constant introduction of new laws and regulations led to great confusion within the *Reichsmusikkammer*, whose president was Richard Strauss, who, however, was mostly inaccessible at Garmisch. A strong hand at the helm was obviously necessary to steer the department through all this, because every new regulation involved piles of letters and applications from those affected by it. It was above all necessary to have a president on the spot who really attended to the work and not one on the top of some Bavarian mountain.

The confusion and egotism which reigned in the *Reichsmusik-kammer* during the frequent absences of Strauss was unbelievable ; craving for power, rank ignorance, rivalry, envy, all were inter-woven.

In contrast to the easy-going Strauss, Furtwängler took his duties as vice-president of the *Kammer*, as in every matter where his principles were involved, very seriously. He usually opposed every-thing, with the result that the bureaucracy, and last but not least, Strauss himself, began to conceal things from him. This constant and futile underground struggle gradually began to sap his nervous energy, yet he did not relax his efforts for the maintenance of his standards and wrote one memorandum after the other to demonstrate the shortcomings in every field. These memoranda were usually handed to the Minister in question directly. But as they naturally had to be filed, sometimes the very thing to be avoided actually happened : the papers fell into the hands of the underlings. It is significant that one of these documents dealing with the corruption in several departments and their chiefs, disappeared in the Ministry of Propaganda, and all that could be found was the empty file !

The underlings in official positions felt that their jobs were threatened by Furtwängler, and soon he had hardly any friends left in official quarters. Yet he spared no effort to uphold the standards of pure art, inspired by the conviction that it was his mission to fight for what he judged to be *right* as long as it was in his power to do so.

Though the ban on Hindemith's opera was still in force at this time, his concert music was not officially prohibited. Hindemith had arranged part of his opera *Mathis der Maler* as a symphony ; and

Furtwängler had included this piece in one of the programmes of
the Philharmonic Concerts without any objection from the authorities. The performance of the work was an unparalleled success
and the *Philharmonie* was wildly enthusiastic. Cabinet Ministers
and high Party officials attended the concert as usual. Actually,
the serious character of the work did not invite frantic applause,
but the voice of the genuine Germany broke through on such
occasions, and the public enthusiastically supported Furtwängler.
Press reports of the new work appeared all over the world, and
many concert institutions announced its performance on their
programmes.

Such success, especially if nourished by opposition, is of doubtful
value, especially in Nazi Germany; and Hindemith, too, had to
pay for it, being constantly attacked by the Nazi press which knew
itself backed by the Government. He was fast becoming a hero and
a martyr. The ban on his opera remained.

As in April 1933, when Furtwängler was induced to write an
" Open Letter " to Dr. Goebbels on the freedom of the arts, the
necessity now arose for him to expatiate upon problems which were
troubling a great number of intellectual people in Germany—and
probably everywhere in the world, problems of which the Hindemith matter was only a facet. So Furtwängler wrote his famous
article " *Der Fall Hindemith* " (The Hindemith case, November 25,
1934). In it Furtwängler described the battle that had developed
around Paul Hindemith. He showed on the one hand how unjusti-
fied the *political* attacks were which pronounced Hindemith *untragbar*
to the new régime because he had " Jewish connections " and had
recorded music with two refugees. Furtwängler pointed out that
the two " refugees " were the former leader of the Berlin Philharmonic Orchestra, Simon Goldberg, who had only recently left
to devote himself to a soloist's career, and Professor Emanuel Feuer-
mann (now dead), one of the best cellists in Europe, who had, until
lately, been teaching at the Berlin *Hochschule für Musik*. Regarding
the attacks on Hindemith the *artist,* Furtwängler pointed out that
the libretto of Strauss' *Salome,* to take one instance, might receive
similar criticism as Hindemith's early works : but that this should
in no way detract from the recognition of his later endeavours and
his development, or diminish the value of his opera, *Mathis der Maler*

and his distinction as a teacher. Furtwängler concluded with the words : " What would happen if vague political denunciations were constantly to be applied to the artist ? " He declared that in view of the great poverty in creative musicians all over the world, Germany could ill afford to dispense with Hindemith.

From the moment of the publication of this article in the *Deutsche Allgemeine Zeitung*, events moved like an avalanche.

Furtwängler had discussed the article with the music critic of the *Deutsche Allgemeine Zeitung*, the chief editor of the paper had been informed, and saw no objection to its publication.

On Sunday, November 25th, the article was printed on the front page of the Sunday edition ; it was the most widely read newspaper of the " old " Germany. That morning there was a Philharmonic General Rehearsal. People were thronging the streets leading to the *Philharmonie*. The paper was snapped up from the hands of the sellers. A much larger edition had to be printed that day because of the great demand for it. When Furtwängler appeared on the platform, the whole audience rose and demonstrated so wildly, stamping and cheering for about twenty minutes, that it was impossible for him to begin.

Moreover, Furtwängler had to conduct twice on that Sunday, which was a thing he usually avoided. There was to be a *Tristan* performance at the State Opera in the evening. The house was sold out. Goering sat in his box, and Goebbels, too, was present. As soon as Furtwängler appeared in the orchestra pit, the same thing happened as in the *Philharmonie*. Endless applause, not to be stemmed by anything, filled the theatre. An atmosphere of melancholy beauty enhanced the performance and was felt by the whole audience. At the end, the demonstrations were repeated.

Goering realised instantly what all this meant. During the same night he is said to have telephoned to Hitler and told him that Furtwängler was endangering the authority of the State. The public demonstrations were *for* Furtwängler and therefore—in this case—*against* the Government. This *Tristan* performance was to be the last opera which Furtwängler conducted before his resignation ; the Philharmonic Concert on the next day the last in his official capacity.

Meanwhile, Furtwängler's article " The Hindemith case " was reprinted all over the world, sometimes abridged, sometimes in full.

The professional party and the press—the latter naturally under pressure—attacked Furtwängler in the crudest manner and even the daily papers printed articles against him.

All attempts to prevent these attacks on Furtwängler were of no avail. From this moment, nobody was accessible to him at any Ministry. Furtwängler was completely isolated. After calm deliberation he therefore said to himself : " If this State, which controls everything, lets loose such an attack on me and my musical authority, there is nothing left for me but to resign ". He saw clearly that he could no longer remain vice-president of the *Reichsmusik-kammer,* nor continue as director of the Berlin State Opera and the Berlin Philharmonic Orchestra.

He discussed things with many people before taking the final step : with his collaborators, his colleagues from the Opera, the Philharmonic Orchestra, and several people behind the scenes. Intermediaries had interviews with members of the Government. Goebbels, who had not reckoned with Furtwängler's resistance, and who saw a colossal scandal impending which would implicate his Ministry, showed himself in his true colours, and threatened to show Furtwängler who was the stronger of the two. Should Furt-wängler dare to carry out his plans of resignation, he—Goebbels— would break him completely. Of course Furtwängler got to know about this. He did not lose his nerve—on the contrary, Goebbels' cynical attitude towards what was to him a matter of fervent con-viction finally settled the matter for him.

Naturally all musicians professionally connected with Furtwängler fought desperately to alter his decision. How difficult it all was for him ! What had all these political questions to do with music ? They had been artificially thrust between him and his Orchestra and between him and his opera singers with whom he had been connected for so many years, let alone the public which idolised him. They all wanted his art, whatever his political opinions. His public refused to do without him and his Orchestra did not want to lose his artistic leadership.

Urgent appeals from the public reached him, and the Orchestra besieged him day and night. Finally, he made a last effort, putting forward the following proposition :

If he were enabled to continue his work *purely* as an artist, according to his conscience, if he did not have to accept either a politico-musical office or any other political responsibility—he was willing to go on.

This last proposal was handed to Goering, who was to submit it to Hitler for his final decision.

For a few days nothing was heard. In the afternoon of December 4, 1934, however, Furtwängler rang me from the State Opera House : " I am at this moment drafting the statement on my resignation ".

Hitler had rejected the offer. If Furtwängler would not work within the framework of the National State, the Führer would dispense with his art.

In the evening, Furtwängler came to see me. He felt a great sense of relief, and for the first time for a long while he was happy.

Neither of us had any idea of what lay before us.

Chapter 14

THE NEXT few days passed as if in a dream. The statement on Furtwängler's resignation was published by the Government on December 5, 1934. Erich Kleiber, then first conductor of the Berlin State Opera, rang me up the same night and read to me over the telephone his own letter of resignation which he had just placed on Tietjen's desk. He declared categorically that since Hitler had let Furtwängler go for purely political reasons, he himself would no longer retain his post.

Great confusion reigned around us. The subscribers to the Phil-harmonic Concerts stormed the office demanding their money back. Subscription tickets to the value of about 180,000 RM. (£10,000) were returned the day after Furtwängler's resignation. The Ministry of Propaganda at first decided that the money was not to be refunded, but legal counsel later ruled that since the tickets bore Furtwängler's name, the purchasers should be reimbursed.

Meanwhile, Furtwängler's courageous resignation had made a world sensation. Hardly a newspaper failed to comment upon his step in big headlines. Offers from all over the world were showered on him, from the New York Philharmonic Orchestra, the Philadelphia Orchestra, the Vienna State Opera, and others. His flat resembled that of a bride. Flowers were sent to him from all parts of Germany, piles of telegrams arrived, and all sorts of letters. The wife of a prominent diplomat sent him roses with the words : " Long live liberty ! " (I had to reassure her later that her letter had been immediately destroyed and that she had nothing to fear.)

Furtwängler wanted neither offers nor flowers. All he wanted was to be left alone and to be away from it all. He telegraphed to his English friends, the authors John Knittel and Robert Hichens, who for many years had invited him to come to Egypt, and proposed to visit them.

The Berlin Philharmonic Orchestra was desperate, and resolved not to leave it at this. Nothing was heard from the State Opera. Clemens Krauss, who had been hanging about in Berlin, was immediately engaged as director of the opera in place of Furtwängler. This, we were informed, was by Hitler's special request.

Furtwängler thought innocently that with his resignation all would be well. He intended to divide his future activities between Austria (then still independent) and America, and made no secret of his plans. The Nazis, however, had their ears to the ground, and soon it became known that the German frontier was closed to Furtwängler, Kleiber, and myself.

Kleiber was Austrian, and for him the ban had later to be lifted.

In retrospect, one may often wonder at one's errors of judgement in the past. The obvious thing to do at that time would have been for Furtwängler and myself to leave Berlin separately immediately after his resignation. This would have avoided undue official attention, and we might have been unmolested. As it was, we both remained in Berlin. I had been " allowed " to wind up Furtwängler's office unhampered, because it was appreciated that the sifting of correspondence and of the files accumulated during twenty years would require some time. On account of this I spent much time with Furtwängler in his flat. Instead of listening to friends who advised us to leave Germany as quickly as possible, we took our daily walk in the Tiergarten. Of course, we were both being continuously shadowed although, at the time, we were fools enough not to realise it. The porter of Furtwängler's house later told me that he had been ordered to keep his eye on all visitors.

On December 6th, the anniversary of the foundation of the *Reichskulturkammer* was celebrated, and Goebbels delivered the oration which was broadcast. He referred to the Furtwängler affair, and attacked Hindemith and, indirectly, Furtwängler, without mentioning names, in the most shameless manner. Finally, he read out a congratulatory telegram sent by Richard Strauss, from Holland. By implication Strauss supported Goebbels in his policy. (Later on, abroad, Strauss was questioned about this telegram. He is said to have disclaimed all knowledge of it ; explaining that his son had worded it by request of the Ministry of Propaganda !)

I listened in to the broadcast while sorting papers in my office, and could hardly believe my ears. I seethed with indignation, and it seemed to me impossible even to wind up Furtwängler's affairs in an office under the authority of such people. My mother, who had moved to Berlin two months previously to live with me, occupied the second floor in the same building as the office. During the night I took all the documents and papers up into our private flat and left a note asking my secretary, who was allowed to work with me until January 1st, to come up to me in the morning.

Such was my exit from the office of the Berlin Philharmonic Orchestra. Who could have foretold then that I was to cross its threshold again sixteen months later—as a manager of the London Philharmonic Orchestra and as General Secretary to Sir Thomas Beecham !

Meanwhile the Nazis were by no means inactive. Since they had definitely lost Furtwängler, they no longer had any reason to handle me with kid gloves. Their main idea at this time was at all costs to prevent Furtwängler from continuing to use me as a business connection.

All sorts of changes were made in the Philharmonic office. Collaborators of Furtwängler were immediately dismissed. The Italian radio, incidentally, broadcast a full report of the whole matter and of the changes in the Philharmonic management.

The immense public demand for such a great and popular figure as Furtwängler could not, however, be overlooked by the Nazis, and the pressure of public opinion had a sobering effect on the authorities. The public gave them no respite, and started a campaign against the Government. Even the Nazis became worried over the affair, although for other reasons. They maintained that, but for me, Furtwängler would have acted differently. I was the cause of the whole trouble !—of the loss of prestige to Germany !—of the despair of the Orchestra !

Furtwängler and I gradually became aware of how the wind was blowing, and we decided at last that the time had come to part. He engaged a new secretary who was " pure Aryan ", and therefore could represent him before the official world. For the rest, he assumed that where necessary, I would assist him in the background. I agreed to everything that could help this harassed man—my oldest friend, beloved chief of so many years standing. After all, what else mattered now ?

As it happened, Furtwängler, from December onward until April, had accepted no commitments other than his engagements at the Berlin State Opera and with the Berlin Philharmonic, which were now cancelled. It was only towards the middle of the following April that he had to be in Vienna, and so it was possible for him to have a complete rest during the next few months. He could, therefore, more easily dispense with my services.

The Orchestra had asked Furtwängler to oblige them by conducting the English tour arranged for January 1935, but for him this was out of the question. The Ministry of Propaganda, in blissful ignorance of the feeling of the musical world, decreed that the tour was to take place in any case ; they wanted to prove that it could be carried out without Furtwängler. In this, however, they were mistaken. Our English agent, Mr. Harold Holt, did not seem willing to accept a substitute for the great conductor who was so well known to the English public. Sir Thomas Beecham, on being approached to conduct the Berlin Orchestra on its English tour instead of Furtwängler, flatly refused. The Nazis, who then considered me to blame for everything that happened abroad concerning Furtwängler, immediately declared that Sir Thomas's refusal was due to my influence. The suspicion that I, who at that time was not in touch with Sir Thomas at all, should have persuaded him to refuse, was expressed in a bullying letter to me from the Nazi business manager of the Orchestra, in which he threatened that he would take steps to protect the Berlin Philharmonic Orchestra from my sabotage. How fantastic to suggest that I, of all people, should want to damage the Orchestra ! I should have realised before that the Nazis would attribute their own mentality to others. I felt I could not leave it at that, however. I therefore went to the Wilhelmstrasse declaring that I would not submit to such calumny, and would ask Sir Eric Phipps, the British Ambassador, to inform Sir Thomas of this accusation. Sir Thomas would surely back me up. This was most awkward for the Foreign Office, and I was given to understand that I had better abstain from my intention. What did my honour matter to them ! When, much later, I told this story to Sir Thomas, he looked at me in surprise : " Did anybody seriously imagine that I would have taken the place of a colleague under such circumstances ? " The tour to England had to be dropped.

There was nothing to prevent Furtwängler from having a real holiday, and so he prepared for his departure to Egypt. To all attempts at the reopenings of negotiation with the authorities he turned a deaf ear. He spent much of his time with me.

Suddenly one afternoon two Nazis appeared in my flat, declaring that if I did not leave Berlin immediately without informing Furt-wängler, I would be arrested. This time I had no choice. It was icy cold—one of the coldest nights ever known in Germany. A frost after fog had rendered the streets almost impassable. But delay was out of the question, and under cover of night I left in a friend's car for Leipzig. There I caught the express to Munich, where I had relatives and friends.

Furtwängler, of course, was highly indignant at my forced departure, and asked me to return ; and so after a week in Munich, spent in a dull stupor, I took the risk and went back to Berlin.

I was back in Berlin on December 19th. Furtwängler was to leave for Egypt on the 24th. During the few days left to us we hoped to clear up everything. On the evening of the 23rd I went to him to discuss final arrangements. It was late. Suddenly the telephone rang. It was a high Government official, who spoke to Furtwängler and asked to see him forthwith. Furtwängler explained this was impossible, as he was leaving for Egypt early the next morning. But the gentleman concerned insisted, and when Furtwängler would not give way, revealed that he had a message from the Führer. Furtwängler had, of course, to go out to see him. Full of apprehension, I said : " I am convinced that they won't let you leave Germany ". For hours I waited in suspense. Late at night Furtwängler returned. It was as I had foreseen. The Führer had asked him to wait " a little " before taking his journey, until the excitement caused everywhere by his resignation had somewhat abated. He thought that it would not be desirable for Furtwängler if he were made the object of demonstrations abroad. Furtwängler had consented to the delay, and gained the impression that there would be no objection to his departure about a fortnight later. His passport—contrary to all rumours—had not been detained. Nevertheless, he was not able to leave as he had hoped and expected. It was to be a long time before he was free to move again at will.

I had counted on his departure on December 24th. Until then I was prepared to stand the torture and strain that had now lasted for so many months. Any prolongation of this would have been utterly unbearable. I therefore entreated Furtwängler to leave Berlin, to go away—into the mountains, to the countryside, anywhere—as long as it were away from Berlin, and away from myself. He understood, and left on Christmas day.

The day after Christmas an official from the Gestapo came and confiscated my passport.

The old battle was at an end. A new battle had begun.

[1 9 3 5]

Chapter 15

THE BATTLE for my passport was to last for almost a year. My passport was an absolute essential for my future life. The Nazis realised, of course, that it was quite unnecessary to arrest me while they retained my passport. Without it I was paralysed. They knew, too, that as long as I was not free to travel abroad, I was of no use to Furtwängler.

The departure of Furtwängler and the end of our business relationship on Christmas Eve 1934 was, at any rate, the end of a chapter. Automatically, the old life ended. Although I still was not entirely cut off from my friends, my life was altogether abnormal. One day a foreign diplomat's wife appeared suddenly in my flat; she had climbed the backstairs, and told me that she had left her car "round the corner". If anyone noticed that she had visited me, both of us would have had to suffer. For people who were not entirely independent of the Party it now seemed dangerous to be in touch with me. Many and mysterious are the methods of exerting pressure. An impenetrable barrier seemed to be erected around me. For almost twenty years my work had shaped my life, and everything I did converged on this focus. After such activity, passivity seemed impossible. It was like being an invalid all of a sudden. Between one moment and the next, my old world was closed to me, and I found it painful and difficult to adapt myself to the circumscribed new world in which I found myself.

You can teach the brain to grasp something, you can thrust a knife into a body—but you can't impose a thing upon the soul : it won't accept it—it swings on in its own mysterious way. I felt this strongly while I was still trying to understand what was happening to me. What are arguments of reason, compared to emotions.

I felt, too, that I should not think only of myself. I had made up my mind to do my best to facilitate matters for Furtwängler, and to coach his new secretary in her work as far as possible. It may seem foolish to have tried to do this ; it was after all a matter with which I was supposed to have nothing more to do. However, my life had been so bound up with Furtwängler and the Orchestra, my affections and loyalty were so deeply implicated, that I found it impossible to leave them in the lurch at so short notice, and I thought at the time that it was my duty to help them even under such unusual circumstances.

All the authorities concerned, the Ministry of Propaganda and the *Reichsmusikkammer* continuously inquired when the " transfer of the business " would be completed. They could hardly wait, so anxious were they to be able to dispense with me.

Meanwhile, Furtwängler had, after making several detours, arrived in Bavaria. He had taken a room with a piano in it in a suburb of Munich, and had settled there for the moment.

In spite of his persistent efforts he had not been able to get in touch with any member of the Government. The fortnight which ostensibly was to elapse before he could travel abroad had passed without any move from them. Furtwängler's refuge was a few yards from the estate of Rudolf Hess, the deputy Führer. Formerly, Hess and his wife could not do enough for Furtwängler. The fanatical Party leader had even gone so far as to say that he was so devoted to him that he would stop at absolutely nothing to deliver Germany's great conductor from his "Jewish" secretary ! Now, in spite of living so near him, Hess was inaccessible. The result of the Saar plebiscite in the January of 1935 which was bound to increase the Nazis prestige abroad, strengthened their position at home as well. Without this success they would hardly have dared to treat Furtwängler as they did.

Furtwängler was always extremely sensitive, and was moreover accustomed to having everything run on oiled wheels. He had devoted himself to his music, and had become used to my looking after everything else. He was, too, accustomed to all the facilities accorded to a famous man. Now he was ignored and slighted. He had had not only to cancel his trip to Egypt, but it was uncertain whether he would be able to keep his foreign engagements next spring.

He wrote and telephoned to the authorities constantly, but without any result. How well the Nazis knew how to handle people ! They are experts at tormenting their victims. For them nothing was wiser than to ignore Furtwängler ; for him nothing more unwise than his constant petitions. He should, of course, have remained completely passive and taken no notice of *them*. Even if it had meant temporarily not honouring his foreign commitments, he should have left all responsibility to the Nazis. The balance of moral strength would have been on his side, and his would have been the stronger position. But he lacked the nervous stability necessary for this and thus played into their hands, augmenting their power over him. This is more evident in retrospect than it was then.

It is no wonder that this state of affairs was unbearable for Furtwängler in his isolation. One day I was informed surreptitiously that he wanted to see me—and I travelled to Bavaria stealthily, like a criminal. It had been constantly impressed upon me—in an obvious attempt to intimidate me—that I was being closely shadowed, and so I saw ghosts everywhere. My visit may have been necessary for Furtwängler, but it was painful to both of us. Meeting under such circumstances, we both felt, more than ever, the strength of old ties. This did not make things any easier for either of us. This first meeting after the parting of our ways only enhanced Furtwängler's depression. I did my utmost to conceal my own feelings. As we walked through the snow-covered woods he said to me : " We are just like two dogs with our tails between their legs ". I replied : " It won't be *two* for long. *You* will soon be back in harness, but I, never. Anyway, not in Germany ". Two days later I returned to Berlin.

Furtwängler had at first kept his address strictly secret, but as he was only too well known in Bavaria and did not hide himself, his residence was soon known. Gradually members of the Berlin Philharmonic, delegates of the Vienna Philharmonic, the Vienna State Opera, and even of American orchestras found their way to him. Meanwhile, I continued to train his new secretary, and anxiously waited for the return of my passport.

In February Furtwängler reappeared in Berlin. He could no longer bear the suspense and the isolation, and felt he had to be on the spot. He went to his Potsdam home, the " Fasanerie ", in the Sans-Souci park. We met on the evening of his arrival ; but we both realised that things being what they were, with both of us entirely dependent upon the whim of the Nazis, we could not possibly stay in the same town at the same time. As he was in Potsdam, I had to leave Berlin.

With great sadness I said good-bye, and went for a second time to Munich. Our friends there were at least free from the Berlin " psychosis ", and I could speak freely to them. Nevertheless, I did not know how to overcome the emptiness of my life. The constant pressure under which I had lived since 1933 now began to take effect. I grew ill, and began to suffer from insomnia. The truth is that I was completely worn out, mentally, physically, and spiritually. Everything dear to me had been taken from me. The life I had lived so eagerly, with such passionate interest, was shattered.

Everything I had stood for was threatened and overshadowed. I
had no home, no work, no hope. I was at my lowest ebb.

Some days after my arrival in Munich, my mother rang me up
from Berlin in a state of great excitement to say that my passport
had been returned. She was usually very careful, but having lived
for so many months in this witch's cauldron, she probably lost her
caution for the moment. She knew what this meant for me, and
as the official who had brought it back had asked for me personally,
she thought it best to ring me up in his presence in order to prove
that I was within reach. Jubilantly, she told me the good news.

I felt very uneasy, for I would have much preferred her to
accept the passport silently, without any comment.

I decided not to return to Berlin immediately, but went to the
Starnberg Lake to stay with the Lerchenfelds. The Count, previously
Prime Minister of Bavaria, had been German Minister to Vienna
where he and his Anglo-American wife enjoyed much popularity.
Afterwards he had been transferred to the German Legation at
Brussels, where Furtwängler and I had stayed as his guests. Lerchen-
field was a deeply religious man whose faith pervaded his whole
life and never failed him in any situation. He was highly educated,
well-read, and fond of playing chamber-music. The Countess was
an outstanding personality, a strong character, and a devoted friend
of mine. The house, set in a lovely garden, with a view over the
lake, was full of beautiful old furniture, magnificent paintings and
porcelain, and had a fine library containing many rare old books.

I was not allowed to enjoy the peaceful and serene atmosphere
of this household for long undisturbed. No sooner had I arrived
than I received a message from Berlin informing me that my passport had been confiscated again. What was behind all this, I do not
know to this day. I only heard, later on, that its return had been a
"mistake" because it was intended to chain me down until Furtwängler had been abroad on his own, and until the Orchestra, too,
had travelled to foreign countries without me. The myth of my
indispensability had to be destroyed before I was set free. It was also
not unlikely that my successor, afraid of losing her chance of accompanying Furtwängler abroad, may have conveyed to the Gestapo
that it was inadvisable to release my passport at this juncture.

Nothing could have been more soothing than the atmosphere in the Lerchenfeld's house, but when I realised that my hopes for freedom were again frustrated the black horror of my situation again enveloped me.

More troubles were to come. When I returned to Munich, a letter was awaiting me which can only be described as "blackmail". It was from the Gestapo. Here it is.

" 9/III./1935.

"Dear Frl. Doctor,—As you have already heard from your mother, I returned your passport to you through one of my agents. We regret that we had to withdraw this passport again after the lapse of three days because your mother, in the presence of the official, first by telephone, and later in your own home in Berlin, made public the fact that you were again in possession of your passport. The official reported this incident, and thus I was forced to withdraw the document. The happiness evinced by your mother on receipt of your passport gave cause for suspicion that you planned something definite when you had it in your possession.

"As a result of this incident you will not be in a position to obtain it without my help. I therefore request you (if you want to receive your passport) to remit the negligible sum of 1200 Reichsmark, in cash and ordinary notes of 100 Marks, and in such a way that the outside of the letter does not reveal anything of its contents. It is to be addressed to E. Helferich, Berlin-Spandau, poste restante, and to be received by Thursday, 14th March, at the latest.

"I require this sum as hush-money for various officials who are acquainted with your case.

"Should your letter fail to arrive I regret that I shall not be able to do anything further for you, because I have to report to my chief on the 15th of March at the latest, on the matter of your passport, and your activities in connection with Councillor of State Dr. Furtwängler. If the letter arrives I shall draft my report in such a way that you will receive your passport towards the end of the month.

"I further want to inform you that you are under constant surveillance by our secret police, irrespective of whether you are staying in Berlin or Munich. You are also advised to beware of the secretary who occupies your place with Dr. Furtwängler. I have heard much from her that incriminates you.

"I would beg you not to inform anybody of this letter since

this would result in the retention of your passport. If you will follow my instructions, you will receive your passport.

" (signed)   RAUCH
" (Inspector, the Secret Police)."

The English reader will scarcely be able to believe that so crude and blatant a piece of blackmail could go out over the signature of an official of the Nazi Reich, however minor his position might be. This is, however, an actual translation of the letter (the writer used the word *Schweigegeld* for " hush-money ") ; I still have it in my possession. I can only imagine that the gentleman in question thought that I was so helpless, so forsaken, that he could indulge with impunity in this clumsy move in his game of cat-and-mouse.

Of course the letter was sheer bluff ; I had nothing to conceal at all. I realised that the principal thing was not to lose one's head. This was an outrageous affair for a country whose new régime prided itself on its freedom from corruption.

Many people are known to have given way to such tactics in order to attain their purpose, but I was no such easy prey. I immediately went to a solicitor who advised the strictest secrecy. He proposed to take the ominous letter by hand to Berlin. This he did, and he there gave it to a Nazi connection of his who delivered it to Himmler, chief of the Gestapo. I have never understood why the place where the money was to be deposited at a certain date was not watched in order to get the culprit. The careful investigation which was later staged by the Gestapo indicated that the stirring up of the affair was most unwelcome to them.

I myself remained absolutely passive and hoped that after the revelation of this criminal attempt the Gestapo would immediately return my passport in order to hush the matter up : however, nothing happened.

Some months later I was suddenly informed that the Bavarian Police had received instructions to interview me, and one day the fat and honest village constable called on me. A burnt child is afraid of fire, and I grew very nervous at any contact with officialdom. The peaceful and rural atmosphere of this interview, however, would have inspired confidence even in the most frightened person, and nothing of Prussian Gestapo methods could be detected in it. On

Wilhelm Furtwängler at the piano.

(*Photo : Harlip*)

Furtwängler rehearsing with the Berlin Philharmonic Orchestra.

Portrait of Toscanini with dedication to the Vienna
Philharmonic Orchestra.

Reading from left to right : Siegfried Wagner ; Count Biagio Gravina ; Countess Blandine Gravina (née von Bülow) ; Daniela Thode (née von Bülow) ; Isolde von Bülow ; Eva Wagner ; Cosima Wagner. (1894.)

Taken from the book *Cosima Wagner,* by Max Milenkovich-Morold, 1937.

Hitler congratulating the artists behind the scenes after the new
Lohengrin production at Bayreuth. (1936.)

(Photo : Wieland Wagner)

Sir Thomas and Furtwängler working on the plans for the Covent Garden Coronation Season.

(*Photo taken by the Author,* 1936)

Hitler and members of the German Government listening to a concert given by the London Philharmonic Orchestra, in Berlin. November 13, 1936.

Faked photograph, which appeared in the newspaper *B.Z. am Mittag*, showing the figure of Sir Thomas in Hitler's box, though in point of fact he never entered it.   November 13, 1936.

Sir Thomas Beecham at home.

(*Pictorial Press*)

the wooden bench before the little house, under a blooming chestnut tree, sat the rotund and placid representative of village authority.
He was an enormous man with a frank and ruddy face. It took me
some time to make him understand the position ; but when he had
taken it in, he was very intrigued, and instead of interviewing me,
we both, like Sherlock Holmes and Watson, tried to figure the whole
thing out.

Later on I was interviewed twice more in Berlin ; once by a very
decent police official who immediately told me that I was not to worry,
that there was no charge against me personally, but that it was hoped
I would oblige them by helping to find the blackmailer. Although
one letter of his typewriter was faulty, they had not been able to trace
the culprit—or so they said. The last interview I had in this connection took place when I visited Berlin for the first time with Sir
Thomas Beecham. Needless to say, this interview was a model of
civility and politeness.

This was the last I ever heard of the matter. It was never cleared
up, and to this day it remains a question whether the authority
who instigated the inquiry did it in good faith or as a blind.

But this is jumping far ahead. Let us go back to the beginning
of March 1935. Furtwängler was still waiting in Berlin for an interview with Hitler or Goebbels to define his position. I was still living
exiled in the Bavarian mountains. Yet once again Furtwängler
suddenly sent me word that he wanted to see me urgently. Could
I leave the same evening for Potsdam ? I left by a train which arrived
at dawn and walked alone through the snow-covered Sans-Souci
park where Furtwängler's home stood, like a castle in a fairy tale.
I looked about anxiously, lest anybody should detect me, worn out
and harrowed by the Fate which constantly expelled me from my
old life, only to call me back into it again and again.

Furtwängler had sent for me out of a kind of spiritual claustrophobia.
He was, in a way, trapped. He was used to absolute freedom of
movement, to being entirely his own master, but he was now cut off
from his relation to the outer world, had no idea how his own
problem was to be solved, and was in a bad state of nerves. I had
always discussed his troubles with him, and it seemed natural that I
should do so now.

Although there was no external barrier in 1935 between Germany and the outside world, and normal people were free to move in and out of the country, in actual fact he and I, he to a lesser, I to a greater degree, were anything but free. People from the outside world were aware of the conditions in the Reich, and there were many " men of goodwill " ready to run risks to help people out of an intolerable situation. Furtwängler and I discussed on this occasion a proposition which had been made to me, which would have involved getting me out of Germany without my passport. How tempting it sounded ; for it looked as if the Nazis wanted to keep me prisoner for ever—yet how impossible it was. I had to consider that my mother was still living in Germany and that nobody under German jurisdiction could ever risk being in touch with me abroad without suffering the severest repercussions at home. I felt with absolute certainty that I had to " stick it out ", and that I could only leave Germany " legally "—that is, by the tedious and tortuous procedure which was still left open to people like me.

As we discussed the matter from all angles, I felt that there was a world stronger than the Nazi terror which threatened to crush us —a world of principles, a world of faith. We parted in a mood of serenity and harmony : towards evening I stole along in the shadows to the train which was to take me back to Munich.

Chapter 16

THE BAVARIAN countryside was snow-covered at this time of the year. Friends of mine lived in a lonely chalet above the Isar Valley near Irschenhausen. They were a married couple, both Roman Catholic, and the husband, who came of a family of distinguished scholars, had been assistant to Furtwängler's father and was an intimate friend of the younger Furtwängler. I visited them for a day.

The beauty of their retreat was indescribable. One had a wide view over the mountains from the log-house, which was backed by a pine forest. Everything for the household had be to carried up the mountain path. They did everything for themselves, and cooked marvellous meals on a primus stove. An air of calm and of freedom emanated from them. In the evening we went down through the deep snow to the village of Ebenhausen. There, there was a very old inn, the Post—typically Bavarian—which was also the village butcher's shop. In the evening the peasants sat in the smoke-filled parlour, drinking their beer. Everyone said just what he liked in this untouched oasis of genuine freedom.

I had gradually come to realise that my affairs would take much longer to settle than I had hoped, so I decided to move from the town. The old inn at Ebenhausen seemed just the right place for me and so I installed myself there. I was the only lodger, and had a tiny room with an iron stove. The wing where my room lay was bitterly cold as I was the only person living in it. Until the fire was lit in the parlour, the only warmth was at the side of the big kitchen range. In this old inn I found the refuge and solitude I needed, yet my insomnia became worse. Hardly anything from the outside world penetrated to me, and day after day I wandered for many hours in snow and rain through the woods—always tormented by the same thoughts. At night, although very tired, I could not sleep. In the evening I listened to the peasants' gossip and soon their faces became familiar to me, but for weeks on end I never spoke to any-one save an old rough-coated dog who began to accompany me on my walks.

Even an entirely empty day has to be got through somehow, and so I tried to get something definite to do to fill up my time. This was difficult, because it had to be something which I could do alone. A friend from Munich brought me some typing to do. I copied several zoological essays, and the author does not know to this day who did the job. The days and the sleepless nights seemed interminable, but I had quiet, seclusion, and nature's balm. The countryside was peaceful and undisturbed. Often I walked to the nearby Schaeftlarn monastery and sat there for a quiet hour in the wonderful Bavarian baroque church with its onion-shaped cupola. On Sundays I went to church with the peasants. The monks at Schaeftlarn were Dominicans, and their famous abbot was a great scholar and a strong personality.

In Berlin matters remained stationary. Furtwängler was still not

being received, and the uncertainty of his position made him highly
nervous. He again wrote to the Government, to Hitler. He constantly talked to people who all gave differing advice, and then
reported and distorted all he had said. It was clear that the Nazis
strove to cow Furtwängler as much as possible. The longer he was
made to wait the easier it would be to control him eventually,
because of his temperament. They continued to use me as a pawn
in their machinations. The "war of nerves" is a weapon of the
Nazis—not only used in Furtwängler's case. I had cut myself off
from everyone, and lived in retirement among people who knew
neither me, nor of the "Furtwängler case", but he was systematically
harried. Invented utterances attributed to me and alleged to be
harmful to him were constantly reported to him. Everything he
was told was aimed at making him believe that unless he entirely
broke our friendship, he could never hope for freedom. Later on
I was told how much the Nazis—among them Heydrich—boasted
of the net of false rumours which they spread round the impression-
able artist. "The creation of a panic around Furtwängler" they
called it. In their way they were quite successful.

Suddenly things began to move; but they took an unexpected
turn.

One evening in March we were sitting in the parlour of our inn
when quite unexpectedly a special announcement was broadcast
which began with the words: "Reich Minister Dr. Goebbels
received *Stavtsrat* Dr. Furtwängler to-day. . . ." It went on to say
that Furtwängler had declared that he regretted all past misunder-
standings, that he had never intended to introduce political considerations into the Hindemith case, and that, naturally, all final decisions
on this and every other point must be left with the Führer.

Was *this* the end of the whole desperate struggle? Of the
courageous fight for spiritual freedom? My heart missed a beat.
I could not believe it.

The fact that Furtwängler sanctioned this declaration, which was
broadcast from all the stations in Germany, was deplored not only
in foreign countries: countless Germans, too, were aghast that this
man on whom so many had relied—and who, thanks to his achievements was as independent of the Nazis as only few Germans were
—had given in at last.

Much later I learned the true facts about this matter. Furtwängler was constantly importuned by his friends and by his public not to forsake them. He was in great distress of mind, and discussed with various people what conditions he should make, should he eventually agree to a resumption of his activities in Germany. These conditions and proposals formed the text of various *exposés* and rough drafts which he drew up at the time. Not only his own secretary—not a good typist—but various extra helpers typed these drafts, and apparently one of them out of zeal or an aptitude for intrigue, deemed it advisable to disclose to high Nazi quarters what was going on within Furtwängler's four walls ; and a preliminary draft found its way, in this manner, actually to Goebbel's desk.

The cunning Minister of Propaganda was thus able to forestall Furtwängler. Instead of sending for Furtwängler and granting him the long postponed interview, he sent an official of his Ministry to Furtwängler, armed with a written statement for Furtwängler's signature, to be published immediately after the " reconciliation " he foresaw as the result of the draft.

This statement was such that Furtwängler could not possibly agree to it. He refused, and only after a long and stubborn fight a compromise was found to serve as the text for publication after Furtwangler's interview with Goebbels. This text, watered down as it was, nevertheless represented a complete surrender of Furtwängler in the eyes of independent observers.

After the result of the interview with Goebbels had been sufficiently publicised by radio and press, and the prestige of the Nazis thus safeguarded, every obstacle to a meeting between Furtwängler and Hitler was removed. In the meantime, the date approached for Furtwängler's concert in Vienna. If he was to be in time for the *Nicolaikonzert*, he had to leave Berlin not later than April 10th. The interview with Hitler had been postponed several times. Finally it was fixed early on the day in which Furtwängler was bound to leave for Vienna. It should be remembered that he could not leave Germany until Hitler removed the ban on his crossing the frontier.

There is no record of the interview—as far as the basis of Furtwängler's future activity was concerned. He was not compelled to accept any fixed position. He was willing to conduct some of the Berlin Philharmonic Concerts, as well as concerts with the Berlin

Philharmonic in the provinces and abroad. He was prepared to conduct opera performances in the Reich, with the exception of those at the Berlin State Opera. He would also conduct at the Party Rally at Nuremberg in autumn 1935. No mention was made of Bayreuth for the time being.

He further agreed to conduct a concert in aid of the Winter Help Fund in Berlin on April 25, 1935, after his return from Vienna. In this concert he was welcomed by his frantic public with unbounded enthusiasm. Hitler, who was present with the whole Government, was sitting in the front row of the *Philharmonie* and was ignored. He is said to have felt this keenly ; but in contrast to his behaviour at the ovations before Furtwängler's resignation, he accepted the situation with good grace. He rose, went to the platform, and shook hands with Furtwängler. This symbolic gesture was, of course, photographed and received wide publicity.

On the day (April 10, 1935) of Furtwängler's interview with Hitler the wedding of Goering with Emmy Sonnemann took place. Hitler was best man, and the meeting with Furtwängler had been arranged for an early hour in the morning. When Furtwängler drove in his car to the *Reichskanzlei*, he was delayed by cordons—it being Germany and not England—and when he eventually managed to get to the Wilhelmstrasse after many detours, Hitler had already left for the wedding. Hitler had therefore to be approached again, and a later hour arranged. In the end the two met shortly before the train was due to leave for Vienna. The Anhalter station was informed by the Chancellery that the train must not leave without Furtwängler. The train waited. Finally, Furtwängler appeared on the platform and got in. He was free. The Vienna newspapers reported his arrival in heavy type—" unfortunately without his familiar secretary ".

Meanwhile the " familiar " secretary was still waiting for her passport in exile, and was not allowed to go to Berlin, even while Furtwängler was absent from there.

While Furtwängler was meeting Hitler, the German news was dominated by Goering's wedding. This pompous affair was broadcast by all stations in great detail. It was later said that Goebbels had intended to play a dirty trick on Goering by describing minutely the luxurious presents Goering received and the more than princely setting of the proceedings. I do not know what the effect of the extravagant celebration was on people in the Reich. I can only tell how the detailed broadcast description affected the peasants in Ebenhausen.

It was one of the first beautiful sunny spring days. The peasants were sitting on wooden benches with their mugs of beer under the budding chestnut trees in the yard of the inn. The radio had been placed outside the kitchen window, and everybody was listening. The ceremony was described, the presents enumerated. It is no secret that every citizen, however poor he may have been, had been invited to contribute to these presents, even if only one mark. Everything was mentioned, the yacht, the diamond tiara with the swastika of diamonds in the centre, and all the rest of it. The farmers commented on it all dryly. They continued to discuss the Third Reich, so often claimed by its Leaders to be going to last for a thousand years. Suddenly I heard one of them saying : " Well, one morning we'll wake up and find the thousand years is past ".. It was a comfortable thought.

Chapter 17

ON HIS return from Vienna, and for the first time since his disagreement with the Nazis had been patched up, Furtwängler came to see me. We had again to meet in the utmost secrecy. Furtwängler was by no means at ease over his " reconciliation " with the Government ; he was not sure of the consequences of this step and had much to reckon with now that he had given in.

In Vienna he had been criticised for this move, and it was doubtful how his impending opera performances in London and Paris would be received. He was exhausted, and we hardly talked of anything but his own problems. He told me quite frankly that he considered it impossible for me ever to return to Berlin, except to deal with the matter of the " liquidation " of my home. I was aware that he felt very keenly the fact that it was impossible for him to help me in any way.

At the end of a talk that made both of us realise the hopelessness of the situation, he left—alone—to avoid our being seen together. I was myself quite shattered, and remained numb in spirit, till I could muster up enough strength to leave too. It was less the uncertainty of the future than the humiliating conditions of the present, which I felt so acutely.

I had no choice but to remain in Bavaria for the time being. For many weeks there was nothing but snow and rain, and I used to sit in my wretched little room by the side of my tiny stove. How I welcomed the sun when it came ! In spring this part of the country is very beautiful, the woods, the mountains, the scent of the meadows towards the evening, the animals, clouds, and sky—all were idyllic. But everything was marred by the uncertainty and ignominy of my position, which weighed heavily upon me.

While my case was unsettled and I was at the mercy of the Nazis, I abstained from any correspondence with people living outside Germany. My friends abroad, however, rose to the occasion. An old friend of mine, a very prominent man from abroad, frequently came to see me, to find out how I was, and I talked things over with him. It is due to him that I received an offer from the musicologist and collector, A. van Hoboken, who was living in Vienna at that time, to go to America in connection with his "Photographic Archive of Musical Scores", to endeavour to trace new musical autographs. Hoboken had founded these "Archives" and placed them at the disposal of the Vienna National Library in 1927. They were housed in the "Albertina" and consisted of photographic reproductions of manuscript scores of the great musical masters. The "Archives" were designed to enable the student who hitherto could consult manuscripts only where the original happened to be, to find photostats of the music holographs of the whole world united in one place.

Hoboken intended to increase his "Archives" as much as possible, and some American libraries were interested in founding similar collections.

In spite of this offer, which I reported to the authorities, my passport remained sequestered. Eventually I was advised to make a formal application to the appropriate department. For this purpose it was imperative that I should go to Berlin, which until then, I had been told, was not advisable. However, I finally obtained permission to go.

Meanwhile, Furtwängler had left for London to conduct *Tristan* at Covent Garden. I will not describe the feelings with which I followed him in thought. For the first time he was conducting in London and Paris without me ! I, for my part, went to Berlin where, at first, I felt quite intimidated and out of place. A foreign diplomat's wife once said to me : " There is nothing the Nazis know better than how to humiliate people ". How true ! Hardly had I set foot in Berlin when their manœuvres started again. I was warned to keep quiet, to see nobody, and to concentrate on the matter of my passport only.

On the day after my arrival I went to my local police station. The old inspector whispered to me : " Fräulein Doktor, I admire your patience. I have known you for so long. How can you bear it all ? " Finally, I was told what to do, and I made a formal application for the return of my passport in order to be able to accept a position abroad, since I had had to give up my work in Germany.

Meeting old friends was exciting and comforting. It gave me courage and strength and helped me to have patience. Thus, although the visit to Berlin was an emotional strain, I returned to Bavaria refreshed in spirit.

It was now the end of May, everything was in blossom and peace reigned everywhere.

Soon afterwards, Count Lerchenfeld came to see me, and proposed that I should move to the Starnberg Lake near their home for the summer, pending further developments. This was a welcome idea, and one morning in brilliant sunshine I walked over the mountains and took a room in Percha for the middle of June.

Meanwhile, Furtwängler had conducted in London and at the Paris *Opéra*. He had sent me word to say that he would come to see me directly after his last Paris performance.

He duly arrived and stayed some time in Munich, where he conducted several times. We frequently met, and these quiet undisturbed conversations in a remote place were comforting to both of us. Sometimes he forgot how things really stood, and even suggested on one occasion that I should attend his *Tristan* performance at the *Prinzregententheater*. Needless to say, I stayed away.

The Nazis continued to attach an exaggerated importance to Furtwängler's relations with me as will be seen by the fact that even when Furtwängler was in Munich, Herr Hess made anxious inquiries as to whether I was in the neighbourhood.

Soon afterwards I moved into my new home, a charming little Bavarian chalet with geraniums in the window-boxes. It belonged to two highly cultured ladies of the Mendelssohn family. One of them, Fräulein Mendelssohn-Bartholdy, was a direct descendant of Felix Mendelssohn. The other, her cousin, came from the scholarly Dubois-Reymond family.

Although, according to the Nuremberg legislation, neither belonged to the "Jewish race" (one of them had one-eighth, the other one-fourth of Jewish blood, carefully reckoned out at that time !), they did not feel at home in Hitler's Germany, and had retired to the country.

Their home was delightful. Furniture belonging to the Mendelssohn family, and old masters on the walls, gave the rooms a special atmosphere. Here I did not have to be silent as with the peasants, and the profound human understanding and sympathy of these fine women was most comforting.

It was a healthy and refreshing life by the Lake, and quite different from the old one, which I tried in vain to forget.

My friend and neighbour, Count Lerchenfeld, was the nephew of Count Hugo Lerchenfeld-Koefering, who had been Bavarian Minister to Berlin for thirty years and whose reports to the King of Bavaria were considered highly interesting documents of the period, dating from after the foundation of the Reich until the abdication of the Kaiser.

The nephew was working on his uncle's memoirs, the first volume of which appeared in 1935, and the Bavarian royal archives had willingly allowed him access to these documents, and had agreed to his plan of publishing a book based on them. When I moved to Percha, Count Lerchenfeld was just beginning to work on the material for the second volume, and I sometimes assisted him with the typing. This was fascinating, and a new world opened before me.

A highly interesting part of this work was the chapter on Wilhelm II. The Kaiser was originally a great admirer of the elder Lerchenfelds, but varying political phases caused his friendship to give way to a more restrained relationship.

To Count Lerchenfeld senior, as the doyen of the Diplomatic Corps and Minister of Bavaria, the most important State within the Reich after Prussia, fell the duty of advising the Kaiser to abdicate in 1918. He knew him well and wrote about him frankly. This chapter can be counted among the most enlightening documents extant about the Kaiser. However, the Count has made a reservation in his will relating to its publication.

Furtwängler had been staying in Poland and on the Baltic Sea since the middle of June. For weeks I had not heard from him. After all, what was there to say? Now, suddenly, he announced his visit for the middle of August. He arrived by aeroplane and stayed for two days, and although he was a free agent, not at the mercy of the Nazis like myself, he was worried about everything. He was very dissatisfied with my successor, and had found out that his affairs in charge of this lady, so much favoured by the Nazis, were being mishandled. What was he to do now? It was imperative that a more suitable person should be found. What a grotesque situation this was! Here was I, his secretary of so many years standing, living in forced exile, while he was worried to death trying to find a suitable successor to me. After we had discussed the matter, and tried to find some way out for Furtwängler, he left.

In spite of my wretchedness, I had to own that life on the Lake in these summer days was delightful. Yet, even this remote part of the world was not to remain free from intruders. On the Lake, near Schloss Berg, where the unhappy King Ludwig of Bavaria had been drowned, was a beautiful estate with a large park. This house—built in the '80s—had long been for sale. Finally it was reported as sold. An army of workmen appeared. Extensive alterations were carried out, and the whole garden was rearranged. Everybody wondered who might be the Crœsus who could not only buy such a property but also launch out on such a princely scale of renovation and reconstruction.

Who could it be? One soon heard! It was the German Minister

of the Interior, Dr. Frick, whose yearly salary according to Party law was not to exceed 12,000 RMK or £600. Where did these people get their money from? Before he was appointed Minister of Justice for Thuringia, Frick had been a small civil servant in Bavaria and had had no capital. His purchase of this large property made a very bad impression on the local population, and has certainly not added any adherents to Hitler's cause from the shores of the Starnberg Lake.

From the moment Frick took up his residence, various orderlies were to be seen all over the district. His mail was specially delivered to him by a motor-cycle combination. For months he stayed there with his family, " guarded " by a whole gang of Storm Troopers, for whom special accommodation had been built at the entrance of the property.

Now that I have lived in England for so many years, this " guarding " of Nazi Ministers appears to me even more grotesque than it did before. Neither the King nor the Prime Minister is surrounded by such pomp and ceremony as these German " Servants of the People ". A simple style of life only remains—or so it seems, in the much despised democracies.

Chapter 18

AS TIME went on my personal affairs took a turn for the better. From various sides influential friends tried to regain my freedom for me. After persuading the Nazis that there would really be no danger of my doing any " harm " to Furtwängler when abroad, which was one of their pretexts for detaining me, a new inquiry had to be made to find out where the passport actually was. Finally I was informed that if I now applied to the headquarters of the Gestapo, enclosing documents to prove that I had an offer of work abroad, there was a chance that it would be released. This I did, and all the necessary papers were handed in. Hoboken wanted to meet me in Holland at the beginning of December, and I expected to leave for America early in January.

Meanwhile, my second successor had started her work with Furt-wängler. These changes after twenty years of continuous work with me were most disturbing for him. He had yielded to political pressure, but he had neither time nor inclination to deal with the reorganisation of his affairs, which had previously run so smoothly. He therefore declared that if I were not allowed to put things straight for him again, he, on his side, could not promise to devote the necessary time to his musical duties.

Before I could do this, it was necessary to get the permission of Herr Hans Hinkel of the Prussian " Ministry of Culture " who controlled the " cultural activities of ' non-Aryans ' in the Reich ". He " graciously acceded " to the request.

The reader may well ask, who was Hinkel ? Nobody had ever heard of him. Yet in Nazi-Germany people like Furtwängler were often dependent on nonentities such as he. Hinkel issued a pompous permission for me to clear up Furtwängler's affairs on the condition that this was done during his absence from Berlin. And—it was added—if possible, that I was to remain " invisible " !

I arranged to deal with all this while in Berlin on the passport affair, and I immediately started to work my way through the muddle. It was a fantastic state of affairs ! To what had Furtwängler yielded ? A crazy phobia on the part of the Nazis had drawn our unique organisation into the power of unqualified and inept busybodies. Furtwängler's great art, naturally, could not be touched, but the strain on his nerves due to all these complications was increased and this became more and more noticeable. With great distress I saw how completely he had fallen a victim to the war of nerves. How-ever, I concealed my feelings and did what I could.

The Nazis already had more enemies than friends. Soon, my old cronies knew that I was " back " and I had touching proofs of their affection, not only in professional circles, but even from people like taxi-drivers and the stallholders in the old market.

Many people came to see me ; they all grumbled at the régime, and I was well on the way to being drawn into the whirlpool again. I was determined to avoid this, and after having taken all necessary steps in connection with my passport and having put the new office in working order, I took myself off to Bavaria again.

On November 2nd I received my passport, only to find that it had already expired ! How typical of the whole state of affairs ! I thought : " This is a new trap. The Gestapo knows it's useless— so they send it back." More agony ! New applications ! But now I had the firm support of the Dutch Legation, and finally I was informed that if I went to my local police station in Berlin, a new passport would be handed to me.

This time it seemed as if they really meant it. I left Bavaria for good and went to Berlin.

On November 22, 1935, I received a passport valid for five years. I was free at last ! Now I could think of resuming a normal life. These thoughts chased one another through my mind while I held the precious document clasped in my hands.

However, my relief was to be shortlived. The next morning (November 23rd), an official of the Gestapo appeared, and my passport was confiscated again. This setback reflected the complexity of the forces at work behind the scenes. Individual members of the Government were pulling different strings for different ends, and my affairs were consequently tossed about in this extraordinary fashion. Only by exercising great caution could I inform my friends of this new incident, lest I should jeopardise their ability to help me.

However, I found ways and means of communication, and a few days later I was asked to be in a certain side-street after dark to meet a trusty messenger. I went, and was told not to worry—the passport would be restored soon.

This time Fate was kind. By a strange coincidence, Tietjen and Furtwängler had had a conference on matters concerning the Opera with Goering, who had received Furtwängler with the words : " Well, are you satisfied now ? Dr. Geissmar has got her passport again ! " " She did have it, but only for twenty-four hours," said Furtwängler.

Goering knew nothing of this. He swore that he himself would settle the matter immediately.

This was the messenger's tale. I have never found out on whose initiative the passport had been withdrawn again. I wonder what story the Minister for Propaganda could tell ! If the interview with Goering had not taken place at just that time, heaven knows how long I would have had to wait again.

The passport did not arrive at once. Day after day I waited. I said to my mother : " I don't care about anything. I don't care if I ever see anybody from my old world again, as long as I get away —away from Nazi-Germany !—as far away as possible ! "

My mother understood perfectly. She had seen this coming. I packed two small suitcases, bought my ticket for America, and waited day in, day out.

After an interminable fortnight, one day the door bell rang—it was the only too familiar Gestapo agent. Silently he handed me the passport. At that very moment Goering's private secretary telephoned to say that it was on the way. " Thank you," said I. " When do you leave ? " said she. " To-morrow," I replied, although I knew it was to be that very night.

We sent our servants away on some errand so that they should not notice anything, while a friend collected my luggage and had it cleared at the station. Towards the evening my mother went out, and I stayed behind alone. Soon afterwards I left the flat as if for a walk.

I got into the Hague express and went to my sleeper. The Dutch Legation had given me a letter for the passport officer. However, all went well at the frontier, and after a long and anxious year I left Germany and went on to an insecure future.

Chapter 19

ONLY THOSE who have passed through similar ordeals will know the feeling of irrevocability in crossing the frontier. For whatever reason one leaves one's country, when one does so, there is something which one loses for ever and which no new life can replace. There is no escape from this fact, and it must be faced. Everyone has to find out for himself what his relations are to the land of his birth when he leaves it from political necessity. This was not yet clear to me, as Germany and the old life, with its successes and failures, receded.

About the time of my departure the Berlin Philharmonic Orchestra and Furtwängler were due to make a tour in England, for the first

time without me. Furtwängler had asked me to get in touch with
him as soon as I had arrived abroad, and so I sent him word to London
that I was at the Hague.

Early in the morning, two days later, a letter was pushed under
my door, addressed in Furtwängler's handwriting. It was the first
time for more than a year that he had dared to address a letter to me
in his own hand. I opened it eagerly. He wrote that he wanted
to see me before I left for America and would break his journey at
the Hague for this purpose.

Time was short. There were only twenty-four hours between
two concerts—one in London and the other in Dortmund. In order
to make the most of the time, I decided to meet him at Flushing
where he would arrive about five p.m. with the Orchestra.

As things were, members of the Orchestra were under no circumstances to be allowed to catch a glimpse of me. I therefore waited
in the train, and managed to send a note to Furtwängler on the arriving
boat, saying that I was in the second compartment of the Hague
carriage. Whilst waiting, I thought of the many successful journeys
I had made to England with the Berlin Philharmonic Orchestra.
How happy we used to be on arriving at Flushing on our way back.

The train to Germany drew in beside mine. Concealed behind
a curtain, I saw the familiar instrument cases loaded and the well-
known faces of the musicians as they climbed into the train.

A porter came along with Furtwängler's luggage. I said, just
as I had in the old days : " This way, please ". Finally, Furtwängler
appeared, rejoiced to see me free at last.

He began to tell me about the tour in England. Things had not
been the same, and he was not sure whether this was due to general
conditions or to the absence of the old organisation. He was worn
out, and told me he had decided to reduce his conducting. He
planned a long vacation during the winter, which he wished to spend
in Egypt. At the Hague we left the station separately, lest we might
be shadowed. We spent the evening in the hospitable home of good
friends, and in the cultured atmosphere and the warm sympathy
shown to us we completely forgot that Furtwängler was on the way
to Nazi-Germany, and that I was on the threshold of an unknown
future.

Mengelberg invited me to a concert at Amsterdam soon afterwards, and asked me to come to see him during the interval. At that time he was sincerely helping me—to-day he appears to be making common cause with the occupying force in Holland.

It was the first time for a long while that I had attended a concert, and for the first time in many a day I was welcome in the artists' room! It was a French programme. The French Ambassador was present and Mengelberg introduced me, saying : " This is Furt-wängler's famous secretary ". I felt uncomfortable about claiming this particular kind of fame ! Mengelberg was charming ; he told me I was to consider myself his guest while in Holland and make use of his office for everything I might need.

This soon proved to be most convenient. At that time it was not difficult to obtain visas for holders of a German passport, the flow of emigration not having reached full pitch. Foreign countries did not yet have to protect themselves against an uncontrolled influx as was the case later. German children and students were still receiving money for their studies abroad. But at the time of my stay in Holland restrictions began to tighten, in so far as different governments instructed their consulates to grant a visa only in the town where the passport had been originally issued. I had left Germany on the day I received my passport thinking I could easily obtain my visas in Holland. However, not even my Dutch friend, the chief of a world-wide concern, was able to help me. But on one point I was adamant. On no account would I send my passport back to Germany.

My mother communicated with the American Embassy in Berlin and Ambassador Dodd immediately agreed to make an exception in my case, and advised the American Consulate in Holland. Meanwhile, Mengelberg also had vouched for me with the American Consul-General in Amsterdam ; and I received my visa for the U.S.A.

French visas were then not being issued at all to holders of German passports, and I wanted to spend a few days in Paris to gather the old threads together again. The French Ambassador at the Hague could do nothing in the matter, but Mengelberg sent a telegram to the Quai d'Orsay, and the French Foreign Office telegraphed me my visa. Accordingly, the Belgian transit visa raised no great difficulties and I had everything I needed.

Just before Christmas I went to Paris. I was met at the station by Lucienne Couvreux, the daughter of Rouché, and her husband.

She had behaved splendidly during the period of my difficulties, and had always found ways and means to write to me. How wonderful to meet this truly devoted friend ! I felt as if I were living in a dream in the beautiful old house near the Bois de Boulogne, and during the first night we did not go to sleep at all, so much had we to tell each other.

Rouché showed me his correspondence with the new management of the Berlin Philharmonic Orchestra. How clumsily they dealt with the delicate matters, which had formerly been handled so carefully ! And yet, how often have the Nazis got away with their methods, clumsy or not.

At this time, however, things were not so simple. Public opinion in France grew increasingly hostile to Germany especially after the military reoccupation of the Rhineland and eventually caused the cancellation of the Berlin Philharmonic Orchestra Concerts arranged for April 1936 in Paris.

One evening we went to the theatre to see a new comedy. Suddenly I saw that Herr von Hoesch, then German Ambassador to Great Britain, spending Christmas in his beloved Paris—was facing me. It was a shock to see him, but exciting too ; so much of the old life had been connected with him. I felt, however, that things were so changed now—and, that I, as a refugee, had no longer any rights as far as he was concerned. I told him how I felt about this, but he took both my hands in his and said : " Why not, aren't we old friends ? "

These were his last words to me. I did not see him again because he had not yet returned to London when I was there, and he died while I was in America. He suffered as much, perhaps, under the Nazi methods as many who were expelled from Germany on account of their race. Yet he never complained. I sincerely admired his profound wisdom, and have adopted his maxim : *In dubio abstine !* (" When in doubt—don't ! ")

On Christmas Day I had luncheon at the Italian Embassy. The Cerrutis had been transferred from Berlin to Paris, and I had written to them immediately I was free.

How much we had to tell one another ! I often visited them in Paris, even after I finally settled in London. Later, Cerruti fell victim to one of those diplomatic reshuffles which Mussolini was so fond

of suddenly ordering from time to time. As I write this, I do not
know what has become of these charming people.

From Paris I went on to London for a week, and here, too, I met
old friends. Of course, the German Embassy was now closed to
me, but the Austrian Minister, Baron, now Sir George, Franckenstein,
received me, and I shall never forget his kindness at a time when I
was stranded.

On January 4, 1936, I left for New York.

[1 9 3 6]

Chapter 20

AS I write this, when many on the continent of Europe seem to
regard immigration to America as their only salvation, the standards
by which we measure our individual fates differ from those of 1936.
It is surprising how much more the individual can bear when his
fate is the fate of millions.

Writing in blitzed London, after a night thunderous with gun-
fire and the whistling of bombs, I can confirm this. How upset
people used to be by any extraordinary event, such as earthquake
or fire ! Nowadays, bombs scream through the air, buildings crash,
fires and explosions are daily events. One becomes used to them,
as to the rhythm of day and night. Our attitude towards death
and disaster undergoes a complete change.

When I left Germany in 1935, the urge to the West was only
beginning to make itself felt, although many people had left
Hitler-Germany and lived quietly elsewhere. Hitler had come to
power, but the worst had not yet come to pass.

Most of those who, in those days, tried to flee from Europe did so to
escape from force and the enemy. When I went to America in 1936,
I was not escaping from an enemy at war. My enemy was the
country of my birth, where my family had lived for hundreds of

years, and where I had had the roots of my being. Lost now to me was my homeland. I was cut off from all I had cherished and for which I had lived. The future was a sealed book.

When I went aboard at Southampton in a thick fog, the remembrance of my other Atlantic crossings made under such different circumstances rushed through my mind. But I did not allow myself to linger on the past. As the ship drew near to the new world, a deep gratitude rose in me that I was being given the chance to start a new life—hard as it might be. And with the fresh sea-wind blowing around me, I felt coming back to me a new energy and the determination to fight my own battle.

The friend who had intended to meet me when the ship docked sent a telegram to say that she had influenza, and so there I was alone on a strange shore.

I said to myself : I must take this as a symbol for the future : *this* is how it will be from now on. I went to my old hotel where I had formerly stayed with Furtwängler. Old memories flooded my mind as I went out for my solitary stroll.

This first day, however, was to be the only lonely one. During the night, the telephone rang. It was Joseph Schuster, one of the two solo-cellists of the Berlin Philharmonic who had left Germany eighteen months before, and had been in America ever since.

Schuster had been to a recital by Schnabel, and had heard that I had arrived in New York. He was staying in the same hotel, and declared he must come up and see me at once. This was the end of any prospect of a night's rest, for we found many memories to talk over.

Gradually I saw more and more of my friends, and the prospect of living for some time in New York was comforting.

How strange it seemed to live as a free being, to telephone without fear, to enjoy music again, to go to the opera, to the artists' room as in old times, to read newspapers and periodicals from all over the world, to write letters without restraint, and gradually to emerge from the abnormal and cramped conditions in which I had lived for so long !

It was like convalescence after a long and severe illness, like waking up from a bad dream. It took me a long time to recuperate, and even then no recovery completely removed the nightmare of the past.

At this time Sir Thomas Beecham was in America. I had known him for many years and had always admired him. He had an air of independence which had always appealed to me. His first concert with the Berlin Philharmonic Orchestra in my time was in 1930, and the Orchestra took to him at once. At that very concert an amusing incident occurred. When Sir Thomas made his entry his shoe came undone. Instead of bowing to the audience he bent down, turned his back to the public, and leisurely tied the offending lace. The Berlin Press did not know how to appraise this strange guest, and in spite of their admiration for his art, they emphasised the fact that the first thing Sir Thomas had done was to turn his back to the public !

Whenever Sir Thomas came to Berlin we had been delighted with his personality and brilliant, flashing wit. He had remained our staunch friend since 1927, when the Berlin Philharmonic and Furtwängler played in London for the first time. Although there is a rumour (possibly inspired by Sir Thomas himself) that he never attends the concerts of others, he nearly always appeared when the Berliners and Furtwängler played in London, and was joyously welcomed by the Orchestra. He always had time to spare, not only for Furtwängler, but for me, too ; and I remember that it was on account of a luncheon engagement with Sir Thomas that I failed, on one occasion, to accompany Furtwängler and the Orchestra to the provinces—a unique incident in the annals of my work with him !

Stories of Sir Thomas's generosity are legion, and we had had an example in 1932. In those days, concerts of the Berlin Philharmonic Orchestra in England sold out soon after the booking had opened. The advance booking for the English tour in 1932 was also excellent. However, shortly before the tour was to start, our agent, Lionel Powell, died, and his firm went bankrupt. It was said that his death at the height of the concert season in winter had upset the finances of the firm, and that, had this happened in spring, no difficulty would have arisen. Be that as it may, at the time of Powell's death all the takings were part of the bankrupt estate, and therefore the ready money out of which the expenses of the tour and the salaries of the Orchestra were to be paid, had vanished. We decided, if possible, not to cancel the tour, for we did not want to disappoint our British public.

At the suggestion of the German Embassy in London, and their legal adviser, I rushed to London about a fortnight before the beginning of the tour to see what could be done.

Here I conferred with the lawyer at the Embassy, who expounded the facts at length without being able to suggest any practical steps. It seemed hopeless. I did not see how we could get our money in the near future, nor did I see any chance of financing our ten concerts (two in London, eight in the provinces). I had just come to the conclusion that there was nothing left to do but to cancel the tour, when I received a message asking me to go and see Sir Thomas Beecham's solicitor. I immediately went. The solicitor spoke briefly and to the point : " I am instructed to inform you that Sir Thomas does not like this situation, and intends to see to the matter". " What do you mean ? " I asked. " Sir Thomas does not want the Berlin Philharmonic Orchestra to have any trouble in England, therefore he is going to guarantee the tour." " He is what ? " I asked again. " He is going to back the tour, and I have been instructed to settle the details with you," the solicitor repeated. The few formalities were quickly settled. My timid request to be allowed to thank Sir Thomas personally (who, after all, had deposited £3000 for us) was evasively answered, and towards the evening of the same day on which I had arrived, I took the train back to Berlin.

A fortnight later the tour began, and there was a full house at every concert. The complicated accounts involving unavailable box-office receipts I need not go into here. The last concert was at the Albert Hall, and in the morning, during the rehearsal there, we received the final statement. It showed a balance on the right side, even excluding the original advance receipts, so that we had no need to call on Sir Thomas's generous guarantee. Just as we realised this, Sir Thomas appeared unexpectedly. I went on to the platform and told the Orchestra what had happened ; how Sir Thomas had come to our rescue and that fortunately all had ended well. The

Orchestra enthusiastically hailed him with the customary tapping of bows.

The reader will see, therefore, that there was a bond of sympathy between Sir Thomas and the Berlin Philharmonic. Sir Thomas always liked to go where he could have good music, and that is why, up to a certain time, he liked going to Berlin. As a musician he was above politics, and while he had a greater political understanding than most of his colleagues, he kept his musical activities apart from politics as long as this was possible.

In December 1933 Sir Thomas conducted a Philharmonic Concert in Berlin, and while there he engaged some singers for Covent Garden. We lived at that time already more or less under Nazi pressure, and his visit was a great refresher for everyone. Before he left, I had lunch with him. Afterwards I went to see him off, and when he said good-bye he added : " If ever you get into hot water here, you must come and work for me at Covent Garden ".

Often, during the long year that I had waited for my passport, my thoughts had gone to him, as being the only person in the world for whom I would like to work, but I had never written to him or told him of my troubles.

Shortly after my arrival in New York, Sir Thomas gave a concert with the New York Philharmonic Orchestra. I got in touch with him, and he asked me to see him in the artists' room. After the concert, I therefore went to the green room of the Carnegie Hall, already so well known to me, and found Sir Thomas there, still a little flushed from the concert, but as good-humoured as ever. " Hallo ! " he greeted me, " how are you ? I have heard the most romantic stories about you. . . . Are they all true ? " As the room was full of people, I passed over this question, and we made an appointment to meet later.

Two days afterwards I went to see him in his hotel, the Savoy Plaza. Since this visit, I have seen Sir Thomas in many hotel sitting-rooms and have travelled with him to many places. However the room may be furnished, as soon as Sir Thomas inhabits it, it assumes character ; there are music and books all over the place, papers of all sorts everywhere, and even if he is away from England, there will at least be a copy of *The Times*. His travelling chessboard stands somewhere, generally with problems started, there are pencils of all sorts, and his precious pipes which he fills with art and care, and last but not least, his cigars, which have been made specially for him for the last thirty years. He remains faithful to them in spite of the efforts of different makers to beguile the famous connoisseur to other creations. Such is the paraphernalia which usually surrounds him ! and there he was himself, as he likes to be after his work is done, immaculate in his white silk pyjamas with his Turkish dressing-gown —the picture of elegance, comfort, and detachment.

Soon we were engrossed in conversation. " Now, tell me all about yourself," he commanded, his twinkling eyes full of humour, but also full of kindness and encouragement.

How often in later years people have asked me whether I was ever at all afraid of Sir Thomas. The legend is that most people are. I cannot say that I *never* had any qualms. How could this be otherwise, in the close work at the Opera House, and who can cavil if an artist has an occasional difficult mood ? Nevertheless, Sir Thomas is one of those people with whom one can discuss any subject with complete frankness. I have always revelled in the subtlety of his reactions. Any subject I particularly wanted to discuss with him, he clarified—for me at least—with keen penetration.

After I had described my experiences to him, I told him of the work I was then doing. He was very interested, and said that an archive of musical autographs on similar lines ought also to be arranged for England. I said that I did not know how my work would develop. Then I went on : " There is only one job in the world I would really like, and that is to work for you. Could it not be arranged for you to try me out in your Covent Garden Season next spring ? " Sir Thomas thoughtfully stroked his beard. " Why not ? You are just the person I want," he said. " I will return to England in a week or two. I am about to change all the organisation of the Opera and Orchestra and I will write to you in about three weeks' time." I left him, very much consoled about life in general. It was arranged that we were to meet once more at his last concert in New York on January 20th. We did so, and he proposed that I should arrange to turn up somehow during the next Season at Covent Garden.

Meanwhile, I had gradually made a working plan for beginning my search for the " Archives of Scores ". My main task was to trace autograph manuscripts of great composers in American collections and have them photographed for the Vienna archives. The contents of the archives were restricted on general principles to certain composers, mainly Ph. E. and J. S. Bach, Handel, Haydn, Mozart, Beethoven, Schubert, Chopin, Mendelssohn, and Brahms. It was a most interesting task, because in America there are numerous private collections, as well as the many libraries. At root, this work, although not directly connected with active musical life, took me back into my old world, even if it stressed the scholarly side.

I first visited Miss Bell Green, the director of the Morgan Library, whom I had met on earlier visits to America. She had been a student under Furtwängler senior, who had collected a great deal for the elder Morgan. Miss Green had been the latter's secretary and right hand. It is alleged that for many years she influenced greatly the price level of the international art trade.

Miss Green showed me various precious manuscripts, remarking that she had saved her best for the end. It was the score of Beethoven's sonata for piano and violin No. 10 in G major, with his own signature —a holograph which had been thought lost for many years and had never been photographed ; but she immediately gave permission for it to be done. She further gave me a number of addresses, and things began to look hopeful in spite of my complete inexperience.

Another most interesting find was the sketch for the last movement of Beethoven's " Moonlight Sonata ", in the possession of Mr. Ernest Hutcheson, the well-known American pianist. I still have the note where Mrs. Hutcheson describes the treasure !

" You know, don't you, that the Beethoven Manuscript which we have is a sketch for the last movement of the ' Moonlight Sonata '. It was owned by Schumann for a number of years and has been taken out of Schumann's album. It has under it the title written in Schumann's hand."

The music critics knew relatively little about these things. Among many others, I visited the late Laurence Gilman, for many years critic of the New York *Herald Tribune*, and the acknowledged Wagner specialist of America. After a long talk about Bayreuth, he told me that he had heard there was somewhere in America a very valuable Wagner holograph, the text of one of the great operas.

I tried to trace this, and by sheer luck I came across the original, meticulously written in Wagner's wonderful handwriting—the *Meistersinger* libretto. It was the property of a great American collector and dealer who kept it in his strong room. It was priced at a fabulous sum.

This find was much discussed, and when Toscanini heard of it he asked to see it. The research became more and more fascinating. I was given help on every side, and was particularly assisted by a scholar who wrote articles on rare books and manuscripts for one of the great American papers. There was doubtless much to be found in the United States, and there was great interest in the problem.

A plan was discussed for founding similar archives for New York and Washington libraries, and pending the permission, first to copy what was already existing in Vienna, and for the future to co-operate in the photographing of further holographs.

Nothing would have prevented an immediate start of this venture if Vienna had not delayed the decision. The plan had, however, to be shelved for the time being. Subsequent developments showed how regrettable this was ; after the *Anschluss*, when the Nazis entered Vienna, they assumed sole control over the National Library, where the photographic archive was housed, and that was the end of the project.

Since my departure to America I had had no news from Furt-wängler, but in February I received a letter posted in Warsaw, which reached me after a month's journey.

Meanwhile, there was a rumour that Toscanini intended to resign his position with the New York Philharmonic. It was said that he could not be persuaded to stay on, and he was alleged to have named Furtwängler as a suitable successor.

Furtwängler, who had risen to fame with extraordinary ease, had been faced with more difficulties in America during the years of 1924–27 than in any other country. He had been extremely successful there on his first visit, but less so during the subsequent two years. Nevertheless, all musicians well remembered his concerts, and even after twelve years had elapsed many still spoke appreciatively of his performances.

At any rate, in 1936 the board of directors of the New York Philharmonic decided to offer to engage Furtwängler, and sent him a cable to Vienna. Furtwängler was very reluctant to accept. He was not at all sure whether such a move would be wise—particularly as he was still domiciled in Hitlerite-Germany.

Furtwängler had no permanent position at that time, he was only a guest-conductor of the Berlin Philharmonic Orchestra and the Berlin State Opera. Bayreuth, too, where he had agreed to conduct again for the first time after an interval of five years, in the summer of 1936, could not be considered a permanency. He did not hold any official post in the *Reichsmusikkammer*, but was a member of this organisation, as every musician in Germany had to be.

In contrast to the times when he was occupying so many posts in Germany, he now—for the first time since 1934—felt completely free and independent, yet in the eyes of the world he remained rooted in the musical life of Nazi Germany.

On Saturday morning, February 29, 1936, the announcement of the New York engagement was published. It evoked, at first, a favourable response.

Then, however, a strange incident occurred. In the evening papers of that day, the news of the engagement reappeared ; but side by side with it, and in heavy type, an Associated Press report from Berlin was published saying that Furtwängler had been reinstated in his former position as chief of the Berlin State Opera.

The directorship of the New York Philharmonic was one of the greatest musical positions in the world, and even if the acceptance of a post at the Berlin State Opera had been true—which it was not— it would have been in extremely bad taste to announce the appointment on the same day as the U.S.A. nomination. Moreover, the New York engagement had been offered on the understanding that Furtwängler had no fixed position, and was solely a guest-conductor in Germany and elsewhere.

However, an Associated Press report cannot be ignored, and so a justifiable uneasiness arose among part of the public as well as the Press. While all this was happening, the unsuspecting Furtwängler was on his way to Egypt. It seemed most unlikely that he would accept any position in Germany at that time, but had he contemplated such a step, he certainly would have informed New York.

An inquiry at the Associated Press headquarters produced the surprising statement that the Berlin report originated from official sources, a fact which greatly complicated matters. Those Americans who had opposed Furtwängler's nomination saw their suspicions confirmed.

The directors of the New York Philharmonic decided to clarify the situation. They had supported their candidate and wished to avoid any misunderstanding in the interests of everybody concerned. Cables were exchanged, and Furtwängler's cable categorically denied that he was chief of the Berlin Opera. Repeated inquiries, however, at the Associated Press resulted in confirmation of the original Berlin agency report.

Furtwängler, although he had taken up work again as a guest-conductor in Germany, was very sensitive to the conditions there. His constant and persistent endeavours, in interviews with members of the Government and Hitler, to improve things, continued to have very little effect. Great homage was paid to him, but it never resulted in the ceding of one iota of the Party doctrine.

He had for a long time contemplated a whole year's vacation, and had therefore not committed himself to a given number of engagements. Just before he left for Egypt, nothing was left undone in an attempt to tie him down again to a permanent position. When, at this juncture, his New York appointment was suddenly announced, there was great excitement in Germany. While Furtwängler was actually on his way to Egypt and therefore impossible to contact, Goering is alleged to have given out that Furtwängler was re-instated. It was clear that Goering had made this announcement because it did not suit his vanity that Furtwängler should refuse a position which he had offered him, while accepting one in New York.

In pre-Hitler times, the nomination of a German for this important New York post would certainly have gratified Germany. However, when the Nazis heard that Furtwängler had accepted the New York engagement, they used every conceivable subterfuge to prevent him from working in the States.

While in musical circles the battle of opinions on the Furtwängler appointment raged, an event took place which completely over-shadowed this heated dispute : On March 7, 1936, Hitler marched into the Rhineland, thereby breaking the Treaty of Versailles for the second time.

I was walking along Broadway that evening ; crowds were surging to and fro. Films of German soldiers marching in battle-dress, with full military equipment, were being shown. The atmosphere was tense. One almost had the feeling that war had broken out. In view of these events, the fight of the New York Philharmonic Society over Furtwängler was hopeless.

Editors in New York received hundreds of letters for and against Furtwängler. The newspapers printed both favourable and hostile comments. The Trade Unions protested, and it was said that he would not be allowed to land. Among others, the Karl Schurz Gesellschaft protested, although Furtwängler was honorary member of its German branch : the German American Bund did the same, as did the Teachers' Union, the American Federation of Musicians, and the American Federation of Labour.

It would have been wrong to persuade Furtwängler to take the view which some of his friends held—" that it would all blow over ". He had had too many doubts from the very beginning to warrant such an attitude.

Furtwängler cancelled his engagement in a cable published on March 15, 1936 :

> " Political controversy disagreeable to me. Am not politician but exponent of German music which belongs to all humanity regardless of politics. I propose postpone my season in the interest of Philharmonic Society until the time public realises that politics and music are apart.—FURTWÄNGLER."

The next thing I heard from him, still from Egypt, was a warning that people in Berlin were spreading the rumour that I was the instigator of the whole conflict, and that I had incited the Jews of New York against him !

I had made many friends in America during former visits. As well there were artists and other people from Europe, who either lived there permanently or spent some time there, and now I made a number of new acquaintances.

The chief conductor of the Metropolitan Opera House was at that time Bodanzky. As I have mentioned, before going to New York in 1915 he had been principal conductor at the *Mannheimer Hof-und Nationaltheater* which has served as a stepping-stone for so many great conductors. The old friendship which existed between the Bodanzkys and my parents since his Mannheim days had never ceased, and after my father's death my mother and I met the Bodanzkys almost every summer at the Engadine for their holidays.

Bodanzky, who had been instrumental in Furtwängler's appointment as his successor in Mannheim (1915–20), was full of interest and friendship for his younger colleague, and during our visits to America we had spent much time in his hospitable home.

Now I was there on my own, and Bodanzky showed deep understanding for my position, but he was relentless on one point : he would not accept any argument in favour of those who had compromised with the Nazi State. Thanks to him, I was at home in the Metropolitan Opera, and I enjoyed this greatly. There I heard *Lohengrin* and the *Ring*, and met many old friends from European opera houses, among others, Lauritz Melchior—who no longer sang in Germany, but was a great favourite with the New York public—and his popular wife Kleinchen. How pleasant it was to see them again in New York ! Wherever he happened to be, Melchior allows nothing to interfere with his accustomed routine. When I went to lunch at their New York home, they had only just got out of bed. The table was laden with Bavarian delicacies, sausages, beer, and boiled beef. The whole family, including Kleinchen's Bavarian parents, appeared in pyjamas, and one could hardly believe one was in New York. Shortly after this, Melchior had his birthday, and I received an invitation to " spend with them the time from 7 p.m. till 7 a.m ". Their flat had been marvellously decorated for this occasion and there was a big crowd. I remember meeting there, for the first time, Kirsten Flagstad.

Another friend whom I met again was Alma Mahler, who had married the author, Franz Werfel, in 1919. His drama *Der Weg der Verheissung* was being performed in New York, produced by Max Reinhardt.

Alma and I had always been friends. When I went to Vienna for the first time with Furtwängler in 1921, I visited her. She is a strange mixture of contrasting elements, and a deep and powerful personality. The first conversation we ever had rolled over me like an ocean tide ; she had a profound knowledge of life and in comparison with her I felt as inexperienced as a child. In these early Vienna days I often discussed with her the problems which arose from living by the side of a great and sensitive artist. Great as was my devotion to Furtwängler, and deeply bound up with his life as I was, I had had many difficult personal problems to face in my association with him, as well as much happiness to enhance my life. She understood everything, with her fine womanly intuition. After the first meeting in Vienna we had always kept in touch. When I was in Vienna I never failed to visit her, and occasionally she came to Berlin with Werfel.

When we met in New York in 1936 I was stranded, and the former world which had connected both of us was closed to me. She still owned her beautiful house in Vienna on the *Hohe Warte*, and was still considered the " Queen " of the spiritual and political Vienna. Schuschnigg and other members of the Austrian Government were frequently seen in her salon. However, her day came too, and she left Vienna finally the night after Hitler's march into Austria.

When I saw her again in London in 1938, it was Alma who was the pilgrim, while I had settled down at Covent Garden.

However, I am anticipating. In New York, in 1936, things had not yet reached this sorry pass. In the St. Regis Hotel, where Werfel and she were staying, we talked for hours and hours about all that was happening in the world, and the inexorable fate which had overtaken so many. She tried to give me courage by declaring that all would be well again . . . but I doubt if she believed it herself.

Another friend from the past was Lenore von Mendelssohn, whom I had known since I first went to Berlin in 1920. She was a passionate creature, and her great love of Germany had changed into intense hatred for the Nazis. There she was, an exotic being, the daughter of an Italian mother and a German-Jewish father, the well-known banker, Robert von Mendelssohn, who had been a great patron of music, a friend of famous musicians, and a lover of the arts. While we two homeless women talked about the fate we shared, the picture of her beautiful home in the Grunewald came into my mind, with its art treasures ; its collection of paintings—with its wonderful

Rembrandts and El Greĉos. The spirit of the home was now destroyed and its children—like so many—are scattered over the world.

Chapter 21

TIME FLEW, and on April 4, 1936, I embarked on the *Île de France* for Europe. There were several friends on board, notably some singers from the Metropolitan Opera who were going to Covent Garden for the season. The crossing was soon over, and on April 10th we docked at Plymouth.

It was Good Friday, and brilliant sunshine—the fields which I had missed so much in America shone with the pale glow of primroses.

Arrived in London, I rang up Sir Thomas. As is well known, Sir Thomas seldom answers the telephone. If it cannot be switched off, he sits by imperturbably while the bell rings on and on. On the rare occasions when he does take the receiver himself, he emits a terrifying sound in an unrecognisable voice, and the uninitiated caller usually drops the receiver, utterly cowed.

Nothing of the sort, however, happened on the day I rang. Sir Thomas himself answered, and in his most amiable voice said : " Hello ! so you have landed then ? How about lunch to-day ? "

Fate had taken a hand in the game. I had not only got in touch with him straightaway, but he also happened to be free—a very rare coincidence.

In those days Sir Thomas lived at the Waldorf Hotel by reason of its proximity to Covent Garden, and it was there that I went to see him on this April 18, 1936.

He greeted me warmly and kindly, and I felt his real sympathy and interest. After we had spoken of generalities, he began to question me. I told him of my New York experiences. However, he lost little time on these preliminaries, and soon assumed an autocratic expression.

" Now then," he began. " How do things stand with you ? Are you free ? "

" I am not quite free," I replied. " But if you want me, I can be."
" Yes, I do," he said. " Let us settle the matter at once."

He rose from the table, went to his writing desk and wrote the
following letter :

> " WALDORF HOTEL,
> ALDWYCH, W.C. 2.,
> *April* 18, 1936.

" DEAR Dr. GEISSMAR,—I am happy to learn that you are free to
accept the offer I have made to you to act as my General Secretary
for all my musical affairs.

" These, during the last few years, have assumed such an international character that only someone of your great knowledge
and experience of the Continent can fulfil adequately the duties
and responsibilities that such a post carries with it. I am, Yours
very sincerely.—THOMAS BEECHAM."

He said, " I have thought this matter over. It is of no use your
coming for the Season only ". (Even in my wildest dreams I had
scarcely dared to hope for more.) " You must come for good, and
I am now going to tell you of the plans I have made."

He then at once began to explain to me how he thought the opera
seasons and the Orchestra should be run.

My interest was aroused immediately, now that a real task again
lay ahead of me. Sir Thomas was the only conductor of his standard
in charge of an opera house as well as of an orchestra. He seemed to
me the only one with whom I could work as I wished.

I told him then about my legal position. When I had left Germany
six months before, it had been understood by the Gestapo that I
had gone to America on business. But I was only " travelling "
for the Viennese " Photographic Archives ", and had not formally
emigrated. In any event, I had to reckon with the fact that within
a certain time the Gestapo would inquire about my further plans.
At that time they had the charming habit of trapping German people
who were living or travelling abroad, by expatriation, or by blocking
their accounts. The time was approaching for me to make my position
clear to them.

I therefore arranged with Sir Thomas that I would transfer my
residence from Berlin to London as soon as possible. Before I could
do so I had to get an *Unbedenklichkeitserklärung* (Inspector of Taxes
certificate that no taxes are outstanding) from my Income Tax

collector in Berlin, as well as my *Polizeiliche Abmeldung* (notice of change of residence, endorsed by the police).

Without these two certificates I would not be able to register as a resident in London. I arranged with Sir Thomas to send for my legal adviser from Berlin, as only specialists were able to deal with the aggravating and ever-changing regulations of the Nazis.

Sir Thomas and I decided to keep our new professional relationship secret for the time being, so that the Nazis could not frustrate it by complicating the formalities. However, he said he would inform his solicitors in order that the necessary application for my labour permit might be made.

He instructed me to see his lawyer the next day, and before I left said quite casually :

" By the way, Doctor, I never trouble about money, as you may have heard. It doesn't interest me. How much salary would you like to have ? " After all my changing fortunes, I was dizzy and overwhelmed with the turn that things were taking. Money never came first with me either, it was the work that mattered. However, I pulled myself together, and said that for this kind of work, such and such a salary would be suitable.

" All right," said Sir Thomas, and I took my leave.

The next day I went to see the lawyer, who was thoroughly versed in Sir Thomas's affairs, which, as most people know, are not a little complicated. He viewed with some trepidation my naïve exhilaration, and felt it his duty to enlighten me as to what I had undertaken. Apart from this warning, he has always given me the greatest support. When we arrived at the financial question, he informed me that Sir Thomas had defined my salary at twice the amount I had suggested. Never will I forget this generosity. It is possible that I had just the qualifications to fit in with his plans at that time ; but I was in a position of extreme difficulty, and he knew it. Many others in his place might have taken advantage of that.

My legal adviser arrived on the scene in due course. He was a heavily built, phlegmatic Saxon, never disconcerted by anything. Somehow he had managed to keep on good terms with the Nazis, while looking after the affairs of those persecuted by them. (Later, as everyone knows, " Aryans " were forbidden to deal with the affairs of " non-Aryans ".)

He was proud and pleased to have been called to London, and managed to see more of the town in two days than I have since seen in years. Cautiously I began to let him into the secret.

"For God's sake, keep quiet about it until you have the Berlin police exit permit in your hands here," he said, and added ironically, "the Nazis will be especially pleased when they hear this!"

I arranged a code with my adviser for use when he returned to Germany, and we decided that if he sent me a telegram "Bruno has departed", this would mean that my papers were on their way safely, and everything was settled.

By this time, the International Season at Covent Garden was in full swing. Although I still had to keep quiet about my new job, I went to the Opera House every day and was often present at Sir Thomas's lunch hour. His lunch was sent in from Boulestin's and was a bright, and often brilliant, interruption in the day's routine. Enough was always provided for the many interesting people who dropped in.

I also regularly attended all Sir Thomas's rehearsals, and once found myself in a difficult position with regard to my later friend and colleague, Mr. Charles Moor. He had been stage director of Covent Garden for years, and wanted to banish me from the theatre on the grounds that only those connected with the staff were allowed to be present at rehearsals. Timidly I had to offer the excuse that Sir Thomas had asked me to wait for him in the stalls!

It was difficult for me to keep my good news to myself when Herbert Janssen, the famous baritone of Berlin and Bayreuth, who had been to Covent Garden regularly for seventeen years, said to me when we met in the Opera House: "You know, Geissmar, there is only one place where you should work—and that is Covent Garden!"

At these rehearsals, Sir Thomas was a living dynamo. Everything depended on his inexhaustible energy, and it seemed that there was no side of the work which he could safely delegate to anyone else. To spare his voice he used a police whistle which hung round his neck on a black ribbon. To-day, when I have lost most of my belongings, I still possess this whistle, a reminder of happier days.

All this free life seemed incredible to me at that time. I felt as though I had emerged from a tomb into the light of day. I had no real duties as yet and only went to the Opera House when Sir Thomas asked me to. I acclimatised myself slowly to the work, and especially to Sir Thomas, to whom I was not only grateful, but devoted.

The 29th of April was Sir Thomas's birthday. Of course, no interruption of work was allowed, but there was great fun on the stage, and the famous connoisseur was presented with a solitary special cigar, to which the whole personnel had contributed.

In the meantime he had several times discussed his future plans with me. There was talk of a tour of Germany by the London Philharmonic Orchestra under his direction.

Plans were also going forward for the Coronation year to be celebrated by a ten weeks' season at Covent Garden.

This Coronation Season was to include operas in French and Italian, in addition to the German Season, then so popular.

I suggested to Sir Thomas that he should collaborate with my old friend M. Rouché, the Director of the Paris *Opéra*, in his plans for opera in French. Sir Thomas's temperament is such that he reacts swiftly to such a suggestion. He loves quick action, which makes working for him simple and easy. He now said : " You had better go to Paris at once. You will discuss this matter in general with M. Rouché—and then you will proceed to Switzerland while the Berlin Philharmonic is touring there and meet Dr. Furtwängler. You will ask him to conduct the German Season for me next year and I will give you a letter for him." His eyes twinkled significantly. This was just like Sir Thomas. He certainly wanted the co-operation of the great Wagner conductor : but how kind of him it was to create the opportunity for me to go and meet my former chief.

In the highest spirits I set out for my first continental trip on British affairs. Neither my German Change of Residence Certificate nor my English Labour Permit had arrived before I left, but Sir Thomas's lawyer gave me a letter for the immigration officer saying that I was travelling for the Royal Opera House and that no difficulty was expected with regard to my work in England.

In Paris I stayed with Mme. Couvreux, the daughter of M. Rouché. The chestnuts were in flower in the Bois, where she lived in one of the aristocratic old hotels at Neuilly. It was like old times. All that had happened in the interval seemed like a nightmare. I owed an enormous debt of gratitude to Sir Thomas for this turn in my fortunes, but I doubt whether he would have understood my feelings had I tried to explain. How could a Briton, and such an independent one as Sir Thomas, quite understand the experiences of anyone who has been at the mercy of the Nazi régime.

In Paris I called on M. Robert Brussel in the Ministère des Beaux Arts, with whom I had arranged so many concerts and operatic performances from the German side. I told him I was now working for Covent Garden, and discussed tentatively with him the plans for the Coronation Season. Brussel was delighted, and assured me of every support from his Ministry.

In these few days I prepared the ground for much of my future work with Covent Garden. I was infinitely happy to be engaged again in my old activities, and reported daily by letter to Sir Thomas.

Then I left for Zurich. By a strange coincidence, in the same sleeper with me was Miss Ibbeken, secretary to Huberman for many years. She was on her way from America to Vienna to close down his home there, he having a clear presentiment of future developments.

This was a very strange journey for me, homeless wanderer as I was. As I had not received any information from my legal adviser that my affairs were settled, I was still dependent on the German authorities, and felt I had to be extremely careful.

In the morning when I stepped out of my sleeper in Basle, I bought a paper. An enormous headline immediately attracted my attention : " Wilhelm Furtwängler goes on leave for a year ". What a curious prelude to our meeting !

And a very moving meeting it was. Furtwängler came into my room in Zurich, looking pale and drawn, his blue eyes full of an expression of exhaustion. How much had happened since we had parted at the Hague before my journey to America ! Furtwängler had had many ordeals before obtaining his leave of absence, and much trouble still lay ahead of him ; I who had left him on my way to an uncertain future had, after many adventures, fallen on my feet again. Needless to say we both had much to say under these circumstances.

After our first excitement at seeing each other had subsided we decided that it was better for me not to attend his concerts, but otherwise we resolved to make the most of the three days together in Switzerland. Furtwängler had to leave soon for his concert in Lucerne. Friends had put a car at our disposal, and in this car I waited for him next morning at a given rendezvous, in order not to be seen by any members of the Orchestra.

Furtwängler arrived punctually for our drive, and on a radiant spring morning, under a glowing sun in a cloudless blue sky, we left for Basle. On our way we stopped at a little inn and had our lunch, sitting in the garden under an old apple tree in full blossom.

There are moments in life which make up for much. This radiant day was one of them. In peace and quietness, away from all the nagging horror that had ruined our lives in Nazi-Germany, we were able to liquidate the nightmare of the last years and discuss everything on our minds in intimacy and freedom.

Furtwängler felt a great sense of relief on my account. My fate had lain heavily upon him. He had always had a great liking for Sir Thomas and admired him in many ways. We began to discuss musical affairs at once, and he expressed the hope that Sir Thomas would in future conduct on the Continent more often than before.

We spent a day on the Dolder with Furtwängler's English friends —the writers John Knittel and Robert Hichens—with whom he had stayed in Egypt, and who had supported him in every way during his American crisis.

In the midst of all these personal excitements and emotions, I did not forget the purpose of my journey for a minute. Furtwängler's decision not to conduct for a whole year was certainly a happy solution, but I was resolved not to return to Sir Thomas without having fulfilled my mission, and so I bargained with Furtwängler to finish his " non-conducting period " before the Coronation festivities commenced. Needless to say, the two Englishmen supported me very strongly in this endeavour. We all tried to persuade Furtwängler, who exclaimed in dismay: "But who will fix this up with Goering?" One of his greatest difficulties in obtaining the grace of one year's leave had been Goering's disappointment at his decision ; he had hoped to regain him at least as guest-conductor at his beloved State Opera House in Berlin.

I sent a long report on all these details to Sir Thomas, also informing him that while in Zurich I had received a cable from my lawyer saying that " Bruno's departure was imminent ". This indicated a silver lining in the hitherto clouded sky, and I hoped that all would soon be settled.

The next morning I went back to Paris. There I found a letter from Sir Thomas saying that the London Philharmonic Orchestra was soon to receive an official invitation to tour Germany under his direction.

As Furtwängler was expected in Paris the next day for his opera rehearsals, I was glad to be on the spot to discuss this matter with him. Furtwängler, who for so many years had been fêted with his Orchestra in England, greatly welcomed the idea of a return visit. We discussed in detail how it could best be arranged. I stayed one further day for a luncheon which M. Rouché gave for the Polish composer, Karol Szymanowski, whose ballet *Harnasie* had just been given its première, and then left for London.

I could hardly wait to see Sir Thomas in order to give him all the news. He was immersed in his Opera Season and extremely busy, but he always had time for me. It was a treat to hear a performance of *Götterdämmerung* with the old familiar cast, and to have lunch with Frieda Leider and her husband and to hear all the opera gossip.

Sir Thomas informed me of the invitation for the tour which he had received, in the meantime, from von Ribbentrop, who at that time held the post of " Ambassador at Large " of the German Reich. (*Ausserordentlicher und Bevollmächtigter Botschafter des deutschen Reiches !*)

There were a great many points still to be discussed in connection with this German tour, and so Sir Thomas said : " I think it will save a lot of time and trouble if, as Furtwängler is still in Paris, you will go back and discuss the final details with him ". In the same week, therefore, I found myself again crossing the Channel !

In Paris, Furtwängler handed me an official letter from *General-intendant* Tietjen. Tietjen wrote that he had heard that I was now General Secretary to Sir Thomas, whom he wanted to invite to conduct opera performances in Berlin. However, before addressing him directly, he wished to ascertain whether Sir Thomas, who was most independent with regard to such matters as keeping engagements, would be seriously disposed to accept the invitation. This was to avoid possible bad feeling in view of the fact that in the previous

year, Sir Thomas had cancelled a *Tristan* performance at the Berlin
State Opera almost at the last moment. Moreover, Tietjen thought
it advisable that Sir Thomas should write him a letter confirming
my appointment, in order that he could put the matter before Goering,
his supreme chief ! I was both pleased and amused by this letter.
Tietjen, as *Generalintendant* of the Prussian State Theatres had the
protection of Goering, who, although guilty of unspeakable crimes
against his fellow-men, was all tenderness where his beloved Opera
House was concerned. As *Ministerpräsident* he exercised his power
on behalf of his Opera wherever he could and relied completely on
Tietjen. In asking for an official letter from Sir Thomas confirming
my appointment, Tietjen intended to forestall any possible obstruc-
tions that might be put forward later from other quarters and hamper
my new work.

While in Paris, besides discussing with Furtwängler Anglo-German
plans, I also negotiated with M. Rouché on more general lines, and
he stated that he would be willing to co-operate with Covent Garden
for French operatic productions. Moreover, M. Brussel, whom I
visited again, confirmed that such plans would certainly be approved
by the French Government. I also discussed the possibility of a visit
of Sir Thomas to the Paris *Opéra* and was told : " *Nous ne demandons
pas mieux* ". There are times when everything goes according to
plan, and when on my return I reported to Sir Thomas about
the results of my interviews, he declared himself completely
satisfied.

Back in London, a telegram awaited me : " Bruno left to-day ".
Freedom at last ! The transfer of my residence to London had been
arranged without any difficulty. (Incidentally, this cost me over
£5000.[1]) Radiantly, I went to Sir Thomas to tell him. He remarked
casually : " By the way, your Labour Permit is granted, so you can
go ahead ".

The first thing I did was to show him Tietjen's letter which he
read with great amusement. He immediately produced the headed
notepaper which he had had printed. " How do you like that,"
he asked ; I liked it well enough, and on this paper headed " Sir

[1] It was the *Reichsfluchtsteuer*—a sum I had to pay to the German Government for
being allowed to fly the country of my birth and settle in another ! But this was a
detail.

Thomas Beecham, Bart. ; General Secretary, Dr. Geissmar ; Royal Opera House, Covent Garden, W.C. 2, he wrote at once to Tietjen !

"*May 28, 1936.*

" GENERALINTENDANT TIETJEN,
   STAATSOPER, BERLIN.

" DEAR MR. TIETJEN,—I want to inform you that I have appointed Dr. Berta Geissmar as General Secretary for all my musical affairs.

" I intend to send Dr. Geissmar over to Germany at the end of June to discuss plans with you.—Yours sincerely.

THOMAS BEECHAM."

In those days, I really had not the faintest idea whether it would ever again be possible for me to go to Germany. But this did not trouble Sir Thomas in the least. He regarded my misgivings as a joke, and took it for granted that if *he* wished to send me to Germany on his business this would be sufficient reason to overcome all obstacles. And so it proved to be !

The Season was still at its height, and Sir Thomas was very busy in every way. Not only had he to conduct on most evenings, but he had also to run the Opera as its director and was at the same time preparing for the Coronation Season.

He had not the suite of offices then which was later arranged for him upstairs at Covent Garden, but only a room among the other offices downstairs, where it was almost impossible to secure any privacy. I remember that one evening he said to me : " Now let us hide in Melchior's dressing-room—at least we will be undisturbed while he is singing ".

For me, of course, everything was entirely new, but Sir Thomas smoothed the way. He invited me to be present in his room as much as possible while he worked, so that I quickly learned how things were done.

On the other hand, he was most generous in letting me work in the way to which I had been used. I arranged his files in my own way, and applied my old and proven system in my work with him. I tried to avoid talking too much to him on all the manifold questions pouring in from all sides, and typed out everything on a kind of " questionnaire " to which in many cases he could just add " Yes " or " No " or " O.K.".

All his letters were carefully spread out for him on an extra table, in some cases with explanatory notes added by me. But Sir Thomas, with regard to his correspondence, was no exception to other great men, and had a special way of dealing with his mail. He would take up a letter, look at it, turn it round, and put it down again. So far as he was concerned this was the end of his interest in it, and the rest was left to me.

When, however, he considered a matter worth while going into, he gave it his most careful attention ; and if he dictated a letter himself he was most particular with regard to its minutest detail ; and it had, if necessary, to be written out again and again until considered satisfactory by him.

The correspondence, however, was only a small part of my work with him. Much of it was, of course, the routine duties connected with the office of the director of an opera house and of an orchestra. But Covent Garden was a very peculiar place, and occasionally situations arose with which, especially in the beginning when I did not yet know him as intimately as later on, I sometimes did not know how to cope. Sir Thomas rarely gave me any instructions or explanations about anything. Never, for instance, has he helped me with so much as a hint about the innumerable new people I had to get to know ; I had to appraise everybody myself, while he generally contented himself by saying that somebody was either a " damned idiot," or something of the sort.

One day when I had again been compelled to act in a certain dilemma without any hint of my chief's wishes, I asked him why he never gave me any directions ; how could I ever know whether he was satisfied or displeased ? (While other people when displeased say so, Sir Thomas had the unfortunate habit of remaining taciturn in such event.) It was true I had held down a big job before working for him ; but I was a foreigner here ; Covent Garden had its very special and sacred etiquette, and Sir Thomas, without ever raising his voice, could be the most exacting person imaginable. " Well, you see, Doctor," he explained, " when I was a little boy and had to learn to swim, my tutor just threw me into the water, and I have always been an adherent of this simple and efficient method of education. Also," he added with that inimitable self-assurance of his, " if I engage anyone as a personal collaborator, it is, of course, because I trust her, and leave the handling of things entirely to her."

One has to live in England for many years before one realises that such an attitude is a result of that spirit for which a troubled world is now fighting.

Chapter 22

IN THE meantime negotiations for the German tour of the London Philharmonic Orchestra were progressing and Sir Thomas took it for granted that I was to act for him in Germany. I, having learned by experience, said to him : " That is all very well, but I must be sure that after all I have been through nothing will happen to *me*. I will run the tour with the greatest pleasure ; but I want to be able to move about freely and to be certain that while one German department sanctions arrangements, another will not be planning to arrest me at the frontier and another to confiscate my passport again." At this time the Nazis were making an even more frequent practice of retaining passports without any legal reason. Sir Thomas did not take my concern very seriously, and said : " Don't worry, there will be no trouble about *that*". For my part, I did not wish to stress the point more than was absolutely necessary, feeling ashamed that I had to mention such possibilities at all. At this time I was becoming more and more friendly with Sir Thomas, and each day began with a long telephone conversation. One morning he rang me up, discussed all sorts of things, and said finally, " By the way, Doctor, you can go to Germany as often and for as long as you like ; it is all settled". He said this quite casually, just as he might say : " Come to the Opera House at twelve o'clock ".

Later I went to Sir Thomas. I still felt diffident about the matter, but to him it presented no problem. " Well, you see, Doctor," he explained, " yesterday, I had a talk with von Ribbentrop. I told him that you were dealing with all my musical affairs and were running the German tour, and I wanted to be sure that there would be no trouble whatever. He told me that you had nothing but friends in Germany, and that they were proud that I had a German secretary. You see," he concluded, " there is no difficulty at all."

How like Ribbentrop ! It is no secret that he had always been a gambler rather than a man of principle and *Weltanschauung* and that he had readily thrown over his former connections when he promised himself greater advantages from joining Hitler's banner. He, the prototype of a snob and a capitalist, suddenly chose to become an ardent adherent of the National-" Socialist " government, when it promised him a more satisfactory position than that of a rich wine merchant. It must also not be forgotten that at this moment friendship with England at *all* cost was the password of Nazi politics. Hitler, who knew little of the world as it was, believed in Ribbentrop who wore white spats and tried to be more English than the English. The Führer blindly followed his advice—which quickly changed its front after the German Ambassador's catastrophical *échec* at the Court of St. James.

However, at the time when Sir Thomas declared that he did not intend to travel without his General Secretary, Ribbentrop had only one aim : to ingratiate himself with the English ; and so the reader will understand that he did everything to make Sir Thomas believe that things were *couleur de rose*.

I was indeed used to many things, but such a shameless and cynical lie as Ribbentrop's seemed to me the limit. In Germany Furtwängler was still being reproached with regard to his relationship to me. It was constantly hinted to him that it was not considered sufficient that he had terminated his business connection with me, and had not broken off all personal relations. So, while in Germany matters were being handled as I have indicated in this book, the " Ambassador at Large of the Reich ", serenely smiling, expressed himself to Sir Thomas in the manner just related.

The Nazis " played ball " just as it suited them, but the rules of this game were not always dictated by their ostensible principles. What had been declared to be *untragbar* ever since 1933 was now suddenly sanctioned because this suited their politics. A great German musician had not been allowed by them to retain my services ; and yet, before the wishes of a prominent Englishman, they were sycophantic enough to bow down and accept the situation.

It was only natural that all these conflicting elements were very upsetting to me, but Sir Thomas had a philosophically humorous attitude to everything in life, and quickly and with pleasure I began to learn to look at things from a different angle. What did it all matter beside the fact that I was now free to work and live? His sense of humour was contagious, and I was surprised to find myself sometimes looking at life through his eyes, as it were. I was possessed by but one idea, too, at the moment: to assist him as well as possible.

Of course, I had no relations with the German Embassy, but one day the late Baron Fries, former Private Secretary of Hoesch, rang me up. "At last we have got you," he said; "where are you?" I said: "I am in the Royal Opera House". "But why did you not get in touch with us?" "How could I?" I retorted. He understood, of course, and inquired: "But surely you have no objection to meeting an old friend?" I had not, indeed. Fries had been loyally devoted to Hoesch. He had had to suffer severely for that under Ribbentrop. How often had we stayed in the Hoesch Embassy under the same roof! He was now helpful in every way, and told me that Ribbentrop's *homme-de-confiance*, who then was his liaison-officer between England and Germany in all special affairs, was due back from Berlin soon. I confided to Fries: "I shall have to get in touch with this man, for we must get this tour on the right footing at once". Ribbentrop had written a pompous letter to Sir Thomas saying that he had initiated matters, and that he had appointed the appropriate people for the work. I was naturally extremely dubious about all this. Sir Thomas had as yet not been informed as to any details, but I had heard rumours. I had had a visit from the Chairman of the Leipzig *Gewandhaus* who was also the head of the famous firm of Breitkopf & Haertel. What he told me about the preparations for the tour in Germany filled me with apprehension. Things might easily be spoiled before it even started.

Then one day I had a phone call from Ribbentrop's liaison-officer who had just arrived. He asked whether I would come to the German Embassy to discuss the tour. I replied that I would rather not. Here was the first conflict in my new job! I was firmly resolved to do everything possible for Sir Thomas, but I was just as firmly resolved not to set foot in the German Embassy while the Nazi régime lasted. On the other hand, I could not very well invite the gentleman to come and see me at home, because I lived in a garret in order to save up for my new home. At last we arranged to meet in the Carlton Hotel, and there I went, scared and uncomfortable. I was a "burnt child", and felt considerable uneasiness at the proximity of anything or anyone connected with the Third Reich. Very carefully, over a cocktail, the conversation began, and at first I could hardly trust myself to speak at all. However, the gentleman in question was not one of whom one needed to be afraid. He had rather a free function, and had mainly lived abroad. He was a very distinguished and sensitive man belonging to the old German nobility. Two years later, in point of fact, he severed his connection with von Ribbentrop and the Diplomatic Service.

He told me that the Ambassador had left the whole organisation of the tour in his hands, but confessed that he had no experience of such things. Perceiving how little he did actually know, I said : " I will draft a framework for the tour, and when the main points are settled the details will be simple ". This seemed to take a load off his mind, and he then told me that the Ambassador had appointed a representative in Germany for the whole tour. I knew the man. The choice was the worst which could possibly have been made. I was hardly in a position to lay down the law, but I said without hesitation : " This is absolutely impossible. If it were a boxing match he might do, but you simply cannot bring such a person into contact with Beecham. If you *do*, he will just bolt."

Thank heaven, my authority carried some weight, in spite of all my political troubles. So I proposed : " The matter is quite simple. I can manage the tour from England, and the office of the Berlin Philharmonic Orchestra can make the arrangements within Germany. They knew exactly what to do, and have run tours with me for many years. If the London Philharmonic Orchestra tour can be arranged in that way, you can be sure that all will be well." He warmly welcomed this simple solution, but was worried as to how to dispose of the representative in Germany, who had been recommended by the *Reichsmusikkammer*. But this was not my concern. As I left I said : " You can rely on me ; I make but two conditions : I wish to avoid meeting my former secretary, and the Nazi-appointed manager of the Berlin Orchestra. Apart from these conditions, I will draw a veil over the past and consider the whole matter only from the angle of my new work."

The liaison-officer soon returned to Berlin and made the arrangements according to plan. The Berlin Philharmonic Orchestra were delighted with the idea of running the tour for their English colleagues. They had visited England so many times themselves, that it was a matter of honour, as well as a pleasure, to ensure that the arrangements for the English Orchestra were carried out to perfection.

Furtwängler protected the enterprise in every way. He wrote to me in detail about the tour, and at the same time informed me that he had engaged my third successor and hoped that on my visit to Germany I would have time enough to coach her ! I reported the contents of the letter to Sir Thomas. With the expression of a pasha he granted me the necessary leave to go to the rescue of my former chief.

Although Sir Thomas had the greatest regard for Furtwängler as an artist, he adopted a paternal attitude towards him and generally addressed him as " my boy ".

To some extent Sir Thomas is inscrutable, and no one can be sure of what he is really thinking. All our Nazi calamities and catastrophies seemed to be a permanent source of amusement to him. Nevertheless, when a really serious eventuality cropped up, I could always count on him, and be sure of real understanding and efficient help.

Meanwhile, Sir Thomas had made his arrangements for the summer. He was going to Norway for a month and then on to Bayreuth to hear the performances and engage his cast for the Coronation Season. I was to meet him at Nuremberg and go on to Bayreuth with him. According to my old custom with Furtwängler, I had typed out for him his whole travelling plan. Very astonished, he looked at my slip of paper. I was soon to learn that he is an expert in reading time-tables and maps, and does not need anything of the sort. He would have been a genius as a travelling agent ! Yet he did not disillusion me, and only commented dryly : " The only point I see in all this is that we meet on the 24th in Nuremberg ".

He had given me all necessary instructions, and left London at the end of June while I prepared for my departure to Germany.

Hardly six months had elapsed since I had stealthily left the country of my birth in night and fog, convinced that I should never return. And now I was on my way back, conscious of an independent position, a settled income, and a new existence. This was just what I had dreamed of but could scarcely have hoped for.

Chapter 23

WITH VERY mixed feelings I took the train to Berlin. At the German frontier my passport was examined, but no questions were asked.

Berlin lay before me bathed in sunshine, and soon I was back in my home, pouring out my tale to my mother.

Already, before my arrival, officials of the Berlin Philharmonic Orchestra had asked when they might call on me; and there was an inquiry from von Ribbentrop's headquarters asking when I was expected.

My mother is a strong and single-minded character, and ever since 1933 she had felt all my difficulties acutely. Although she was as devoted to Furtwängler as to a son, she would have much preferred that we had parted a great deal earlier, before all this agony began. She had become used to the fact that I was treated like an outcast. I had not even been permitted to keep my own files. Communication between the Berlin Philharmonic Orchestra and myself had been forbidden. She knew also that my old gem of a servant, who in former times had looked after the office of the Orchestra and myself, had been threatened with the loss of her job unless she broke off any connection with me. No wonder, therefore, that she was dumb-founded by the circumstances of my return, and after the first joyous meeting she said to me: "Now tell me, what does this all mean? Are we in a lunatic asylum?" I replied: "Far from that. The explanation is simply that I am Sir Thomas Beecham's secretary."

"You must get used to the idea," I went on, "that we are neither in a lunatic asylum nor for the moment are we personally subject to the Nazi terror—at least for the time being—but are just normal people."

" I cannot really take it in," she answered. " It seems impossible, after all we have suffered."

" I have stopped thinking about that," I replied. " I have a job to do and I am going to do it."

Soon the telephone rang. It was the Berlin Philharmonic office inquiring whether the management could come to see me at once.

" There is no reason whatever to call on me," I replied. " I am here on business, and I will be at your office in half an hour."

As I have mentioned, I had stipulated that I was not to meet my old secretary nor the Nazi manager. This condition was strictly observed.

The chairman of the Management Committee in my time had been dismissed immediately after Furtwängler's resignation. The next chairman, who had been appointed by the Goebbels Ministry, was a failure. He had held a post abroad, but had lost it owing, it was alleged, to his being a Nazi. He, therefore, had had to be rewarded, which fact alone proved to be no qualification for this highly responsible post, from which he, too, soon had to be dismissed. The present chairman had been on the *Rundfunk* before the Nazi régime, and had joined the management of the Philharmonic Orchestra after the debacle with his predecessor. I had known him a long time, but had not seen him since he was with the Philharmonic.

At the appointed hour I took my heart in my hand, went to my old office, and rang the bell. The odd-job-man—" ex-unemployed "— whom I have mentioned before, opened the door. He was in Storm Trooper's uniform and said, " Heil Hitler, Fräulein Doktor, how nice to see you again ".

He ushered me into my old room. It was now occupied by the chairman. How changed and bare it looked ! The comfort, ease, and elegance of the old days had gone, the atmosphere of culture dissipated. As a recompense for vanished beauty, an enormous picture of Hitler greeted me from one of the walls.

Almost before I had had time to take it all in, the chairman and my old collaborator, Höber, came in, grinning with embarrassment, and shook hands heartily with me.

" Well, you have made a marvellous recovery," they said. " We are so delighted about it all."

"So am I," I replied, "but now you must tell me all your news."

This they did, and then they asked me whom I had seen of the former Orchestra members in the outside world. I had seen them all, some in New York and some in London.

Very soon my dear old *Trudchen*, whose services I had shared with the Orchestra, appeared bringing coffee and the cinnamon cake which had been my favourite in the old days. She was absolutely radiant and, strange to say, no one threatened her now that if she were in touch with me she should lose her job. She declared with decision : "I am coming to see you this evening". This time she was *not* prevented.

After our excitement died away we got down to work.

Höber and I, who had in the past arranged innumerable tours, were in our element, and very shortly the whole plan was clear. We began to discuss details, and I said decidedly :

"Do see that this great musical occasion is not exploited for purposes of Nazi display, and don't, whatever you do, let the *Bier-Abend* of the two orchestras after the Berlin Concert be interfered with." Both were only too glad to concur, and were proud and touched that in spite of all that had happened, I had advocated their collaboration.

Two days later I left for Bayreuth. It has always been a peculiar place, the scene of impassioned cross-currents and interests, in which one was embroiled whether one wished it or not.

In 1931 when I had last been there, the old and the new Bayreuth, the Bayreuth of Cosima, and the Bayreuth of Winifred Wagner, clashed hard. The Bayreuth of which Furtwängler, who looked up to the *Festspielhügel* as to the Grail, dreamed, was a different Bayreuth from that of Toscanini, who had collaborated with Siegfried Wagner before his death. Again the Bayreuth of Richard Wagner, as visualised by Furtwängler, the serious conscientious musician, stood in contrast to the Bayreuth of the present—a Bayreuth conditioned by the period and by the people there.

Only by realising the existence of the undercurrents resulting from these different points of view can Bayreuth as a whole be understood.

Whatever views one may hold regarding Bayreuth, no one can

escape its atmosphere : the tradition of a great cultural epoch, the spell of the gentle and dreamy landscape which surrounds the poetical old baroque town, and—in spite of everything—the *Festspielhügel*.

All my recollections of former days awoke within me on my journey, but it was yet another Bayreuth which awaited me. In spite of the fact that even in Nazi times Bayreuth was protected from interference, it was nevertheless the Bayreuth of Adolf Hitler to which I was on my way on this radiant June morning.

In 1936 nearly all the remaining members of the Wagner family lived in Bayreuth. After the death of her husband, Siegfried Wagner, Winifred Wagner was the principal heir and ruler of Bayreuth. She directed the Festival, and was a trustee of the whole Wagner estate for her four children who were at that time minors. Winifred Wagner was British born, but had been brought up in Germany. She has a beautiful face, a clean-cut profile, and can be bewitchingly charming. In spite of her great position, her life was difficult, and I believe that her inaccessibility and occasional brusqueness arose rather from an inner uncertainty than from inherent hardness. It was no easy task for this young woman to lead Bayreuth forward to the future, under the very eyes of the past.

The four Wagner children were all very pronounced personalities. They had grown up in utter freedom, in that unique atmosphere, and no one had ever tried to discipline them. When I spent the summer of 1931 with Furtwängler in Bayreuth, nobody was safe from their tricks and no one knew what they would do next.

Wieland, the eldest, was then—in 1936—nineteen years old. He had many artistic inclinations, but had not shown any particularly strongly developed talent so far. He was very interested in painting, and at this time was planning new settings for *Parsifal*, which he later on partly completed. He was a strong young man with unmistakable Wagner features. Hitler had a great affection for him, and it was said that when war broke out in 1939, Hitler forbade him to enlist on account of his sacred Wagner blood !

The next was Fridelind, generally called " Maus ", who retained the features of her grandfather, even down to the differently-shaped ears, and had the slim, long, aristocratic hands which she had inherited from Liszt through Cosima Wagner. " Maus " was in many ways the image of the great Richard. She was gifted and courageous ;

but she was not an easy character, and has gone her own way in life.

Verena, the third, was an enchanting being, with a slim, willowy figure and big melancholy eyes. All those who were able to judge, always said she was the image of Cosima, and in her looks she certainly took after the Liszt side of the family.

Wolfgang, the youngest, was an exceedingly good-looking boy with Wagner features, but he of all the children took most after his mother. Even then, when still quite a little chap, he showed a pronounced ability for technical matters and was the shadow of the famous technical director of the *Festspielhaus*, Herr Eberhardt, to whom the perfection of the Bayreuth stage is due.

These four children, with their young mother, were the future of Bayreuth ; but the past was still alive, demanding loyalty to tradition and almost suspiciously scrutinising events within *Wahnfried* and the *Festspielhügel*.

This past was personified in the older generation, the aged Blandine, Countess Gravina, the highly cultured Daniela Thode, and Frau Eva Chamberlain, who followed the panorama of events with the keenest interest, and whose very existence in Bayreuth often made things difficult for Frau Winifred.

All these members of the family, then, lived in the Bayreuth to which Adolf Hitler gave his passionate devotion. Ever since his youth Hitler had been a fanatical Wagnerite, and for him it certainly must have been a great experience to meet the young and beautiful daughter-in-law of Richard Wagner at Frau Bechstein's house in Munich. Winifred had felt deeply the conditions in Germany after the last war. She was therefore very sympathetic to Hitler's ideas, but it was a long time before her husband, Siegfried Wagner, consented to receive Hitler in *Wahnfried*. " Maus " told me that she had never forgotten Hitler's first visit in 1922 : how starved he looked, and how poor he was. She remembered perfectly all the controversies about his person, and she also remembered that her grandmother, Cosima, who was then still alive, but very infirm and nearly blind, refused to receive him. Long after this first visit, Hitler was still only able to come to *Wahnfried* at night under cover of darkness. To-day he has his own pompous quarters in the former *Siegfried-Haus* in the garden of *Wahnfried*, and for the visitor nowadays, it would seem that not Richard Wagner but Adolf Hitler is the dominating spirit of Bayreuth.

Hitler gives the famous place every possible protection. Thus Bayreuth—like the State Opera House of Berlin—is exempt from the authority of Goebbels, upon whom all the other theatres in the Reich depend. The blind confidence of Goering in Tietjen, his *Generalintendant*, was shared by Frau Winifred. Thus a valuable and intimate collaboration developed between the Berlin State Opera and Bayreuth, Tietjen gradually assuming the same authority on the *Festspielhügel* as in Berlin. Frau Wagner even nominated him guardian of her children.

This was the Bayreuth at which I arrived. I stayed at the *Post* as I had done so often previously. The Falstaffian landlord greeted me as an old friend : the *Festspielhaus* had ordered my room—that was sufficient ! He asked me at once : " Fräulein Doktor, what would you like to eat ? I will cook anything you fancy." " For me there is only one thing : *Kalbshaxe mit Kartoffelsalat*," I replied, and so it was. He brought in the biggest knuckle of veal I had ever seen, and in spite of the swastika in his buttonhole, he sat down and kept me company. A number of the singers usually came in the evening to the *Post* and had supper or a glass of beer there : and so we all met again.

In the meantime I received a message that Tietjen expected to see me at nine o'clock the next day. So, on a radiant morning, I strolled up the well-known path to the *Festspielhaus*, where I found Tietjen and Frau Wagner. Tietjen took me for a little walk around the hill, and I told him how much I loved being in England, and I also, quite frankly, told him all my ideas regarding the political situation.

I then gave him Sir Thomas's message, told him his plans for the Coronation Season, and last, but not least, informed him how many German singers Covent Garden would need for the 1937 International Season. Tietjen glanced at me humorously and said : " You seem to expect that the Berlin State Opera House should be closed for the English Coronation Season ! " But he promised all the support he could, and was very pleased that Sir Thomas was coming to Bayreuth to discuss matters with him personally.

I then sought out Frau Wagner, and conveyed Sir Thomas's greetings to her. *Au fond*, I always liked her, but previously, especially when I had stayed with Furtwängler in Bayreuth in the summer of 1931, our relationship had been strained. Now I came back to Bayreuth independent of all its undercurrents, and all was well. I discussed with her details regarding Sir Thomas's lodgings, and she invited him to share her box for all the performances. The lodging question was very difficult, von Ribbentrop having booked half the available accommodation, as he had invited innumerable English people, who actually failed to arrive at the last moment. Finally, however, everything was settled.

I informed Tietjen that Sir Thomas wished me to accompany him to Bayreuth and then declared :

" Under no circumstances, however, will I attend the performances. After having been Furtwängler's assistant for twenty years, and then having been forbidden to show my face in Germany any more, I can't be present at a performance now."

" Of course you will," said Tietjen, " and you will also be invited to the luncheon which Frau Wagner is giving for Sir Thomas to meet the Führer. It is all arranged for the free day between the *Ring*."

I really felt as if I were losing my reason ! I certainly had not counted on this last development, and began to get extremely uneasy as to where events were leading. I was told later that Hitler had decreed that I was to be treated as a member of the British party. I can hardly believe it even now, nor can I ever verify it. In any case, I was determined to avoid Hitler at all costs, and I counted on Sir Thomas to come to my rescue.

After his rehearsal, Furtwängler appeared at the *Festspielhaus* to call for me in his new car. We drove to the *Feustelmühle* outside Bayreuth where he had his romantic quarters ; had our lunch in the old-fashioned garden, and then took a long walk over the hills. I spent the evening with him in order to meet his new secretary, " successor No. 3 ", who had arrived with a dog. I must admit that my zeal to coach my successors was gradually diminishing. There are certain things which one cannot instil into others, and among these are love and devotion to a cause. However, the present outlook seemed fair, and I hoped for the best.

All my affairs were now settled and I went off for my three weeks' holiday on the Starnberger See while Sir Thomas was in Norway.

Time passed quickly. I had written several times to Sir Thomas to the address in Norway he had given me. Later I was to learn that although he gives addresses, he seldom collects the mail which has been sent there. It seems highly probable to me that my letters are still at the bank address in Oslo which he gave me, unless they have fallen into the hands of the Germans in the meantime ! Among them was an amusing letter written from the Bayreuth Information Bureau regarding accommodation for Sir Thomas, starting, " Concerning Mr. Beecham, English Furtwängler ! "

The first cycle of the *Ring* began on July the 23rd and Sir Thomas was to arrive on the 24th for the *Walküre*. When I arrived in Bayreuth two days before, there was already great activity at the station, and the little place, so quietly poetical in normal times, was scarcely recognisable. The town was bedecked with blood-red flags stamped with swastikas, particularly on the way to the *Festspielhügel*. What had become of the old Bayreuth ?

This time I stayed with Frau Schuler, the widow of the former director, and intimate friend of Cosima, in my old quarters in her lovely home on the *Festspielhügel*. Soon Frau Schuler had told me all the Bayreuth news ; Preetorius dashed over to see me in the interval of the *Rheingold* general rehearsal ; then Furtwängler called for me, and we went for a drive in the country.

At that time everything at Bayreuth was at boiling-point. Furtwängler seemed to be at loggerheads with all sorts of people, and the whole place was seething with gossip. There was also much indignation about myself, because I had declared that the principal of the Foreign Department of the *Reichsmusikkammer* was a *Rindvieh*, which can perhaps best be translated as a " bloody fool ", and which, in my opinion, was the exact truth. This gentleman was continually seen pottering about the *Festspielhügel*, and had already cut me. In former times I might have taken this very seriously, but had no need to do so now. I soon realised that if I were to get through the next few days alive, I would have to go very carefully indeed. I longed for the moment when Sir Thomas would arrive and I could find protection behind his broad shoulders.

On our drive Furtwängler and I discussed many things, including the plans for the Coronation Season. He drove me back through the fields on a wonderful moonlit night at a very late hour. Frau Schuler was waiting up for me, and we talked till dawn was near.

She was kindness itself, and her friendship warmed my heart. We both remembered the summer of 1931 when Furtwängler and Toscanini had been in charge of Bayreuth together and I had lived in her house.

Early next morning Ribbentrop's liaison-man appeared in Bayreuth and came to see me, asking for news of Sir Thomas, who was due to arrive that afternoon. Hardly had he left me when I received a telegram : " Sorry, cannot come. Greetings. THOMAS BEECHAM ". *Now* what was I to do ? I cannot say I felt particularly happy at this moment, and immediately put a call through to Covent Garden. Although Sir Thomas's telegram had been sent from London, the Opera House had not the slightest idea where he was, nor had anyone else. Later I learned that it is part of the etiquette of Covent Garden that if Sir Thomas does not report to the Opera House no one ever dares to try to locate him.

" All right," I said to myself, " I will go and find him. I will not stay another single day alone here. I will return to London straightaway." No sooner said than done. I asked to see Tietjen, which was very difficult on that particular morning, as he was rehearsing, and I told him about the telegram. I said to him : " Under no conditions will I remain in Bayreuth alone ". He understood, but begged me to go and see Frau Wagner before I left. Frau Wagner was considerably displeased. " But this is impossible," she said. " The Führer expects Sir Thomas, and wants to sit with him in my box." I replied : " I have not the slightest idea what has happened, but I will return to London at once and, if possible, I will fetch Sir Thomas over ". This proposal relieved Frau Wagner's mind. In the meantime the liaison-man appeared again, very much disturbed by Sir Thomas having cancelled his visit. He said : " I am sure that something has happened. Possibly the Italians are behind all this ". At this time Sir Thomas was believed to be a friend of Edward VIII, and the Germans seemed to measure the political situation by his conduct. I do not know what game, if any, Italy was trying to play then. My own politics were sufficiently complicated to keep me busy.

This little incident may demonstrate the naïveté of the Nazis with regard to English politics. They thought, in all seriousness, that they could draw safe conclusions of the general situation from the behaviour of one man, because he was said to be acquainted with the King. It was the same mistake, in essence, that Ribbentrop made. His goal at that time was certainly an Anglo-German Entente, but his mistake was that he apparently thought that by courting certain Mayfair salons he would make sure of British goodwill. His attitude while German Ambassador to the Court of St. James shows that he had no idea of what the English character and English politics really are.

The same fundamentally wrong conception of the problem was found in Hitler himself, who proposed to present the Royal Opera House, Covent Garden, for the Coronation Season with a similar *Lohengrin* décor as that of Bayreuth's new magnificent production of 1936. The tale goes that Edward VIII on hearing of the Führer's plan to embellish the Coronation festivities had declared that he did not mind personally as long as he had not to go and attend the —— Opera ! Whereupon the plan was dropped.

In any case, the master of Covent Garden having apparently let everybody in Bayreuth down, I left at two o'clock in the afternoon in the boiling sun in order to catch the Hook of Holland boat the same night.

Everything went smoothly on the journey, and greatly relieved, I passed the frontier. As soon as I had reached Holland, I sent a telegram to Sir Thomas at his usual address : " Am coming to London to fetch you. Hitler expects you. Greetings. GEISSMAR."

I arrived in London, full of fighting spirit. I had one idea only, and that was to find Sir Thomas. Unhampered by considerations of Covent Garden etiquette, I telephoned half London trying to trace him. Now it is one of Sir Thomas's amusing but not always convenient tricks to disappear in this way. He maintains that this is the only method by which he can secure the solitude he considers necessary. It seemed that at this moment he was experiencing this curious urge again. Everyone I asked warned me : " For God's sake, don't ring him up ! ", or, " You had better wait until you hear from him ". However, I was not at all inclined to wait until I heard, and Fate allowed me to find out where he was. Incredible, but true—he had betaken himself to the Euston Hotel ! I rang him up there, as though it were the most normal thing in the world to do. Smith, his indispensable manservant, was helpful and Sir Thomas came to the phone. " Did you get my telegram ? " I asked. " Yes,

I did," said Sir Thomas. "You had better come straightaway and see me." "All right Sir Thomas," I said, and jumped into a taxi.

In the Euston Hotel, serene and immaculate, sat Sir Thomas in his usual white silk pyjamas, with his Turkish dressing-gown and the inevitable cigar, having breakfast.

"Well now, Doctor," he commanded, " tell me all about Bayreuth."

"There is a lot to tell about Bayreuth," I replied. "But the principal point is that they have asked me to bring you back at once, as Hitler expects you to be his guest next Sunday in the Wagner box."

I looked at him expectantly and continued to describe the situation, but nothing impressed him. He did not care a damn whether Hitler expected him or not.

"Look here, Doctor," he said. "I simply can't go immediately. I have much to do in London just now, and you must understand that when I do go to Bayreuth I shall be very busy. Will you please convey my regrets to Frau Wagner and tell her that I will come later on for *Lohengrin* and the whole of the second *Ring*, and you will come with me."

"I think," he continued, " that during the second *Ring* it will be easier to work than during the first round." Not a word about Hitler! His features were sphinxlike. Only his eyes twinkled mischievously, and I had no doubt that he had changed his arrangements to avoid politics altogether, and to go to Bayreuth in the service of art—art alone.

Chapter 24

SIR THOMAS intended to remain in London until his journey to Bayreuth. One day he told me that he had decided to give up his room on the ground floor in the Opera House and to take over three adjoining rooms upstairs. I was to have the first room, then came Sir Thomas's large office, and behind this was to be his private room with his music library. Apart from a small iron door to which Sir Thomas held the only key, and which opened directly into the theatre, this inner room was inaccessible except by passing through his office. The normal entrance to the whole suite was through my room, the door of which bore a nameplate inscribed with both our names.

At the end of July I was again sent to Berlin. It happened to be about the time of the opening of the Olympic Games. When I arrived at Liverpool Street Station there were bills and banners everywhere inviting people to visit Germany. All trains to the Continent were running in three parts. Not only were there the Olympic Games, but it was the time of the year for continental travel. All my fellow-passengers were on the way to Berlin, and on the boat we were packed like sardines.

In Berlin my taxi had to make an enormous détour. In spite of the Olympiade many roads were up in connection with the gigantic plans of the Führer to leave to posterity a city bearing the stamp of the "architectural culture" of the Third Reich. The chauffeur talked to me very confidentially in the broadest Berlin slang. "They are turning Berlin inside out, lady, I can tell you. We can afford anything now as long as the people pay. God knows where it will end!" The angry irony in his voice was unmistakable. Finally, having driven through much beflagged Berlin, he deposited me at my mother's house. Soon I was immersed in my work with the Berlin Philharmonic office on details for the London Philharmonic tour which, of course, was the principal reason of my trip.

On August 7th I went back to England. I nearly missed my train at the Bahnhof Friedrichstrasse, the Linden being up and the Brandenburger Tor blocked, because Hitler wanted to widen the Charlottenburger Chaussee leading from the Brandenburger Tor past the *Reichstag*, through the Tiergarten. Again my chauffeur, in a confidential rage, made it difficult for me to keep a neutral attitude. The "voice of the people" was anything but pro-Hitler!

On August 11, the appointment of von Ribbentrop as German Ambassador to Great Britain was announced.

The weeks passed quickly and soon I left again for Bayreuth. I had to take the *train-de-luxe* because Covent Garden, which had ordered the sleeper for Dr. Geissmar, had omitted to say that I was a woman, and there was a man in the second bed!

Finally I arrived, and formalities and friendly visits over, I was handed my tickets for the performances—in the first row of "the relations box". I accepted without further demur on account of my work for Covent Garden.

Sir Thomas was to be a permanent guest in the Wagner box. Furtwängler was to sit with him (Tietjen conducting the second cycle) in order to discuss the singers.

Next morning, at seven o'clock, I went to Nuremberg to meet Sir Thomas, who in spite of the train's two hours' delay stepped fresh and rosy from his sleeper. While we had breakfast he listened to all my Bayreuth gossip, and then we drove on to the residence allocated to him for his visit. This was an octagonal baroque tower outside the town. It had belonged to one of the Margraves of Bayreuth, and soon became known as "Sir Thomas's tower". A most romantic kind of "cavalier's house" with panelling and furniture of the period had been built round the tower. This delectable little château had been renovated luxuriously later on, retaining, however, the old baroque style. The tower itself was transformed into an enormous music-room with a gallery. All sorts of guest-rooms and living-rooms had been added. It stood alone on a hill, far away from the "madding crowd" and was surrounded by an old-fashioned garden with a beautiful old well. Sir Thomas was entirely alone in this place except for the necessary servants. He was very pleased with this idyllic spot, and greatly appreciated its romantic beauty. No less did he appreciate his solitude.

The first performance was *Parsifal*. Furtwängler conducted, and the French dramatic soprano, Germaine Lubin, was singing Kundry for the first time. At first I felt a little awkward, especially as many old friends sat around me to whom my transition from the service of the foremost German conductor to that of England's unique Sir Thomas caused no small sensation. Soon, however, the solemn music held our rapt attention and all else was forgotten.

Sir Thomas spent the first interval with Frau Wagner and Tietjen, while I had been invited by the singers to have coffee in the restaurant. The "singers' table" is always very amusing, and everything would have been all right if one of Goering's sisters had not been sitting opposite me. Goering's sisters played a certain rôle at that time. They were bourgeois and rather commonplace, especially this one, who was plump and dowdy. They gossiped a lot, and Berlin was always quoting what one or the other had said.

This sister, Frau Riegele, worshipped the tenor, Max Lorenz. She had no objection to his wife (the famous Lotte) who was a Jewess, and was on very friendly terms with both of them. I had, of course, to be introduced to her; but no one will blame me if I failed to direct my conversation to her. Though I ran into her continually in the intervals I made a large détour whenever possible. Later I was told that she had complained: "I do not know what is the matter with Doktor Geissmar. I always try to greet her amiably, but she always avoids me." Lotte Lorenz, with her Berlin bluntness, is said to have replied: "You don't seem to know that Dr. Geissmar was deprived of her passport for a whole year. You cannot blame her if she is reticent."

In the second interval Sir Thomas wanted to see Furtwängler. We climbed up to Furtwängler's room and found him resting and very scantily clad because it was extremely hot. The contrast between the two conductors with whom I was so closely associated struck me very forcibly: Furtwängler, half-embarrassed because he was having his airbath, and yet pleased to see me and his British confrère: Sir Thomas, elegant as ever, in his beautifully cut light grey suit and silk shirt, the complete man of the world. "How do you like your new secretary?" Furtwängler asked. Whereupon Sir Thomas generously replied that "she was a marvel".

After *Parsifal*, I drove with Sir Thomas to his tower. For the whole time that he stayed in Bayreuth, he always went straight home after the performances, and I spent the rest of the evening with him. It was wonderful to return to this peace from the *Festspielhügel*.

Generally he played the piano a little, and I remember one special evening listening and leaning over the instrument, on which his travelling chessboard stood. A world chess tournament was taking place at that time and Sir Thomas, who is a passionate chess player, was following the games. While listening to him I fidgeted unconsciously with the chessmen and upset the problem. When he had finished playing, he turned to his chessboard and discovered the havoc. "My God, what's this?" he exclaimed. Quickly and painfully I became aware of what I had done. "I am afraid it is my fault." I apologised, "I have moved the figures quite unintentionally.

I am awfully sorry ". Anyone else might have made a scene. But Sir Thomas, with the greatest amiability, said consolingly : " Don't worry. It is quite all right ".

Next morning, Sir Thomas and Furtwängler completed their plans for the Coronation Season peacefully sitting in the latter's garden. It was a formidable task, and Sir Thomas, who has a special talent for this sort of thing, drew up a wonderful chart in his neat handwriting. I assisted, and also took photographs of them both at work.

Lohengrin was to be given that afternoon. The first *Lohengrin* produced by Furtwängler, Tietjen, and Preetorius together had been performed in the Berlin Municipal Opera House in 1929. This performance was quite unique. In the old days when Siegfried Wagner was still alive, there had never been any connection between Furtwängler and Bayreuth. In spite of Furtwängler's incontestable genius as an interpreter of Wagner, he was never invited to the *Festspielhügel*. Instead, the strangest choices were sometimes made. However, once Siegfried Wagner attended one of these Berlin *Lohengrin* performances incognito. He was impressed to the highest degree, and decided at once to bring this production to Bayreuth. Fate decreed that he should not live to see this carried out.

There was a system in Bayreuth, by which the *Ring* and *Parsifal* were performed every season, while the other operas took their turn. In 1936, it was *Lohengrin's* turn, with a magnificent new production. Furtwängler conducted the first performances, while Tietjen had the direction in the second half of the Festival.

Marie Müller sang Elsa, and Franz Völker was—at least so far as his voice was concerned—an ideal Lohengrin. The perfect ensemble of singers, the Festival Orchestra and the combined choruses of the Berlin State Opera and Bayreuth, united with a superb *décor* to make a *Lohengrin* unknown outside the world of dreams. At the Bayreuth *Lohengrin* première Hitler is said to have been moved to tears and went backstage to shake hands with everyone. (Incidentally, this was the *décor* that Hitler had wished to present to Covent Garden for Edward VIII's coronation.)

Sir Thomas was soon very popular on the *Festspielhügel*. His poised, detached, yet amiable manner, to which his halo as master of Covent Garden was no slight addition, soon won public enthusiasm.

After each act I met him in front of the Wagner box, when he came out with Furtwängler. Several times we three were photographed together. Even the official house-photographer of Bayreuth took a picture of us in conversation, and this was openly sold as a postcard in spite of the inclusion of such a notorious "non-Aryan" as myself.

Hitler and the members of the German Government who had been present at the first cycle had departed, but meanwhile everyone else concerned had arrived, including innumerable musicians and many faithful old Bayreuthers. Sir Thomas frequently used the intervals to discuss his impressions with Furtwängler, and so we sat sometimes at one of the little tables outside the restaurant. It disgusted me to see how people for whom I had ceased to exist during my troubles now approached our table.

Very rarely have I felt so strongly as I did in Bayreuth what a fraud all Hitler's racial doctrines are, and how unnatural is the cleavage which he has thrust between human beings. I was exactly the same person who hardly a year before had been a pariah. *I* had not changed, but the Nazis now chose to disregard their principles because it was convenient to themselves. I sensed a relief on the part of many that there was at least one case in which the absurdity of Nazi theories had been quickly demonstrated. In spite of all this, I remained fully conscious of the true state of affairs, and of the appalling dominion of the Nazi régime over even those who, at heart, rejected their ideology. It was delightful to meet old friends and to see how little Hitler had actually succeeded in convincing some people, but nothing can acquit them for their passive outward acceptance of Nazi-ism.

Of course, there was plenty to do in Bayreuth. The day was short, and the performances began at four o'clock. Everyone looked forward to the London Season, and great curiosity prevailed as to the final cast for the German operas.

Sir Thomas always endeavoured to get the best talent for Covent Garden, and although Preetorius, the famous stage designer, knew hardly any English, they got on very well together. To his great delight, Sir Thomas invited him to do a new *décor* for the *Fliegende Holländer*, and to come over at once in order to have a look at the Covent Garden stage. Sir Thomas himself was shown all the latest innovations behind the scenes at the *Festspielhaus*, and the opinion was freely expressed that he knew a good deal more about the stage than most other people of his profession.

Meanwhile the *Ring* was going on and Sir Thomas listened to every performance from beginning to end, but afterwards he escaped quickly to his car before we were engulfed in the stream of the traffic. We often went for drives in the surrounding country. On one of them he told me how, in the summer of 1899, when he had stayed in Alexanderbad near Bayreuth, the feud between the Wagnerians and the Brahms-ites was at its height. This induced him to make a thorough study of Brahms' compositions.

Finally, our visit came to an end. An *entente-cordiale* had been made between the Berlin State Opera and the Royal Opera House, Covent Garden, for the Coronation Season. All the singers required for London were to get leave to come if they possibly could. Furt-wängler was to conduct two cycles of the *Ring*, with Tietjen as producer. Preetorius was to make a new *décor* for *Der Fliegende Holländer* and *Orphée*. Sir Thomas was to conduct a new production of *Orphée* in Berlin, and this production was later to be repeated in London. He had made many new friends, and was very satisfied with the result of his Bayreuth visit.

The day after *Götterdämmerung*, Sir Thomas went to Paris, while I left for London—and a good sleep.

Chapter 25

IN LONDON we had to confirm and record the arrangements made in Bayreuth. The casting of the *Ring* is always a difficult matter, even in normal times. For the Coronation Season, of course, Sir Thomas wanted the very best. London has no permanent opera, other than Sadlers Wells, and yet the public is more exacting than any other.

The most critical choices to be made for the *Ring* are always Brunhilde and Siegfried, and these important rôles had to be dealt with first. Lauritz Melchior, who had ceased to sing in Germany, was a great favourite with the Londoners. He was to sing Siegfried in one cycle and Max Lorenz, the Bayreuth and Berlin Siegfried, in the other.

For the Brunhilde, in spite of their old admiration for Frieda Leider, Londoners wanted the newly famous Norwegian dramatic soprano, Kirsten Flagstad, for one cycle. This was rather difficult on account of Mme. Flagstad's heavy bookings in America. One morning, when Sir Thomas and I were working, it suddenly struck us that we were getting nowhere with the Brunhilde problem and were, indeed, in danger of falling between two stools.

Mme. Flagstad was then in Vienna, rehearsing for her first appearance in *Tristan* at the Vienna State Opera. Sir Thomas, as usual, decided quickly. " What is the time, exactly ? " he asked. It was noon. " Now, look here, Doctor," he declared, " I have had enough of this Brunhilde nonsense and I do not intend to waste any more time upon it. The boat-train for the Orient Express leaves at three p.m. There is plenty of time for you to get ready. I shall send Smith for your ticket, and in the meantime I will give you a letter for Madame Flagstad, and you will go to Vienna at once and get this thing settled."

Soon I was sitting in the train. I arrived punctually in Vienna the next day, and on my way to the Hotel Imperial, my old head-quarters, I passed the Bristol where Mme. Flagstad was staying with her husband and sent her a message that I had just arrived with the object of seeing her.

Mme. Flagstad is a tall and beautiful woman, with a fine Scandinavian profile and beautiful brown eyes. Her quiet and unassuming manner gives no hint of her regal stage presence. When I arrived she was sitting with her husband, a tall Norwegian. Her room was full of the loveliest flowers, and there was also a liberal provision of whisky, obviously for husband and guests. It was just two hours before her first appearance in the Vienna State Opera, so I tried to be brief. I said straightaway : " Sir Thomas wants this matter cleared up, and he wants you. Here are his dates for the *Ring*." Owing to complications arising from her many engagements it was not easy for her to fit the required dates in, but she was most anxious to appear in the Coronation Season and promised to adjust her plans. I cabled Sir Thomas accordingly, and received his imperious telegram :

" Stop until matter completed ". His instructions are always un-equivocal, which makes it very simple to carry them out.

It was the beginning of September. The warm rays of the late summer sun streamed over Vienna. One heard much of the desperate situation in Austria, but the Vienna one saw seemed beautiful and unconcerned. The hotels were full of cosmopolitan visitors. Many had remained there for a while after the Salzburg Festival. Edward VIII was there with his friends, staying at the Hotel Bristol. He was very popular, and what he said at the opera or at the Turkish baths was the talk of the day. As in former times, I was very much under the spell of this beautiful town. Many old friends turned up. The Vienna press, sniffing sensation, "tactfully" asked me to give them an interview about my work with Furtwängler and Sir Thomas Beecham. I was wise enough to avoid this. Deliberately misinterpreting their question, I answered : " Sir Thomas Beecham is not coming to Vienna at the moment, and so I am sure it is not necessary for you to trouble about an interview ". I had not dreamed that I should ever set foot in the Vienna State Opera again, but the irresistible charm of this beautiful theatre, so rich in tradition, came over me again when I called on Dr. Kerber, its director.

Vienna was then brimming over with musicians. Many celebrities went there, and each had his own adherents. Among conductors there were Boehm, Furtwängler, Kleiber, Klemperer, Knappertsbusch, Clemens Krauss, Toscanini, Bruno Walter, Weingartner, and many others. It was a great time for the sensation-loving Viennese, for whom everything concerning music is of the first importance.

I visited museums and saw for the last time all the treasures in the archives of the *Gesellschaft der Musikfreunde*. Sir Thomas was always searching for rarely performed classical music. At that time he was especially interested in a concerto for hurdy-gurdies by Haydn, which he wanted to perform. " Please try to find out something about this piece in Vienna," he said to me when I left. " I intend to do it at one of my concerts and to ask Sir Henry Wood and Sir Hugh Allen to play the hurdy-gurdies. It will be very interesting." He said this with a deep seriousness, so that I had not the slightest idea that he was pulling my leg. I therefore did my best to investigate the matter and found the original of the work, which had been composed in 1786 and was dedicated to the King of Naples, in the archives of the *Gesellschaft der Musikfreunde*, whose librarian had it photographed for Sir Thomas.

Meanwhile, my business with Mme. Flagstad had been completed, and I had also started negotiations for Sir Thomas as well as for the London Philharmonic Orchestra to go to Vienna.

Furtwängler was still at Bayreuth. The Festival was over and Bayreuth was empty. The Wagner family were in their country house on Lake Constance, and Furtwängler had decided to stay on until the beginning of September and to complete some work in solitude in these beautiful surroundings.

As he was then in constant touch with Covent Garden he knew that I was in Vienna in order to contact Mme. Flagstad. The telephone operator in the Hotel Imperial was the same one who, for many years, had often put calls through for Furtwängler to me in Berlin. She had greeted me at once when I arrived, and our old acquaintanceship was renewed. In the middle of the night she suddenly rang my room. " Here is Bayreuth coming through, Frau Doktor. I believe it is the Herr Direktor." I have never found out why Furtwängler was invariably called the " Herr Direktor " by the staff of the Hotel Imperial. However, it was he, and he asked me whether I could spend a day with him in Bayreuth on my way back to London. This was easy to arrange, since I had in any case to change to the Ostend train in Nuremberg.

At dawn I reached Nuremberg, where I had to take a local train. When I arrived Bayreuth lay veiled in a light morning haze. How quiet were the places of many memories, how different from the turmoil of the summer! I drove through the sleepy little town, through fields and autumn-tinted woods, and eventually arrived at Furtwängler's romantic abode. The present solitude was better suited to him than the commotion of the *Festspielhaus*. Although he towered above the others there as a personality, he was not skilled as they were in the craft of contending with the intrigues arising from the trivial round and common task. His " reconciliation " with the régime had not in any way emasculated his critical faculty, and he regarded the evergrowing encroachments on cultural life with great apprehension.

Next morning he had to go to Jena, and I accompanied him on a drive through the country of Goethe and Schiller. From Jena I

intended to take a train back to Nuremberg and there catch the
Ostend train. Being preoccupied with Covent Garden's affairs, I
had entirely forgotten that the Nuremberg Party Rally (*Parteitag
der Ehre*) was to begin that week, and when at last I boarded the
overcrowded train at Jena, I was pushed into a compartment overflowing with elderly women on their way to the *Parteitag*. They
were ecstatically discussing the Führer. Their attitude was typical of
a certain class of German women. They were all " petit bourgeois "
suburbanites, and I doubt whether they had ever had any real contact
with political life. They were nourished by a propaganda exactly
attuned to their mentality, and they passionately discussed what the
Führer would do on the first day ; whether he would be seen in
the morning, remembering that he had been seen on the first day
the year before, and so on. It was easy to perceive that their
whole fantasy revolved round a Hitler fixation, which had given
them a renewed sense of life.

No one will doubt my discomfort in these surroundings. and it
was with inexpressible relief that I left the train at Nuremberg. On
Nuremberg station pandemonium was let loose. It was only noon
and yet the place was full of Nazi uniforms. Special trains filled with
Nazi contingents continued to arrive : Party comrades greeted each
other pompously. Back in the mad house ! I thought : " If I have
to wait here until evening, something will happen ". I saw a local
train to Würzburg draw in at my platform, and as I could just as
well catch the night train to Ostend at Würzburg, I decided immediately ; I jumped in and was soon on my way. The train passed
through beautiful and peaceful country, untarnished by any sinister
trend of humanity.

In the famous old diocese of Würzburg some quality of quietness
seemed to transcend the turmoil of the ordinary world. In the old
churches there prevailed an atmosphere of eternal peace and beauty
which the Nazis could neither emulate nor destroy. I spent the
afternoon there. How beautiful were these baroque churches, the
cathedral and all the wonderful buildings, dating back to the time
of the Bishop-princes. The contemplative life seemed to have left
its mark for ever on the old, dreaming town. The quiet atmosphere
gave me strength and courage. Late in the evening I took my train
to Ostend. In considering all these experiences and impressions, a

great feeling of gratitude arose in me for the turn my fate had taken, and I looked forward eagerly to my return to England.

Chapter 26

SOON AFTERWARDS the Orchestra left with Sir Thomas for the Norwich Festival, and I was again sent to Berlin.

This was my third trip to Berlin since June, so I was getting used to it and was no longer nervous. Most of my friends had continued difficulties with the Nazis, and were relieved to discuss them with somebody from the outside world. Though they had in a way become resigned to the present conditions they all declared that it was impossible for such a state of affairs to last, and were convinced that sooner or later this nightmare was bound to come to an end.

I still had the same interests, but my main thoughts were beginning to take root in my new work. Although I imagined that in London things could hardly continue so rosily as they had begun, I saw clearly how much simpler my task was than my old one had ever been. Principally I realised how much less time was lost in England than in Germany, where everything was discussed interminably—a nerve-racking process. Covent Garden was certainly no smooth sea, but in comparison with the work in Germany, between the Philharmonic and the State Opera, the Nazis and non-Nazis, Goering and Goebbels, Furtwängler and Tietjen, the life with Sir Thomas and Covent Garden was like a pleasure cruise. Even more important was the fact that I was a free human being again.

Before I left London, a plan had arrived from Germany, enumerating the entertainments which were to be offered to the London Philharmonic between journeys and concerts. Dutifully I had submitted this scheme to Sir Thomas. "Now, look here, Doctor," Sir Thomas had said politely, but decisively, "I don't think this will do. If this amusement guide were to be followed, I should have to get the Berlin Philharmonic Orchestra to play for me after the

second concert of the tour ! " I therefore had the awkward task
of explaining this to our overzealous hosts. Consequently, the
Orchestra's free time was left a little less crowded.

Englishmen will always do as they please, and will not suffer too
much dictation. I doubt whether it would have been possible to
persuade the London Philharmonic Orchestra to accept similar
instructions to those imposed on the Berlin Philharmonic Orchestra
on the occasion of its first visit to Paris after the last war. This was
in 1928, and this first concert in France was considered of paramount
importance. The Orchestra arrived the day before and had a free
day, which meant also a free evening ! It was, however, decreed
that the musicians (who were all billeted in the same hotel) should
not go out in the evening so that they might be in their best form for
the concert. At a certain hour one of the executives, the principal
double bass, Herr Pingel, went to all the doors to verify that all his
colleagues were duly in bed ! Characteristically German, he remarked from the bottom of his heart : " Here we have order !
Here we have discipline ! " *After* the concert, however, the
Orchestra disappeared from the hotel for the night, and they
arrived on the departure platform next morning still in their dress
suits !

The days in Berlin were fully occupied with the final preparations
for the London Philharmonic Orchestra tour, which was to start in
November. The Berlin Philharmonic Office had scheduled everything down to the last detail, the towns were fixed, the itinerary
arranged, and the hotels booked.

I called on Sir Eric Phipps, who had been British Ambassador in
Berlin since 1933, and who was very pleased about the impending
visit of the London Philharmonic. He knew my history, and, very
amused about my transfer to the English Orchestra, proceeded to
deal with the matters in hand.

There was much to discuss with Tietjen, notably the exact date
for the singers' leave from the State Opera and also the casts for
Sir Thomas's Berlin performances. All the offices of the State Opera
had been luxuriously enlarged and extended on the most lavish
lines—notwithstanding National-Socialism. There was an enormous
bureaucracy and innumerable officials. Many whom I saw during
those days unburdened their hearts to me. It was not only the Jews

who complained of the régime, but many others, especially really cultured and intellectual people.

I had been on the telephone to London to Sir Thomas several times, and he had proposed that I should have breakfast with him immediately upon my return. This I did with pleasure, and enjoyed reporting the fruits of my labour to so understanding a listener.

Hardly had we finished when Sir Thomas suggested, " You had better come straight to the Theatre with me ". So off we went. While I had been away the new offices had been completed. They were beautifully furnished with grey fitted carpets and new curtains. In my room was a big desk, with all the necessary equipment, and a large wall-cupboard for Sir Thomas's private files. In the next room, his office, was his wonderful Chippendale desk, his piano-forte, gramophone, and radio, his lovely old prints of musicians, and his cupboard of reference books. In the third room was a fine old carved oak refectory table, and his music-library of priceless scores covered three walls. There he could work un-disturbed, and slip through his little private door directly into the theatre.

From my room one could go out on to the flies and look down on to the stage to see how far the rehearsal had proceeded. It was a practical as well as a comfortable suite of rooms, and Sir Thomas had arranged all the details himself. " How do you like it ? " he asked me expectantly, and naturally I could only answer, " It is simply perfect ".

One would think that nothing could now hold up the progress of normal office work, but until all was settled for the Coronation Season, one continually had to deal with the Continent, and Sir Thomas preferred that such matters be arranged personally rather than by interminable correspondence. Hardly had I settled in London than I was sent abroad again. " You see, Doctor," he said, " you are now a kind of Ambassador at Large for Covent Garden. You had better go to Munich and settle the outstanding questions with our friends, and from Munich you will go to Paris and see M. Rouché." On October 6th I found myself crossing the Channel again.

In Munich my principal task was a conference with Preetorius regarding the scenery for *Holländer* and *Orphée*. Preetorius knows what he wants and is very easy to work with, and so all went smoothly.

In Paris I cleared up many outstanding questions, including details of the French scenery for *Alceste* and *Pelléas et Mélisande*. The date for the Paris visit of the London Philharmonic Orchestra with Sir Thomas was provisionally arranged for the following March. I saw Ministers, committee ladies, etc., and returned to London as quickly as possible.

The Orchestra was about to leave for Sheffield, and Sir Thomas left for Sweden and Norway, spending an evening on his way to Stockholm with Furtwängler and Tietjen in Berlin. Both wrote to me about him in glowing terms. The three of them, it appeared, had very thoroughly enjoyed their evening together. Their meeting was to have served as a final conference on the Coronation Season, yet not one of them had made any note of their decisions, which I only obtained later by exercise of secretarial assiduity and clairvoyance! Matters were the more complicated because Sir Thomas was now in the remote North, and only available when he happened to ring us up from Stockholm or Oslo.

My life in London at this time became a continual round of interest. In his lovely house, full of Gauguins and other treasures, I discussed the Paris concert of the London Philharmonic Orchestra with Monsieur de Margerie, the First Secretary of the French Embassy. We were old friends from Berlin days, and renewed our old co-operation with pleasure. One day he told me that Sir Austen and Lady Chamberlain were going to lunch with them and proposed that I should come too, as Lady Chamberlain was the chairman of the Anglo-French Art and Travel Association, which was highly interested in the Paris visit of Sir Thomas and the London Philharmonic Orchestra.

I accepted the invitation, grateful for this opportunity of meeting such an eminent statesman as Sir Austen. He was an unusual type of man, with curiously chiselled features. In his conversation with me he made no secret of the fact that he did not wholly approve of Sir Thomas's visit to Germany with his Orchestra.

I explained that Sir Thomas was going purely as an artist. When the Berlin Philharmonic came to England for the first time in 1927, there had been great enthusiasm, and the public and Press could not do enough to show their appreciation. Since then—in 1932—Sir Thomas had founded a new Orchestra, the London Philharmonic. Although a real Briton, he was a man of international experience and knowledge, and knew the orchestral life of the Continent. He knew, too, that his own Orchestra—although young—could stand comparison with any other. That was why he wanted to travel with the London Philharmonic Orchestra. He wanted the British orchestra to show its quality in places renowned for their own old and famous orchestral tradition. In Germany—in spite of the Nazis—an orchestra still mattered.

I told Sir Austen about my former work, how the Berlin Philharmonic had started to tour Europe, how they had won success, and how—when there was a difficulty—the Foreign Office of pre-Hitler times had discreetly assisted with the expenses. I told him how much it was to be regretted that British cultural enterprise abroad was either officially announced as being done for the British Council, or generally left entirely to its own devices. Except for rare cases, when the very heavy expenditure was financed by the other side, the crippling cost of merely getting to the Continent was itself sufficient to ensure that if Sir Thomas, for instance, did not personally secure the necessary funds, it would hardly ever be possible for this great Orchestra to travel abroad — and incidentally enhance British prestige.

Sir Austen then discussed Nazi Propaganda, which he naturally despised. I said to him : " No one knows better than I how untrue, vulgar, and insidious Nazi Propaganda is. Yet, I could wish that the English might take a middle course between this and their own method of understatement, which frequently results in non-support of their most valuable assets." The conversation then took another turn, and he was pleased when I told him about our other continental plans, especially those for the Paris concert.

Chapter 27

AT THIS time London was a centre of musical life. Sir Thomas conducted his Beecham Sunday Concerts every week at Covent Garden. The Royal Philharmonic Society gave their concerts with the London Philharmonic Orchestra in Queen's Hall, where the Courtauld-Sargent Concerts were also held. The B.B.C. had their Symphony Concerts at Queen's Hall on Wednesdays. In addition to all this activity, internationally famous conductors, soloists, and chamber-music players visited London. With genuine catholicity visitors from abroad were welcomed and were free to perform, unhampered by political restrictions.

The Dresden State Opera had taken Covent Garden for a fortnight, and had on their programme, *Tristan und Isolde*, *Figaro*, *Rosenkavalier*, *Don Giovanni*, and *Ariadne auf Naxos*. Richard Strauss was expected, and was to conduct *Ariadne* as well as a Royal Philharmonic Concert where he was to receive the Gold Medal of the Society.

By the end of October the producers and stage personnel arrived from Dresden. This was fortunate, because the scenery had been badly damaged during the crossing and needed repair. Upstairs in front of my office, in the flies, and in the paint room, the Saxon workers moved about. They were highly delighted suddenly to find someone on the spot able to help them with the language.

In the meantime, Strauss arrived at the Opera House and attended the rehearsals. For a long time, I had had a grudge against him for his highly questionable behaviour during our troubles in Germany, and I intended, if not to avoid him, at least to be in no hurry to run into his arms. However, Jackson, the famous and beloved stage door-keeper at Covent Garden, whose memoirs would certainly be more interesting than all of ours put together, suddenly telephoned from the stage door : " Doctor ", he said, " Doctor Strauss has just asked for you. He has this minute gone on the stage." I went down, therefore, and greeted the famous composer, who assured me how delighted he was that I had ended up at Covent Garden. He wanted to know when Sir Thomas was expected back from Sweden. Sir

Thomas had introduced and conducted most of the first performances of Strauss operas in England. He and Strauss had been friends since Sir Thomas had conducted the first English performance of *Elektra* in 1910. His story of all that happened in connection with the first night of *Salome* in London is one of his best tales, and has found a place in his own memoirs in a chapter called "The Episode of *Salome*". He is an excellent interpreter of Strauss' music, and Strauss was well aware of this.

It was intended to arrange a small Anglo-German opera season at Covent Garden after the Christmas of 1936, where, amongst other operas, *Salome* was to be performed. Strauss knew of this plan and said to me now: "Where could we have a quiet chat?", whereupon I proposed to him that we should go up into Sir Thomas's office. Upstairs, Strauss looked pensively at the nameplate outside the office suite:

> " SIR THOMAS BEECHAM, Bart.
> DR. GEISSMAR."

Strauss sat down in Sir Thomas's comfortable chair and began to talk. He was still very good-looking in spite of having aged a little; he had the same fine head and guileless Bavarian expression. Many thoughts shot through my mind as I sat opposite him. He had known my parents' house and myself for many years. Yet in spite of the fact that he was President of the *Reichsmusikkammer*, he had not made the slightest move to help either Furtwängler or me during all our difficulties in Germany. It had been out of the question for me to ask him then for even so little as to intervene in order to get my passport back. He himself made use in foreign countries of his Jewish publisher, Herr Fuerstner, who had emigrated to London. Stefan Zweig and Hugo von Hofmannsthal had written wonderful libretti for his operas, and enthusiastic Jews had furthered and supported his work; but he only remembered these things in so far as they contributed to his own interests. Now, solely to get into touch with Sir Thomas, he came to talk to one who had been in such distress hardly a year before, assuming for the purpose a manner of the greatest charm. For many reasons it did not seem politic to ask the questions that passed swiftly through my mind. Why had he behaved as he had in the Third Reich? Why had he not, in his position as President of the *Reichsmusikkammer*, supported all of us who were by tradition and merit entrenched within the traditional musical culture of the genuine Germany ? Why had he not protected artists like Furtwängler and Hindemith, and also people like myself, against the Government ? Why had he not protected the principles vital for Germany's musical life ? I burned to express my opinion that had he not played into the hands of the Nazis, many tragedies in the field of music might have been avoided.

Yet I refrained for two reasons. First, because I considered it wiser to remain neutral in regard to these problems—as the conversation was taking place in Sir Thomas Beecham's office ; secondly, and I must admit it, I was entirely bewitched by his fabulous charm. We discussed many topics, among which were casts for his operas, but the dangerous problems were carefully avoided. He expressed the wish to meet Sir Thomas as soon as possible after his return, and left me in ostensible friendship.

Another visitor to my office was the Dresden stage designer, Professor Fanto. After he had once come to see me, he often found his way up again. I said to myself : "Funny, one can never be sure of anything, but if Fanto is not a Jew, I am a Chinese". Soon afterwards a story was repeated to me in this connection. Strauss spent his free time in London, as everywhere, in playing cards. He had his card-playing friends all over the world, and just as in former days he used to send for my father directly after his arrival in Mannheim, he had now summoned in London his traditional *Skat* party. One day, when playing, they questioned him about Fanto, whereupon Strauss innocently, or perhaps cynically, explained : "Well, Fanto, you see—Fanto has been clever, he has simply declared that he was a foundling and does not know anything about his parents. So the Nazis had to leave him where he was."

Considering the agonies which other people had endured on account of just one Jewish great-grandmother—at that time—it must be admitted that this statement direct from the President of the *Reichsmusikkammer* seems a piece of incredible cynicism. What desperate letters addressed to Furtwängler had I seen in the years 1933–34 from people whose private and professional life had depended on the handling of the question of their parentage.

Of course Strauss was enormously fêted. At the performance
of *Der Rosenkavalier* he sat in von Ribbentrop's box. Ribbentrop
saw fit to give the Hitler salute while the British National Anthem
was played—a piece of effrontery which caused great annoyance.

Chapter 28

IN THE meantime, Sir Thomas had established the organisation
of the Orchestra within the Covent Garden Opera House, and he
decreed a new plan of work. Those charters of his are always very
characteristic, and I cannot resist inserting here the document concerning the management of the London Philharmonic Orchestra
which was handed to each of us.

November 2, 1936.

MANAGEMENT OF ORCHESTRA

G. C. Reynolds—*Business Manager.*
Dr. Berta Geissmar—*Organising Manager.*
Frederick Laurence—*Orchestral Manager.*

MEMO :
    The functions of these three respective officers of the Company
are to be clearly defined for the purpose of practical administration.
    (*A*) Mr. Reynolds and his department are to occupy themselves
exclusively with financial control, especially in the important
matter of the relationship of the Orchestra with the Opera Company.
For the purpose of entirely satisfactory co-operation, this department
will make use to the fullest extent of the services of the Orchestral
Secretary, Mr. Laurence, whose functions are such as to bring him
into continual daily contact with the Orchestra itself.
    (*B*) The Organising Manager, Dr. Geissmar, will undertake and
control the entire task of organising the year's work of the Orchestra
in respect of its various dates of engagement. This involves the
co-relation of all the activities of the Orchestra in respect of concerts
in London or elsewhere, together with Tours, both in this country
and abroad. It will be apprehended that these duties, performable

by an official who is also my General Secretary, will come largely under my own personal supervision and control and that, therefore, Dr. Geissmar will be responsible to myself alone for their adequate accomplishment.

(C) Mr. Laurence ; the duties of the Orchestral Manager are to be limited to the supervision and management of all that daily and regular business in connection with the Orchestra which is apart from either financial control or organising preparation. For example, all that involves the due and punctual appearance of the Orchestra at concerts, rehearsals, or upon railway stations, is his particular function, together with the competent control of library of music, such as required. A further essential part of his duties is the arrangement in conjunction with such conductors and other persons who may be involved, of the times and occasions of rehearsals and gramophone sessions.

The above-mentioned allocation of duties is intended to produce the following results :

(1) The business administration shall be independent of and free from the embarrassing burden of having to worry or concern itself with any form of activity other than that which it is most competent to deal with.

(2) The organising department can pursue its industrious career, unhampered by the dread that it may be committing itself or any other part of the establishment for financial obligation.

(3) The department represented by Mr. Laurence, severed from any preoccupation other than that of the purely domestic life of the Orchestra, will be enabled to devote its energies to the maintenance of that pleasing amenity and content among the players themselves, which its experience and disposition is so well qualified to achieve.—THOMAS BEECHAM.

Meanwhile, the time had arrived for the German tour about which there had been so much controversy. Sir Thomas, who used to keep his artistic activities entirely separate from political considerations, was strongly criticised, and many people disapproved of the tour to Hitler-Germany. Sir Thomas had accepted the invitation as I have said for purely artistic reasons, and I, for my part, was determined to assist him in every possible way, and to try to forget my past wretchedness in Germany.

It was in my new capacity as Organising Manager that I gave my first interview, which appeared on November 1st in the *Observer*, and dealt with the imminent tour to Germany. As I had asked not to be mentioned by name, I was referred to in the article as " the enthusiastic organiser ".

About twenty other German towns beside those we had arranged to visit had asked for the London Philharmonic Orchestra, but as the available time was limited and the Orchestra had to fulfil engagements in England, they could not accept these invitations.

The programmes had been designed with careful consideration. Sir Thomas said to me : " I will not do any Beethoven or Brahms in Germany. That would be carrying coals to Newcastle. But I will give them something else." Sir Thomas's healthy self-esteem told him he could afford to do without the usual box-office attractions.

His first suggestion for programmes included Mendelssohn's Scottish Symphony. No sooner had von Ribbentrop received the draft than his A.D.C. arrived at my office, somewhat embarrassed. " The programmes are excellent," he said, " but do you think you could tactfully suggest to Sir Thomas that it might be advisable to leave out the Mendelssohn ? " I informed Sir Thomas—not, I am afraid, tactfully, but frankly (as was always my way with him) that this work seemed hardly to be desired on the German programmes. " Why not," flashed Sir Thomas—although perfectly aware of the implication—" it was a favourite piece of Queen Victoria's ! " However, having accepted the invitation to go to Nazi-Germany, he decided not to make this point a *casus belli*, and so the Mendelssohn Symphony was dropped.

Sir Thomas and the Orchestra were to arrive in Berlin on the morning of November 12th, but I had been sent on a week beforehand to deal with the final details.

The Berlin Philharmonic Office had made all the arrangements in the grandest style. Two executives of the Berlin Orchestra were to accompany the London Philharmonic Orchestra on the tour, while von Ribbentrop had appointed a gentleman of his staff to act as A.D.C. to Sir Thomas.

Sir Thomas and the Orchestra duly arrived early in the morning. From that moment until we left Germany, I scarcely knew whether to laugh or cry. Everything, including my own position, seemed strange and unreal. At the station there were several deputations, amongst them the Committee of the Berlin Philharmonic Orchestra, most of whom I had not seen since my troubles in 1934. When we greeted each other they appeared somewhat embarrassed, and one of them, whom I had known for twenty years at least, stepped forward quickly and whispered in my ear, " It was not us, Fräulein Doktor ". It was only possible to whisper, for we were in the company of the " big noises " from von Ribbentrop's office, from the Foreign Office, from the Reich Chancellery and others who had come to receive Sir Thomas. Press photographers crowded the platform, and there was an enormous commotion.

No one who has not accompanied Sir Thomas on such an occasion can imagine in the slightest degree his inimitable dignity. While he greeted me with a secret twinkle, he received the ovations of the deputations with the condescension of a potentate who has spent his life doing nothing else.

We drove to the Esplanade Hotel, where we enjoyed a comfortable breakfast in peace and privacy, before plunging into the vortex of the tour. Sir Thomas had been allotted a princely suite. He and myself (!) were the guests of the German Government on the whole tour, and all hotels had officially been so informed.

In every town the Government had put a car at the disposal of Sir Thomas. This car bore not only the Swastika flag, but also a kind of eagle to indicate its important status. Even before Sir Thomas arrived, a similar car was placed at my disposal in Berlin, and it was with very mixed feelings that I drove about in it.

Sir Thomas spent his first day in all sorts of conferences. Moreover, he was besieged by the Press. The English journalists arrived on the scene too, and looked at the matter from their own angle. Of course, I was used to dealing with Press affairs, and still knew most of the foreign Press then in Berlin. Indeed it was my good relations with the Press which had at first aroused the displeasure of the Nazis. It had soon been conveyed to me in the Third Reich that it would " harm " Furtwängler if I continued to act for him in Press matters. All this, however, was now forgotten. I was repeatedly told by officials how pleased they were that I was there, as this greatly simplified the relationship to the Press. There was much official coming and going, and continuous telephone calls from Government quarters were put through to me. Yet it had been considered one of my greatest offences that, while still in my old job, I had spoken on the telephone to one of these exalted beings, who had then complained of my presumption.

On the following morning, on the day of the Berlin concert, there was a rehearsal in the *Philharmonie*. The whole of the Berlin Philharmonic Orchestra was assembled to hear it. I had not set foot in the *Philharmonie* since the fateful Sunday morning, November 25, 1934, when Furtwängler's article on the Hindemith case had appeared, before his last concert preceding his resignation. Even while I was his secretary, it had been hinted to me that it would be wiser not to be seen there, and it would have been entirely out of the question, after my resignation, to have attended a concert— even as a private person. Now that I came in the company of Sir Thomas, this honoured and much courted guest, all doors were suddenly opened to me again. It will therefore be easily understood that it was in the *Philharmonie* that I lost my self-possession for the only time on this tour. I was never more aware of the grotesqueness and hypocrisy of the whole Nazi ideology than when I entered the *Philharmonie* as Sir Thomas's secretary.

Here I was—received because of my great English chief—in the very place in which my presence had been held to be so injurious to Furtwängler! The Berlin Philharmonic Orchestra crowded round me affectionately, and it was as though we had never been separated. Jastrau, the Orchestra attendant, still grimy from un-loading the English instruments, took me in his arms : "But, Fräulein Doktor, you really must not cry", he said simply. He was so comical in his dismay that he helped me to recover.

Sir Thomas did not wish to make any other appointments on this day. In the afternoon he was to see Hitler. The meeting had been arranged for five o'clock. A message came, however, that the Führer had a conference and would send his car as soon as it was over. No car came. When five o'clock had passed, Sir Thomas said : "Now look here, Doctor, if this wretched car does not turn up soon, I am not going. I have to conduct a concert to-night. After all, I am an artist. What does this man think, I wonder ? " He meant exactly what he said. Sir Thomas was rightly proud of his Orchestra, and it was going to play in Berlin for the first time. What did he care for Hitler at that moment ? I am convinced that had the delay been a little longer, he would have cancelled his visit, but finally the car from the Chancellery arrived and off he went. Later on, in initiated circles, the following story was told.

Hitler, after expressing satisfaction that Sir Thomas had come to Germany with his Orchestra, is reported to have said :

" I should have liked so much to come to London to participate in the Coronation festivities, but cannot risk putting the English to the inconvenience which my visit might entail."

" Not at all," replied Sir Thomas innocently. " There would be no inconvenience. In England we leave everybody to do exactly as he likes."

Hitler is reported to have been nonplussed by this reply. Soon the story was told everywhere, and it was whispered that never in his life had the Führer been so bewildered as he was by the ready-witted Sir Thomas.

Meanwhile the hour of the concert was approaching, and our English friends had arrived by aeroplane. The *Philharmonie* was sold out and presented a brilliant scene : the *Corps Diplomatique* was present in full force, led by Sir Eric Phipps. All the civic authorities, all the musicians, and the whole *Reich-Government*, headed by Adolf Hitler, attended. The Government occupied the " *Philharmonie* box ". I had been given the box above, and sat there with all our English friends.

The programme of this memorable concert was Dvorak, Rhapsody No. 3 in A flat major ; Haydn, Symphony No. 5 in D major ; Berlioz, le Carneval Romain ; Handel-Beecham Suite, the Gods Go a-Begging ; Elgar, Enigma Variations.

The concert went very well, and Orchestra as well as conductor had every reason to be satisfied with the success. After the first item, Hitler applauded, full of enthusiasm. Sir Thomas, who had entirely forgotten that this concert was to be broadcast, said to his Orchestra in an audible voice : " The old bloke seems to like it ! " This informal comment was characteristic of Sir Thomas's intimacy with his Orchestra, but it was not only the Orchestra who heard what he said. It was, in fact, heard wherever the broadcast was received, and an English paper wrote an amusing report about this incident with the headline, " Mysterious voice on the wireless during Sir Thomas Beecham's concert in Berlin ".

In the interval there was much coming and going. I remained

in my seat, but many came to my box. Several Press photos were taken, which were published all over the Reich next day. To our great astonishment there was also a photograph published of Sir Thomas in Hitler's box surrounded by Hitler, Goebbels, Neurath, Blomberg, and others. This was inexplicable, as Sir Thomas had not left the artists' room during the interval. Many had gone to see him there, such as the British Ambassador, Furtwängler, and, if I remember rightly, Goebbels ; but Sir Thomas had certainly not set foot in Hitler's box. The Nazis, however, had apparently found it necessary that he should be seen surrounded by the German Government and so *photomontage* had been called into action.

The next morning, throughout Germany, the Press was full of accounts of the concert. In every paper the photo of the *Reichsregierung* could be seen, while the music critics dealt with the English Orchestra and its conductor in long serious articles. There were special articles about Sir Thomas and the Orchestra, and long descriptions of all the personalities who had attended the concert.

The Berlin Philharmonic Orchestra treated the occasion as an artistic event only, and so they and Furtwängler had asked their colleagues and their conductor to a *Bier-Abend* in the *Philharmonie* ; only musicians were invited. The members of the Berlin Orchestra were already well acquainted with the London players, having met them frequently in London. The sections of the two orchestras quickly linked up with each other, joining in technical conversations about their instruments. It is amazing how quickly the flutes always find the flutes and the cellos the cellos. Soon there was great merriment, and in the early hours Sir Thomas is said to have danced on a table, sung, and told some of his inimitable stories !

Next day we left for the provinces. All the concerts of the tour were entirely sold out. In Dresden there was no incident, and the following day a concert was given in the famous *Gewandhaus* in Leipzig. After the rehearsal there was an informal reception in the *Gewandhaus*. I saw many old friends there : among them were Max Brockhaus, the well-known publisher, Herr von Hase, director of Breitkopf & Haertel, and Dr. Karl Straube, the venerated and famous *Thomas Cantor*, a successor to P. E. Bach at the *Thomas Kirche*. They all attended the concert at which the performance of the second

Symphony of Sibelius—hardly ever heard before in Leipzig—was a great success.

Outwardly Leipzig had been adapted to the Nazi régime, but at this time its citizens were seething with indignation. Hardly a week before Sir Thomas arrived with the London Philharmonic, the Mendelssohn monument had been spirited away by the Nazis in the middle of the night from its plinth at the entrance of the *Gewandhaus*. No one could trace it. The inhabitants of Leipzig were stunned and shocked. I believe that the question of the monument had been discussed before, and the then Mayor, Dr. Goerdeler, had pledged his word that the statue should remain where it was. At this time, however, Dr. Goerdeler was on an official journey to Sweden. In his absence his authority became vested in his deputy who was one of the "new people". So the monument disappeared.

There was an atmosphere of freedom around Sir Thomas, and the people instinctively turned to him. In the interval of the concert he pressed some envelopes into my hand. "You had better keep these, Doctor," he whispered. The envelopes contained the following two letters which give a vivid picture of what was really passing in the hearts of the Leipzig people.

"Leipzig,
November 1936.

" Sir Thomas Beecham,
Gewandhaus, Leipzig.

"A week ago, at night, the great monument of Felix Mendelssohn-Bartholdy, which stood in front of the main entrance of the *Gewandhaus* was pulled down and taken away. Nobody knows where it is, and there was not a word in the Press about it.

"In 1835, Mendelssohn, at the age of 26, assumed the direction of the *Gewandhausconcerts*, a position which he kept until his death. He died at the age of 38 in 1847. His life was an uninterrupted chain of triumphs as composer, virtuoso, conductor, and as a cultured, universally beloved man. He often visited England, and in 1846 the English public accorded him their last festive acclamations.

"The town of Leipzig erected the above-mentioned monument and unveiled it with solemn honours. The third generation, now ruling, destroys it, because Mendelssohn was a Jew.

"The bronze statue of Mendelssohn (more than life-size), with its goddess and two little angels with music-scores, will probably be melted away for guns.

238

"But his music is immortal, and will continue to be played in all civilised countries with the exception of Germany where it is strictly forbidden.

"Honour to his memory!

"The whole cultural world of Germany thinks and feels as I do and bewails much that is lost. It includes in its daily prayers the cry for help and freedom.—(Unsigned)."

The envelope addressed to Sir Thomas Beecham, bore the words : "Please do not give this letter to any German, because it might be very dangerous".

Sir Thomas gave the letter to me, and I have preserved it to this day. The other letter also deserves to be recorded. It reads as follows :

[*Without date.*]

"SIR THOMAS BEECHAM,
  GEWANDHAUS, LEIPZIG.

"When you conduct to-morrow evening in the *Gewandhaus* you will see in the first row, exactly as in Berlin—the 'Leader-personalities' (Führer-Persoenlichkeiten) assiduously applauding. You will be in a better position to judge the real musical culture of these gentlemen when you have been informed of the following facts which, perhaps, nobody else will tell you :

"Some days ago, late at night, the monument of Felix Mendelssohn-Bartholdy, the immortal composer and conductor of the *Gewandhaus*, was pulled down and removed.

"May you, dear Sir, be comforted by the fact that the thought of this act of racial hatred brings the blush of shame to the cheeks of millions of music-loving Germans.

"For your wonderful music—my heartfelt thanks.—A GERMAN."

These were the serious sides of this tour, of which, however, the Orchestra was little aware. They were immensely fêted in every town. The German orchestral players were especially interested in them. Léon Goossens, particularly, probably the finest oboe player in the world, created a great sensation. Of course, everybody was in high spirits, and it was only with the greatest difficulty that they could be persuaded to go to bed at all in the night-train from Leipzig to Munich.

In Munich the advice to treat the London Philharmonic Orchestra's visit as a purely musical event was unheeded. We arrived very early in the morning. At the station there were deputations for Sir

Thomas from the *Gau*, from the *Partei*, and so on. On the platform speeches were made to him, which he listened to with more dignity than pleasure. It was only seven o'clock in the morning, and he wanted to go to his hotel, for which no one could reproach him.

The provincial Nazis were not particularly pleased, I am sure, to be forced to receive me with politeness. Sir Thomas, as everyone knows, has the most impeccable manners, and lived up to his reputation on this tour. On this occasion he alighted from the train with my fur coat on his arm. The Munich Nazi dignitaries looked forward with pride to driving the famous Englishman to his hotel, but with an inviting gesture Sir Thomas waved me into the car—" Get in please, Doctor." Only those who know something of the internal workings of the Party can realise the sinister humour of the combination—the Munich Nazis, Sir Thomas, and myself starting off together in a car beflagged with a great Swastika !

We arrived at the Hotel *Vier Jahreszeiten* where I had stayed so often for so many years. Herr Walterspiel, the proprietor, came at once to greet Sir Thomas. The old hall-porter said encouragingly to me, as he handed me our mail : " You see, Fräulein Doktor, times change ".

The hotel was flying the Union Jack *and* the Nazi flag. Sir Thomas noted this, and mischievously commented : " The Swastika seems to be for you, Doctor ! "

We arrived in Munich on a " free " day. There had been all sorts of invitations for Sir Thomas, but he had stipulated that he wished to be free. It has been arranged between us beforehand that we were to go to the Starnberg Lake to visit the Lerchenfelds. The famous car was again at our disposal carrying the ominous flag.

There was great joy when we arrived, and the Count and Countess with their dogs came to meet us as we drove in. The house with its old furniture, its family pictures, its library—the hosts, with a culture belonging to a family hundreds of years old—all this represented something beautiful and precious which had almost vanished in Germany.

A strange spell surrounded us. Sir Thomas was very much at home, and the little circle had a great deal in common. They all belonged to the same world. Sir Thomas seemed very sensitive to this, and as we drove back, he said to me : " What will become of Germany if the voice of such people as these is stifled ? "

We arrived at the hotel to find, in addition to the two flags, a further adornment consisting of a sentry complete with sentry-box. " Still more honours for us ? " inquired Sir Thomas, with malicious humour. This time, however, it did not concern us. Goering had arrived, and as we had the flags he had to have the sentinel !

In the late afternoon we went to see Preetorius. It had long been arranged that he was to show Sir Thomas his treasures of Chinese art. Walleck, then *Direktor-General* of the Bavarian State Theatres, and Frau Winifred Wagner, were also present—the latter having come from Bayreuth especially to attend the concert. Preetorius showed Sir Thomas and Charles Moor, the Covent Garden stage director, who had joined us, his sketches for the proposed *Fliegende Holländer* performance in Covent Garden. There followed a passionate debate as to the position of the ship. Preetorius had set it with its blood-red sail right in the centre of the stage, creating a sinister effect. It was a very animated hour, only too short ; but the programme did not allow any alteration. In the *Residenz Theater*, so ideal for Mozart performances, *Don Giovanni* had been put on for Sir Thomas because he was very much interested in the scenery by Preetorius. The *décor* was most striking and unusual. Frau Wagner, Preetorius, Sir Thomas, and myself sat together in a box. However, soon A.D.C.s from some high official came to take Sir Thomas to the Town Hall, where many notabilities had assembled and where everything possible in the way of banquet and entertainment was offered to the Orchestra and its chief—including, of course, rivers of beer. It was only with considerable force that the Orchestra were persuaded to leave their beds next day.

Munich proved its right to be called the capital of the Nazi Movement. It would be impossible for a normal mortal to find his way through all the different authorities of Party, Town, State of Bavaria and Gau. Each had its own cultural department. Whether they had any real culture is another matter ! Such was the demand for seats for these functionaries that only with great difficulty did I contrive to get any for the English Press.

The British Consul-General came to see Sir Thomas, while I talked to the journalists. Everywhere there was great activity, and the pomp with which all these Party affairs were staged could not be reconciled with the attacks regularly made by the Nazis on the subject of extravagance by the Weimar Republic.

At this Munich concert almost everyone of importance was present. The concert hall was completely filled, and it was a brilliant spectacle. In the centre of the front row Hess, the Führer's deputy, sat in state surrounded by his staff. There were the leaders of the army and of the Bavarian Government, and there were many uniforms of high Nazi officials. The concert was excellent, and great ovations were given to the artists.

Sir Thomas had asked me to come straight to the artists' room after the concert, as I was to assist him in his negotiations with the Munich bass, Ludwig Weber, whom he wanted to engage for Covent Garden. However, I found my passage suddenly barred by a double line of black Storm Troopers. "Nobody is allowed to pass here," they declared pompously, "until the Minister has left the hall." How ridiculous this seemed to me when I reflected that the King of England can leave the Covent Garden Opera House and scarcely disturb the policeman on duty !

I said to the S.S., " Please let me pass. I am secretary to Sir Thomas, and he expects me." Then with the greatest energy I elbowed my way past them ! A year before, the sight of the S.S. uniform alone would have been enough to unnerve me.

Sir Thomas would have preferred to have gone back to the hotel this evening, but was told that the deputy of the Führer, who had invited him to his house after the concert, would be "hurt" by a refusal. He therefore decided to go for a short time, and Frau Wagner accompanied him. The evening took a strange course, for Herr Hess had no better idea for entertaining the long-suffering Sir Thomas, than to provide another concert.

Hess tried to ingratiate himself with Sir Thomas by declaring how he admired the discipline of the Orchestra, a quality he had not expected to find in a group of Englishmen. "Well," replied Sir Thomas loftily, "we English have our own brand of discipline, but it is not always recognised or comprehended elsewhere ; for instead of accepting it from others, we impose it on ourselves."

At the party, Sir Thomas played the piano. When I told him next morning that everybody was full of praise for his amiable humour in entertaining Hess's guests, he replied : "What could I do, Doctor; I was bored to death—so I played to amuse myself."

While we travelled next day to Stuttgart, through the romantic part of South Germany which I knew so well, Sir Thomas declared : "I have had enough of all these festivities, and I will attend no more. After all, what is the use of always listening to speeches which are probably all concocted in the same kitchen in Berlin." Hardly, however, had we arrived, when we were informed that another banquet had been arranged. It was obvious that the object of all this was to make Sir Thomas meet the principal Nazis in every town, to get him photographed with them, and to report in the papers whom he had met.

In Stuttgart the same comedy went on as before, and when trying to escape, Sir Thomas was told that the *Gauleiter* would be offended if he, the guest of Herr Hess in Munich, refused to accept the hospitality of Württemberg's Leader in Stuttgart.

Gradually, Sir Thomas began to lose his serenity through the constant pressure of engagements. At last he said to me decisively : "Doctor, please, will you kindly convey to Baron von G. (the gentleman from Ribbentrop's staff who was acting as the liaison-officer between Sir Thomas and the different authorities), that this nonsense must stop. I want to conduct my concerts and do nothing else. This is to be the last occasion on which I am dragged into that sort of thing. No artist who has to conduct every night would stand this." I replied : "I will certainly tell him, but I am sorry that your decision comes just before the concert in Ludwigshafen, where you would certainly meet the most interesting people of the whole tour". "Can't be helped," said Sir Thomas. "I wish you would get me *The Times*. That is all I want."

The next concert was to take place in Ludwigshafen in the concert hall of the I.G. *Farbenindustrie*, the famous chemical works which are so often mentioned in the R.A.F. communiqués nowadays. This Company was an organisation of great importance. Some of the finest scientists in the country worked for it, and the staff was chosen so carefully that mere association with the firm was a distinction in itself. The social institutions of the I.G. were most progressive, and for many years first-class concerts were given there for the

Trust and their staffs. The demand was so great that every concert had to be given twice. The I.G. had long been opposed to any interference by the Nazis, and one knows of several battles which the scientific director, the late Professor Bosch, had to fight, not least of all with Hitler himself. When the London Philharmonic Orchestra's tour was first projected, the I.G. Trust of Ludwigshafen was among the first to ask them to give a concert. It proved one of the most interesting of the tour.

Owing to the superiority of the hotel there, we were billetted in Mannheim, the Rhine alone separating the two towns. It was with mixed feelings that I arrived at the Mannheim station. Sir Thomas was received by the usual deputations on the platform. The Mayor of Mannheim, feeling himself at a disadvantage because the ovations for the exalted guest were to be presented by Ludwigs-hafen, endeavoured to share the honours and provide new ones, but the experienced Sir Thomas had now the necessary technique, and resisted his advances with energy.

Sir Thomas and I stayed in the *Mannheimer Hof*, a new hotel which had been built during the Hitler régime. Great was my amusement when Sir Thomas was informed that a singular honour had been bestowed upon him, namely, that he had been allotted the " Hitler Suite ". This suite, which was reserved for visits of Hitler himself, or of members of the Government, consisted of several rooms which were equipped and furnished in perfect taste, and had some fine pictures on the walls, beautiful floral arrangements, etc. Sir Thomas chuckled. Nor did I lose my composure : nothing could further impress me, after the display of flags which had greeted us everywhere.

In Ludwigshafen a two hours' rehearsal had been arranged. Sir Thomas is very considerate and is not a rehearsing-sadist, but when he demands a rehearsal he really needs it. When he had arranged his programme, he had announced that a rehearsal to cover the last three concerts was indispensable, and was not to be put off under any circumstances. Hardly, however, had we arrived at the concert hall of the I.G. Trust, than the Mayor of Ludwigshafen appeared on the scene, and, taking the floor, addressed the exasperated Sir Thomas for at least half an hour. Finally the rehearsal began, and Sir Thomas's irritation was quickly dispelled by his interest in the superb acoustics of the hall. He was told by officials of the organisation that these were due to an especially constructed wooden screen placed behind the Orchestra. Sir Thomas was so impressed that he ordered a screen of similar construction for Covent Garden. The plans were supplied by the directors of the I.G.

In the course of this conversation, one of the technical directors mentioned a new method by means of which music could be recorded on a film. It was a most interesting matter, and Sir Thomas, always open to new ideas, immediately arranged with the inventor for the experiment to be shown to him after the concert.

An enormous audience was drawn from Mannheim and Ludwigshafen, and the concert was a sensational success. Afterwards Sir Thomas went with the chief engineer to the laboratory, and was soon so deeply immersed that it seemed as if the world no longer existed for him.

The I.G. had organised a banquet for six hundred persons in his honour that evening. Time went by and he was still in the laboratory. One of the directors, whom I had known since childhood, came and anxiously reminded me : " Six hundred people are waiting for Sir Thomas, Fräulein Doktor ". But what could I do ?

As I have stated, Sir Thomas had emphatically announced his refusal to attend any more festivities, whereupon I had drawn his attention to the fact that this particular evening with all the famous scientists in attendance would certainly be one of the most interesting experiences of the whole journey. Nothing further had been said about the matter. Throughout the tour Sir Thomas had, up to the present, submitted to everything like a lamb, but if in consequence people imagined that they could, with impunity, go on compelling him against his will they were mistaken. He is the last man in the world to be coerced. Once he has made up his mind he never wastes a word. Baron von G. probably felt uneasy on this point. " Would it not be advisable," he asked me, " if I were to accompany Sir Thomas to Mannheim when he changes, so that people need not wait too long ? " Now it was my turn to feel uneasy. " Certainly," I replied cautiously, " it would be a good plan, but you had better take your own car, as Sir Thomas likes to be alone after a concert." At last, Sir Thomas went to his car—as it was thought—to go to his hotel and change for the banquet. In the car we talked about music only, and I did not skate over the thin ice of the question of his attendance at the banquet. Nor did he.

Arrived at the hotel, I went with him to his suite. He was in very good spirits and said to me : " Now, Doctor, we will have a very comfortable evening. Just let me change, and ask the waiter to come up here." Of course this prospect was delightful, although rather awkward. Not only Baron von G. was waiting downstairs, but also *my* old Mannheim friends with whom I had promised to spend the evening. Diffidently I remarked : " I suppose you know that Baron von G. is waiting to take you to the banquet ". Sir Thomas, however, replied incisively : " Don't worry about that ".

I went downstairs to speak to my friends. Baron von G. saw me and presumably took my presence as a sign that Sir Thomas was soon to appear. I, however, had only informed my friends that I was not able to join them. The A.D.C. had seen me coming downstairs, but I did not want him to see me going up again, so I crept up the service staircase back to Sir Thomas. He had changed in the meantime and looked as though he had just come out of a bandbox. He sat there peacefully and serenely reading his newspaper, the picture of elegance and unconcern. " Here I am," I said, " but what about the man waiting downstairs ? " Sir Thomas took a piece of paper and wrote a few lines. He wrote that with the greatest regret he was not able to attend the dinner this evening, being over-tired by the strain of the last few days, and that he was afraid that if he were not careful he might be unable to finish the tour. It was a masterpiece of politeness, but those who wished could read the implications between the lines.

" Now then," said Sir Thomas, for whom this episode was definitely shelved, " what are we going to have ? " He lost himself in contemplation of the menu and after he had ordered an epicurean feast with champagne, the waiter was at last permitted to give the still waiting A.D.C. his message.

Had Baron von G. possessed the slightest subtlety, he would have realised that it would have paid him to rescue Sir Thomas from the festivities at Stuttgart, and thus the Mannheim fiasco might have been avoided.

The evening with Sir Thomas in the " Hitler Suite " in Mannheim was one of the most amusing I have ever spent, and I told him on this occasion of how in the April of 1933 Furtwängler had also refused to attend a banquet held in his honour in Mannheim and had spent the evening with me—but for more serious reasons, and without champagne and *foie gras* !

The next morning was less amusing. When I came down I was greeted by long faces. The Nazis, steeped as they are in intrigue, always imagine that everybody else is playing some subtle game for their own ends. They never attribute a simple motive to any occurrence : devious themselves, even in small matters, they imagine that everyone else is full of thoughts of complicated revenge. On this occasion they taxed me in the most bitter way with having been the cause of last night's debacle, seeing in it a sequel to the " Furtwängler affair " of 1933 !

In the meantime, Sir Thomas had sent for me. He was smoking his cigar and studying *The Times* with an imperious expression. " Now look here, Doctor," he said, " I have had enough of all this, and I am not going to stand any more. I will not continue the tour by train. Please get me a private car and we will travel very comfortably, and alone." I saw that this was his reaction to all the fuss made by the Nazis and the incessant demands on his time. He was pleased with his artistic success, and was full of admiration for the way in which the organisation of the tour functioned ; everything else he resented with growing irritation. It was useless to debate a decision with him.

We drove on the new *Autobahn* to Frankfurt, where the next concert took place in the famous *Museumsaal*. The concert was sold out and the hall was full of old friends.

Before retiring for the night, Sir Thomas proposed that we should leave early the next day. " I want to have a look at Frankfurt," he said, " and then we shall have lunch somewhere on the Rhine on our way to Cologne." So we started early and drove to the *Roemer*, to the *Dom*, to the *Goethehaus*, and to the *Schirn* in the old town, where the Frankfurt sausages are made. It is a great pleasure to look at things with Sir Thomas. He is neither a dry academician nor a sight-seeing tourist ; he observes things precisely and remembers clearly what attracts him. In this sense his outlook and erudition are highly individual, as he has learnt mostly from experience, not from books alone. Similarly he preferred, as a young man, to go and hear

fine musical performances rather than to acquire his musical knowledge through interminable years in a musical college.

He now looked at his watch. " I would like to see the Cathedral
of Mainz again," he said. " Let us leave for Mainz *now*."

Off we went to Mainz. First we looked at the *Dom* alone, and
then a Catholic priest came and talked to us. It was inevitable that
one should sense in a Catholic church all that the people were suffering
under the new régime, and it was strange, as were many other little
incidents on this tour, to see how a man could relieve his heart once
he was satisfied as to the views of his listeners. We did not introduce the subject of politics, but the priest, without saying much,
conveyed to us the strain through which he and his fellows were
passing.

Sir Thomas astonished me by his exact knowledge of the history
of the Cathedral. He knew that there had been two churches of
different periods. He showed me where the different periods were to
be traced, and looked with loving reverence at the manifold beauty
of the architecture. How lovely was this quiet day, how far away
from the world, from all the fuss and vulgarity of the Nazis. Here,
we were in the midst of that eternal Germany which testified through
her buildings and her beauty to the nobility of spirit which reigned
in former times.

We then drove in the direction of the Rhine, and in a little hidden
village, the name of which I do not recollect, we stopped for lunch.
There was no one in the dining-room of the little inn, which was
surrounded by chestnut trees. Sir Thomas studied the wine card
with great care. He is a connoisseur of hock, and soon a whole
battery of bottles stood before us, all of which he wanted to sample.
I assisted with my weaker powers, and it was really a very amusing
lunch. He was in a happy mood, for he loves anything unusual,
and after the last week under the shadow of Nazi régime, this day
of freedom was indescribably pleasant. But soon the seriousness of
life asserted itself ; to our dismay, we discovered that it was rather
late. A light mist began to rise from the Rhine, and we could
scarcely expect to reach Cologne, where the last concert was to be
held, within the next few hours. We therefore started off at full
speed. The spell of the Rhine valley charmed us. Sir Thomas
seemed taciturn, and I did not disturb his gravely quiet mood.

While we drove through this beautiful country at the approaching close of the German visit, he must indeed have had much to reflect upon.

At last we arrived in Cologne and drove to the huge *Messehalle* (it holds 10,000 persons) where the Orchestra had already assembled.

Besides the Orchestra, there were the inevitable " other people ", and during the rehearsal I was informed that von Ribbentrop had arrived in order to meet Sir Thomas before he left Germany. This evening a reception in the Town Hall awaited the conductor and his Orchestra. Sir Thomas had had no intention of joining the festivities, but I was told that it would be very much appreciated if he changed his decision in order not to offend Herr von Ribbentrop, the host of the tour.

After the rehearsal we returned to the hotel. Here there was such a commotion that one would have thought an army command had taken possession. It seems that a Nazi minister cannot move without a whole staff of A.D.C.s and a number of S.S. for his protection.

When, after the concert, we drove over the Rhine bridge, the town of Cologne was flood-lit in honour of the English guests. The cathedral and the old churches gleamed in a strange magic light. It was an indescribably wonderful sight ! I was deeply moved—this was the lost land of my birth.

In the hotel, however, the charm was soon dispelled. People surrounded us, and Sir Thomas consented to go to the reception on account of Ribbentrop. I went to bed.

Late in the evening somebody knocked at my door. " Doctor," said Sir Thomas's indignant voice, " what do you think ? Herr von Ribbentrop was not there at all. He fell asleep and forgot all about it." On this note of absurd anti-climax the much-talked-of reception had ended !

Sir Thomas then declared : " I have changed my plans. I won't return with the Orchestra to England, but we'll go to Paris. Please make all the necessary arrangements, and we will leave in the morning by the Nord Express."

This we did, and the A.D.C. who appeared with an embarrassed face on account of the Ribbentrop contretemps, drove us to the station. Sir Thomas, however, was all smiles. Everything was now over, and he could afford to relax. And so once again I crossed the frontier of my so strangely changed country.

On this last stage of the journey an amusing incident occurred. Besides their agreed fee, it had been arranged with the Germans that members of the Orchestra were to receive a certain sum in marks every day as pocket money. As the Orchestra had, however, provided for their private expenses before leaving London by buying " travel marks ", the management decided that it was more practical to retain this " pocket money ", and every day a sum was therefore handed out to me to keep. This was becoming an increasingly heavy package, and from Munich onwards I tried hard to place it with a bank in order to avoid having to carry it about ; but with the German currency laws, this was a difficult matter. Anybody taking charge of marks belonging to a non-German resident was liable to the heaviest penalties, while any money put into a bank in the name of a non-German resident was automatically " blocked ", and it was only possible to release it by the most complicated manipulations.

I had no choice but to continue to carry this ever-growing bundle about with me, and to change the notes into bigger ones as the amount grew.

As the tour neared its end, I grew increasingly uneasy over the matter, and trusted that some miracle would occur to solve the problem. It did not, however, and meanwhile there I was, with my marks.

Before leaving Cologne, the last stage of our tour, I had consulted Sir Thomas. " What shall I do," I wailed. " If I leave the marks here they are lost to us, and to take them out of Germany is forbidden under the heaviest penalty." He was just packing his attaché case. " Give the damned parcel to me," he said. " I am fed up with these rotten marks." Calmly he put them on top of his other papers in his case. " But, Sir Thomas," I remonstrated, " you really cannot . . . what about the penalty." One knows that with Sir Thomas nothing is impossible ; but there are limits, and everyone will sympathise with my feelings when he took the marks as if they were a packet of cigarettes.

" What are you talking about ? " he said quite unperturbed,

" nothing will happen, you'll see. Leave the marks to me and don't worry."

As mentioned above, Sir Thomas had decided to travel via Paris, and not to return directly to England with the Orchestra. This change of plan was made late at night before the departure from Germany, arranged for early the next morning. While the frontier had been instructed about the Orchestra, nothing so far had been arranged for Sir Thomas and myself, who were to travel by another route. " My God," I said to myself, " if our luggage is examined, we're certainly done for." I decided to avoid any possible risk, so I hunted up the Ribbentrop A.D.C. and asked for special instructions to be sent to the frontier with regard to Sir Thomas in the Nord Express. The Ribbentrop man, very embarrassed by the fact that his master has been asleep when he should have been entertaining Sir Thomas, promised to do his best.

So we left and sat comfortably in our reserved first-class compartment, the ominous case between us . . . open ! Most people at least hide their treasure ; not so Sir Thomas. His self-esteem is such that he deems it out of the question that any Customs' or other official would really dare to approach his sacred person ! On the top of the open case, quite unconcealed, were the precious marks. He sat there calmly smoking his pipe.

We arrived at Aachen. A very polite Customs' official opened the door. I—in a cold sweat—mumbled : " This is Sir Thomas Beecham who has just been touring Germany with his Orchestra by invitation of the Government." " Oh yes," said the man, " we have been advised." A click of the heels, a deep bow, " Heil Hitler ! ", and out he went. Triumphantly, Sir Thomas looked at me. " You see, Doctor ! " he said, knocking the ash from his pipe, with the familiar movement of his expressive hand. . . . I saw.

One would imagine that with this the story of these marks was at an end. Not at all. As they were not in my charge any more, I can only repeat what I have been told. Nobody in London would change them. Somebody had to take them back into Germany and use them there. It was again Sir Thomas who undertook this. There was a rumour that he spent them all in an incredibly short time. This subsidiary German tour was *not* under my management !

The results of the German tour were in every way satisfactory. No one was converted to Nazism, and all the players were glad to be back in England. On the other hand, they had been very proud to show their art in places where the musical tradition was so old and so famous. Sir Thomas shared this feeling. His sensitive mind recoiled from the vulgar panoply of the tour, but he felt that it had been an artistic success, and this made him happy. It had been an auspicious time for me, and I had been delighted to put my knowledge of the Continent at the service of such a cause.

Shortly after the return of the Orchestra, to England, a musical party was arranged in a big London house for the Orchestra to meet Herr von Ribbentrop. Edward VIII was expected to be present. The party took place without him, however. The crisis leading to his abdication was coming to a head, and it is more than likely that he had more pressing engagements. Many rumours were current at this time, and on this very day it was said that the abdication had become inevitable, as indeed was confirmed on December 10th.

About me, personally, there was much comment, both in Germany and in England. A foreign diplomat rang me up at Covent Garden. "You have had a real triumph," he said. While with Sir Thomas in Germany, this opinion had been expressed by many, but I was far from feeling any elation—quite the contrary. The Nazis had never contested my efficiency; but, having no charge other than my race against me, had tried to malign and humiliate me and to accuse me of lack of national sentiment—their usual pretext. Now, when it suited their purpose, I became again a person of credit.

Shortly after our return, the *Manchester Guardian* published a report of the tour, mentioning that much as the German Ambassador boasted about his responsibility for the enterprise, the successful arrangements for the tour were made by Sir Thomas Beecham's German-Jewish secretary, Dr. Geissmar. I read this with considerable uneasiness. I had never met von Ribbentrop, and have never seen him to this day. Now, fortunately, any encounter between us seems less likely than ever!

Chapter 29

AS SOON as I began working for Sir Thomas and the London Philharmonic Orchestra, I tried to use my old business relations with continental musical centres on their behalf. It was only gradually that I learned how much more difficult it was to achieve this from England. The geographical situation of Great Britain necessitates an expensive journey even before the Continent is reached, and it was difficult to finance ventures which involved a risk, as such international enterprises were bound to do. There was in England, however, more chance of private patronage than on the Continent, and often on a very generous scale, but it was only a very limited group which was prepared to allocate money for cultural purposes.

The then-existing semi-official organisations concerned with the propagation of British culture abroad, seemed to have aims different from those of corresponding institutions in pre-Hitler Germany, Italy, or France. Government support for cultural ends on a big scale did not exist in England. This had at least one advantage : as no one paid the piper, no one could call the tune.

During the time when Sir Thomas was devoting the whole of his time and energy to the musical life of Great Britain, he did not regret this fact, even if it meant an increased burden on his own shoulders. But there is no doubt that many valuable enterprises could have been achieved if the circumstances had been different.

During my first visit to Paris in my new job, I had started negotiations with M. Jacques Rouché regarding a visit of the London Philharmonic Orchestra to Paris. The Paris *Opéra* was only available on Tuesdays or Thursdays. To find a suitable day for Sir Thomas and the London Philharmonic Orchestra between all their booked dates in England was a puzzle, especially as the Royal Philharmonic as well as the Hallé Concerts—both then mainly conducted by Sir Thomas—were taking place on Thursdays. Finally, a date was found for March 1937—but this did not mean that all technical questions had been settled.

Ever since 1927 when, for the first time after the Great War, I arranged a Paris concert for the Berlin Philharmonic Orchestra, I had worked in conjunction with the *Association Française d'Expansion et d'Echange Artistique*. This department of the French Government was under the patronage of the *Ministère des Affaires Étrangères et de l'Instruction Publique et des Beaux Arts*, and was the centre of French cultural propaganda. The offices were in the Palais Royal, and from its windows one could look into the wonderful old courtyard of the famous building. Scarcely any of the officials or ushers had changed since my first visit. The whole organisation seemed incredibly old-fashioned ; but it had a style of its own, and exceedingly clever work was done in these historic surroundings.

In 1936 I went for the first time to the Palais Royal on English business. The official Government department had then been linked with a semi-official society, *Art et Tourisme*, which was to assist the official cultural propaganda in a more private way. This Societé had a corresponding organisation in Great Britain called " Art and Travel ", whose chairman was Lady Austen Chamberlain.

I had scarcely realised how many " committees " on both sides were involved in the plan for the concert of the London Philharmonic Orchestra and Sir Thomas in Paris. It seemed to me that too many people had their fingers in this pie, and so I steered unconcernedly through all these " auxiliary " forces. It seemed unlikely that they could add anything essential to the practical preparations for the concert. The French at that time were most keen on cultural collaboration with England, and this was very fortunate for my purposes. Paris was full of life. There were innumerable cliques and interests. Needless to say, the French were much more subtle than the Nazis : so were the methods which they used to achieve their ends. Everything was done with elegance and dignity. I met many people I had not previously known, as the circles interested in Anglo-French activities were other than those concerned with Franco-German relations.

M. Rouché took me one day to a performance of Gluck's *Alceste* at the Paris *Opéra*. The French had a special way of presenting that kind of opera with their ballet, of which they were so proud. Rouché broached the question as to whether this performance of *Alceste* might be presented at Covent Garden, and I proposed to submit this plan to Sir Thomas. The dramatic soprano of the Paris *Opéra*, Madame Germaine Lubin, was especially suited for parts like *Alceste*. She was a great artist and a beautiful woman.

At the end of a very busy week I returned to London. I found that during my absence a major political crisis had developed with regard to the young King's proposed marriage. I sensed a great tension everywhere. The freedom of Press comment amazed me. I thought that at such critical moments even in a democracy a certain line would be indicated to the Press in order not to confuse public opinion. Yet no such direction was apparent, and I was filled with admiration for the moral strength and independence of a people which could be trusted to form its own opinion about such grave events.

Sir Thomas, who is extremely patriotic, followed the events with great interest ; but he never discussed the situation.

In these days there was much work for us to do, and Sir Thomas hardly ever left the Opera House. He ruled over his theatre with an iron hand, and insisted that everything should be submitted to him. However, he naturally did not like to be disturbed when he was working. For such occasions we had prepared a big signboard " No Admission ", which I hung outside my door with special delight, for thus, undisturbed, we could discuss at length many subjects for which our busy general routine afforded no time. Among other things, I was able to report fully to him my deliberation over the French business, the many committee ladies, and so on. Sir Thomas is generally in a genial mood, and the best way to get on with him is by using one's native wit. But nobody should be deceived by this veneer. He can suddenly switch round to deadly earnest and then—be on your guard !

Such a *volte face* occurred when I discussed the Paris concert. After having listened to me in silence for a considerable time, he suddenly cut in : " Now look here, Doctor, this won't do. The only solution of all this muddle is an official invitation. If I am not invited by the French Government, I will not conduct this wretched concert, and that is that." He was right, as he knew by experience how smooth a Government invitation can make things.

I realised at once that he meant what he said, and that he would throw up the whole Paris project if it could not be arranged as he wished. I, for my part, was very anxious that the concert should take place, and so I replied : " It's all quite simple. The French want this concert. Let me go back to Paris, and I will settle the matter within two days." " All right then," agreed Sir Thomas, " but please understand, I will have no nonsense."

Thus it happened that within a few days I left again for Paris. The journey was rather exciting. I travelled by the ferry night-boat with Madame de Margerie. The whole train was full of well-known people, and everybody discussed the King's impending abdication which seemed to be inevitable. When I arrived in Paris the platform was thronged with newspaper boys waving the special editions announcing the accomplished fact.

I was deeply impressed by these events, but my principal obsession was the object of my Paris visit—the formal Government invitation to Sir Thomas. I went straight to the *Ministère des Beaux Arts* determined to secure it. The Ministry agreed at once to my proposals. The French Government invited Sir Thomas and the London Philharmonic Orchestra over, and were prepared to pay all expenses. Armed with a letter from the French *Ministre de l'Instruction*, I returned to London. Triumphantly I handed Sir Thomas the Minister's personal invitation. " Very good," he said, and wrote a letter to Lady Chamberlain, the chairman of Art and Travel, telling her that he was pleased to inform her that the Paris concert was now settled between himself and the French Government.

Meanwhile, Sir Thomas worked with great intensity on the details of the Coronation Season which, as mentioned above, was to include French, German, and Italian operas. There had already been some preliminary *pourparlers* with prominent French singers ; but France and Great Britain being on such friendly terms, the French had informed me through M. Rouché that they themselves wanted officially to contribute to the festivites by presenting some operas in French. This contribution of the French Government added to the importance of the Coronation Season. The French proposed to give *Ariane et Barbe-Bleue* by Dukas, *Pelléas et Mélisande* by Debussy, and *Alceste* by Gluck. They were particularly keen on presenting *Alceste* in spite of the enormous costs involved in bringing chorus and ballet to London. For a long time they had wanted to

present their ballet at Covent Garden and were all the more eager
to do so on this special occasion. All this was discussed during my
short visit to Paris at the beginning of December, and when I
returned, not only the concert of the London Philharmonic Orchestra
in Paris but also the official contribution of the Paris *Opéra* to the
Coronation Season had been settled.

When I arrived at Boulogne on my return to London on a dreary
foggy evening with a misty rain drizzling down on us, there was a
strange atmosphere prevailing in the port. I asked my porter what
was the matter, and he told me that they were expecting at any
moment the British destroyer carrying the former British king into
exile.

I well remember how agitated English public opinion was in those
days, and how individual opinions clashed. But calm was quickly
restored. The Press behaved with dignity. The new King had come
into office and from that moment everything was at his service.

Life went on, and as far as Covent Garden was concerned, the
preparations for the Coronation Season did not suffer in the slightest
degree by the fact that the king for whom they had been intended
was not to reign.

[1 9 3 7]

Chapter 30

EVER SINCE I had settled in England I had been looking for a
home. This was not so simple in London for one who had no pre-
dilection for the very comfortable but impersonal modern flats. I
was on the look-out everywhere, especially around the Bloomsbury
neighbourhood, near Covent Garden. Here there were many lovely
old houses with beautifully proportioned rooms.

At last my search ended in Red Lion Square, where there were
stately old houses and a fifteenth-century church. Although the
City had almost encroached on the Square, it still retained an old-

fashioned dreaminess, especially on Saturday and Sunday afternoons, when there was not a soul to be seen. Lovely old trees adorned the Square, including a plane tree many hundred years old, in which a multitude of pigeons nested. In winter, the branches were silhouetted against the sky, and in spring it was a delight to watch the young green shoots. One could hardly believe that one was in the heart of London.

I went to live at No. 36, which was an eighteenth-century house. One of the first things the owner told me was that Charles Dickens is said to have lived there for a short time before he moved, as history records, to the house nearby.

I had the two top floors of the house which was otherwise used for business purposes only. The previous tenant had redecorated the rooms with a perfect feeling for the period. Lovely old Georgian panelling extended up the top staircase and to all the rooms. The paintwork was of a mellow ivory, and a small hall led into a large bright room with three windows facing the Square. Here the morning sun flooded in. The long, low-ceilinged room made a charming setting for my old furniture, and was acoustically perfect for our evenings of chamber-music. Next to it was a smaller room, delightfully raftered. On the top floor there was a big studio with two doors leading to a roof garden. Here, again, the proportions were perfect, and the beauty of the studio was enhanced by an authentic Tudor chimney-piece which had been cleverly incorporated by the previous tenant. From the roof garden there was a marvellous London panorama, dominated by St. Paul's.

At the beginning of January, my furniture arrived from Germany. I stood on the roof garden waiting for the van to turn the corner. At last it came, carrying the beloved belongings I had missed so much. We unpacked at once, and all my friends assisted, including some helpers from Covent Garden. At that time, I had no idea how bitterly cold and draughty these old houses could be, but an experienced friend thoughtfully sent round an oil stove. At intervals, while unpacking, we all gathered around this stove, as little chickens gather round the lamp in the incubator.

Soon Sir Thomas arrived to inspect the flat. He loves old English things and greatly admired my furniture, which was mostly Sheraton bought in England by my grandparents. The place appealed to him immensely. "This is really unique," he said, seating himself. Then he proceeded to give me a comprehensive history of Red Lion Square and the famous people who had lived there.

Every morning I took my seven minutes' walk to Covent Garden. Soon I knew every house on the way, and every day I made this journey full of gratitude that " the lines had fallen unto me in pleasant places ".

The old Square is no more. The church was demolished by two direct hits ; only a column or two and a ghastly skeleton is left. No house in the Square remains intact. My own home was hit three times and with the adjoining three houses was first burnt out at the top, and later blasted and razed to the ground. (This happened on May 10, 1941, the date on which the Queen's Hall was also destroyed.) Of all the things rescued from Germany with so much love and care—of all the books, music, furniture, family belongings, nothing remains. What had been my home is now just charred, discoloured bricks.

But to mention this is to jump far ahead. Even if the political commentators of to-day state that the war could have been pro-phecied years ahead, in our sphere there was no indication of this, and work went on undisturbed. Sir Thomas was full of enterprise and swept others along with him.

I was at this time in continuous correspondence with Furtwängler, Tietjen, and Preetorius regarding the coming season. In consequence of Hitler's unexpected decision that Bayreuth should give its third consecutive Festival in the summer of 1937 instead of taking the traditional third yearly rest, Tietjen had to cancel his promised co-operation as producer for the Coronation Season. He had handled this refusal very cleverly, however, and so his friendship with Sir Thomas remained unimpaired. He continued to be very helpful in the matter of releasing his singers for Covent Garden, and made only one condition—that by June 17th they were all to be back in Bayreuth for their rehearsals.

Meanwhile, Sir Thomas had returned from a short visit to the Continent. He had been living for a long time at the Waldorf Hotel, and now finally decided to take a house again. One evening, while we were working at the Opera House, he suddenly said :

" Come with me, and see my new home ". He had found a house in St. John's Wood which was reputed to be the oldest in the neighbourhood. It had a little old-fashioned garden in front, which was protected by a high wall. He had re-engaged Mrs. Olivia Samuelson, his Swedish cook-housekeeper, who had been with him for many years in the past. Mrs. Samuelson cooked marvellously, and always officiated dressed in white like a chef. She looked like a dowagerduchess and attended all Sir Thomas's concerts with great interest. Smith, the inevitable, was, of course, on the scene.

There are those who allege that Smith is as famous as the master after whom he looked for so many years. He certainly belonged to that class of English servant which is dying out. Only a " gentleman " like Sir Thomas could evolve such a factotum as Smith and maintain such an exacting and perfectly balanced relationship for so many years with no hint of friction. Smith was a tall, rosy-faced, blue-eyed Briton. He never fussed or hurried, but moved with quiet dignity about his duties. " Smith ! " called Sir Thomas about a hundred times a day, and " Yes, Sir Thomas ", replied Smith just as often, with an imperturbable face.

Smith had certain qualities which I used to admire. As Sir Thomas never answered the telephone on principle, Smith had to deal with everybody and to know everything. He, however, always assumed an ingenuous lack of information and never showed the slightest ambition to be " in the know ". If one rang up, he gave the impression that one was highly welcome, even when Sir Thomas was heard to say in the background : " What on earth does he want ? I am not in." He treated all telephone callers with a mixture of dignity and intimacy, and with an unvarying politeness whether he was in sympathy with them or not.

If one came for a meal and had to wait for Sir Thomas, Smith made conversation in a dignified way and offered refreshments. When one sat at table with Sir Thomas, Smith behaved with the same dignity as Sir Thomas himself. He was, however, never familiar, never offered a personal opinion on anything, and in spite of all he must have known and heard, he was always impenetrable and invariably non-committal. His inborn diplomacy would have graced a cabinet minister.

Smith was a very clever mediator between Sir Thomas and the

outside world, and last, but not least, between him and his personal collaborators. Sir Thomas was only human, and so it may have been that sometimes in the early morning he was not as serene as usual. One morning I arrived; Smith, on opening the door, put his finger to his lips and crossed his arms. Thus he tried to warn me that Sir Thomas was "cross" and I had better be on my guard. On entering Sir Thomas's room the first thing I did was to tell him this little incident; he could not help laughing, and the clouds were soon dispelled.

In one matter, however, Smith was adamant. He would not be responsible for any scores or other music in the household. The eternal mislaying and retrieving of music filled him with alarm, and he once said to me in heartfelt tones: "All would be well if it were not for this damned music!" Nevertheless, he appreciated the soothing influence of music on his master. Once when receiving a guest (when Sir Thomas again seemed cross) Smith whispered, to him *sotto voce*, "For God's sake give him a piece of music!"

To return to the first time I visited him in his new home; we arrived late and there were no servants about. Sir Thomas never says what he intends to do, and his household adapts itself accordingly, whether he comes alone or with guests. On the sideboard there were always several different cold dishes, which he carved with virtuosity. He considers carving a special art, and I have often heard him discussing at length with Smith alternative methods of carving a certain joint. Although Sir Thomas provides an endless variety of drinks for his guests, he generally contents himself with milk.

Whenever I spent an evening with him, we both tacitly avoided the routine questions of our work and were glad to turn to other subjects. If he is in a good mood, there are few persons who are so stimulating. He may play the piano or pick up at random a favourite volume—Milton, Shakespeare, or Beaumont and Fletcher, and read aloud in his admirably modulated voice.

It had been arranged that Sir Thomas should conduct two new productions of *Orphée* and *Il Seraglio* at the Berlin State Opera about this time. As usual, I went on a few days in advance. Sir Thomas arrived in splendid spirits, and the whole of this Berlin visit is associated in my memory with his holiday mood. We stayed in the Esplanade and were very well looked after. In such a hotel, comparatively little could be sensed of what was going on in Nazi-Germany. The reflected glory of Sir Thomas and the " benevolent " attitude of high quarters had the result that, just as on our German tour, I had no cause for uneasiness. As usual in Germany, the rank and file followed the direction of their superiors like sheep. I accepted the situation, not for private reasons, but on account of my work.

The Berlin State Opera placed its best resources at the disposal of Sir Thomas. The *Orphée* was an interesting production. Preetorius was responsible for the *décor*, and Tietjen was the producer. The singers were the best available. The zeal of the Berlin State Opera to make the performance an artistic success can be gauged by the fact that for the part of Amor they specially engaged Madame Cebotari, who excelled in this rôle, from the Dresden Opera House.

Sir Thomas strode into work within an hour of his arrival, and was passionately interested in the production, the scenery, and last, but not least, the singers, whom he rehearsed most carefully. The days were filled with rehearsals and conferences. Everything else had to be fitted in with these.

Hardly had I arrived when I was asked to see Baron Holthoff, who combined with his other functions that of a kind of master of ceremonies for the State Opera, so far as these ceremonies concerned the social arrangements of Goering, the Chief of the State Opera and then Prussian Prime Minister. The Baron informed me that the *Ministerpräsident*, the " M.P. ", as Goering was then usually called, intended to give a reception for Sir Thomas, and he wished to go with me through the list of those who were to be invited. " Let us begin with the ladies," he said, placing my name at the top. " What ! " I protested, " have you gone mad ? How can I go to a reception of Goering's. Please don't be ludicrous ! " " I beg your pardon," Baron Holthoff replied. " The M.P. especially inquired whether you would accompany Sir Thomas on his journey to Berlin, and has asked me to tell you that he particularly wishes to invite you." " All right," I said resignedly. " Things seem to get more and more crazy, and in this case I will leave the decision to Sir Thomas." The reception took place after the performance of

Il Seraglio. Sir Thomas had decided that I was to go, without any more fuss. To my boundless relief, however, this reception took place without our host, who at the last minute had to leave on a diplomatic mission to Poland . . . *tempi passati* ! There were about fifty people present. Frau Wagner was there, having come specially from Bayreuth with her eldest daughter to attend the performances. She sat at the centre table with Sir Thomas and Tietjen. The singers, who were soon to go to London, were also there and crowded round Sir Thomas. Tietjen lifted his glass to me : " Prost, Geissmar ", he said. I was very moved—but embarrassed and ill at ease all the same.

Finally we left, and in a very dubious state of sobriety arrived back at our hotel in the early hours !

A very original evening was spent with Preetorius and some of the singers at the old and legendary tavern of " Luther und Wegener ". This historical *Weinkeller* in old Berlin, between the Opera and the *Schauspielhaus*, was the original of the first scene of *Contes d'Hoffmann*. It had always been a famous meeting-place of authors, musicians, and actors. E. T. A. Hoffman, among many other celebrities, had been a regular visitor. Having been informed of the identity of the illustrious guest, the old waiter conducted us to the very table at which E. T. A. Hoffman used to sit with his friends, and from which he never left stone-cold sober.

All sorts of old relics and pictures of famous actors who had been habitués of the place were shown to Sir Thomas, who was enraptured by the atmosphere. Once again we revelled until the early hours, and towards the end someone mounted a table and made a speech. I couldn't swear that it was not Sir Thomas.

Another evening Furtwängler came to see Sir Thomas alone, and they had a long conversation about musical and political questions.

All the Berlin performances were a great success. The *Orphée* especially made a deep impression. The State Opera Orchestra loved Sir Thomas, and the singers followed him well. As he had been very pleased with the choreography of the " Orcus " scene, Sir Thomas engaged the *prima ballerina*, Lizzie Maudrick, who had been responsible for it, in order to obtain the same effect in the *Orphée* performance with the Russian ballet at Covent Garden in the coming summer. Sir Thomas's wide and detailed knowledge of Gluck impressed all who came in contact with him to a high degree. Nobody had expected to find behind the mask of the elegant man of the world such expert knowledge.

It was said after the *Orphée* performance that Sir Thomas's conducting was the true experience of the evening, and that his rare dramatic instinct enabled him to achieve a performance at once strong and sensitive, which was neither overloaded by obvious operatic effect nor emasculated by sentimentality. Sir Thomas, as a conductor, was said to be just as strict, dramatic, and unsentimental in his way as was the great Christoph Willibald von Gluck as a composer. The Press extolled him as a born man-of-the-theatre, a first-rate technician, and a pronounced " leader-personality ".

The *Seraglio* was just as great an artistic success. The whole performance was permeated with the spirit of Mozart. The combination of objectivity with temperament, and the firmness of the never-dragging *tempi* were especially admired. One was delighted with the discipline of the performance, with its polish, as of finely tempered steel, and with its extreme grace and flexibility.

The visit was unclouded in every respect. The atmosphere of the only Opera House of the Reich outside Goebbels' orbit was much less stifled than in the theatres depending on the radical and fanatical Minister of Propaganda. The old Prussian State Opera House attendants officiated with the same dignity as they had done under the Hohenzollerns. The staff at the administration was mostly of the old régime. Wherever possible, the artists had remained unchanged. Tietjen himself was of the old school, Preetorius and all the leading spirits were artists of the first rank, and Goering, who held his protecting hand over this institution, was in this instance not such a " good Nazi " as he had been on June 30, 1934.

His Berlin engagement over, Sir Thomas returned to London, while I went on to Dresden on business for Covent Garden. I then returned to England, and on the Flushing boat I met Preetorius and his two assistants. Sir Thomas had especially taken to Preetorius. Although the latter did not know one word of English they had a very amusing way of understanding each other, and Sir Thomas had invited him to come and get acquainted with the Covent Garden stage before the finishing touches were put to his scenery.

In London we were met by Mr. James Smith, one of the directors

of Covent Garden. Jimmie Smith—as he is known by everybody—
was a most generous man, and always ready to help if anything was
needed. It was he who had at first suggested that Preetorius should
be engaged to do the scenery for *Der Fliegende Holländer*, and this
scenery he presented to the Opera House as a gift for the Coronation
Season.

Chapter 31

AT THIS time of the year Covent Garden woke up. Of course the
house was in use all the year round; for the Beecham Sunday
Concerts, shorter Opera Seasons, the Russian Ballet, and so on.
But the climax was the International Opera Season in the early
summer, especially in the year 1937 in view of the approaching
Coronation, when many visitors from all parts of the world were
expected. The management of the Orchestra, the Covent Garden
Estate Company, Sir Thomas Beecham's office, and a small staff of
the Covent Garden Opera Company were permanently housed in
the Opera House. Some time before the Opera Season the permanent
staff was augmented by various collaborators who returned every
year.

The Royal Opera House, Covent Garden, can look back on a
glorious past. What memories of great artistic emotions it holds !
A patina of associations seems to cover the fabric—whether it is the
bare boards and iron rails of the high, old-fashioned gallery, or the
gilt and red plush and cream-painted woodwork, the thin pillars of
the boxes, the awkward staircases, the odd, high, glass-roofed bar
and foyer, and the red curtain bearing the coat of arms of the reigning
King. Then . . . lights down, baton raised, the great curtain
sweeps up, and once again for the hundredth time the tense magic
holds us in its hands.

Covent Garden was always difficult ground for a singer, because
the English public, used to the best, was always particularly exacting
in so far as singers were concerned. In some parts of Italy and France
and in all the larger towns in Germany, the State-supported opera
performs all the year round, the public subscribes for the whole year,

and thus the repertoire can be planned in advance for the whole period. In contrast to this, Covent Garden, dependent on private subsidies, had to cram performances within the short space of two months, May and June. During this time, however, the opera was not only a musical event of the highest order, but also a social one. English society appeared in Town after having spent the winter in the country " hunting and shooting ". Visitors came from all over the British Empire, and diplomats preferred to take their leave at this period. In normal times, boxes were unobtainable a full year before the Season began. For months in advance all restaurants round Covent Garden were booked for the dinner intervals of the performances of the *Ring*; and after the opera people sat till the early hours of the morning in big hotels such as the Savoy, and there met " everybody ". All this has vanished now, probably never to return.

For all that, the true music-lovers were not to be found in the boxes alone. They sat in the lower-priced seats in the upper circle, the amphitheatre, and in the gallery. Leaving the theatre the night before the performance of a favourite opera, one could see a long queue, equipped with stools and sandwiches, waiting to be admitted to the gallery seats the following evening.

It was still a strange experience for me in 1937 to be working in this famous opera house, which functions so differently from those I had known. My office had been installed in Covent Garden for seven months when preparations for the International Season began. Just as I had had to learn my way about the many annexes, corridors, and wings, I had gradually come to know everyone in the house.

SIR THOMAS BEECHAM directed the fortunes of the Opera House, and undoubtedly it was owing to his persistent efforts, his untiring devotion, his personal sacrifices and superb ability that this opera house in the heart of the British Empire could maintain its high level. It is not easy to realise how difficult the financing of an opera season was. Consider, for example, the enormous rent which had to be paid even before a budget could be planned.

Sir Thomas is regarded as a cynic, and likes to appear as such in the eyes of the world. Actually he is exactly the opposite. He is a passionate idealist, and highly sensitive. Under cover of the biting

266

irony of his famous speeches, in which he exposes unsatisfactory
conditions and demands support from the British public in his effort
to promote musical life, he has given to the British nation not only
a fortune but also his heart's blood.

The Coronation Season, of course, received his closest attention,
and he prepared for it with great care. He patiently rehearsed all
operas with the Orchestra alone. During these rehearsals never a
harsh word was heard. Only when a mistake occurred one could
hear him exclaim, " Hey ! " The relationship between Sir Thomas
and his London Philharmonic Orchestra, which played for his opera
seasons, was unique. So much was understood between them that
little needed to be said. About what *was* said, innumerable stories
are told.

When more than one mistake was made at a rehearsal, more than
" Hey ! " was necessary. For instance, at a rehearsal one day, an
unfortunate player missed his cue several times. With ominous
politeness Sir Thomas put down his baton.

" Mr. So-and-so," he said with the greatest urbanity, " we cannot
expect you to follow *all* the time, of course, but perhaps you would
kindly keep in touch with us occasionally ! "

If Sir Thomas was obliged to be exacting at a rehearsal, he never
missed an opportunity to refresh the Orchestra with a remark in
lighter vein before the close of the session. One day the rehearsal
had been long and strenuous ; the Orchestra and Sir Thomas had
worked indefatigably at some great passage of Wagner. At last,
Sir Thomas took out his watch.

" My God ! " he said, " we have been playing for two solid hours,
and we're playing this bloody tune still ! "

Occasionally a contretemps would arise, in the solving of which
the Orchestra would take a hand. For instance, one of the *répétiteurs*
was supposed to play the organ in *Lohengrin*. When his moment
came, he was either absent or missed his cue. After this had happened
several times, Sir Thomas shouted : " Throw him out ". The
répétiteur disappeared and was never seen again. Sir Thomas then
turned to the Orchestra. " Gentlemen," he said, " what are we
going to do now ? Can any one of you play the organ ? " " Bill
can," replied the Orchestra in unison, and amid great acclamations
Bill Coleman, normally a trombone player, took his place at the

267

organ. When war came and we had to leave Covent Garden, Sir Thomas entrusted the electronic organ, which was his personal property, to Mr. Coleman, who retains it to this day.

When the general rehearsals started, things naturally became a little more hectic. One day in particular, at the dress rehearsal of *Götterdämmerung* everything went wrong on the stage. The scenery was not ready. The lighting was not correct. The Siegfried had refused to come to the rehearsal on some pretext. Sir Thomas walked about on the stage, roaring like a caged lion. The atmosphere was at white heat. The Orchestra, in their pit, sensed the tension, and relieved the situation by striking up " The Blue Danube " !

Sir Thomas, ever at one with his orchestra, responded at once, and rushed down to the pit. Taking up his baton he conducted " The Blue Danube " at full Wagnerian strength, tubas included. The stage was nonplussed for the moment. The German prompter, making for his box, was heard to mutter : " In Dresden, this would be absolutely impossible."

During the preliminary orchestral rehearsals the music, scores, and parts were held in readiness, and many amusing conversations occurred between Sir Thomas and the elderly librarian, Mr. John Primrose, father of the well-known viola player, William Primrose. Mr. Primrose was a Scot, and one of the few people who could always speak his mind to the rather awe-inspiring Sir Thomas. When Primrose made jokes in his soft Scotch accent, he was irresistible. Sir Thomas had a fund of original names for this old character, who at rehearsals used to sit, silent and attentive, in the background. He was, on occasion, either " Mr. Daffodil " or " The Wild Caledonian ". After a particularly good rehearsal one day, Sir Thomas is said to have commanded Primrose to kneel down, and " knighted " him with his baton. From this time he always liked to be called " Sir John ".

The librarian had his perplexing moments, particularly when receiving requests for the loan of Sir Thomas's scores, which were especially sought after by conductors. One day he was approached by a lady who wanted to borrow a valuable score. Primrose demurred, but the lady assured him that Sir Thomas " wouldn't mind ".

When the librarian told Sir Thomas of the request, he said : " Mr.

Primrose ! You're not to lend my score to Moses, Tubal Cain, the Queen of Sheba, or God Almighty !"

At this preparatory stage scenery was erected and lighting tested. It seemed natural that all departmental activity should be centralised in Sir Thomas. He had to see to everything : how the dragon in the *Ring* was to appear without arousing laughter, how a lighting problem had to be solved, or when the cost of a new production was estimated. As director, of course, he had the last word, but beyond this he had established a natural and undisputed authority over the whole house—an authority coveted in vain by certain other people in the theatre. He was literally a dictator, but a very charming and fascinating one.

PERCY HEMING was assistant artistic director of that Season. He had been connected with Sir Thomas since 1915 when he joined his company, the Beecham Opera Company, at the Shaftesbury Theatre.

He is, by the way, a direct descendant of the John Heming, who was a fellow-actor of Shakespeare's and part editor of the *First Folio*.

Percy, as everybody called him, was always cheerful, and always ready to give help wherever it was necessary. His experience as singer, actor, and producer, from grand opera to music hall in the provinces, gave him a wide knowledge of "both sides of the curtain".

Percy had the special gift of being a "good mixer". He behaved in the same way with the foreign celebrities, producers, or singers, as with the stage hands from the Opera House, and he was equally at home lunching with some of the stars at the Savoy, or at the "Nag's Head" opposite the stage door of Covent Garden, where the stage hands used to assemble. Between these two hostelries every problem of the theatre was discussed, and when Percy on the following morning picked up the "Guv'nor" at St. John's Wood and drove him in his car down to the Opera House, he was able to discuss many details, thus saving much time during the day.

The Stage Director, CHARLES MOOR, who was a Scotsman, had worked at Covent Garden for twenty years. He had been trained as a musician in Leipzig and Vienna, and had had ten years of experience as a conductor before he took up opera production. Early association with Bayreuth, where he was one of the musical assistants, brought him in close contact with Cosima Wagner and the great conductors of the early century. His command of languages greatly assisted his work, which took him to all parts of the world, but he always came back to Covent Garden. He knew this old theatre like the palm of his hand, he knew its shortcomings, and was familiar with its gradual innovations. He knew his collaborators thoroughly too. In fact, he had trained many of them for their special duties—artists, chorus, stage hands, electricians, and flymen. He called the stage staff by their Christian names, and they behaved like one large family. Moor was responsible for most of the performances, and nobody could override him ; every visiting producer was helplessly at his mercy. He held the secrets of the stage. During the Season, he slept in the Opera House on a divan, as he preferred to be always on the spot and to supervise the scene-shifting at night. He appeared where he was least expected, and his flying white overall was not always welcome. There were famous singers who suffered agonies of fear, believing he disliked them. Moor had, of course, his eccentricities. If a singer refused to rehearse because the stage was said to be dusty, or on some similar pretext, he could be really unpleasant ; and he held no brief for singers' wives who arrived with scarves for their husbands or to inspire encouragement from the wings. Kleinchen Melchior, however, the wife of the famous tenor, was notorious for her refusal to submit to any stage discipline, and always cunningly frustrated any order of Moor's. (I record among the first impressions during my work at Bayreuth in 1931 that at the dress rehearsal for *Tristan* she suddenly appeared quite placidly on the stage—strictly against regulations—dressed in the height of Paris fashion, topped by a completely crazy hat, such as only she could wear !) In the disputes regarding admission to the stage Moor fought relentlessly, blindly supported by the firemen, who usually refused admission to the wrong people. Moor and I cooperated perfectly. He was very experienced, and both of us, knowing how much Sir Thomas had to get through during a season, tried to assist him as much as possible. Sir Thomas had complete confidence in him, and when Moor wanted an interview he was given immediate audience.

Although the time-table was worked out well in advance, the call sheet was only completed at the last minute. Sometimes an American boat was delayed, a singer's leave was postponed, or an unforeseen rehearsal became necessary. Conductors always wanted a great many rehearsals, the singers, however, especially the famous ones, wanted large fees and few rehearsals. No wonder that sometimes we were at a loss, and gathered round Sir Thomas awaiting a judgement of Solomon. On such occasions he used to sit at his desk in his grey linen coat. "Now, let me see," he would say, adjusting his glasses. "Why not do it in this way?" His solution generally proved to be "the one and only one". Nobody appreciated this quality of his more than Furtwängler who, once on such an occasion, admiringly said: "The ease with which Beecham always finds a way out is incredible".

Moor ably assisted Sir Thomas in these manipulations and between them they solved the most intricate problems in a harmonious way.

I had always maintained that in comparison with opera houses on the Continent, there was very little gossiping in Covent Garden. When, however, rumours spread through the house, they stopped short at Sir Thomas's door. Moor was certainly great at straightening out difficulties before they reached his chief. He often telephoned me at eight a.m. about some imminent mishap which he wanted my co-operation to prevent.

HAROLD BARRETT was stage manager and Moor's right-hand man. He was called Harold by everyone, and was a real child of the theatre. As a small boy he took the rôle of the baby in a performance of *Butterfly* with Emmy Destinn and Caruso. He possesses a watch presented to him in 1910 by Destinn which he highly treasures and which is still in working order. He started his work with Sir Thomas when he was the " rabbit " in Sir Thomas's production of *The Golden Land of Fairy Tales* in the scene *Puss in Boots* in the Aldwych Theatre, in 1912.

Harold was a small dark fellow, a very quaint type, who constantly pottered about the house and kept his people in order. He had manifold duties, among the most difficult of which were the compilation and confirmation of the call-sheets. He had to know every person in the house, and where to find everyone day and night. He was charged with maintaining peace in the theatre, and when rumours cropped up he had to be in a position to confirm or deny them with authority. He was indefatigable and always in good spirits. Very proudly he tells you that Sir Thomas once said to him : " My boy, you are a pillar of the theatre ", which he took as a cue to ask for a rise in salary. He never lost his good humour, and his Cockney dialect was marvellous—if you understood it.

FRANK BALLARD was stage machinist, and BILL MITCHELL his assistant. Ballard was an elderly man and he, too, was part of the house and knew the ropes. He was in charge of the technical side of the stage. He was taciturn, and his reign over the stage was unchallenged. It was he who decided the earliest possible moment at which rehearsals could begin after a performance of *Götterdämmerung*. One had to be on good terms with him. He was a very conscientious man, and if he was asked whether the stage could be ready at a certain time he invariably replied : " I don't think so ", or " I couldn't promise it ". Actually nothing was ever impossible for him, and Sir Thomas knew he could rely on him in any of the unexpected situations that are unavoidable in theatrical life.

His assistant MITCHELL was a very reliable and gifted stage-hand who had worked his way up from property-man and was an excellent draughtsman. Nothing was too much trouble for him, even if it kept him up the whole night. The same applies to JACK CROXFORD, the chief electrician, and his assistant SIDNEY CHENEY, who had grown up in the place. One needed such enthusiasts in Covent Garden, and Sir Thomas had a knack of gathering them around him.

In the paint-room upstairs was to be found Mr. LYNHAM, with his assistants, mixing colours in dozens of Woolworth chamber-pots. Mr. Lynham was a true Dickensian figure. He looked rather like an Italian with his dark skin, black eyes, and a mass of black hair. He was always splashed with paint, especially his face, and under his chin where his hand used to rest, there was a many-coloured stain. He knew much more about the painting of scenery than the man nominally responsible for it, whose instructions he often ignored. If Lynham thought that he had a better idea for the execution of the scenery than that indicated to him, he quickly got into touch with Moor. If Moor agreed, Sir Thomas was besieged : "'E knows," Lynham used to say, "I want to speak to 'Im". Sir Thomas then came to look at the great canvas, Lynham standing next to it, stained from head to toe, but very sure of himself. Sir Thomas took things in at a glance and used to say briefly : "Very good" or "I quite agree". Whereupon a triumphant Lynham eagerly resumed his work and the head of the department was faced with a *fait accompli* when he returned. Sir Thomas appreciated the veiled tactics of the paint-room but diplomatically ignored them. His verdict, at any rate, was frequently given in favour of suggestions submitted to him in the manner described.

In 1934–35 the *Ring* and *Parsifal* were presented in new *décors*. Some of the *Ring* costumes, especially those of the Valkyries, were, I thought, appalling, while the flower maidens in *Parsifal* seemed more like tumbling autumn leaves than spring flowers. Some of the scenery, too, left much to be desired, though things were gradually improved where it was possible. The end of *Götterdämmerung* was horrible, the *Halle der Gibichungen* crashed in such a way as to resemble a slow-motion film. Considerable argument arose over the rock in the first act of *Rheingold*. Many were the protests it engendered. Its height prevented the gallery-ites from seeing either the summit or the gold, and Alberich from regaining breath after clambering up to his treasure. He usually attained it with his tongue hanging out of his mouth, while the rock shook dangerously as he climbed. Sir Thomas had been aware of this deficiency for some time, and suddenly decided at a rehearsal—at which the scenic artist was not present—to have the rock lowered by about one-third. This innovation was carried out with great enthusiasm. A few days later, as I was crossing the stage with the designer, he caught sight of his rock at the new level and straightaway broke into loud lamentations, reminiscent of the Rhinemaidens wailing "Rheingold, Rheingold". "What has happened to my rock?" he quavered. As, however, the alteration had been made on Sir Thomas's authority, he was sensible enough to accept the inevitable.

MISS NEWBERY, the very capable wardrobe supervisor, knew her business from "A to Z". She had a dignified appearance, with a great deal of poise. Once she and I together dressed an actress. In the famous performance of the *Rosenkavalier* on May 4, 1938, when Lotte Lehmann collapsed on the stage, the performance could only continue because Hilde Konetzni was in the audience and agreed to act as a substitute immediately. The public was asked to have a little patience. I went back-stage at once to look after Lotte Lehmann and then went to Konetzni's room. She was, of course, much plumper than Lotte Lehmann, and when I entered her room she was just being " sewn " into her costume ; but there was still a large expanse of her back uncovered. I happened to be wearing a long black velvet cape over my evening dress and Miss Newbery suggested : " If you would not mind, Doctor, I think your cape will be just the thing ". We draped it down Hilde's back, and she walked on to the stage, an imposing Marschallin.

Some singers came regularly every Season, and since the dressers remained the same for many years, unwritten laws came into being in the legendary dressing-rooms of Covent Garden, which were honoured by everyone. Melchior, a great favourite with Londoners, had his special foibles, and it was out of the question for him to have any dresser but his beloved " Bill ". Melchior's room was always the scene of all sorts of events. When he was not on, he sat there comfortably, scantily clad, drinking pints of grape-fruit juice, and expecting his friends to keep him company. Meanwhile Kleinchen, his wife, caught up with her correspondence or dealt with her finances with her London banker, who was a great opera enthusiast, and was always in the Opera House when Melchior sang ; or she wrote dozens of autographs for her husband, an accomplishment she had mastered to a high degree. It was always pleasant and peaceful in the Melchiors' company—as long as nothing untoward happened.

This applied also to the professional side of things. It is said of Melchior that at the beginning of the first act of *Tristan* he never remained on board the ship, but after his first scene used to slink back to his dressing-room and have another pint or two of grape-fruit juice, returning to the ship in time for his second scene. Owing to the reconstruction of the ship, it had become impossible to do this unnoticed by some part of the audience. Melchior demurred, and

wanted to wade through the ocean ; but when Sir Thomas told
him that he wished him to remain aboard, he said, or so the story
goes, that he could not refuse Sir Thomas's wish, but for his
" sacrifice" demanded a bottle of champagne for every *Tristan*
performance. Sir Thomas is reported to have faithfully honoured
this not strictly legal but otherwise binding agreement.

The Kurwenal to his Tristan, Herbert Janssen, is probably the
most moving interpreter of Amfortas in the world. But during the
endless intervals between his appearances in *Parsifal* he has to be
amused, so as to relax from the strain of his rôle. It is difficult to
reconcile the monumental and tragic Amfortas with the placid
Janssen, serenely sitting over his crossword puzzle, cracking jokes
with his dresser Horace, who was a genius in producing tea and the
innumerable sandwiches Janssen used to have during his intervals,
or enjoying a congenial chat, while his wife sat by quietly knitting
or reading.

Covent Garden has always been politically neutral. But as events
moved on many singers came to us who had left Nazi-Germany.
On the other hand, there were some who—at home at any rate—
were rabid Nazis. And yet these ardent Hitlerites were quick to
switch round when they noticed that things in England did not
work as in Hitler-Germany. All of them wanted to be invited to
London for the Season.

After Hitler came to power Covent Garden was one of the few
Opera Houses where old friends of long-standing from Berlin and
Bayreuth could still meet. Sometimes some skirmishing took place
in the men's dressing-rooms, quite harmless as a rule, and many
memories of old times spent together were revived. There were all
shades of political opinions, but only very few visitors were ever
really unpleasant. Sir Thomas, although well-informed of everything, never seemed to notice any diversity of opinion. He was
only concerned with the voices, not with the political opinions of
his singers. Usually all went well. Only on one occasion there was
a " diplomatic incident ". One of the few really troublesome visitors
had been accommodated in the same dressing-room as a singer who
had emigrated from Germany, and who had formerly sung in the
same opera house. This fact created great excitement, and somebody
rushed up breathlessly to my office asking me to approach Sir Thomas

to get these two separated. I refused, saying : " Sir Thomas is on the stage rehearsing. I would be ashamed to bother him with such a matter. To him all guests in his theatre are equal. This is most disgraceful behaviour. Political differences exist all over the world without causing such disturbances." I did not mention the affair to Sir Thomas and quiet reigned back-stage. It was not the *émigré*, but the singer domiciled in Germany who had made a nuisance of himself, believing he could use the same methods in London with which he terrorised his opera house at home. It is significant of the authority Sir Thomas enjoyed, that this dispute could be settled with him in the background and in complete ignorance of it.

The legendary Stage-Door-keeper JACKSON was one of the most important persons in Covent Garden. He was a gentleman in the true sense of the word. Many were the celebrated artists he saw come and go during his long régime. Everybody spoke to him in their own tongue, although Jackson invariably replied in English. He was in charge of the artists' mail, knew everyone, and remembered every name. Jackson was not only interested in his stage-door, but took deep interest in the artistic aspect of the Opera House. Immediately after a performance he made up his mind if it had been good or bad.

Sometimes it fell to Jackson's lot to regulate matters outside the hallowed walls of the Opera House. The gallery queues used to attract all sorts of itinerant musicians and entertainers to Floral Street where they displayed their art to the patient onlookers. Sir Thomas's windows were directly above, and often a hurdy-gurdy or public acclamations made too much noise. On these occasions it was Jackson whose assistance was sought. His tact in dealing with such matters was infallible, and within a short time no more untoward sounds would be heard, while the queuers were in no way offended by the interference.

He guarded the House inexorably and was relentless on questions of admission. With unerring instinct he distinguished between friend and foe, and was renowned for his way of treating the Yellow Press, with its nose for scandal. He is said once to have unceremoniously deposited an over-enthusiastic reporter in the street with no uncertain force, after having refused a very considerable sum of money for permission to photograph a fainting prima donna. Jackson was connected to my room by a direct telephone line, as nobody was allowed up to Sir Thomas's quarters without having been announced. He also informed me when Sir Thomas was seen to approach. "Sir Thomas has just come in, Doctor. I believe he is coming up."

I used to say that Sir Thomas's arrival could be sensed in the whole House at once. Sometimes, however, he slipped in through a side-door and appeared quite unexpectedly. On leaving, too, especially if he suspected that people were lying in wait for him, he preferred to avoid the stage-door, and disappeared mysteriously through one of the other exits. As a rule he liked to vanish suddenly. At work he used to speak to me through the open door from his room. In the middle of such a conversation, he sometimes vanished through his library, and whilst I waited respectfully for him to return he had quietly stolen away. Because of this Jackson was often hard put to it, and the question, "Where is Sir Thomas?" was frequently heard from this veritable Angel Gabriel at the gate of the Covent Garden paradise. But Jackson was first and foremost an Englishman. In 1938, when Mr. Chamberlain went to Berchtesgaden to see Hitler he whispered to me as I was leaving the Opera House that night : "Doctor, I don't like our Prime Minister going to see *that* man ".

Mr. C. A. BARRAND was the oldest official in the House, its business manager and head of the box-office. He started in Covent Garden thirty-five years ago as box-office assistant. He and Mr. REYNOLDS (who died in 1941 and who was responsible for the finances) managed the business affairs of the Opera House and the different companies housed there. Their sphere of activity and power was indefinite and varied with the situation.

As private secretary to Sir Thomas I had my office upstairs, as I have said, in communication with his rooms. It was my duty during the Opera Season, when no concerts took place, to assist him in every way, to receive visitors, to have details of everything at hand, to keep all important files of their copies, to know the artists' movements, their dates of arrival and departure, and to keep the opera programmes and rehearsal sheets in readiness. On my wall were pinned programmes of Covent Garden and of the important continental Opera Houses, which I had had sent to me so that in an emergency we could know where to get hold of a singer.

Having no permanent opera in London, the cast was not easily assembled, nor was a substitute readily found. People naturally demanded international artists at an International Season, and so it was often a hazardous thing to have no understudy for a special part. If a star fell ill, we were at a loss. The following story illustrates the difficulties and the necessity for rapid action.

Richard Tauber had achieved his long-standing ambition and had been engaged at Covent Garden for *Il Seraglio* and *Don Giovanni* (1938). One evening, just before the first performance of *Elektra*, which Sir Thomas was to conduct, I returned to my office and there found Frau Tauber, a red-haired and most elegant tornado, steaming fury at Sir Thomas. She reported that her husband's vocal chords were inflamed, and declared emphatically that on no account would she permit him to sing the next evening. Now I considered myself an adept at dealing with the turbulent wives of tenors and so was Sir Thomas, but there was no pacifying this one, and Sir Thomas instantly saw that he had to change his plans. On the point of leaving for a very difficult performance, he was compelled to issue his instructions quickly. So he commanded : " Doctor, either you get me another tenor for to-morrow night's *Il Seraglio* or you will try to get the whole *Rosenkavalier* cast from Berlin for to-morrow night instead of the day after. I can't be bothered with anything now. I have to conduct *Elektra*. After the performance I expect your full report." Saying this, he disappeared. I flew to the telephone and attempted at once to find a tenor. Rosswänge from Berlin was not available, so I called Munich in an attempt to get Patzak. The Munich State Opera informed me that he was free, but that he usually spent this time of the day at Tegernsee. I had to abandon hope of Patzak, for when I rang Tegernsee I was told he was on the lake. When the quest for the tenor proved hopeless, I called the Berlin State Opera to find out about the *Rosenkavalier* cast. The State Opera was very obliging and Frau Lemnitz, the leading soprano, was—thank heaven !—available, so I rang her. One realises in such moments how dependent one is on the goodwill of singers. She told me she was willing to come and bring the others with her, if they could find accommodation in the seven a.m. Lufthansa air-liner.

It was arranged that she would try, and would ring me back at two a.m. at my home.

Sir Thomas then appeared, stimulated by the performance of *Elektra*. He took my report, and immediately offered me a glass of champagne to fortify me. In the middle of the night, Lemnitz rang. All was arranged, they would all come together, having secured seats in the air-liner, through the goodwill of other passengers who had sacrificed their places for the sake of Covent Garden.

Such was life in the Opera House during the Season, and Sir Thomas was present almost day and night. Grave and gay went hand in hand, but everybody was heart and soul in the work. For many of the staff their whole professional life was concentrated every year in these few months of work at the Opera House.

Sir Thomas reigned over the whole, inspiring everybody, always energetic, hardly ever ruffled. He always saw the humorous side, but was adamant in serious matters, and everybody knew it. We were a happy working community, full of pride and enthusiasm for our work.

Chapter 32

BY THE middle of March I was again on my way to Paris in order to assist with the final arrangements for the concert of the London Philharmonic Orchestra with Sir Thomas, fixed for March 16th at *l'Opéra*.

I had been familiar with the ritual of gala performances at *l'Opéra Nationale* since 1928 when I had arranged the first visit of the Berlin Philharmonic Orchestra with Furtwängler, but this English gala concert had a different atmosphere from the German concerts. A different stratum of society was interested. The peculiar reserve of the English, which shows itself in every aspect of life, struck me again in my dealings with the British Embassy in Paris. While, in fact, every support was assured to me, the discussion of this matter took place in a more aloof atmosphere than I had been used to at the German Embassy. Naturally I do not mean the repugnantly aggressive Nazi-Germans ; but, for instance, the Embassy presided

over by the former German Ambassador, von Hoesch. With him
music was an *affaire-de-cœur*, and his whole staff took the warmest
interest. The success of the Berlin Philharmonic and Furtwängler
in Paris, and to some extent even in London, was doubtlessly due
in the first place to their great art, but also to the warm and efficient
support of von Hoesch, who was wise enough to enlist the sympathy
of those who were ready to encourage music and musicians from
abroad.

The English took comparatively few steps to display their achievements in other countries. Having a higher general standard of living
than other nations, they seemed in some ways too complacent.
Thus certain cultural matters which, abroad—before the rise of
Fascism—would have been considered essential and of paramount
importance, were here seemingly of no value and in apparent danger
of being handled merely socially. It was the outlook of those who
feel independent and secure, but one which is so dispassionate as to
seem almost indifferent.

At all events, it is certain that the official British attitude towards
such an event as this visit of the London Philharmonic Orchestra to
Paris was very different from that to which I had been accustomed,
and I felt it acutely. With a fervour equalling the importance of the
occasion, I did my very best to prepare for the concert to the last
detail.

Sir Thomas arrived in Paris, and in place of the pompousness of
the Nazis, was greeted with the fine elegance and gracious courtesy
of the French ; no flags, no swastikas, no speeches ! He responded
in the same dignified manner with which he had submitted to the
loud Nazi demonstrations. An habitué at the Ritz Hotel, he was
treated by the staff, his valet, and his *garçon* with that confidential
yet distant intimacy which is a special French quality.

On the evening of the concert, the Paris *Opéra* presented itself
in all its splendour. Members of the *Guarde Republicaine* with their
picturesque uniforms stood on each step of the famous staircase.
The whole French Government, headed by President Lebrun, was
present, and the house was filled with an audience from a world
which has ceased to exist. Representatives from all the official
Government departments and the *Corps diplomatique* attended the
performance.

It had not been easy to design the programme. At such a concert, which is a political as well as an artistic affair, many points of view have to be considered. The concert opened with " *La Marseillaise* " and " God Save the King ". The programme was as follows :

Haydn	.	.	Symphony D major No. 93
Elgar	.	.	Enigma Variations
Handel-Beecham	.	Ballet Suite : The Gods Go a-Begging
Delius	.	.	Summer-Night on the River
Berners	.	.	Fugue in C Minor
Berlioz	.	.	Overture : Le Carneval Romain.

Paris lavished frantic applause on the artists. By a tragic coincidence the news of the death of Sir Austen Chamberlain, the spiritual father of Anglo-French cultural activities " *se glissa dans la salle au commencement du concert* " as somebody wrote. During the interval, Sir Thomas was invited to the box of President Lebrun, who, in the presence of the British Ambassador, Sir George Clerk, decorated him with the Cravate de la Légion d'Honneur. This was perhaps only a gesture, but it was performed at a time when a gesture still meant something.

Besides this political element, the concert was artistically very successful. Paris had always enjoyed visits of world-famous orchestras. The Berlin Philharmonic Orchestra came every year, and so did the *Concertgebouw* Orchestra from Amsterdam. The New York Philharmonic Orchestra and the Vienna Philharmonic had also given concerts in Paris. With regard to the London Philharmonic Orchestra, it was unanimously declared that the British Orchestra at least equalled these other orchestras of much longer standing. There were even voices which preferred the London Philharmonic Orchestra to the orchestras from " *outre-Rhin* ". The wind section created a deserved sensation in the country where the finest wind-players are to be found, and the *bois miraculeuses* were mentioned as being both rich and delicate. People admired the fine unobtrusive musicality of the Orchestra, the deft way in which everything was played, and the great and natural exactitude. Sir Thomas was understood and acclaimed for his musical sincerity. The subtlety of the feelings and of his directions, as well as 'the naturalness of his interpretation were greatly admired. It was noted with what little apparent effort he obtained magnificent results from the Orchestra, and how close was his affinity with each of the different works he conducted. As one writer put it, " *Il devient plus Italien que Toscanini, plus trépidant, plus frémissant qu'un danseur de tarantelle*". It was in every way a stimulating experience.

Meanwhile in London, the big private houses, Embassies, and Government departments all prepared to entertain in the Coronation Season. Many guests from all over the world were expected, and brilliant social and artistic gatherings followed each other ceaselessly during Coronation time, and did not lessen until the summer was over.

On April 1st, the Royal Philharmonic Society gave its Coronation Concert under the patronage of the late Duke of Kent. The London Philharmonic Orchestra played, and Sir Thomas conducted.

One of the most hospitable houses in London was Kent House, the home of Sir Saxton and Lady Noble. The house, with its big concert-room, was famous for its jade and Chinese art collection, and the opening reception of the French and Chinese Exhibitions had been held there.

One afternoon we were invited to Kent House for " one hour of poetry and music " which had been arranged under the patronage of the French Ambassador in conjunction with some prominent English people. This was in memory of the Comtesse Anna de Noailles. A select circle had assembled. The Princesses Marie Louise and Helena Victoria sat in the front row. I sat in the background and discussed with the brilliant Roland de Margerie my impressions of our Paris concert.

It was about this time that I spent a memorable evening at Kent House. I met Princess Marie Louise at dinner with Lady Noble. I felt it was a great privilege to meet a granddaughter of Queen Victoria. The Princess had known many great people, and as there were only three of us present she was able to tell us of things belonging to the past. She had known Cosima Wagner and Hans von Bülow : she talked about the Sunday lunches with the old Kaiser Wilhelm ; she had known the Kaiserin Friedrich, who was her aunt and eldest sister of her mother. And she had known Bismarck.

The Princess loved music and Covent Garden, and had her definite views about operas, conductors, and singers. She was a great Wagner enthusiast, and told me that her love for Wagner's music dated from the time when with Cosima she went to the rehearsals on the *Festspielhügel*. She attended the performances of the Covent Garden Season whenever she could, and at Wagner operas sat with her sister, Princess Helena Victoria, in the stalls, which they preferred because they found the acoustics there to be better than in the Royal box. Her true appreciation of music and her great human understanding have warmed the hearts of many of the international artists who came to England.

Shortly afterwards there was a very small dinner-party at Lady Noble's, where Princess Marie Louise and Princess Helena Victoria were present. The chief topic was the coming Coronation. Even as a child I had venerated our old Grand-Duke Friedrich von Baden, and was brought up in the days when the State was represented by a monarch. "The whole symbolism of the Coronation moves me deeply," I said, "and I shall go to the cinema to see the whole cere-mony." "But why have you to go to the cinema?" asked Princess Marie Louise. "Why do you not go to your Ambassador?"

How could I explain to her that "my Ambassador" would never invite me? The complications arising from Nazism are difficult enough to explain to foreigners, let alone to royalties. So I said simply: "My Ambassador is certainly the last man in London to invite me to see the Coronation". Whereupon I was promptly told: "Then *we* shall invite you". I remember to this day how the blood rushed to my cheeks, so embarrassed was I. I had taken part in the conversation without any such thought.

The Princesses kept their promise. A few days later I received an enormous envelope with an invitation marked, "Guest of the Princesses", directions how to reach my seat, a brown label for my car, and so on. I was deeply touched by this kind gesture and the Coronation Day with its symbolical display of the might of the British Empire was an unforgettable experience to me.

Meanwhile, the Covent Garden Season approached. It was to open with a performance of *Otello* on April 19th. Singers appeared from all over the world. The Berlin State Opera took their participa-tion in the Season so seriously that in the spring they put on the whole of the *Ring* under Furtwängler's direction with the London cast. This served as a rehearsal for Covent Garden.

In the last week before the beginning of the Season, the Opera

House began to be like a dove-cot or perhaps more like a Tower of Babel. All kinds of languages were heard. A Press reception took place at which we all did the honours of the House, and at which artists who had already arrived participated. Covent Garden had a charming and informal way of managing such functions.

It must be understood that the Covent Garden Season was a true London occasion and the glamour and excitement of it extended to all the streets of the district, right down to the Strand, making a strange contrast with the cabbage stalls, stray potatoes, and the smell of vegetables lingering on from the early market. The always-to-be-admired London police were in control of all approaches, directing the endless stream of cars which drew up in the famous covered way under the portico. They ceremoniously took care of arriving pedestrians, and I had a special friend in the bobby at the corner of Bow Street and Floral Street, who came to know me, and would smilingly hold up even the most pretentious and impatient traffic to let me go through in time to carry out my last-minute duties before the curtain rose.

The opening night of the Covent Garden Season was a unique occasion like no other social function as regards the display of dresses and jewellery. It was a curious mixture of private elegance and public excitement. The National Anthem, played with *élan* and conducted with especial pride by Sir Thomas, rolled its chords round the great Opera House before the overture started, and brought the whole house to its feet before the lights faded out.

At the entrance flashlights exploded on every side, photographing the new arrivals. If one was in doubt as to the degree of celebrity which any particular person enjoyed (or was ambitious to possess), one had only to watch the Press photographers leaping like huntsmen on the prey they valued—or disdainfully failing to notice the attempts of some eager parvenues to manœuvre themselves into the centre of the picture.

The richly uniformed porters at the main entrance were men of quite formidable authority. They had a stern ritual for ensuring that the desire of departing members of the audience to linger on the steps in conversation did not hold up the traffic. If one of the first peers of the realm lingered more than a moment over his adieux, a stentorian voice would ring out with the accusing words : " The

Duke of Blankshire's car stops the way ", a cry which would quickly be repeated until their Graces bundled themselves into their seats and drove off.

One knows that not all the visitors came purely on account of the music ; for many only the social element mattered ; but how we others enjoyed the opening performance of *Otello* conducted by Sir Thomas.

The second day all honours were directed to the French official presentations. It was *Ariane et Barbe-Bleue* by Dukas, conducted by M. Philippe Gaubert, first conductor of the Paris *Opéra*. M. Rouché and other official French personalities, who had come over from Paris, were formally received in the foyer. The performance of *Ariane* could hardly be a popular success on account of its sinister subject, nevertheless Germaine Lubin as Ariane made one of the deepest impressions of the Season. Lubin is a beautiful woman, tall and blonde with blue eyes, incalculable and capricious, yet charming. Whether she impersonates Isolde, Ariane, or Alceste, she has always a regal dignity, simplicity, and greatness.

Another French performance a few days later was the only performance of *Alceste* which was, with the exception of the Orchestra, entirely presented by the French, Gaubert again conducting. Chorus and ballet came from the Paris *Opéra*. I vaguely recall a very turbulent day.

The superb performance of *Alceste* was one of the finest events of the Coronation Season. Lubin as Alceste was unsurpassable, and the part seemed to have been written especially for her. The ballet aroused the greatest admiration. The unity of style throughout the performance was remarkably impressive. In these days Paris was unexcelled in staging operas such as *Alceste* and *Castor et Pollux*. In June 1939 I saw a performance of *Les Troyens* of Berlioz similarly presented in their own characteristic style.

In the first week there was a *Parsifal* performance with Torsten Ralf as Parsifal, Herbert Janssen as Amfortas, Ludwig Weber as Gurnemanz, and the wonderful Kerstin Thorborg as Kundry. As with the rôles of Siegfried and Brunhilde, it was getting more and more difficult to find the ideal Parsifal.

Another of the German performances *Der Fliegende Holländer* was scheduled for the end of the Season. Preetorius, who was in charge of this *décor* as well as that of *Orphée*, was then very busy in Berlin and Bayreuth as well as in London. His scenery was superb, and many people came to attend his scenic rehearsals.

The 29th of April was Sir Thomas's birthday, and I decided to prepare a " birthday table " for him in the continental fashion. At a Viennese confectioner's I ordered a big chocolate cake (a *Sachertorte*) in the form of a heart, which was decorated with white icing sugar. It bore the enormous initials " T. B. " and had a huge red candle in the middle. Sir Thomas was very astonished at this unusual ovation. However, he was much impressed by the cake, which had the hearty approval of the other Covent Garden folk and soon existed no more.

We also invited him to a luncheon-party in his own office, which he was not allowed to enter beforehand on account of the preparations. Some of the singers whom he was then rehearsing joined us. There was no limit to the wit and fun at this party until a Press photographer, complete with equipment, knocked at the door, the Press having in some mysterious way got wind of the event as usual. This brought us down to earth, and work was resumed.

Sir Thomas had originally planned for an International Music Festival at the time of the Coronation Season. The interesting idea of inviting several continental orchestras was shelved in view of the numerous activities on foot. All that remained of this ambitious plan were two concerts of the Berlin Philharmonic under Furt-wängler's direction. This had been arranged so that Furtwängler could start the *Ring* rehearsals immediately afterwards.

Sir Thomas did not forget the hospitality shown to him and his Orchestra in Germany, and he devoted much care to this visit of the Berliners. He sent me to Victoria Station—probably with conscious irony—to meet Furtwängler and the Orchestra, and to receive them in his and Covent Garden's names.

At the first evening Furtwängler conducted Beethoven's Choral Symphony, for which he had brought his soloists from Germany, the chorus being English.

A performance of the Ninth has always been a sacred occasion for Furtwängler since his earliest days. During the Great War, while he was conductor in Mannheim, he never allowed this work in his programmes. It was only after 1918 that he conducted again this

286

great masterpiece, which he treats as a holy ritual. In later years a performance of the Ninth was given by Furtwängler only on special occasions. After he had succeeded Richard Strauss as a conductor of the Berlin State Opera concerts in 1920, a performance of the Choral Symphony was always the feature of the last concert of the season. When he became the successor to Nikisch at the Leipzig *Gewandhaus* and Berlin Philharmonic Concerts, it became the tradition that the Pension Fund Concert of both Orchestras was a performance of the Ninth Symphony, which was given at the end of the regular cycle and was sold out for months ahead. While Furtwängler was in charge of the Vienna Philharmonic Concerts, and also later on, the Vienna Orchestra always asked him to conduct their Pension Concert. In Vienna, too, for many years, it was the Choral Symphony which was given on that occasion. These Vienna performances of the Ninth were unforgettable. Prominent singers gave their services, the *Sing-Verein*, the chorus of the venerable *Gesellschaft der Musikfreunde* sang, and the Vienna Philharmonic played with fervour. The Viennese public, which eagerly awaited this special concert from year to year, listened with that rapt attention which they give to music, while Furtwängler himself, during the days that he devoted himself to this great work, seemed entirely to forget the real world.

This was the first time that he had given the Ninth in London, and a very wonderful performance it was. The sincerity of the slow movement, especially, in its holy simplicity, was deeply moving, and felt to be so by all who attended the concert. The second evening was a mixed orchestral programme.

Although happily settled in England, these days were an emotional strain for me. I had not heard this Orchestra with which I had been so intimately connected for so many years, since 1934. I had not been allowed to hear it.

The evening after the second concert was devoted to a banquet given by Sir Thomas and the London Philharmonic Orchestra to the German guests, for which purpose the members of the London Philharmonic Orchestra had been making weekly contributions for many months past. Sir Thomas, unrivalled in the planning of festivities, had arranged this dinner in the most charming way. The two Orchestras were invited to the Savoy Hotel, where in a special room everything was arranged in characteristic English style. Enormous joints of beef were wheeled on trolleys by white-capped chefs, and wines flowed abundantly. The musicians, sitting at small tables, quickly joined their counterparts, as they always do on such occasions, and renewed their old friendships. There was, at the top table, a combination of guests which—considering Nazi times and principles—could only have been assembled by the independent Sir Thomas. He made one of his spiciest speeches at this dinner. Recounting his experiences on the German tour, on which he had been bored by the uniformity of all the addresses made to him which he always maintained emanated from one source, and all stressing the " cultural link between the two countries ", he said :

" I made thirty-nine speeches, as many as there are articles in the Rubric, and all of them were different. On the other hand, our German hosts made thirty-nine speeches too, but all of them identical ; which only goes to show the superior organisation of the Teutonic mind."

Friendship and serenity still reigned. Hitler had not yet been able to cast his shadow over all international musical life ; but with inevitable tragedy, the gulf between the Germans and the world widened, and was becoming increasingly difficult to bridge.

When the concerts were over, the main rehearsals at Covent Garden were devoted to the *Ring*. Valkyries, Rhine-Maidens, and choruses were rehearsed and scenery was tried out. Many of the singers, were, of course, used to Furtwängler, but the whole ensemble had to be rehearsed together. Performances of the *Ring* and their preparation are a strenuous and exhausting task and so Saturday afternoons and Sundays, usually free of rehearsals, had to be sacrificed to go through the principal scenes, and especially the *Mannenchöre* of *Götterdämmerung*. At the close of these rehearsals, we would gather, talking all through the night about former performances of the *Ring*.

As is his nature, Furtwängler took these rehearsals with the deepest seriousness, and had little time or thought for anything else. Between and after rehearsals, however, we all met a great deal, and one or the other of the singers was always appearing in my office—rather too often, I am afraid, to please Sir Thomas. But if it was so, he never showed it. He was always very kind, and when Furtwängler used

to come up and peep through the door, he would call out cheerily :
" What can I do for you, my lad ? " He greatly liked the serious,
sensitive musician, and, with his talent for making people comfortable, he invariably put even the shy and reserved Furtwängler
at ease.

About this time the B.B.C. had just begun its television programmes. They wished to combine propaganda for television with
a compliment to the famous German conductor, and so they asked
whether Furtwängler would be willing to talk with Sir Adrian
Boult in a television programme. After the text of their talk had
been finally agreed upon, I accompanied these two gentlemen to the
Alexandra Palace where the session was to take place. Furtwängler
felt most uncomfortable, while Sir Adrian submitted to the proceedings with all the unconcern and self-assurance of a Briton. The
whole programme was endangered when Furtwängler was told that
he had to be " made-up ". This worried him so much that he nearly
lost courage for the talk ; however, the ordeal eventually came to an
end, and he was very relieved to be himself again.

The 12th of May was Coronation Day. In the Opera House *Aida*
was being performed. At 7.20 p.m. all the Prime Ministers of the
Dominions were to broadcast, and a speech by the British Premier
was to conclude the programme. Finally, at 8 p.m., the King spoke.
Between these speeches and the performance, " God save the King "
was broadcast from the Royal Opera House, Covent Garden. This
was sung by Eva Turner, the great favourite of the Londoners,
accompanied by the London Philharmonic conducted by Sir Thomas.
The chorus and principals, numbering some five hundred, and the
overflowing house, joined in. The Royal box was decorated with
roses.

The day after the Coronation was fixed for the beginning of the
Ring. Owing to the great demand, there was always a separate
Ring subscription at Covent Garden and for many London opera
lovers the Cycle has always been the chief interest of the Season.
This was certainly so in the Coronation year, when the occasion was
enhanced by Furtwängler's superb direction. He does not like
conducting this work too often, but the feeling in him for the heroic
is close to the spirit of the great trilogy. He passionately lives the

music while conducting, forgetting all else and keeping his audience as breathless as himself.

His wonderful handling of the Orchestra was universally acclaimed, while many of the singers excelled in their parts. In *Rheingold*, Erich Zimmermann as Mime was the sensation of the evening, and in *Walküre* Völker, the Bayreuth Lohengrin, was a wonderful Siegmund, with Frieda Leider as Brunhilde, and Marie Müller as Sieglinde. Max Lorenz was the Siegfried of the first *Ring*, with Bockelmann as Wanderer. In *Götterdämmerung* Ludwig Weber, the magnificent Hunding of *Walküre*, was a sinister Hagen.

In the second *Ring* Lauritz Melchior, beloved for many years by his Covent Garden public, was the Siegfried, while the sensational feature of the second *Ring* was the first appearance of the new Brunhilde, Kirsten Flagstad. She was a born Wagnerian dramatic soprano, and had everything necessary for a Nibelungen heroine. Her voice mounted to its highest registers without trouble. She was extremely adaptable and collaborated well with Furtwängler who was fascinated by her voice. In the new *Holländer* she sang Senta but with less success than Brunhilde. In *Tristan*, however, which came on in the last week of the Covent Garden Season, she was simply superb, and the triumphant ease of her fresh and effortless voice put all her colleagues in the shade.

With the second *Ring* Furtwängler's days in London were finished. He had a farewell lunch with Sir Thomas, and the two conductors parted on the best of terms.

Although Furtwängler was entirely preoccupied with the *Ring*, other problems had been pressing in upon him. His relation to Bayreuth was very unsatisfactory. One would have thought that Bayreuth would have appreciated a man of Furtwängler's standard. However, in spite of its great artistic possibilities, the *Festspielhügel* has, as I have indicated, always been difficult ground. At Bayreuth a great personality always ran the danger of being attacked on the grounds of "not serving the cause". It is interesting to note that while this was a traditional habit of Bayreuth, it later became the usual method applied by the Nazis whenever a strong character arose who threatened to be inconvenient to them. Frau Wagner was not always adroit in handling great artists. Even Toscanini, who was otherwise worshipped in Bayreuth, bitterly complained in 1931, when he conducted *Parsifal* there for the first time. Of course, Frau Wagner was in a difficult position. However, it was her weakness that she tried to give excessive consideration to the foibles of her *entourage*, and the ill-balanced dealing in questions of authority disturbed Furtwängler's enthusiasm for the work to which he had brought such serious devotion. He knew the ground, and felt that he had to insist that his position should be defined before starting the work. Frau Wagner seemed as yet hesitant on this point.

After long and careful consideration, Furtwängler therefore wrote a letter from London offering his resignation to Frau Wagner should she not see her way to accord him the authority which was his right. This discord was resolved—but only superficially.

It was during his memorable performances of the *Ring* at the London Coronation Season that this correspondence passed between Furtwängler and the trustee of the spiritual heritage of Richard Wagner. And it is one of history's ironies that this period marked the beginning of his estrangement with the *Festspielhügel*.

The world has condemned Furtwängler because he conducted in Bayreuth after Hitler had come to power. The artistic possibilities of Bayreuth are unequalled, but working and living there was difficult for a sensitive artist, and—whatever the current opinion may be on that point—carried neither personal nor political advantages. Furtwängler engaged in the work there out of idealism and patriotism. Nowhere has he suffered more than in Bayreuth, and neither Bayreuth nor the Nazis have ever thanked him for the fact that, out of loyalty to the cause of Richard Wagner, he tried to persist in his duty as he saw it.

During this time, the Royal Philharmonic Society had redecorated their offices and invited their friends to a house-warming party in Berners Street. The festivity was arranged for twelve o'clock midday, a time when I could usually not leave my office. However, I asked Sir Thomas for permission, on account of this special occasion, which, of course, be graciously granted. (He grants everything with condescending politeness, but he wants to be asked.)

The Royal Philharmonic Committee were perhaps a little conservative. The soul of their organisation was then Miss Dorothy

Wadham, Secretary to the Hon. Secretary, Keith Douglas. Miss
Wadham is a clever woman, with a cool and aloof temperament.
She and I are to-day good friends, and when war broke out, I even
lived in her house for a while. At this time, however, we were
only at the beginning of our relationship. I passionately represented
the interests of Sir Thomas, while Dorothy had formed an *a priori*
conclusion (whether with reason or not) that the Royal Philharmonic
Society must be protected from the encroachments of the "tyrant".
Like some of his colleagues, Sir Thomas had the perturbing habit
of changing his programmes at the last moment. In such cases
Dorothy seemed to develop into a lioness ; especially when Sir
Thomas with nonchalant sadism wanted to change an item which
was to be broadcast did Dorothy manifest a strength of will against
which even I—a warrior myself—was utterly defenceless. To my
discredit—and I must confess it happened several times—I must
own that after having been sent to the telephone as a forerunner to
discuss some such delicate matter, I could not save Sir Thomas from
fighting his own battle.

On this morning, however, all was sunshine. The last season of
the Philharmonic was happily over, and the future season as yet
cast no shadows. All the friends of the venerable Society were peacefully united and were having sherry in the bright new offices. Sherry
at twelve o'clock in the morning is not everyone's "cup of tea",
certainly it is not mine. After I had taken several glasses, an oil
painting on the wall began to take my fancy. This picture had been
painted in memory of the visit of King George and Queen Mary
on the occasion of the performance of Handel's *Solomon* which
had been conducted by Sir Thomas. It shows the famous old double-
bass player, Winterbottom (who had celebrated his jubilee, twenty-
five years in the profession) being presented to their Majesties, the
Society's familiar Beethoven bust looking down on the scene, and
Sir Thomas in the background. The picture was rather original and
amusing. The sherry had confused my sense of "mine and thine"
and I decided that I wanted to have that picture. Then and there
I took it down and tucked it under my arm, being interested to see
what reactions this would have. There was a certain amount of
laughter, for the kindly and polite hosts did not imagine that my
intentions were serious. I profited by this and quickly escaped with

my booty. Triumphantly I arrived at Sir Thomas's office at Covent Garden. "God help us ! What have you got there," cried Sir Thomas. "Isn't it wonderful ? " I said enthusiastically. "I have stolen this picture, and now I'm going to hang it on the wall opposite my desk." I proceeded at once to do so, and there it remained throughout the whole Coronation Season, an object of conversation for all my visitors ! I was not, however, to enjoy the fruits of my robbery permanently. After several admonishments by letter to return the picture to its owners (to which I replied by silence), one morning I found the wall empty ! All my inquiries as to who had taken the picture away were fruitless. By the cunning smiles on the faces of all members of the Philharmonic Committee alone did I gather that this had been a concerted action, and as I was in the wrong I had to submit. Only in the summer of 1941 did I learn that the Philharmonic Society had commissioned Percy Heming to rescue their property.

Chapter 33

MEANWHILE THE opera season proceeded, sometimes smoothly, sometimes not. At the end of May came the first performance of Debussy's *Pelléas et Mélisande*, under the direction of the French conductor, Albert Wolff, from the *Opéra Comique*. It was a French cast with an English Mélisande, Lisa Perli, who had just the poetry for this part. The *décor* came from the *Théatre des Champs Elysées* in Paris, where I had discovered it, and where Sir Thomas had inspected the *maquettes* put up for him when he was in Paris. However, when the scenery arrived, it had to be entirely overhauled. Among other deficiencies, it proved to be much too dark, probably owing to grime. The designer, a Russian, arrived, and it was necessary to work on the scenery day and night. Once Sir Thomas did not go to bed at all, and did not leave the Opera House until this problem seemed on the way to solution. The performance was a very interesting one, though perhaps caviare to the general. Toscanini, who, to the delight of the Italian singers, occasionally visited Covent Garden, attended the performance. He planned to give *Pelléas* in Salzburg later on.

At this time, I had some dramatic adventures, and although they had nothing to do with music they deserve recording. As I have mentioned, I lived on the top flat in an old business house in Red Lion Square. After five o'clock the business premises were vacated and I was alone in the strange old building, except for a friend who kept house for me. The house was built of timber, and it was probably about a hundred and fifty years old. When I returned from the Opera House in the evening, I began to hear queer noises, but dismissed them, supposing them to be made by a young kitten.

One evening we heard these sounds again. "Do you know what that is?" my friend asked me. "It is rats!" I felt anything but happy, because the sounds suggested rather a large number of rats! The noise continued to increase, and during the night strong gnawings could be heard.

One evening, an enormous rat greeted me when I came in and rushed up the stairs in front of me whipping her tail, whereupon I scarcely dared to go up at all.

From that day the rat appeared every evening when the house was quiet, and gradually I became afraid to go into my flat alone. When I did enter the house, I banged the door, made as much noise as possible, and did not dare to look round until the rats had had time to scuttle away. I might have been a Chinese making a noise to frighten away the evil spirits. Meantime the symptoms increased and rats began to appear even inside my flat. One day when Furtwängler was sitting up on my roof garden eating his salad, a rat was seen peacefully walking round the flower boxes, which did not, however, disturb him in the least. This particular rat was later on caught by us in a trap hidden in the flowers, and was found one day hanging down from the boxes by her long tail.

During the nights the situation grew worse and worse, and terrible noises developed. I said to my friend: "Now they are in my room, and that is the limit". My phlegmatic friend refused to be disturbed, and tried to convince me that the acoustical properties of the wood made the rats appear to be in my room, when actually they were only between the timber-joists.

From this day events proceeded apace. One day, when going to my bathroom, an enormous rat jumped over my naked foot. Night after night, on the curtain pole of my bedroom, always in the same place, a rat appeared and sat there quietly with her long tail hanging down. Neither the light, nor the frantic noises I made succeeded in disturbing her, and I lay in bed sweating with fear and utterly unable to sleep. The noise started every night at the same time. I made intensive inquiries as to how to deal with this plague and unburdened my heart to Jackson, my friend at the stage-door at Covent Garden. Jackson, usually so sympathetic, was not very encouraging : " You cannot help it. There are lots of rats in London " was his blunt reply. " The other day we had one in the Royal box." He seemed to hold the view that a rat having been seen in the Royal box was quite sufficient to reconcile me to all my personal rats. Sir Thomas, who, of course, had no rats of his own, characteristically took the matter from a humorous point of view, and greeted me every morning : " Doctor, how are your rats ? " Smith was full of sympathy, but the rats continued to gnaw.

I was absolutely at my wits' end. One morning I was still in bed and wanted to use the telephone. When I took up the receiver it had a strange, heavy feeling. What was the matter ? A rat was hanging on to the telephone cord and was just starting to gnaw it through. No one will blame me for dropping the receiver and jumping out of bed with horrified shrieks. I was nearly demented. At long last, however, I was told of a way out of my troubles, and so it came about that I telephoned to Mr. Dalton, London's famous ratcatcher, who came at once to see me. He was a Dickensian figure indeed ! I told him of my troubles, which did not move him in the least. On the contrary, he said to me : " Well, you know, Madam, rats are increasing in England, especially in the City, and we have just ascertained that the percentage of rats at the moment is higher than ever before ". There he sat, a little thick-set man, with a rosy face and blue eyes, and promised to help me. " But how do you get them ? " I anxiously inquired. Whereupon he showed me his enormous fists. " You wait, Madam, millions of rats have been killed by *them* ! "

Here I must interpolate a true story. Mr. Dalton gave a talk on the radio on the subject of catching rats, and in consequence he received a large fan mail. By a delightful mistake the fan mail addressed to Mr. William Dalton was forwarded not to him, but to the composer William Walton, who later on confirmed to me the truth of the story.

Mr. Dalton promised to send his son and his assistant. Accordingly, the two young men called. They informed me that for a whole night they were to be entire masters of the flat. If I intended to be at home at all during this night, I had to withdraw from the battlefield into one room, which so far seemed to be have been free from rats. I was not allowed to make the slightest noise, and to put a light on was out of the question. When I arrived after midnight from the opera, I gave an arranged signal and was silently let in. What had these men not done in the meantime ! On the ground floor, neatly arrayed in serried ranks, were twenty-eight dead rats ! I retired, and according to our agreement, at seven o'clock in the morning I made some good coffee and had breakfast with the rat-catchers. Eighty-six rats had been caught. Some had been killed and the others were in cages, and were to be used for medical research. All possible holes were filled with twisted wires, and the strictest instructions were given to me how to protect myself from any threatened invasion in the future.

Full of gratitude to my saviours, and with the greatest respect for their profession, I parted from them.

One fine day Friedelinde Wagner—then seventeen years old—the eldest daughter of Siegfried and Winifred suddenly arrived at Covent Garden. She had been sent to a school near Arundel, and had got bored there. Apparently, any independent action on her part had been strictly suppressed. During the *Ring*, the Bayreuth cast were, of course, all present, but there had been no sign of Friedelinde. However, the *Holländer* and *Tristan* were still to come—and so was Friedelinde ! I had always had sympathy for " Mausi " as she was called in private, a girl whose rebellious spirit, quick brain, and natural feeling for music had ever attracted me. When I first went to Bayreuth, she was twelve years old, and one of the most amusing and unmanageable of children.

My surprise at seeing Friedelinde can be imagined, knowing that she should have been at school, where, of course, even pupils of seventeen years of age do not usually make independent excursions. "Here I am," said Mausi as she walked into my office at Covent Garden. "Good gracious," said I, "but what are we going to do with you?" "*Um Gottes Willen*, be careful," warned Frieda Leider, then the Brunhilde and Isolde of Bayreuth, and the confidential friend of Frau Wagner and Tietjen. "If they hear in Bayreuth that Mausi is in London, there *will* be trouble. She must get back to her school at once!" But to return Mausi to an unwelcome destination was easier said than done. She definitely knew what she wanted. Not only did she want to hear opera in Covent Garden, but she wanted badly to meet Toscanini, her paternal friend, again. In spite of the latter's rupture with Bayreuth, there existed between these two a close and charming friendship. (Toscanini had a number of concerts with the B.B.C. Orchestra during the Coronation Season and was accompanied to London by his whole family and many friends.) Mausi behaved comparatively unobtrusively at Covent Garden. Sir Thomas gave instructions that she should be well looked after. All publicity was to be avoided, out of consideration for Bayreuth, but there is little discretion in an opera house, and one day I received an S.O.S. from Mausi who was sitting in her box and about to be photographed. (Incidentally a pressman had just asked her how her father was, he having been dead for seven years, and I arrived just at the right moment to prevent some pointed remarks from her on the intelligence of pressmen in general!) She was taken to the Royal box, where she met the Princesses Marie Louise and Helena Victoria, who had known her grandmother Cosima so well.

Mausi remained in London as long as she wished before returning to her school. Later on, from the autumn of 1938, when she left Hitler-Germany for good, she made London her headquarters before she went on to America in spring 1941.

The *Holländer* and the *Orphée* and the English opera *Don Juan de Mañara* by Eugene Goossens were to be the last new productions of the season. The *Orphée* had been wonderfully staged, and the Russian ballet danced in it. It was sung in French, with a tenor instead of the usual alto. Maggie Teyte was Euridice. The *Orphée* was a superb performance, especially so far as the staging and the scenery was concerned, yet Press and public failed to appreciate its high artistic merit.

In these days Sir Thomas took me as his guest on an occasion which interested me greatly. Lionel Tertis, the famous English viola player, connoisseur, and teacher, intended to retire from concert work on account of his rheumatic arm. British musicians arranged a farewell dinner in his honour, and this was held at Pagani's, the celebrated restaurant where many musicians had been at home for fifty years. Many important people in English musical life foregathered here frequently. I must confess I felt a little embarrassed and alien on such an occasion, but the natural hospitality of the British quickly dispels such feelings. It was most interesting to me to contrast the English festivity with the German counterpart of such a celebration. Somehow in England, everything is more relaxed and natural. There are, of course, petty jealousies and occasional grumbling among the English, but these things are more superficial with them. What *does* go deeply with them is the capacity for team spirit when the occasion arises. Thus it was that on this occasion there were assembled over a hundred musicians of very varying interests, all of them united by a sense of solidarity and friendship, so strong that one felt it like a warm wave. They had but one idea, to honour the guest of the evening, Lionel Tertis, who was overwhelmed by their kindness.

The speakers of the occasion were Sir Hugh Allen, Sir Thomas Beecham, and Dr. Ralph Vaughan Williams. Each was brilliant in his own characteristic way. Again I noticed how all these men spoke in a manner far less pompous and much more natural than Germans would have done. The same applied to the reply of Tertis, who was so overcome that he was hardly able to speak. This was a most instructive experience for me, and I was very grateful to Sir Thomas for having taken me along.

Slowly the Covent Garden Season came to a close, and towards the end of June other celebrations began to thin out. The last new production of Covent Garden was the opera of the British composer and conductor, Eugene Goossens, *Don Juan de Mañara*, in which the principal rôle was sung by Laurence Tibbett. Goossens himself conducted ; the whole Goossens family assembled for the occasion. The Goossens are a great English musical tribe of Flemish origin. The composer, Eugene, is already the third generation of Eugene

Goossens. His grandfather, Eugene I, had been a conductor, his father, Eugene II, was conductor of the Carl Rosa Company, and Eugene Goossens No. III is a composer, and for years has been conductor of the Cincinatti Symphony Orchestra in America. His brother, Léon Goossens, one of the world's finest oboe players, makes a great sensation wherever he is heard. Until the outbreak of the war, he was first oboe of the London Philharmonic Orchestra. Both his sisters are harpists, one of them, Marie, was formerly the London Philharmonic Orchestra's harpist and was married to the late Frederick Laurence, who was for years one of the London Philharmonic Orchestra's managers. The other sister, Sidonie, is harpist for the B.B.C. The Goossens are a devoted family, and it is said that every week Eugene sends a cable from America to his old parents. The whole family, and a vast number of Goossens' fans, followed the performance with keen interest and satisfaction.

Finally, the 30th of June arrived, and with it the end of the Season. The last performance was *Tristan*, conducted by Sir Thomas, with Walter Widdop, Flagstad, and Thorborg (all Bayreuthers having left London on June 17th for their own rehearsals).

At the end of this memorable season there was a great scene of enthusiasm. Prevailed upon to speak, Sir Thomas appeared before the curtain after it had fallen for the last time and indulged in some irony at the expense of the critics of the Season :

"The Season has been longer than usual and has had several distinguished features. The most remarkable thing of all has been the Press. Never before in the history of Covent Garden has the Press attained so high a state of excellence.

"We on our side have not been able to live up to it. We propose to devote the next six months to a careful reading of every word of abuse that has been written in the newspapers. We have become sadder and wiser people, for you know how seriously we take everything that is said about us. We only hope that you do the same—though the vast attendances suggest, I am afraid, that what they say has had no effect on you." (June 30, 1937.)

After this, Covent Garden quickly changed its complexion. The Russian Ballet made its entrance, and beautiful men and women were constantly seen running about the corridors. In the evening the stage was always full of the loveliest flowers which were sent to the dancers by their admirers. The stalls, especially the first rows, were always full of men, and I have noticed that the older they are the nearer to the front they sit. I myself was absolutely fascinated by these wonderful folk, who for many years had been intimately connected with the Royal Opera House. They had the exclusive right to perform in the theatre and no other ballet company was allowed at Covent Garden without their consent. Only those who have seen these women in their training kit, practising relentlessly, can form any idea of the overwhelming cost to themselves of their brief glamorous hour before the public.

Apart from the Covent Garden Season and other special musical events, Toscanini conducted during the Coronation summer a series of concerts at Queen's Hall for the B.B.C., with which he had the most cordial relations. His concerts in London were always eagerly awaited by his large following and friends, many of whom, Italians, had especially come to London for this occasion, as they could no longer hear him in Italy.

For a long time the public and Press have acknowledged the magic qualities of Toscanini's baton and have accorded him a unique position. Toscanini has always cast a spell. The glory of his name is enhanced by his strong and unflinching attitude in the face of the Fascist peril, and his moral strength in the cause of freedom.

Boundless enthusiasm reigned at his concerts ; yet the enthusiasm of the moment, great as it was, was no measure of the lasting impression made by such an event. His genius raises and stimulates a special brand of interest among musicians. I remember remarking the same phenomenon after Toscanini had toured the Continent with the New York Philharmonic in 1929.

It is perhaps the fact that he has to conduct independently of the score which has led Toscanini, the fanatic of musical truth, to adhere with utter conscientiousness to the greatest accuracy and exactitude. His optical memory of scores—he even conducts all Wagner and Verdi operas by heart—is such that he knows exactly the place on the sheet of every bar, every marking on the paper ; it is a kind of unique phenomenon of memory. Then when he stands before the orchestra, he " hears " acoustically what his memory " knows " visually. His preparation of a concert piece is like that of the producer of an opera where every detail is fixed beforehand ; everything is rehearsed *with the orchestra* in minute and careful work. Nothing is left to chance at the time of the actual performance, which is thus protected from the risk of the moment as far as possible. Yet, when the moment comes, the performance appears an inspired improvisation of persuasive truthfulness.

In all the centres of musical life much discussion followed his London performances, and it was interesting to note that the problem of the " impeccable execution ", the faithful reproduction of the composer's intentions, that from time to time occupies musical minds, now again engaged the interest of many.

This is no place to go into this much debated subject. The reader may, however, be interested to hear something about the London Toscanini concerts from quite a different angle. The box-office management of Queen's Hall was beset by other problems than those of music itself. It was the manager of Queen's Hall, Mr. Charles Taylor, who told me of *his* side of things : " Our chief difficulty ", he said, " was the enormous public interest in Toscanini, and it soon became plain to us that we had to find special means to deal with it ". The B.B.C. and the Queen's Hall management soon agreed that it would be unfair to sell the tickets only to those who could afford to sit on the Queen's Hall doorsteps before the box-office opened, and so it was decided to ballot for them. Orders for seats were accepted by written application only. Over 17,000 letters were received. These were all numbered, and tickets were finally drawn from a drum ; the inquiries were dealt with in the order in which the numbers were drawn. " Don't you believe that this story is a blind," Mr. Taylor concluded. " It was all done correctly, and there was no other way for anybody to get into a Toscanini concert."

There was, however, a way to listen to his rehearsals, to which a number of people were admitted on presenting a card with his own signature. I went as often as I was able to snatch a moment from my Covent Garden duties, and again felt that there is nothing more interesting than to listen to the rehearsals of a real master. These rehearsals had a special atmosphere of their own ; it was like the gathering of a huge family assembled around the Toscaninis ; Signora Toscanini was the centre of many friendly demonstrations, and had a kind word for everybody.

The Toscaninis left in the middle of June and until the outbreak of war the *maestro* always managed to come back to London for a few weeks to his faithful and enthusiastic audience.

The last prominent event in the chain of Coronation festivities were two concerts by the Vienna Philharmonic under the direction of Bruno Walter at the end of June.

The Vienna Philharmonic had a special etiquette for all they did. This was particularly felt when they were on a tour, and had I not known it before, I would have learnt it when I once accompanied them on a short English visit in 1930, while Furtwängler was their principal conductor as well as of the Berlin Philharmonic. The superb self-assurance of every member of the Orchestra and their ostentatious pride in belonging to this famous body of players was quite unique. As a matter of fact, every member of the Vienna Philharmonic feels himself to be a god, and expects to be treated like one, be he in Vienna, London, or anywhere else.

Wherever the *Wiener Philharmoniker* may be, they are a demonstration of the fact that music and everything affected by it plays a special rôle in Vienna's life, where, from the café-waiter and the taxi-driver, to the oldest aristocracy, music and musicians stand first.

Furtwängler had been a great favourite in Vienna for many years, and the Viennese from time to time clamoured for him for themselves. He had decided for Berlin in 1929, but when he resigned from all his German positions at the end of 1934, an intermediary was sent from Vienna to offer him for the second time the direction of the Vienna State Opera. Alma Mahler, the widow of this institution's most famous director, and at this period a kind of uncrowned Queen of Vienna, strongly supported these endeavours, and telephoned to me in Berlin at midnight from Vienna urging me to persuade him to accept this offer. I am sure that the Nazis, who tapped the lines, were not too pleased by this conversation.

Furtwängler had all his life wanted to settle in Vienna, but at the last minute decided otherwise. However, he has been connected all through his career with Viennese musical life. So, through many years and experiences, I was closely linked with the Vienna Philharmonic, and when I met Buxbaum and Rosé, these patriarchs of the Orchestra, at Oxford Circus on their way to Queen's Hall, we simply fell into each others' arms.

The first programme comprised Beethoven's Emperor Concerto, played by Schnabel, and Bruckner's Eighth Symphony. A prominent and distinguished audience was present. Baron Franckenstein, then not yet Sir George, did the honours with exemplary unobtrusiveness and was full of pride for the Viennese Orchestra.

Afterwards, I went out to Soho with some of the players and heard all their news. The ever-fluctuating musical fortunes of Toscanini, Walter, and Furtwängler were the very centre of their world, and these questions exclusively occupied the evening.

The visit of the Vienna Philharmonic to London had its termination in one of the most brilliant gatherings to take place during the Coronation Season. It was a reception at the Austrian Legation where Baron Franckenstein was always a perfect host. On this occasion, the great music-room of the Legation was filled with royalties, diplomats, and other distinguished people. A number of great artists and scientists had also come to hear the music which was to be provided for them. A section of the Orchestra played Beethoven's Wind Sextet, and then Elisabeth Schumann sang, accompanied by Bruno Walter. Finally, the new young leader of the Vienna Orchestra, Odnopossoff, whom Furtwängler had discovered, played. His teacher, Professor Carl Flesch, listened, filled with pride and satisfaction. In the first row sat the Princess Royal with the Princesses Marie Louise and Helena Victoria. After the concert the whole audience intermingled with the ease and informality so characteristic of Baron Franckenstein's house. Nearly all the ambassadors were present. Ribbentrop was noticeably absent. I wonder what his representative, Baron Doernberg, thought of this gathering ! His red head towered, in any case as far as material height was concerned, above all other heads present.

So ended a most interesting and eventful time. Sir Thomas was already busy with his plans for the next opera season of 1938, and with all his concert programmes for the winter. In the middle of July I left for the Continent with instructions to visit Bayreuth and Salzburg.

Chapter 34

IRRESISTIBLY drawn by memories and the need to learn how the fine old university town had fared since the Nazi days, I stopped at Heidelberg on the way to Bayreuth. How far-off seemed my old university days !

During the period after 1910, when I had studied philosophy there and also after 1918, Heidelberg had been a haven of intellectual life. Great scholars taught there, and students from all over the world came to this shrine of culture. Not even the Nazis had yet been able to drain this oasis completely, and there were still certain " springs " reminiscent of former times.

The way the Nazis tried to put their stamp on even such a traditional institution as this ancient university, may be illustrated by the following true anecdote. In 1929 a new university building was added to the famous old one, founded in 1386. It was built with money collected in America by the late Ambassador Schurmann, who was himself a Heidelberg student and enthusiast. Friedrich Gundolf, Germany's great historian of literature, and authority on Shakespeare, had devised a motto which was inscribed on the front of this new home of learning. It was : " *Dem lebendigen Geiste !* " (" To the living spirit ! "). What was that to the Nazis ? " *Lebendig* " must become " *Deutsch* " ! And so Gundolf's fine motto was changed to the jingoistic cry—" *Dem deutschen Geiste* " (" To the German spirit ").

After completing my studies, I had often stayed at the old place. Heidelberg was not only a university : it was renowned for its concerts, and one of the most impressive festivals given by the German Brahms Society took place there in 1926 under Furtwängler's direction. He and the Berlin Philharmonic frequently visited the romantic town on their tours, and thus contact with the friends living there had never been lost.

Heidelberg meant almost more to me than my native town of Mannheim ; and when, after my long Odyssey, I came back again and was met at the station by friends, I felt transported back to another life.

In spite of the indestructible beauty of the place, one soon sensed the changed atmosphere. The Heidelberg of the past was no more, and I was by no means alone in recognising this. One of Heidelberg's famous scholars, who had voluntarily left Germany and spent some time in London studying Oriental manuscripts at the British Museum, once said to me : " There is no escape, we must see things as they are ; the symbol for the present-day Heidelberg is its castle ruin ".

During my short visit I saw different friends, who in retrospect seem to have mirrored the clash of the " new order " with the old university which had tried manfully to defend its tradition.

I visited Furtwängler's aged mother, daughter of Brahms' great friend, the classical scholar Wendt. She sat in the library of her late husband, the famous archæologist, closely following the life of her son, thus uniting interest in the past and the present—a survival of the intellectual and spiritual Heidelberg !

I met again the courageous Protestant theologian, Professor Martin Dibelius, who in spite of being a " pure Aryan " had suffered much at the hands of the Nazis, and this only because he adhered to his religious views. The simplicity and honesty with which this great scholar behaved, and the way he remained calm, serene, and unflinching in the face of his trials, reflects a heroism which may have passed unnoticed in our sensation-loving times. Yet history is made by such men.

My visit to the economist, Professor Alfred Weber, was different. He, like his late brother Max, was an ardent democrat. Max was the more famous of the two, and was husband of the champion of women's rights, Marianne Weber. The Webers were " Aryan ", and Alfred, like so many others, could have drifted with the tide in order to save his position. However, he resigned from his post at the university soon after the advent of the Nazis and devoted himself to private work.

When I had met him last in 1938, he had been still brimful of life. In contrast to the serenity of the theologian Dibelius, and the conscious resignation of the philosopher Jaspers, he was full of active determination. At the time of writing I cannot say how he has fared in the years of his isolated existence. This life of isolation has become the fate of many of those non-Nazi intellectuals in Germany for whom it was not absolutely necessary to emigrate, or who had no opportunity to do so, and who live a kind of life of exile in their own land, a more tragic fate perhaps than that of those who left it.

One of my teachers, the philosopher Professor Karl Jaspers, was another type. He was the most prominent of the present-day pre-Hitler German philosophical school. Ever since the beginning of his career he had had a large following, not limited to Germany alone. He had originally been in medicine (psychopathology) and his lectures on the psychology of religion, on Kierkegaard, on Jesuitism, on figures like St. Theresa, Ignatius of Loyola, and similar subjects were so original in their treatment that students flocked to them. On account of the enormous attendance, they could only be held in the famous and ancient *auditorium maximum*. His fate was determined by his Jewish wife, his faithful collaborator, secretary, and nurse, for his health was delicate, and he would scarcely have been able to keep up his strength for his work but for her devoted care. Now he was a recluse, living within his home, which was full of books. Gradually all his ties with the world had been severed ; that world in which he had been venerated by an enthusiastic young generation and by sympathetic colleagues. He was the same man that I had left a few years ago. His Greek philosophers, his mystics, his Kierkegaard, his Goethe, and his Kant were the same. An hour spent with this noble man of unchanging integrity was the same wonderful experience. Now, however, my visit to him did not leave me elated and fortified as formerly, but filled with shame and despair over the fate awaiting great minds of the genuine Germany.

Heavy at heart and yet soothed, I said farewell to Heidelberg and went on my way to Bayreuth.

This time I was less self-conscious on arrival than in 1936. In the meanwhile I had been to Germany frequently on business, and many German artists had visited London. In the joint work at Covent Garden I had lost some of the complex feelings aroused by Nazi conditions.

Mausi Wagner was at the station to meet me, in an exciting *Dirndl* dress with red heart-shaped buttons. I had looked after her at Covent Garden, and she took me under her wing in Bayreuth. We went off for a ride immediately on the recently constructed *Autobahn* in her new car. Of course, we did the *verboten* things, such as turning at the wrong place. We were promptly stopped by the police. " Heil Hitler ! Your name and address please ! " " Wagner, Wahnfried," said Mausi, and the overawed policeman withdrew. We drove on to the *Eremitage*, the old palace of the Margraves of Bayreuth, where the unhappy Bavarian King Ludwig II had stayed during his last visit to Wagner, and Bayreuth with its gently undulating landscape enthralled me again.

In the evening there was a rehearsal of the *Ring*. Frau Wagner invited me to sit with " the family "—an event unheard of according to Bayreuth etiquette. (When I was there as Furtwängler's secretary, this would have been unthinkable.)

The Wagner children and the " aunts ", Countess Gravina, Frau Daniela Thode, and Frau Eva Chamberlain sat together. This was the last time I saw the old Bayreuth generation—all have since died. The youngsters were in great form. Verena, the second girl, was more fragile and Liszt-like than ever ; Wieland, the elder boy, had tried his hand at the new *décor* for *Parsifal* and was fully absorbed in his work. Little Wolfgang, passionately interested in the technical side of it all, rushed from one part of the theatre to the other. What opportunities these children had !

The next day I resumed my business. Sir Thomas had given me a letter for Tietjen explaining his tentative plans for the 1938 season in regard to German operas. He wanted suggestions for a cast for *Meistersinger*, *Rosenkavalier*, *Lohengrin*, and *Fliegender Holländer*. He was looking particularly for a new Senta. The cast for the *Ring* was as usual dependent on the Siegfried and Brunhilde. He wanted Furtwängler to conduct the *Ring* again, and proposed that Tietjen should come as producer.

After the oracles of Bayreuth had given utterance, I sent a detailed report to Sir Thomas. He had refrained so far from expressing his own opinion or wishes. Actually, he wanted to hear the views of the others. Sir Thomas does not disdain to ask other people's opinions, and does so perfectly frankly. If the advice proves suitable he makes use of it ; if not, he ignores it. He never feels it to be a loss of prestige if he utilises experiences gained, in some way, by other people. " Go and find out from your friends what they think," he said to me when I left, " that will save me a lot of trouble." This was the main point for him !

His hand-written reply to my long report from Bayreuth came by return. It was a characteristic Beecham document. Once he had clear-cut suggestions in front of him he began to comment on them. He is never unwilling to change his opinion if he is convinced that this is justified, but when he has definitely made up his mind on the cast for an opera, he goes his own way.

Although he has very strong views about singers, he shows much human understanding, and is very skilful in handling them. Never, for example, during an opera season would he let a singer feel that he had already decided not to engage him again. His comments on singers who had the ill-fortune to displease him are most amusing—I am afraid, less so for the artists concerned. There is a rumour that Sir Thomas definitely dislikes opera singers. I cannot confirm this, as I have always particularly noticed the kind, even paternal way he treats them. Whatever the singer's foible, Sir Thomas remains unruffled. Yet the rumour is supported by the following story :

During the last act of Massenet's *Don Quixote* Madame Sadowa, who sang the part of La belle Dulcinée, failed to synchronise the concluding passage accurately with Chaliapin (Don Quixote) and Petrov (Sancho Panza). After repeated expostulations on the part of Sir Thomas she finally exclaimed :

" I cannot help it, Mr. Chaliapin always dies too soon."

" Madam, you must be profoundly in error," said Sir Thomas, " no operatic star has yet died half soon enough for me."

His reply to my Bayreuth report contained a number of " friendly " comments such as I have hinted at above. But it also contained his own ideas on the casts in question. Some of these did not fit in at all with the views of the *Festspielhügel* and it was difficult to reconcile the divergent opinions.

Of course, I was only the mediator in all these negotiations, but my friendly relations with both sides often eased the situation. Between Bayreuth and Covent Garden, Sir Thomas and the musical powers of the Continent, and last, not least, between Nazi-Germany and Great Britain, I had to tread warily.

From Bayreuth I went to spend my holidays on the Starnberg Lake. Things had altered greatly since last summer. Definitely, although scarcely perceptibly, the screw had been tightened. How difficult things were for the Catholics who had always sent their children to the convent school ! How depressed were the peasants who did not want to see their children in the " Hitler Jugend " ! What rumours and stories we heard at the hairdresser's, in the little shops, and in the wayside inns where we stopped for a glass of beer on a cycling tour.

Bavarians were in distress, and although National Socialism had arisen first in Bavaria, there is no doubt that in 1937 it was already declining there. Every time I returned to Germany I clearly saw the growing terror, and also the growing but helpless opposition.

Seen superficially, things were quiet, and a stranger, unless very alert, might have been oblivious to the trend of events. Personally I was unmolested. Sir Thomas wrote and telephoned frequently, and this gave me a feeling of security. I enjoyed every quiet and peaceful day amidst those lovely surroundings.

At the request of Sir Thomas, I went next to Salzburg. The Salzburg turmoil was a great contrast to the quiet Bavarian village. The surroundings were indeed beautiful, as was the old episcopal town, but it seemed that the spirit and atmosphere of Mozart's birth-place had undergone many changes.

Many musicians and intellectuals had their homes just outside Salzburg, safely protected from the bustle of the festival for which people from all over the world had gathered. It presented a strange mixture, this Salzburg public. There were the native Austrians and there were Germans who no longer had a home in Germany ; there were the international music-pilgrims who would not miss their Salzburg visit for anything, and there were the sensation hunters who did not come for the performances only, and who filled the place with their worldly activities.

The festival community itself was divided into many cliques and coteries. The Vienna Philharmonic, with their complicated interests, dominated the battlefield. Then there was the Reinhardt clique, the Walter clique, and last but not least, the Toscanini following, with its enthusiastic music lovers, its Italians, and other Toscanini " fans ".

Immediately after my arrival, I was dragged to the Café Bazar, where members of the Vienna Philharmonic were waiting for me.

Our old ties of friendship had only recently been renewed on the visit of the famous Orchestra to London, and before long we were deeply engrossed. Again conversations revolved round the customary subjects, the eternal Viennese problems whose aspect changes according to whoever holds the balance of power at that precise moment, and the temporary political and financial state of affairs. How remote those times seem now ! Many members of the Orchestra, as well as their chairman, have been dispersed all over the world since the *Anschluss*.

I discussed Covent Garden business with the director of the *Festspielgemeinde*, Dr. Kerber, who was also the director of the Vienna State Opera, and, of course, attended rehearsals and performances.

The programme was rich and varied, and I heard a magnificent performance of Verdi's *Requiem*, conducted by Toscanini, and saw him and his family afterwards. I was also interested to hear Gluck's *Orphée* under Bruno Walter, wonderful as far as the music was concerned, though the production did not appeal to me. Much simpler and more impressive were the Berlin and Covent Garden productions of this opera. The Hades scene had been far better in Berlin, and even more so in London, thanks to the Russian ballet.

On leaving Austria I almost got into trouble. The Gestapo official on the German side, an unpleasant type, suddenly refused to let me re-enter Germany. Although my passport, valid for five years, gave him no grounds for this, he began to question me in detail. He wanted to know why I was living in London, and many other things. He was the sort of person against whom one is quite helpless, and my mind was in a turmoil. I tried, however, a method I had never been able to use on earlier occasions when dealing with the Nazis, because I had up till now always been the weaker party. I was cool and rather rude. " I am staying in London because I have been appointed to Covent Garden." " Why have you been appointed there," the man then wanted to know. " You had better ask Sir Thomas Beecham," I answered. " I am on a business trip to Salzburg and Bayreuth, and you will see from my papers that I am expected in Bayreuth during this week." It worked. But he scrutinised me with great suspicion until the train left.

Sir Thomas having decided after all that it was unnecessary for me to meet him on the Continent, I was free to arrange my return journey as I liked, so I accepted the invitation of an old friend to stop at Mannheim. It is always strangely moving to return to the place of one's childhood, yet it is still more so to return after having been exiled. Coming back to Berlin had been exciting ; but Berlin was a big city, and everything there had been more or less connected with my work. It was a different matter in a small place where everybody knew one from girlhood.

The old Mannheim had vanished. Only a few old friends remained. The children of many of the elderly people were scattered over the four corners of the earth. There were many ancient and distinguished Jewish families in South Germany. From many of these I learnt of the fate and the wanderings of the younger generation. Everywhere the story was the same. The older people, although restricted in many ways, were as yet unmolested. Very few of those whom I met at this period wished to face emigration in their old age.

No one could foresee the future. The pogrom of November 1938 took a heavy toll in Mannheim ; people were killed, and homes I had visited in 1937 were burnt down or destroyed. A year later, masses of people were dragged into concentration camps, to be released only on producing a foreign visa. Whoever could do so left after these November days, but many were still unable to go. For those who remained, there was no mercy. Jews still domiciled in Baden and the Palatinate one day in 1940 were told to be ready within a few hours for deportation to an unknown destination. Sick and very old people only were left behind, husbands and wives were separated ; many people whom I knew personally died on the journey. They had to leave everything they possessed behind— where it was, of course, seized by the Nazis—with the exception of what they could carry, and they were finally confined in camps in unoccupied France, Vichy apparently having consented to this atrocious proof of the gulf between Hitler's new order and the rights of man.

Worse was to come, and in early 1942, these unfortunates were moved to eastern Europe, and later still in that year were among the victims of the Nazi's sinister " extermination programme ".

On my visit to Mannheim in 1937 interference and lack of freedom were certainly felt, but this merely enhanced the old friendships. I went to all the shops with whom my parents had dealt, and in many of them the old owners were still at work. The butcher who had served my mother's household immediately presented me with an enormous sausage of the kind that he remembered as being my favourite. The florist who had supplied my grandparents would hardly let me leave when the time came, and insisted on giving me a present for my mother. It was difficult to make him understand that I was returning to my home in London and not to Berlin.

I went to the Mannheim cemetery, which lies outside the town on the banks of the Neckar. It is hundreds of years old, and very lovely. I visited the graves of many friends, of my great-grandparents and grandparents. I stood beside the grave of my father and my only brother, profoundly thankful that they were spared the ordeals of our age.

About this time Sir Thomas was due at Vichy (not yet infamous), where he was expected to conduct a concert. However, he wrote to me that he had cancelled his engagement. Sir Thomas sometimes does not keep exactly to the letter of the truth, for reasons of his own, and so I was not in the least astonished when on the evening fixed for the Vichy concert, I heard the French announcer say that we were now going to hear Sir Thomas Beecham conducting, this also having been announced in the wireless programme. To show him that I was *au courant* I sent him a telegram on hearing this announcement, telling him that I was just going to listen in. It was not Sir Thomas, however, who conducted ; and for once it was not Sir Thomas, but the Vichy Radio, that had told the untruth.

Returning to London according to plan, Sir Thomas spent some days working at the Opera House. His main concern at this time was to secure the London Philharmonic Orchestra financially for the coming year. A schedule was drawn up for the whole year, week by week. All engagements were correctly entered, and then it was calculated how much money was still lacking to ensure the financial solvency of the Orchestra. Nobody who is not intimately acquainted with Sir Thomas can imagine the diligent and meticulous way in which he evolves schemes such as this for a year's activities. It never fell to him to enjoy the artistic side of his orchestra only.

I reported at length the result of my negotiations for the opera season to Sir Thomas. Fortunately, he has great human understanding, and so I could tell him quite frankly how I had found things in Bayreuth, as well as in Munich and Salzburg. Sir Thomas wanted an assurance, however, that Furtwängler was again going to conduct the *Ring*, thus repeating the beautiful performance of the Coronation Season, which had been so carefully rehearsed. Furtwängler had not yet definitely agreed. He had done so with reservations, and so had Tietjen.

Sir Thomas, after having listened to my report, simplified matters at once. For him reservations did not exist. " Now, listen, Doctor," he said very decidedly, " what you are trying to convey to me is all very well, but I have to consider only one thing, namely, what London wants, and with all due respect to our friends, I must make my decisions according to London only." " Well," I replied, " you alone can settle things. I am at the end of my wits." He was not, and drew up a letter for me indicating exactly what I was to say in order to remove the obstacles. This was effective, and the situation was clarified.

Chapter 35

IT MAY be premature to attempt a survey of the tragic circumstances which led to the present war. However, by the end of 1937 milestones on the road to catastrophe were becoming clearly visible, even to those previously unaware of the trend of events. An incident which for many may at the time have had only a sensation value, seemed to be symbolic for what was to come.

While we in London were already preparing for the winter season, on the Continent the summer festivals were still in full swing. The Salzburg Festival of 1937 lasted until September and included widely different elements. The principal figure was Toscanini, who, in spite of the fact that all the other musicians were linked with Austria's musical life by old tradition, was doubtless the greatest attraction of the festival.

After the assassination of Dollfuss on July 25, 1934, and at the time of the consistent underground Nazi activities in Austria, when bridges were blown up and other acts of sabotage committed, matters in Salzburg went from bad to worse. In addition to this, the receipts were reduced because the influx from Germany was stopped by the closing of the frontier between Bavaria and the *Salzkammergut*, and by the German passport regulations with regard to Austria.

Toscanini was on very friendly terms with the Austrians at the time and conducted frequently in Vienna. He helped to collect funds for the rebuilding of the Salzburg *Festspielhaus*, and was the motive power, as well as the leading figure of the festival. Hardly a room was to be had in the neighbourhood of Salzburg, because a public from Paris, London, and New York, and many Italians and other adherents of Toscanini had flocked to the *Salzkammergut*.

For many years Furtwängler had been invited to conduct at Salzburg but he had always declined, preferring a quiet and restful summer. In 1937, however, he had allowed himself to be talked over by the persistent entreaties of the Vienna Philharmonic, and had consented to conduct Beethoven's Ninth Symphony at the end of August. From all accounts this magnificent performance was one of the highlights of the festival.

Rumours then current that Toscanini had openly disapproved of Furtwängler's invitation to Salzburg cannot now be checked. Doubtless some discussions had taken place, and the idea had been expressed that one who conducted in Bayreuth would have done better to avoid Salzburg. As soon as he heard of this, Furtwängler went straight to discuss the question with Toscanini, who, with his forthright nature, told his confrère (with whom he and his family had always been on friendly terms) his ideas on this delicate matter. Toscanini, in his conversation (as told to me later by Furtwängler himself), concentrated his point of view into a kind of ultimatum: " Salzburg or Bayreuth ". For Furtwängler such an ultimatum would normally have presented no problem at all. He, so much in need of quiet and rest in the summer would actually have been relieved to have "neither Salzburg nor Bayreuth ". Somehow this incident and the exchange of opinion between the two conductors leaked out, and became for some time the topic of the day. The problem ." Salzburg or Bayreuth" was symbolic of the whole European situation. It was to be solved in a manner as unexpected as it was tragic. In March 1938 Hitler marched into Austria.

While this controversy of Salzburg preoccupied all those concerned, matters were also on the move at Bayreuth. The customary tradition of pausing for one year in three was broken by Hitler's request, and the next festival was fixed for 1938. Furtwängler, though he had decided not to return to the *Festspielhügel*, had not officially resigned, but had in conversations with friends and collaborators made no secret of his intentions. Winifred Wagner, well aware of what Furtwängler was contemplating, forestalled him by presenting him with a *fait accompli*. The *Festspielprogramm* for 1938 was announced ; among the conductors Furtwängler's name was missing. Only after that did she explain to him the reasons for her decision in a letter, a strange and curt document, doubly strange if one considers that it was written by the trustee of Bayreuth to a Wagner conductor of Furtwängler's rank.

Musical life in England at that time was flourishing, and developed a more international character than ever before. No political forebodings yet marred plans and their execution.

Sir Thomas Beecham concentrated his interest and energy on English concert and opera life. For the 1937–38 season he had a number of invitations to conduct on the Continent, but he cancelled the whole list with one stroke, much to my regret, saying : " I am needed here, not elsewhere ". England benefited greatly by this loyal attitude, which inspired all the musical activities connected with him. Each successive day was filled with work for the London Philharmonic Orchestra, for Covent Garden, the Royal Philharmonic Society, and the provincial societies.

In addition to old-established events, such as the Russian Ballet Autumn Season at Covent Garden, there were many new enterprises.

A group of young enthusiasts and artists had decided to give a series of Mozart Concerts at the Cambridge Theatre. Sir Thomas Beecham, to whom much of the increasing popularity of Mozart in England was due, was elected president. This was his first musical co-operation with his wife, then Miss Betty Humby. She, a keen Mozart player, approached Sir Thomas about her plan for the new Mozart series. The plan met with his full approval, and he launched the enterprise with a short article in the *Daily Telegraph*, September 4, 1937, which I will quote here :

"The artistic world generally has for long been of the opinion that Mozart is the greatest musical genius that has yet appeared among us. But beyond the pious acceptance of this belief, it has not begun to adventure. In other words, it is not paying him the more practical compliment of playing or listening to him.

"Of course, everyone is acquainted with a limited number of his works, mostly of the latest period—four or five operas and about the same number of symphonies and concerts. These and little else constitute the acquaintance of the bulk of people with the immense output of this unique prodigy.

"But very few, I venture to say, outside the small circle of genuine Mozart lovers realise that the catalogue of his achievement runs into nearly seven hundred pieces, of which to my own knowledge, something like two hundred are of striking originality and beauty.

"The aim of this new organisation, as I understand it, is to make a beginning in the direction of redressing this balance of neglect ; and it is because I heartily approve any enterprise of the kind that I have accepted the office of President.

"The larger revelation of the transcendent gifts of Mozart is a crying need in our present condition of dubious culture and civilisation. His spirit, more than of any other composer, is made of that stuff which can provide the most telling and efficacious antidote to the chaotic thought and action of a blatant age !

"If I were a dictator, I should make it compulsory for every member of the population between the ages of four and eighty to listen to Mozart for at least one-quarter of an hour daily for the coming five years."

Sir Thomas gave his services for one of the Mozart Concerts with the London Philharmonic Orchestra, and on this occasion made a speech in which he jocularly referred to the Glyndebourne Mozart performances conducted by Fritz Busch, saying : "Mr. Christie with his knowledge of wine and music should know that good Mozart, like good wine, needs no Bus(c)h".

One of the great events in English musical life is the Leeds Musical Festival. At the end of September, Sir Thomas Beecham had gone to Leeds with the London Philharmonic Orchestra to rehearse. The Leeds Choir is one of the world's finest, and Sir Thomas had arranged to repeat with them Handel's *Dettingen Te Deum* and Beethoven's *Missa Solemnis* at the Royal Philharmonic Society's first concert of their 1937-38 season in London.

316

According to the statement of a committee member of the Royal Philharmonic Society, Sir Thomas had omitted to inform them of his intentions regarding the Leeds Choir, and when the committee proposed to discuss finance he told them that it was not their concern. Accordingly the Royal Philharmonic Society, when confirming the programmes of the Season in a note to Sir Thomas, stated : " It is understood that the Society is not responsible for any cost in connection with the Choir ".

In Leeds there was great enthusiasm for the plan, but less financial support than had been anticipated. Sir Thomas had apparently also informed Leeds that the financial question was not their concern ! As the day of the concert approached, the Leeds Choir found themselves between Scylla and Charybdis, so Sir Thomas, with quick decision, settled the matter by defraying the whole of their expenses out of his own pocket.

The performance of the *Missa Solemnis* was magnificent—one of those rare occasions when a flawless technique supported the interpretation of a work of art, the rendering of the inner meaning of which is well known to be infinitely difficult.

A great authority on Beethoven, and the author of a notable Beethoven book, Dr. Walter Riezler, was in England at that time and attended the concert. The mere perfection of the Choir alone overwhelmed him. He declared that only at such a high level of technical proficiency could one begin to approach the spirit of this masterpiece.

Among other interesting autumn events in London were the visit of the Czech Philharmonic, with the conductors, Jan Kubelik and Vaclav Talich, and that of the *Orchestre des Concerts Colonne*, under the direction of Paul Paray. The concert of the French Orchestra was accorded official honours, a rare occurrence in England. Mr. Neville Chamberlain and Mr. Anthony Eden attended. Afterwards there was a reception by Monsieur Roland de Margerie, First Secretary of the French Embassy.

The English *première* of Schumann's posthumous Violin Concerto also took place that autumn. It was performed by Jelly d'Aranyi and the B.B.C. Orchestra, directed by Sir Adrian Boult.

At this time Herbert Janssen suddenly turned up in London. He was one of Germany's greatest baritones, a "pure Aryan", and a wonderful lieder-singer and interpreter of Wagner. For many years a member of the Berlin State Opera and Bayreuth, he was always the first to be asked wherever the parts of Kurwenal, Wolfram von Eschenbach, and Amfortas were to be sung. He had been forced to quit his home within two hours and to escape to England. What was the reason for this flight? I doubt whether anybody in England could really understand it. Intrigues, denunciations, envy, jealousy, all flourished in the soil of the Third Reich, and all had played their part in forcing Janssen into exile. It is true he had brought his main asset with him, his wonderful voice ; but it is one thing to have the background of one's country and two world-famous Opera Houses, and quite another to have to start life afresh in exile.

When I had come to England as a refugee in 1936, and no one yet knew of my appointment, Janssen had been one of the first to befriend me. Now that I had taken roots in my new habitat, I was glad to invite him to stay with me, and to help him to overcome the shock and grief of this upheaval.

Sir Thomas characteristically asked few questions and acted decisively. For seventeen years Janssen had come regularly to sing at the Covent Garden International Seasons. Now Sir Thomas engaged him for a "Beecham Sunday Concert", thus laying the basis for his new financial security.

At the beginning of November I went to Berlin. Sir Thomas had a concert with the Berlin Philharmonic, and also made records for *Zauberflöte*. The whole opera was being recorded ; the carefully selected cast came mainly from the Berlin State Opera ; and the Berlin Philharmonic was the orchestra.

The State Opera was just preparing a new production of *Tannhauser* with Furtwängler conducting, and Lorenz in the title-rôle, the dress rehearsal of which I attended. My time in Berlin was filled to overflowing ; but, as usual, personal problems cast their shadow over them.

Inquiries made on behalf of Herbert Janssen were either met with vain promises, or with icy politeness and impenetrable faces. It was heartbreaking to notice how integrity and the sense of right and wrong were now completely banished, while servility to superiors and the bullying of subordinates had become *de rigueur* in the Third Reich.

No sooner had I returned to England than another political exile confronted me—my old friend, Pau Casals, who had come to London to play Tovey's Cello Concerto with the B.B.C. Orchestra under Sir Adrian Boult. This small stocky man, with his thick spectacles and his pipe in his mouth, looks more like a clerk than an artist. The moment he begins to play, however, he is transformed. His face softens, and assumes the expression of a visionary. This is always so with him—never for him does Art become routine, but invariably the same mysterious inspiration. Nevertheless he was a firm and determined character, and a fervent patriot. He was indomitable and unyielding even in small matters. The uninitiated could not possibly know what an iron will lay behind requests made in his soft and mellow voice.

When in 1933 many international soloists refused Furtwängler's invitation to the Berlin Philharmonic Concerts for the 1933–34 season, one of the most beautiful, and certainly the most dignified letter, was from Casals, wherein he declared he could not return to Germany until the work of artists there was unfettered again. To this day he has not returned.

In 1937 he had had to leave his own home with a sad heart. A passionate Catalan, and an ardent democrat, he had been driven out of Spain by Franco's forces, and was now living near the Spanish prison camps for refugees at Perpignan. Our friendship was of long standing, but we had not met since the Brahms Centenary in Vienna in 1933. I went to see him on the day he arrived in London. It was difficult at first to find any words—so much had happened in the meantime, and so tragic were the present circumstances.

Later we talked for hours and hours : of Germany, Spain, himself, and myself. In the end we came round to music, and I said : " So often since we last met I have longed to hear you play Bach's D Minor Suite—for once heard, it can never be forgotten ". "*Attendez*," he said, unpacked his cello, and there in the prosaic hotel room, he began to play. The sublime music of the old *Kapellmeister* of Coethen banished for a while the despair we both felt in face of the tragedies of our countries.

However, our time was not entirely taken up with the tragic pre-occupations of our age. An amusing incident occurred when Sir Thomas went to Cambridge with the London Philharmonic Orchestra. The concert was to take place on a Sunday, and I had gone on in advance. When the concert was due to begin the hall was crowded and the Orchestra assembled, but there was no sign of Sir Thomas. After a pause of some little duration, it was announced that he had had a breakdown with his car, and would arrive shortly. Eventually he appeared and the concert started ; during the interval I went to see him. " Hallo," he said, " please come in and close the door." " Are you all right ? " I asked anxiously. " It was rather dangerous to come down by car in this fog. I thought you were coming by train." " I did come by train," Sir Thomas explained, " but I did not get out at Cambridge ". " How is that ? " I asked curiously, noticing a twinkle in his eye. " Well, you see, Doctor, one of the concert promoters was in the train and so I didn't bother about anything and played a bit of chess. After all, why should two of us concern ourselves with such details ? So I passed Cambridge—you had better ask *him* why ! By chance, looking out of the window at a station, I found we had reached Ely. There was only just time to jump out of the train before it went on again." " Goodness, how did you get back so quickly." " Oh," replied Sir Thomas, " that was very simple. There was a local train on the other platform and I got in." " But where did you change your clothes ? " I wanted to know. " There was no time to go to your hotel." " Never mind," he laughed, " trains have their conveniences after all ! "

I went to Berlin for the Christmas of 1937. There were not yet any codified regulations relating to such journeys by holders of German passports, and so the train was crowded with those travelling to spend Christmas at their home. Some of them lived abroad normally, and others had only left since Hitler's seizure of power.

The passport control on the train was in the hands of the Gestapo. It was my first experience of this. Several people were detained at the frontier and not permitted to enter. Many had their passports taken away after entering, and were fortunate indeed if they were able to get out again after weeks of waiting. I suffered no mishap, but I realised that the absence of regulations is always a double-edged sword.

[1 9 3 8]

Chapter 36

THE LONDON musical calendar for 1938 was complete ; there was hardly a day without a musical event.

Mengelberg came to England at the beginning of the year, and rehearsed with the London Philharmonic Orchestra the *Vorspiel und Liebestod* from *Tristan* for his Royal Philharmonic Society Concert. He treated the Orchestra as if they had never played or heard this music before. The London Philharmonic is an orchestra which does not show—at any rate for a long time—what it thinks ; but it does think a good deal, and very independent thoughts they are ! The relations between the Orchestra and Sir Thomas were always easy and cordial. He always treated a rehearsal as a joint undertaking with the Orchestra. " Let *us* do this again," he would say. " Let *us* try it this way." The musicians were entirely unself-conscious with him. Instinctively they accorded him the artistic authority which he did not expressly claim. Thus he obtained the best from them, and they gave it without reserve.

Mengelberg did not respect this tradition. His rehearsal manners are notorious, and his interminable lectures are torture to orchestral musicians. I was on tenterhooks throughout the rehearsal, and was not in the least surprised when a member of the Orchestra said to me : " If he goes on like this there will be a hell of a row."

I had known Mengelberg ever since 1924, when I had met him in New York with Furtwängler. He had been in charge of the New York Philharmonic for many years, and was a great favourite with the New Yorkers. Apart from his musical qualities, he was a very sociable man, who did not mind sitting up talking the whole night after a concert. He entertained very lavishly—a thing which the Americans greatly appreciated. It may be remembered that

America at that time was dry, while it is no secret that a good drink is enjoyed in the U.S.A. just as well as anywhere else. Mengelberg, who travelled on a diplomatic passport, kept this in mind and brought plenty of the necessary liquids with him, a fact which greatly added to his popularity. In the 1927 season, the New York Philharmonic had three conductors : Mengelberg, Furtwängler, and Toscanini. Furtwängler came after Mengelberg in point of time. We went on tour with the Orchestra, and when we arrived at our first stop, Washington, I remember the well-known baggage master of the New York Philharmonic, Mr. Salter, when dealing with Furt-wängler's luggage, asking me : " And where is the case ? " Naturally, I failed to understand, and only gradually did I grasp that " the case " meant the crate of liquor which Mengelberg took with him when going on tour with the Orchestra. Unfortunately, Furtwängler —who was a teetotaller—could not compete in this respect.

In other respects, however, he could compete with him only too well : for the New Yorkers, in spite of all their enthusiasm for Mengelberg, who, after all, had for many years trained their New York Philharmonic, took to Furtwängler and afterwards to Toscanini, which resulted ultimately in Mengelberg's eclipse.

Years later, on the occasion of a banquet in Amsterdam given by the *Concertgebouw* for the Berlin Philharmonic Orchestra, Mengelberg, who sat on my right, complained bitterly about this lack of gratitude. This was the first personal revelation to me of his human foibles, and ever since it has been a link between us which was renewed when I arrived in Holland as a refugee.

In the above-mentioned rehearsal I therefore felt as if I might now do something to ease the situation, and went to talk to him in the interval. In the course of this conversation I managed to mention casually that this Orchestra had played *Tristan* under Beecham, Furtwängler, and Bruno Walter. I think he understood.

At the end of January Furtwängler arrived in London with the Berlin Philharmonic. Nobody could foresee that this was to be their last visit before the outbreak of the war.

Some of his old friends came to meet Furtwängler after the concert. From February onwards sinister political shadows were to fall on life in England. On that occasion, however, none of us imagined what was going to happen in the near future and that within two short months, Baron Franckenstein, who was among those who had joined us, would be homeless, like the many exiles who had shared the warmth of his hospitality.

That particular evening deepened my misgivings about Furtwängler's position. I realised that his apparent toleration of the Nazi régime was superimposed on his deep loyalty to all that remained of the real Germany, but even this superficial acceptance of a system that was betraying our country grieved me deeply. After he had left for the Continent I wrote to him about what I felt, quoting the following moving passage from Stefan Zweig's new book, *Magellan* :

" The man of creative temperament is guided by other and higher laws than those of nationality. One who has a task to perform, a discovery to make, or a deed to do on behalf of mankind, is not truly a citizen or subject of any country, for his loyalty is given to his work. To one authority alone will he bow, that which the task itself imposes on him and he will find it permissible to ignore the interests of one State or one epoch, providing he is true to the obligations laid upon him by his destiny and his peculiar talents."

Later Zweig's own fate rang a knell over these words. He and his wife committed suicide in February 1942, the terrible year when so many people decided not to " tolerate the intolerable ".

The fateful month of March 1938 continued to be full of musical activity in England. The concert season was at its height. At this time Sir Thomas was often in Manchester, and he occasionally went to Sheffield, Liverpool, or Bradford with the Hallé Orchestra. The preparation and dispatch of his music and personal orchestral parts, always meticulously marked by him, was a very responsible task. However, sometimes scores were forgotten, or orchestral parts mislaid. Not always were we in London the real culprits, and I recall that one day, Mr. R. B. Hesselgrave, for many years Secretary of the Hallé Society, rang me up, insisting that a set of music was missing which later turned out to be in an unopened parcel already safely delivered in Manchester. On another occasion it was no false alarm. The scores and orchestral parts of Delius's Hassan Intermezzo and Prelude, which were required next morning in the North, really were missing.

Very late at night, when already in bed, I had a 'phone call from Manchester. " Sir Thomas," said Mr. Hesselgrave, " is extremely displeased." I was frantic. Sir Thomas had complained that the constant mislaying of music was a perpetual nightmare to him. Although I had nothing whatever to do with the supervision of the Orchestra library, I had made a bet with him that this nightmare was going to be ended, that no more mistakes would occur. Now I had failed lamentably. However, despair gave me strength. I tried to get in touch with the late Frederick Laurence, at that time manager of the London Philharmonic Orchestra, who had packed the music. The library in Covent Garden was closed at night, and Laurence had the key. I rang—no reply—his telephone was out of order. What could I do? I sent an urgent telegram to him at Finchley. After several hours of suspense, he telephoned back from a local call-box at two a.m. We arranged that I should 'phone the fireman at the Opera House to warn him that we were coming ; about four a.m. we met at Covent Garden and there was the missing music, beautifully packed, lying on the library table ! We took it to Euston Station in time for the early morning train to Manchester, where it was collected by the relieved Secretary of the Hallé Society.

Such are the alarums and excursions that go on behind the scenes, and of which, luckily, the concert-going public is seldom aware.

Chapter 37

EARLY IN 1938 there were certain new portents of trouble to come. Hitler had not made his usual traditional speech on January 30th, the anniversary of his becoming German *Reichskanzler* (an omission not to be repeated until 1943). There were many rumours about discontent in German military circles. A reshuffle took place in the Army and high Government posts. This did not receive much attention outside Germany, but was to be of far-reaching importance.

The cautious Foreign Minister, von Neurath, who advised against any violent action was removed, and rendered innocuous as President of a new " Cabinet Council ". Ribbentrop was appointed to his office, and was recalled from London, where indeed he had hardly ever been seen in public.

As far as Ribbentrop was concerned, Hitler was blind and would not listen to advice. Many people tried to explain to him that Ribbentrop had completely failed in England. The German ex-Ambassador had a few English friends, it is true, but his conceited manner, and the snobbish luxury with which he had rebuilt the formerly dignified German Embassy — where men like Prince Lichnowsky had lived on a third of his budget—only revealed him as a *parvenu* in the eyes of the British. He was an object of ridicule, known to the people as " Brickendrop " or " Ribbensnob ".

Meanwhile, the already precarious and delicate Austrian internal political situation was being threatened by perturbing influences of German origin. After some preliminaries, the Austrian *Bundeskanzler,* Schuschnigg, was inveigled to Berchtesgaden to see Hitler. The facts of this interview are known. Schuschnigg was forced to agree to reorganise the Austrian Cabinet by February 15th, and to accept Seyss-Inquart as Minister of the Interior. This did not only open the Cabinet to the Nazis, but—and this is the important point—it secured their control over the police.

Historically important events are not always seen as such when they occur. How little did the world seem to realise that the desperate struggles which were taking place in Austria were the last agonies of a free nation ! Yet, in America, some seem to have had a better prophetic sense, because on February 17th Toscanini had informed the Austrian Government by cable from New York that in future he would not conduct in Salzburg nor anywhere else in Austria.

On Sunday morning, the 20th of February, two paragraphs appeared in the *Sunday Times.* One reported a telegram which Bruno Walter, then musical director of the Vienna Opera, had sent to Toscanini urging him not to desert Salzburg, where everything was to remain unchanged. The other announced that Bruno Walter's contract with the Vienna State Opera was renewed for three years ! What a moment to announce this !—with the Nazis at the door. So far as the musical world was concerned, this news reassured some ; but those who were not blind saw that Austrian life was fated to pass through the same vicissitudes as that of Germany.

The Austrian situation and the political commentaries had their effect, and at last England began to grow restive. After some heated parliamentary debates, the British Cabinet was summoned to meet on a Sunday. "A Cabinet meeting on Sunday!" a friend, with relations in the Foreign Office, exclaimed to me with bated breath. These words mean more in England than anywhere else. Only a very critical situation calls for the break-up of the week-end and the holding of a peace-time Cabinet on Sunday.

On the same Sunday (February 20th) Hitler delivered a speech which had been tensely awaited in Austria, and which, although couched in vague, general terms, showed the Austrian Nazis which way the wind blew. Hitler had solemnly declared to the Reichstag on May 21, 1935, that he did not intend to interfere with Austria's independence, and in February 1938 he reaffirmed his recognition of Austrian sovereignty, which had been already expressed in the Austro-German Agreement of July 11, 1936.

The independence of Austria had always been strongly supported by Mussolini, yet during the days of the Berchtesgaden summons Austrian envoys tried in vain to reach him. While the late *Bundeskanzler* lived, and even shortly after his death, there was no doubt of Il Duce's friendly attitude towards Austria; the widow and her children were his official guests for some time. Now, when Dolfuss's friends urged him not to desert Austria, he smilingly changed the subject; in the meantime his line had been decided for him.

From that time onwards distressing letters from Austria poured into England. In London it was not yet possible to form a clear idea of the situation, but one sensed that the Austrians felt themselves threatened by the sword of Damocles.

On February 26th I visited the Austrian Minister about some musical matter; outwardly he was calm and no one would have gathered from his manner what must have been passing through his mind. He was a passionate Austrian, and for seventeen years had represented the interests of his country at the Court of St. James. We talked about his beloved Salzburg, also about the Walter and Toscanini question, and I felt how clearly he realised the imminent danger. "How is it possible, your Excellency, that you can be so calm?" I asked. "Crises make for calmness," he replied. It was certainly a crisis—he knew it. Nevertheless he did not cancel the reception for the Opera Circle planned long ago to take place in his

house, at which Mr. John Christie of Glyndebourne was to speak.
It was to be the last reception at the Austrian Legation.

During all this time, contrary to the agreements between Hitler
and Schuschnigg, intense Nazi propaganda was flooding Austria.
The whole Austrian Nazi movement had long been completely
organised underground. Every Nazi had his membership card, his
number, and his badge. Schuschnigg did all he could to counteract
these activities, and feeling ran high in Austria.

On March 5th a friend wrote to me from Vienna : " *Hier ist dicke
Luft* " (" The air here is thick "). It seemed to get worse from hour
to hour. The situation was such that only rapid action could have
saved Austria's freedom. Schuschnigg therefore called upon the
Austrian people to decide on the future of Austria as a free, independent, Christian state by a plebiscite fixed for Sunday March 13th.
Germany, at first, remained completely silent, and this ominous
silence filled many Austrians with foreboding.

Meanwhile, much happened behind the scenes. The German
Army was said to be on the move, and on the morning of the 11th
of March the Austrian Federal Army was mobilised. The plebiscite
was cancelled. On the same day it was suddenly announced on the
wireless that Schuschnigg would speak. We listened to him in
London at 7.30 p.m. He offered his resignation to avoid bloodshed
between Germans, and ended with the words : " God save Austria ".
Then the variations of the famous Kaiser Quartet by Haydn, the
theme of which forms the beautiful National Anthem of Austria,
were played. After this speech, records of Austrian classical music
were broadcast for some time. The Austrian radio was controlled as
long as possible by loyal officials ; then suddenly the *Horst Wessel
Lied* was heard. Austrian freedom was dead.

Every possible pressure had been used to compel Schuschnigg's
immediate resignation, because the Nazis realised that the plebiscite
fixed for the 13th had to be prevented at all costs. This plebiscite
would undoubtedly have decided against the Nazis. Experts were
of the opinion that at least seventy per cent of the population would
have voted for Schuschnigg's free and independent Austria.

Schuschnigg himself was arrested within an hour of his broadcast.
Immediately after his arrest, a torchlight procession, in which

hundreds of thousands took part, marched through the streets of Vienna. Everything had been prepared in advance—even the torches.

During the same night, Hitler entered Austria. Next day, when I was tuning in to the radio, I happened to hear a broadcast of the "enthusiastic welcome" the Austrian people gave the arriving troops. This entry was organised with all the appearance of a peaceful act. Triumphal arches and flowers greeted the arriving soldiers. Every house in Vienna which was "entitled" to it hoisted the Nazi flag (Jews, of course, were not permitted to display the swastika). It was said that all the Nazi flags had been sent by air from Germany. In reality it was an invasion, a military occupation, and eye-witnesses have told me how strangely cowed the population was by the dull drone of hundreds of aeroplanes "peacefully" circling over Vienna, and how disturbing was the effect on the public of this ocean of crimson banners.

On the day originally planned for the plebiscite the incorporation of Austria within the Reich was proclaimed. Oesterreich became Ostmark. Austria was soon "nazified". What had taken five years in Germany was accomplished there with ruthless determination within a few weeks. Mass arrests, mass shootings, dismissals, "Aryan" legislation, suicides, persecution—despair. None of the concomitants of Fascism were missing.

The Nazis, wherever they set their feet, never showed the slightest regard for any tradition. They only know the "present", the past does not exist for them. This is what Thomas Mann said on the anniversary of the bombing of Coventry (April 11, 1942) : "Hitler-Germany has neither tradition nor future ; it can only destroy. Let us hope that from its ashes a Germany will arise that will be able to think and hope, to whom will be given the retrospective love of the past and the anticipatory love of the future of mankind. Thus it will earn love instead of the mortal hatred of all peoples."

Emigration from Austria started at once—at least, those who were able to do so left. There were not many of them at the beginning. Soon all the neighbouring countries (Hungary, Switzerland, Czecho-Slovakia) shut their frontiers against those refugees who could not prove that they could eventually find homes elsewhere, and terrible tragedies occurred.

Many refugees from Nazi-Germany had already built up a new

life in Austria, and with one stroke this was ended for them ; those who had emigrated once, again found themselves on a pilgrimage into the unknown. Many Austrians, not driven by actual necessity, also prepared to leave their country.

The Gestapo and its passport department took possession of the Rothschild Palace in the *Heugasse*, and long before the doors opened, people flocked there from early in the morning onwards and waited patiently in the open air, moving slowly in an endless queue. Their Austrian passports were retained, and only on receipt of a German one, usually marked with a " J " for *Jude*, were they able to proceed on their journey into exile.

All who valued Austria and its traditions were deeply concerned at the changes wrought by the Nazis. German cultural life had been " co-ordinated " by the Nazis in a slow and painful process, but " co-ordination " in Vienna was no longer an experiment : it was merely a question of technique.

The *Wiener Staatsoper* was one of the first institutions to feel the change. Bruno Walter, for the second time in a prominent position in a country which was in the grip of Hitler, was fortunately not then in Austria, but staying in Holland. As he conducted a great deal in France at that time, he went there, and received French citizenship by a special decree. He did not enjoy his new nationality long. In 1940 he was again on the move, and has now found a new home and a richer field of activity in America. As the Nazis could not find him in Vienna, they sealed his flat, and when he became a Frenchman confiscated his belongings and sold them by auction.

The *untragbar* members of the State Opera immediately disappeared from the scene, while others seized the opportunity and pushed themselves into the foreground. The Vienna Philharmonic, this world-famous orchestra which celebrated its centenary in 1942, succumbed at once to Nazi control. Their active chairman, a great admirer of Toscanini and of Bruno Walter's, vanished immediately and appeared soon afterwards in Canada.

A number of members were pensioned off at once, among them the aged Professor Arnold Rosé, who had been the leader of the Vienna Philharmonic for fifty-seven years. He—the patriarch of the Orchestra, as he was called in Vienna—was the only one of the Philharmonic members on whom they had conferred honorary

membership. He and Professor Friedrich Buxbaum, the renowned
and witty principal 'cellist of the Vienna State Opera, came to London
shortly afterwards. A new Rosé Quartet was founded here, and,
deeply moved, an audience, with the ex-Austrian Minister, Baron
Franckenstein, in the front row, heard them play Haydn's Kaiser
Quartet.

The *Musikvereinsgebäude* in the *Canovagasse* also fell an immediate
prey to the Nazi spirit. During the many years when I had accompanied Furtwängler on his journeys to Vienna (1920 to 1933), and
also on my visit to Vienna on behalf of Covent Garden (1936), my
first errand had always been to pay a visit to the *Musikvereinsgebäude*,
to the *Generalsekretariat* of the *Gesellschaft der Musikfreunde*, founded
in 1812. There I used to see the enthusiastic Secretary of the Society,
Dr. Friedrich Dlabac, a passionate devotee of music generally,
and—like so many Viennese—an excellent chamber-music player
himself. Here everything concerning music was known even before
it happened ; here was the hub of the musical world ! Here, too,
were the archives of the Society, administered by people to whom
this work meant everything ; their priceless manuscripts, the portraits,
of musicians, and their letters. Here was the office of the Philharmonic,
a shrine testifying to their great tradition, with their *Ehrenwand*—the
wall displaying the photos of all the artists who had taken part in
their work during their century-long existence. Here was their
legendary attendant, Effenberger, himself a great crayon artist.
Here lingered the air breathed by Beethoven, Schubert, Bruckner,
and Brahms.

Soon it transpired that most of those who had worked in the
Musikvereinsgebäude were denied access to their offices. They were
rapidly replaced. Dlabac did not survive the fact that strangers
were working havoc in his office sanctuary. Soon afterwards he died
of heart failure.

In Germany the Mendelssohn monument in front of the Leipzig
Gewandhaus had been removed, as was the bust of Joseph Joachim
from the *Hochschule für Musik* in Berlin, and from the *Beethoven Haus*
in Bonn, where the Joachim Quartet contributed unforgettable hours
of musical inspiration to the Beethoven Festivals. In Vienna, too,
much was sacrificed to the idea that with the removal of symbols
the spirit could be destroyed. Thus—among others—the portraits

of Mahler and Walter, and the fine engraving of Rosé by Schmutzer disappeared from the historic wall of the Philharmonic office. The famous bust of Gustav Mahler by Rodin was removed from the great foyer of the Vienna State Opera, and the *Gustav Mahlerstrasse* was renamed *Meistersingerstrasse.*

Yet for many people there life went on as before. At the Opera many artists, not affected themselves, continued their work, and everything had settled down to the new order when, on Hitler's birthday on April 20, 1938, Furtwängler conducted in the presence of the Führer a gala performance of *Die Meistersinger.*

When Austria ceased to be an independent state, the Austrian Legation in London was immediately occupied by the Nazis, who hardly gave the Austrian officials time to pack in peace. Some of them were taken over by the German Embassy, a few went back to Austria, and some remained in England.

The Nazis naturally tried to get as many members of the Austrian Legation as possible to go back to Vienna. On March 15th I was a witness as to how dramatic such a summons could be. I was spending the evening with the Press attaché of the Legation, the late Count Huyn and his wife. A small number of friends were assembled, and throughout the evening the 'phone rang and messengers arrived from the Legation, which was in process of liquidation, telling him that Vienna insisted on his return—a summons which nevertheless he indignantly refused.

The period during which the Nazis were taking over the Austrian Legation was very trying. The Minister, Baron Franckenstein, moved out as soon as he could, although he was given a fortnight's grace to settle his affairs.

As a sign of protest against the annexation he refused to return to Austria and applied for British citizenship, which was granted immediately. His Majesty King George VI, who had conferred the C.V.O. on him at the end of the Coronation year, received him in audience, and knighted him Sir George Franckenstein.

On April 10, 1938, the plebiscite to confirm the incorporation of Austria into the German Reich finally sealed Austria's fate. A plate bearing the words *Deutsche Botschaft* was displayed at the former Austrian Legation in Belgrave Square, London, and the swastika fluttered from the roof.

Chapter 38

AT THAT time Covent Garden was inundated with letters from singers, *correpetiteurs*, and conductors who wanted to quit Vienna. Moving letters arrived even from members of the Vienna Opera—chorus and ballet appealing for help. As far as was possible at that late hour we responded ; Sir Thomas was always willing to assist in real need and distress, as I knew from my own experience. A number of international artists who could actually have remained in Vienna left as soon as possible. Kerstin Thorborg, for instance, the excellent Norwegian contralto, left on the night of the Nazis' entry, never to return. The incomparable Elisabeth Schumann, whose art was a high light of Viennese musical life, immediately left for London with her family. Lotte Lehmann, who soon after Hitler's advent had ceased to sing in Germany and concentrated on Vienna and Salzburg, was in New York at the time of the *Anschluss* and never went back ; instead we welcomed her and many others at Covent Garden that summer. On the day she landed from America she sang in *Rosenkavalier*, and it was said that her breakdown during the performance was due to the news she received about her family in Vienna.

More than ever was this Opera House a last sanctuary, not only for artists, but in many respects for the public too. Among the audience there were many people for whom their own soil had become dangerous, and who were grateful to find a fragment of their own lost world in the Royal Opera House, Covent Garden. Anna Mahler, a highly gifted sculptor, the daughter of Gustav Mahler, the composer and former director of the Vienna State Opera, came to London as a refugee, and seeing a poster advertising *Zauberflöte* for the night of her arrival, rang me up immediately and came to the Opera House. By a strange coincidence she shared a box with Friedelinde Wagner, who, though in a different position with regard to the Nazis, was quite determined by this time to sever her connection with Germany.

This Covent Garden Season was actually the last real Season before the war.

Although the casts were selected as far as possible without regard to the political situation, life at the Opera House reflected the trend of events more than it had done formerly.

A number of great artists who had in the old days been too busy at Vienna and Salzburg now came to Covent Garden and enjoyed the fresh air of freedom. There was Richard Tauber, the great favourite of the Viennese, and Erich Kleiber, who has been a wanderer since his voluntary departure from the Berlin State Opera, the day following Furtwängler's resignation on December 4, 1934. He had taken root again in Austria, the country of his birth, whence he sallied forth from time to time to conduct in South America and other countries. Now he was an exile again. Rose Pauly, the inspired interpreter of Elektra and Salome came to us too.

The Season started with a performance of *Zauberflöte* conducted by Sir Thomas Beecham.

A first night at Covent Garden still presented the same splendid picture. The German Ambassador, von Dirksen, who had taken a box for the whole Season still sat as a matter of course among the representatives of all the countries menaced by Nazi-Germany.

The London production of *Zauberflöte* took place under a lucky star. Artists and audience equally enjoyed the immortal music. Tauber sang Tamino. The scenery had come from Berlin. When Sir Thomas decided to do this work, I remembered the performance under Bruno Walter in 1926 at the *Charlottenburger Opernhaus*. The scenery for this Berlin performance had been painted after the water-colours and engravings of the poetical old *décor* by Schinkel. I made the necessary inquiries, and found that this *décor*, which was ideal for the *Zauberflöte*, was not being used at present, and possibly therefore available to us. Sir Thomas went to see the *maquettes* at the Berlin *Theatermuseum*, and decided immediately to use the Schinkel *décor* for his London production.

Schinkel had drawn twenty-six sketches for *Zauberflöte*, the first of which he designed in 1815. On January 18, 1816, a performance of this opera took place at the *Berliner Königlichen Theater*, and it was reviewed in the *Vossische Zeitung* on January 20, 1816. The Schinkel scenery is reproduced in the catalogue of the interesting *Zauberflöte Ausstellung* of 1928 at Salzburg. The originals of two of the most beautiful designs, a copper-coloured plate of the period,

the entrance to Sarastro's Temple, Act 1, Scene 5, and Sarastro's
Garden on an island, Act 2, Scene 7, are in the Music Library of Paul
Hirsch, now housed at the University Library, Cambridge. This
great collection, consisting of about 25,000 volumes of music and
books on music, is considered to be the most important of all
privately owned music libraries. It was transferred in 1936 from
Frankfort-on-Main to England, and is now on loan at the University
Library, Cambridge. Richard Capell, in an article written in 1937
in the *Daily Telegraph*, called it a " windfall for Cambridge ". The
collection comprises, amongst other notable sections, a great number
of rare theoretical works, over 1000 opera full-scores from 1600
to our days, etc. etc. It is especially rich in Mozart literature and
early printed editions ; a few original manuscripts by Mozart, including the string-quintet in D major—Koechel 593—may also be
mentioned.

For connoisseurs, however, the event of the Season was Strauss'
Elektra. Who could resist this marvellous performance, in which the
first-rate cast—Rose Pauly, Kerstin Thorborg, Herbert Janssen, and
Hilde Konetzni—co-operated with the magnificent achievement of
the orchestra, conducted by Sir Thomas Beecham.

The reserved Englishman was keyed up to an unusual pitch.
Elektra (Rose Pauly), intoxicated by the vehemence of the conductor, at the most dramatic moment gripped her delicate sister
Crysotemis (Hilde Konetzni) so hard that the poor woman burst
into tears. The public was in an ecstasy, and Rose Pauly declared
that she had never sung Elektra under such brilliant leadership.
After the performance she stormed in with me to see Sir Thomas,
taking him by surprise. Sir Thomas invited us to have drinks with
him, and we stayed talking for hours.

Many musicians and musical enthusiasts from all over the world
were present at this performance. The late Stefan Zweig, the
intimate friend of Gustav Mahler, Richard Strauss, Toscanini, and
many other famous musicians, wrote to Sir Thomas :

" *May 6, 1938,*
49 HALLAM STREET,
LONDON, W. 1.

" DEAR SIR THOMAS,—Allow me a sincere word of congratu-
lation. I have heard many a performance of *Elektra*, from the very

first one. I have heard those of Mahler and Richard Strauss himself (with the unforgettable Bahr Mildenburg)—but never in my life have I heard a more perfect than yesterday evening. I shall remain thankful to you for ever.—Sincerely yours,

STEFAN ZWEIG."

On the occasion of the 1938 performance of *Elektra* Sir Thomas wrote a few notes about some incidents at the occasion of its English *première*, which he conducted in 1910. He refers to this in his own book, *A Mingled Chime*.

When Richard Strauss heard of Sir Thomas's intention to give *Elektra* during the International Season in 1938, he presented him, on the occasion of his birthday, with the first and the last page of the full score, in his own handwriting, and bearing a very appreciative dedication. During the air raids of September 1940, Sir Thomas's house had a direct hit, and this document of a life-long friendship suffered the fate of so many irreplaceable treasures.

As I have said, the Covent Garden public was very exacting. It demanded its International Opera Season. However, when the Season was arranged with great difficulties and financial sacrifices, dissenting voices were heard. Some did not want Italians, and others objected to Germans. It was, after all, 1938 !

Sir Thomas never mentioned to me that—as I later heard from another source—he had been reproached for engaging the normally very popular Furtwängler for the *Ring*. He had invited him solely for artistic reasons—because he wanted to have the famous Wagner expert as conductor for his Season. However, the net profits of the *Ring* fell in 1938 by several hundred pounds in comparison with 1937.

It had never been the custom of Sir Thomas to discuss things while they were in a state of flux. He always considers matters for himself, makes his decision, and presents it to his entourage as a *fait accompli*. Nor would the hectic life at the Opera House have permitted long deliberations. So far, he had not discussed the European political situation, but one day in June he suddenly broached the subject.

I remember this conversation because it represents a milestone.

We were sitting in his office at Covent Garden. We were working and he began to talk. He told me that opinion in England had changed completely with regard to the Nazis—even in those circles hitherto friendly towards the genuine Germany. Diplomatic relations were the only link between the two countries; otherwise there were few friendly feelings left. The inhuman acts perpetrated by the Nazis in Germany and Austria, passively tolerated by the German people, were too outrageous to a free England.

He told me quite plainly that he would not acccept any future invitations to Germany. This was a hint to me to see that no such invitations reached him. He wanted to avoid having to hurt the feelings of his German colleagues, with many of whom he was on friendly terms.

Despite these stormy portents Covent Garden carried on, and artists from all over the world continued to participate in the International Season of 1938 which ended with a performance of *Die Meistersinger* on June 17th, under the direction of Sir Thomas.

Plans for 1939 were made immediately.

Chapter 39

ON MAY 21, 1938, the first Czech crisis occurred. There were rumours of German troop concentrations near the Czech border. England and France thereupon declared that they would not tolerate an invasion, and the British Ambassador to Germany made preparations for his departure from Berlin. Hitler, the great gambler, had not reckoned with this! He gambled, but there was yet no necessity to risk everything in one throw of the dice. Thus the danger was temporarily overcome; yet Germany did not relax its pressure on Czechoslovakia, and at the beginning of June there was no doubt that Henlein's demand for the Sudeten Germans could no longer be ignored. Inevitably the last democracy on the Continent opened its doors to the Nazis.

On July 9th I went to Germany on holiday and business combined. This was to be my last visit to Germany. My personal friends seemed unchanged, and all business transactions went as smoothly as ever. Yet, no sooner had I set foot on German soil than I had the feeling that great changes were taking place, and abnormal trends developing, and I knew instinctively that I would never return.

After a short stay in Berlin I went to Bayreuth for three days and there saw the general rehearsal of *Tristan* with the new scenery by Preetorius. Once more I saw all my friends, once more I succumbed to the charm of the *Festspielhügel*. I was not tempted to go to Salzburg, which was being quickly and radically reorganised, as if Max Reinhardt, Hofmannsthal, Bruno Walter, and Toscanini had never existed. Of course, it was easy to carry on with the united Austro-German artists, and the Italians were only too eager to take part. Furtwängler, who originally had wanted to refuse, after lengthy negotiations agreed to conduct four *Meistersinger* performances and one concert.

As usual this represented a compromise between his original decision and the pressure of the Nazis. It was all the more regrettable since the performances did not turn out as well as they ought to have done. Bayreuth was not well disposed to the production of Wagner operas in Salzburg. Furtwängler, who had broken with Bayreuth, had consented to go to Salzburg only on condition that he should conduct *Die Meistersinger*. However, he was not able to get a first-class cast. The artists required, most of them members of the Berlin State Opera who also sang at Bayreuth, could not obtain the necessary leave. Hitler is alleged to have supported this Bayreuth policy against Salzburg, although for many reasons Salzburg was also a useful tool to him.

On July 24th the world *première* of Strauss' new opera, *Der Friedenstag*, took place in Munich. On this occasion music-lovers, publishers, and music critics from all over the world assembled in Munich, probably for the last time before the war.

Germany was full of war rumours. Friends insisted that I should leave—"one never knows". At the Starnberg Lake people could not sleep at night because of the trains incessantly rolling towards the Czech frontier. Nevertheless, I could not accept the monstrous idea of another war.

On the 22nd of August I left Germany for the last time. On this journey back to England I had a pretty and amusing protégée. She was the seventeen-year-old great-granddaughter of Bismarck, Countess Beatrix Bismarck, who had been invited to England by a school friend. Her mother preferred her adventurous daughter to make her first journey to England protected by a friend. Beatrix, who could have melted a heart of stone, was one of these rare beings who can entrance even the most cold-hearted individual. We had reserved a sleeper together, but as soon as we got into the train at *Bahnhof Zoo*, the attendant, even before being tipped—most obsequiously offered us two first-class sleepers, and looked after us in every way. He was deeply impressed by the illustrious name of my companion, and her reflected glory shone on me.

No regrets weighed me down on this journey. I had long realised that the "eternal home" which one always loves, and to which one belongs, had ceased to exist for me in the present-day Germany. I had long left behind me the sorrow of parting and of renunciation. I had suffered enough.

However, my own experience enabled me to sympathise with others. An incident at the *Bahnhof Zoo* seemed to be symbolic of our time. In our coach one compartment was filled with flowers. On the platform a crowd had gathered round a distinguished-looking woman and a young man. The lady had a small bunch of violets in her hand. When she leant out of the window I heard her say: "This is from my garden". Next day, I saw her on the boat; she was sitting in a deck-chair, and she still held the little bunch clasped in her hands. The sleeping-car attendant had whispered to me confidentially: "This is Frau G—— (one of the best known names in the Berlin Jewish commercial world), she is emigrating with her son. We have passengers like that daily now!" My thoughts went back to the time when alone, and without flowers, I had stolen away in the night, and as always when on my way back to England I was filled with a deep gratitude.

My protégée and I arrived safely. The English Customs' officer was especially benevolent. I have always found that the innate English decency is reflected, in no small measure, in the Customs' officials and police constables. Representatives of these two classes are quite different in Great Britain from anywhere else in the world— especially the customs officer. However, if you are not honest, beware! We had brought a bottle of brandy with us, which we had opened during the crossing. It was a little more than was actually permitted ; but I immediately took it out and declared it, while Beatrix smiled a bewitching smile, and the official forthwith decided that if this bottle was our *common* property he could let it through. How different was this attitude compared to that of the Germans who, on our arrival at the Dutch frontier, had knocked at our compartments, and then started shouting because Beatrix could not open the door quickly enough.

In due course we arrived in London, and Beatrix went on to her hosts. I was relieved of my responsibility but missed her sunny smile. However, there was no time for regrets, as I had plenty of work and immediately became engrossed at the Opera House. A few days later my telephone rang : it was Beatrix : " Can I come and stay with you ? " " Of course," I said, " but I thought you were hunting ? " " Yes, I meant to, but the horses are too bad ! " said she. Not for nothing was she the heiress of the stud-farm of Varzin, the famous Bismarck estate !

She returned and did some sight-seeing, but her main concern was to get a pair of riding breeches such as only London could provide. Besides, she did not come alone, but was accompanied by an admirer. The rest of the story does not belong to this book. The young Englishman was even at that time in the R.A.F., and has now been decorated as one of the heroes of the Battle of Britain, and Beatrix shortly after returned to her native country.

About this time I had a strange visitor. He was a collaborator and friend of Pastor Niemöller. He had always been one of those personalities who emanate strength and serenity. In times of need and distress it is imperative to help one's self, but one is always grateful for any support from outside. When I thought my life was hopeless and finished, this man's moral strength, his unshakable belief that what is right and good is bound to survive all evil, had imbued me with the humble but fervent belief in that mysterious power which, unseen and unknown to us, guides our fate. Never can I forget how at midnight of New Year's Eve, a wintry and snow-covered night, just after the Christmas of 1934 when Furtwängler and I had parted, I felt myself irresistibly drawn to the old church where this man was officiating. There were many unknown faces there, but I also recognised many whom I knew to be in deep trouble. Never will I forget the overflowing church, and the priest himself, unfalteringly preaching what he deemed right—giving strength and hope to all of us.

Now he had come to England on the invitation of the Bishop of Chichester. Everything had been arranged so that he and his family could come over—for England was at that time really the promised land. However, he was determined to go back to Germany after a short visit, and to stick to his flock as long as possible. As far as I know, he is there still. How brave these people are and how little is really known of their steadfast courage.

Nothing is more grotesque and more improbable than some of the hazards of life. One afternoon, an English friend of mine suggested that we should go and dine with some friends in Surrey. After about an hour's drive we arrived at a beautiful English country house.

When we entered the hall, whom did I find among the guests . . . ? Dr. " Putzi " Hanfstängl, who after his flight from Germany had settled in a London suburb. Immediately on seeing him, memories of the sinister first months of the Hitler régime thronged my mind. Hanfstängl had then been Hitler's Press chief and had a great influence over the Führer, who listened eagerly to his gossip and his piano playing, and accepted his " musical judgement ". Hanfstängl, besides his official function, was a kind of court jester, until the jealousy of the Führer's entourage almost cost him his life. He was generally present at Hitler's notorious luncheons, and during the first few uncertain months people continuously reported alleged conversations between Hanfstängl and Hitler. He had enlightened Hitler on German musical life as it was, and as it should be. Because of him, Hindemith's head had " rolled ", and according to my information my own head, too, had fallen at this strange round table.

Hanfstängl had used his political power to push his musical friends. One day—a concert having been arranged with a famous pianist as soloist—he had rung the Berlin Philharmonic office, shouting through the telephone : " You must have Wilhelm Backhaus (then the favourite of the Führer) and no one else ! "

Without awaiting a reply, he had slammed down the receiver. I had taken the call and that had been, so far, my only personal encounter with the famous " Putzi ".

Hanfstängl, as a Bavarian, felt particularly called upon to interest himself in Furtwängler's affairs because the latter had grown up in Munich. Thus he was said to have been obsessed by my " case ". He had not the slightest idea of the work he felt it was his duty to interfere with, nor of the difficulties he was creating for his beloved Furtwängler, when he hinted to Hitler that Furtwängler's reliance on me was rooted not in my work but in my being indispensable to him in other respects. The Führer, always an easy prey to informers and soothsayers, apparently swallowed every word of this nonsensical myth, which, of course, had the same effect on him as a red rag on a bull.

Nobody will blame me that I could not bring a faked politeness to bear on this surprising encounter. However, Hanfstängl, whom I was meeting personally for the first time, warmly shook hands with me, saying : " Dear Fräulein Doktor, I am so happy that things turned out well for you after all ", as if he were my lifelong friend.

" What ! " I cried. " How dare you say such a thing, you, who always told Hitler that I have had three children by Furtwängler, and who were instrumental in making him treat us as he did ! " I was in a great state of excitement, but our hostess had the situation well in hand. She took my arm and said : " You two had better have a talk alone in the other room, here you are, and here is some sherry. . . ."

Meanwhile, the ominous month of September arrived. It was a golden English autumn. The Russian Ballet started in Covent Garden on September 1st, and the London Philharmonic Orchestra was playing. Sir Thomas, who always declared that September is the finest month of the year, had retired to the country because the Orchestra did not need him for the moment. Nevertheless, he was quite likely to appear at Covent Garden just when he was least expected.

London was sweltering under the autumn heat, and as usual hardly anyone had remained in town. Yet things were not as quiet as they seemed : a restlessness hung over the people. The question was asked on all sides, " How will events develop in Czechoslovakia ? " In spite of the radiant weather the clouds were gathering, and the distant thunderstorms were rolling towards the horizon.

Chapter 40

AS THE year grew older, people were pouring into England from the Continent. Many Czechs foresaw coming events, and some Austrians were still able to get out. Hungarians came, too, and a number of " non-Aryan " Germans who had emigrated to Italy in 1933, and were again homeless as a result of Mussolini's newly introduced racial law.

On September 8th the Nuremberg Party Rally began ; it was called the " *Parteitag Grossdeutschland* ". A number of prominent foreigners went—as guests of the Nazis ; but not all diplomatic envoys to Germany attended this rally.

Hitler was silent at first, and the programme was taken up with other items. Finally, on the 12th, the Führer delivered his long-awaited speech. He declared that Beneš would have to come to terms with the Sudeten Germans. If the differences were not settled " peacefully ", war seemed inevitable.

Meanwhile, life went on in Covent Garden as usual. Every morning I went to my office. There I sat, aloft, day after day, alone with my thoughts. Who was causing all the trouble ? " My country." Conceptions became confused. It is true I had left Hitler-Germany ; but I often noticed that some people failed to distinguish between refugees and other Germans. " Germans are Germans," they said. Again I was plunged into a conflict. Although our country had discarded us, according to International Law we were still Germans. This was difficult enough in peace-time—but now war was imminent. Nobody could blame the English if in their own difficult position they labelled us according to our passports. I saw the inevitable clearly enough. Three years of Nazi persecution had sharpened my senses.

There I was, in the Royal Opera House, Covent Garden, the secretary of the chief. Ghostlike, the old agony which had torn me away from my home and work arose again. Would I again be an outcast—now in the very land which had welcomed me so kindly, and this time because I was " German " ?

However, I kept these thoughts to myself. Who would have really understood my problems ? At such times, however, the high culture and kindliness of the English are much in evidence. While I could easily avoid contact with people in the Opera House because of my secluded office, collaborators frequently came up to my eyrie to see me. I never felt isolated. The Germans would have made one feel such a situation acutely, but the English, without words, did all they could to reassure me.

Rehearsals for the English Covent Garden Season had begun. There were to be three weeks in London, and performances later in the provinces. Amidst great difficulties private patrons had provided the funds for this undertaking. The spirit of the rehearsals was lamed by the uncertainty of the situation, which weighed upon everyone. The English seldom bother one with their personal troubles, and they expect the same reticence from others. But even the English are only human, and one day when the tension had become well-nigh intolerable, one of the secretaries came to my office. In her distress she told me that during the last war her father had been reported " missing ", and that her family had never had any further news about him. Her mother had never quite recovered from her tortured hopes, but had gradually become resigned. She herself was engaged, and her fiancé had to report immediately on mobilisation. " Do you believe there will be a war ? " she asked me in despair. All barriers were swept aside. I do not know who was more desperate, she or I ? We embraced each other without words.

On September 14th the tension had reached a climax. Minutes dragged like hours. The atmosphere was leaden, and nobody knew what was really going on. Towards lunch-time, hope for a peaceful solution had been given up. The chorus was rehearsing in the foyer for a performance which might never take place. In peace-time I had rarely listened to the news, but on the afternoon of this day I was tuning in on Sir Thomas's radio absent-mindedly, when suddenly a special announcement was made. " Mr. Chamberlain is flying to Berchtesgaden ! ! " What a respite ! If the Prime Minister flies to Berchtesgaden there may be a way out. I rushed to where the rehearsal was still going on and shouted : " No war for the moment, Chamberlain is going to Berchtesgaden." Everybody stopped, the terrible suspense was over, and the rehearsal then enthusiastically continued.

The September drama ran its course. The war of nerves in Czechoslovakia began. Hitler himself, in a circle of friends, boasted cynically of how the Czech " hostile acts " were manufactured. The Nazis were trying out a technique that they perfected later in other lands. They seized on the most trivial episode and magnified it till it became a mysterious and overwhelming threat. A man watered his window-boxes, the water overflowed, and the pavement was splashed. Before this minor occurrence had been finished with, it became a " poison-dew " falling from the heavens. Rumour was piled on rumour till the brain reeled and nerves cracked.

Mussolini proclaimed himself on Germany's side in the event of a conflict. Chamberlain, Halifax, Daladier, and Bonnet met on September 18th in London and agreed that all Czech districts with more than a fifty per cent. German population should be ceded to Germany. This was more than Hitler had demanded. The Czechs at first refused to accept these conditions. The tension was renewed. Chamberlain flew to Godesberg. Anxiously we waited in London. News was confused. Rumour of a deadlock at Godesberg was current. Again the spectre of a near war haunted us.

On September 24th, Chamberlain, then the symbol of hope for peace, came back from Godesberg. It was said that he had not been able to come to an agreement with Hitler and that war was inevitable.

On September 25th the *Observer* published an article by Garvin which epitomised the change of opinion that had taken place in England.

The situation grew more tense. The Allies, although ready to be conciliatory concerning the Sudetan question, threatened to declare war if Hitler tried to invade. Hitler delivered one of his notorious speeches in the Berlin *Sportpalast*. " The Sudetenland is my last territorial demand in Europe."

However, nobody could ignore the gravity of the situation. Immediately after Hitler's speech in the *Sportpalast*, Chamberlain broadcast a speech to which, among many millions, I listened. I felt that he was at the end of his tether and had given up all hope when he said : " How terrible, fantastic, incredible it is that we should be digging trenches and fitting gas masks here, because of a quarrel in a far-away country between people of whom we know nothing ".

We drew our own conclusions.

It became known that Hitler had ordered mobilisation of the German army at two a.m. on September 28th. The British fleet was mobilised. This meant war. We bowed to fate.

On the same day it was suddenly announced in the House of Commons that through the good offices of Mussolini, Hitler had invited the French and British Premiers to a conference at Munich. The sequel is known to everyone.

On September 29th " Munich " was signed. . . .

Mr. Chamberlain's umbrella was the symbol of " peace in our time ". Woolworth's sold small editions of it made of candy and black tissue paper. . . .

Chapter 41

SIR THOMAS had been absent from Covent Garden during the crisis. He reappeared for the first time at a *Faust* rehearsal at the beginning of October. Not a word of politics or of the nerve-racking past three weeks! On October 10th a short season of " The Covent Garden English Opera Company " began. On the programme were : *Faust, Madame Butterfly, Tristan and Isolde, Rigoletto, I Pagliacci, Cavalleria Rusticana, The Serf* by George Lloyd (first performance) and *Fledermaus*.

Normal life was resumed, but England had suffered a severe shock. It was a miracle that in spite of all the previous excitement the opera season was able to take its normal course. Nevertheless, everything went smoothly.

345

A torrent of orchestral concerts and recitals began. The performances of the Brandenburg Concertos and Orchestral Suites of Bach by Adolf Busch and his Chamber-Orchestra were especially high lights for lovers of this *genre*.

London was overflowing with an International public. Frontiers were still open then, and besides many Austrian, Czech, and German refugees who continued to flock to England, more and more visitors from all parts of the Continent arrived who seemed to feel happier and safer in England.

Germany's bloodless victory in Czechoslovakia after the annexation of Austria strengthened her hand, not only with regard to foreign but also to home policy. As always, Hitler immediately took advantage of this political success abroad to push forward his programme at home. "Non-Aryans" in Germany and Austria were suddenly ordered to report at their local police-stations, where their passports were confiscated. Thus they were prisoners in Germany and at the mercy of future measures.

Shortly afterwards it was announced that "non-Aryans" in Germany and Austria ("Greater Germany") would in future have passports issued to them for the purpose of emigration only. In other words, a new way was found of expelling undesired people, and of seizing their property under the cloak of patriotic sentiment. It was further announced that these emigration passports would be stamped "J" for *Jude*. Every "non-Aryan" would be compulsorily named "Israel" or "Sarah".

Even "non-Aryan" bearers of German passports domiciled abroad were requested to report at German Consulates to have the "J" stamped on them, and to have the conspicuous additional first name inserted.

Perhaps people within Germany had gradually become immune to such humiliations, incredible as it may seem. But for those living abroad, such a measure was bound to arouse indignation and protest. Sir Thomas had always been full of understanding in all my Nazi troubles, but I usually avoided burdening him with sordid details. This time, however, it had gone too far. Everything in me revolted at this new indignity, and I was determined to ignore the new measure. I wondered what he would say, and so I put the case before him. "I don't want my passport stamped with a "J", and I am not going

346

to be called Sarah. It isn't my name, and I don't want it," I protested excitedly. " But why are you so scared," Sir Thomas laughed, " Sarah is a very beautiful name, it was my great-grandmother's." However, in spite of his jocular reply, Sir Thomas understood me perfectly. And I did not hand in my passport to be stamped.

Although his duties as president of the Hallé Society took him frequently to the North, the centre of Sir Thomas's activities was naturally London. Apart from the Beecham Sunday Concerts at Covent Garden, he had organised a number of Saturday Concerts with famous soloists, and selected programmes for the season 1938-39 at Queen's Hall.

All the time remaining from these activities was used for making recordings with the London Philharmonic Orchestra.

The Columbia discs of Beecham with the London Philharmonic have a world-wide fame. The art of orchestral playing for recording has been more thoroughly mastered by this combination than by any other. The quality of the recordings that it has made here is acknowledged even in America, a country famous for its electro-acoustic achievements, as well as for its orchestras.

About this period, flawless recordings were made of Chabriers's *España*, Mozart's Haffner Symphony, Rossini's William Tell Overture, Bizet's Carmen Suite, Sibelius' *En Saga*, Grieg's Peer Gynt Suite, and of Berlioz's *Damnation de Faust*.

Enthusiasts are always delighted as well as amused to hear from the final grooves of the disc devoted to the *Danse des Sylphes* from the Berlioz work, the voice of Sir Thomas saying : " Thank you, gentlemen " to the Orchestra.

Sir Thomas, as " the *entourage* " knows, does not share the common tendency of conductors to hold inquests after their concert performances ; but it is a different matter where recording is concerned. With infinite care the same piece has to be recorded over and over again until it seems good enough for him. The same careful attention is given to the test records when they arrive. They are all played many times before Sir Thomas consents to their release. Only by such meticulous care is he enabled to combine the exigency of the recording technique with his artist's vision of how the music should sound.

As an example of his fastidiousness over the making of recordings, the following story has been told. After a concert performance in America of *The Dream of Gerontius*, he was approached with a view to recording it. The engineers said they were prepared to give Sir Thomas five hours for this.

"Five hours, my dear sirs," he replied, "just time for me to start a headache in."

If he did record "The Dream", five months would be nearer the mark, and then he would probably scrap the records and start again.

In spite of his brilliant social talents, Sir Thomas liked best to spend a quiet evening at home, reading or playing his records, sometimes a friend being invited to listen. On such occasions the records were scattered all over the place, and the morning after one could not safely enter the room, so great was the danger of treading on some precious disc. This state of things was a nightmare to his servants who dared not touch anything, and finally it was arranged that I was to look after the records. I stored them methodically in boxes, labelled in big letters, so that he might easily find what he wanted and easily put it back—but somehow they were never put back in their places and the perpetual hunt for mislaid discs continued.

Sir Thomas had long been recognised as a leading protagonist of Sibelius, and now felt that the time had come for British music-lovers to honour the great Finn. His idea in planning the Festival was that by hearing a great number of the works by Sibelius in a concentrated space of time, the public would gain a better impression of the magnitude and versatility of his achievement.

An introductory article by Sir Thomas for this festival appeared in the *Daily Telegraph* and began with the following characteristic opening :

"I have been asked more than once why I am giving a Sibelius Festival. I remember that nine years ago, when I organised the Delius Festival, the same question was put to me. Of course the simplest answer in either case is : 'Why not?' and as far as I am concerned it would be satisfactorily final."

Sir Thomas had rehearsed with the London Philharmonic Orchestra over a dozen works not previously included in their large Sibelius

repertoire. During this time of preparation he was so obsessed with
the music that he had neither time nor thought for anything else.
Even his habitual courtesy deserted him—for courteous he is always
—though his icy politeness when he is angry is not always pleasant
to encounter. He was very rarely brusque to me, as, after all, he
realised that I simply had to get out of him the necessary approval
for many things dependent upon his decision. But when I once
approached him at the time of the Sibelius rehearsals, he flashed
back at me : " To hell with anything but Sibelius ".

The Sibelius Festival was supported by a large list of patrons, and
the London Philharmonic records that one day, at a rehearsal of one
of the most delicate passages of *The Death of Mélisande* one of
them, a famous London hostess, burst into the hall with a clatter and
a bang. Sir Thomas turned round and hissed savagely : " My dear
lady ! Do you think this is Waterloo Station ? "

The Festival opened with the first concert of the Royal Philharmonic Society's 1938-39 season, which was attended by the
Duke and the Duchess of Kent. The Festival programme consisted
of six concerts which were to include all seven symphonies, most of
Sibelius's greater works and selected smaller works and songs.

Sibelius, who had been expected to attend, was not well enough
to make the long journey, but his daughter, Mrs. Ava-Paloheimo,
attended all the performances. As far as was possible, Sibelius
followed the progress of the Festival by radio and later conveyed
his thanks and admiration to Sir Thomas by letter and telegram.

Gradually, almost imperceptibly, the development of events began
to overshadow the world. At the end of January 1939, one of the
customary foreign tours of the Berlin Philharmonic under Furtwängler was to take place. Although Furtwängler's reconciliation
with Hitler in April 1935 had seriously dimmed his halo, and lessened
the admiration which his earlier heroic resistance had evoked, his
great and unique art still had its devoted adherents.

Ever since 1935 life had become difficult for him outside as well as
inside Germany. By November 1938 he was worn out. In spite
of all the honours which the Nazis showered upon him, they never
quite trusted him. Yet he did not realise that abroad the fact of his
remaining in Germany was resented, and that he was regarded as

one who, for the sake of personal benefits, tolerated Hitler-Germany, rather than one who—as *he* thought—stayed on to fight.

Furtwängler's hypersensitiveness often made his life difficult, but when it came to the point he had always a very subtle instinct. He had at that time strong doubts with regard to the impending visit of the Berlin Philharmonic to England. Events were certainly taking a course which would soon make compromise impossible. Since "Munich", much had changed. However, it was not simple for him to drop of his own accord the English tour, which had become a kind of tradition for so many years, especially so as the Nazis were frantically opposed to its abandonment. Soon, however, fate facilitated his decision : on November 7, 1938, a Polish Jew, Herman Grynspan, shot the secretary at the German Embassy in Paris, Herr vom Rath. As a "punishment" the Nazis staged a pogrom, and an enormous indemnity was demanded of every "non-Aryan". Thousands of people were thrown into concentration camps, from which they were only released on the production of a foreign visa.

A wave of indignation swept the world, and it was not surprising that even those Germans who did not condone these actions were held responsible. After all, the entire German people had passively witnessed these happenings, although a number of them had felt despair and shame. Gradually it was becoming more and more difficult to draw the line between Nazis and other Germans. Furtwängler would now have had to cancel his English visit in any case.

Reaction to these events was strong even in Germany. A Nazi Party member of long standing with a very low membership number, one of those who did not foresee the course of developments when joining the Party, wrote to me quite unexpectedly when abroad on a short business trip. We had never been in correspondence before. He wrote : "In view of what has happened in Germany and what must disgust every decent person, I want to assure you of my friendship. Believe me," he added, "millions of others feel as I do."

Whatever the non-Nazis may have felt—it was too late. Thousands of German "Aryans" and "non-Aryans" endeavoured to leave after November 1938.

My mother was seventy at that time. She was living in Berlin, still unmolested, but she had been shocked and unnerved by recent events. There was still a number of the older generation of her friends in Germany, and we had thought that it was better for her, at her age, to stay in her country. Many emigrants had made similar decisions about their own families. But after these last events, she wrote to me that she was quite determined to leave Germany, no matter under what conditions she might have to live in future. I immediately took the necessary steps. Although this was fairly easily arranged on the English side, because conditions for people over seventy who wanted to immigrate had been simplified, many difficulties had to be overcome.

A little incident may illustrate the unnatural conditions which prevailed as early as 1938 in Germany. The British Chargé d'Affaires, whom I had met when in Berlin with Sir Thomas, was kind enough to advise my mother, and rang her up one day asking her to come to see him at the British Embassy in the Wilhelmstrasse. My mother had to inform him that she was unable to do so, as she was not allowed to set her foot in that particular street, nor Unter den Linden. The British Consulate, where the visas were dealt with, was, unlike the Embassy, not in a forbidden street. He therefore very kindly asked her to have a drink with him at his house at Charlottenburg, where he could talk to her, and tell her what to do. Nevertheless it took fully nine months before her affairs were settled in Germany, and my mother was able to join me, having to leave practically all her property behind.

The English concert season traditionally finished before Christmas with a performance of Handel's *Messiah* conducted by Sir Thomas, and it did so this year as well.

For Christmas I went to Paris, where I spent a little time with friends. An unusually cold spell had swept over England. The water-pipes, especially in an old house like mine, could not stand up to it. They had all burst, and I had been left without water. A failure of the gas supply added to my discomfort. It was with genuine delight therefore that I boarded the *train bleu*. In a comfortable Paris hotel with the central heating which the English do not very much care for, but which strongly appealed to me, I gradually thawed.

I spent Christmas Eve with Herbert Janssen and his wife. Janssen, after his exodus from Germany to England, had been engaged by the Vienna State Opera. With the *Anschluss*, this engagement had come to an end, and he had been very busy in London during the 1938 season and had later gone to Paris for a few months. For the summer of 1939 he was to return to Covent Garden and was then to go to Buenos Aires, and later on to the Metropolitan Opera, New York.

We had a tiny Christmas tree, and the evening, although melancholy, was on the whole comforting and sweet.

Paris in these days was full of refugees. Besides the Germans who lived there since 1933 there were now many Austrians and Czechs as well, and somehow the physiognomy of the town seemed changed.

Furtwängler was in Paris just then and conducted two performances of *Siegfried* with German singers at the Paris *Opéra*. He was grave and thoughtful through all this time. He still held the view that it was his duty not to leave his country and his orchestra ; but once away from Germany he had a clearer perspective and saw everything more objectively. He was greatly depressed, and the strain of the times lay heavily upon us.

After the New Year I went back to London. It was my last meeting with Furtwängler. His Paris performances at Christmas 1938 were to be his last before the war, because the Wagner Festival planned for June 1939, at the Paris *Opéra* under his direction, was cancelled by order of the French Government.

[1939]

Chapter 42

THE YEAR 1939 had a fateful start with the visit of Mr. Chamberlain and Lord Halifax to Rome. As an accompaniment, sinister with foreboding, was the Spanish War with the fall of Barcelona, which was to be followed by the fall of Madrid in March. These events were given less attention in England than in France, across whose

frontiers refugees were pouring. The Continent had forced its
traditions farther and farther to the west, and more and more London
became the haven of the old world. Bruno Walter, then already
a French citizen, came in January and conducted a programme at
Queen's Hall, which included Mahler's First Symphony which was
received enthusiastically by his friends, especially his old Viennese
followers.

Felix Weingartner also came over and conducted his traditional
concerts in England. It was amazing to see how much he still got
out of the orchestra—one sensed the master. In spite of his seventy-six
years, he was full of vigour and great charm. Every morning, when
other people were still asleep, he went for a walk in Hyde Park. I
sometimes accompanied him, and on one of these occasions he described
to me a curious state of affairs. Although his " ancestry " was fully
satisfactory, he had never been permitted to conduct in Nazi-Germany.
Shortly after the *Anschluss* while still receiving his salary as guest-
conductor for the Vienna Opera and Philharmonic, he was prevented
from conducting in Vienna, although his contract was still operative.
No one gave him a reason, and when he turned to Berlin for an
explanation, he received the evasive reply that everything was
" all right ". This went on until one day he thought it advisable
to move to Switzerland, his wife being Swiss and he a Swiss
citizen.

After war broke out, Weingartner occasionally wrote to me. I
had just received a photo of him, taken in his seventy-ninth year,
and had been delighted to see the unchanged, young, and fresh expression of his fine features, when his death was reported on May 7,
1942. With him the last representative of a generation of great
conductors passed away.

The gloom of the political horizon was by no means lightened
by Hitler's " peace speech " on January 30th. Sir Thomas, however,
was determined to give his International Season. To stir the British
public up he wrote one of his peppery articles which appeared in
the *Daily Telegraph* on January 28, 1939. I give excerpts from
it here :

SEASONABLE THOUGHTS

Shall not Covent Garden Stand Where it Did?

By Sir Thomas Beecham

" An eminent personage is of an opinion that the world is growing madder and madder ; and there is some ground for it. Each day sees the leaders and prophets of differing political creeds proclaiming more noisily and vehemently the superiority of their own pet superstition over that of any other.

" Here we continue to vaunt the blessings of democratic institutions without staying to reflect whether or no we are an actual democracy.

" It is not so long since we viewed the unedifying spectacle of a British Prime Minister confessing, in the House of Commons, that he had concealed for years the facts of our weakness in national defence for the reason that the public, in his view, was too pacifically minded to endure the truth. If this is not the entire negation of democratic leadership, then I should like to know what is.

" Last September there was a crisis, and the nation was taken by surprise to the extent that no man or woman knew in the least what to do. Had there been war we should have found ourselves in a condition of chaos and unpreparedness far greater than that of 1914. Whatever may have been the causes of this state of things, no one in his right mind can maintain that they are worthy of either a great or free people. Yet to transform ourselves into a modern State capable of defence at all points against the concentrated forces of nations otherwise ruled or controlled will necessitate, if not surrender, at least the modification of some of that individual freedom and privilege which is apt to be mistaken for indiscipline and irresponsibility.

" This must inevitably lead to closer regimentation and an approximation to the idea either of the classical or of the modern totalitarian State. That is not to say that we shall not preserve for many years to come far more both of the semblance and of the reality of a democratic State than perhaps any other country in the world : but the divergencies between ourselves and some of our Continental neighbours will, as time goes on, become less pronounced. They will obtain a larger measure of personal liberty, and we shall lose something in the direction of individual licence.

" It is safe to prophesy that the ideological lunatics, who abound in every country will, both in the Press and out of it, continue their unhappy endeavours to widen the breach between one country and another. I look forward therefore to a highly ironical and diverting climax to the current epoch of political myopia.

"Just about the time when the rulers of the nations have organised their followers into two or three gigantic groups, all ready to fight and die for what are represented to be irreconcilable philosophies of life, then it will be discovered that in essence there is very little difference (if any at all) between Tweedledum and Tweedledee. A vast wave of unextinguishable laughter will overcome the opposing sides, who will then probably fall upon each other's necks and live happily ever afterwards in international concord.

"I do not know if the eminent personage to whom I have alluded intended to include this country in that portion of the world to which he imputed a condition of comparative lunacy. But whatever we may think among ourselves of the aberrations of our neighbours, we should not be able to defend ourselves very successfully if the charge were levelled against us.

"For how else can one explain the almost general state of apprehension and nerves which now prevails among us? The carefree optimism of past years has yielded to black pessimism. Each of these moods was, and is, without true foundation, but the latter is the more dangerous of the two.

"Masses of otherwise sensible people have gone to the extremity of wondering whether in this dread time we ought to be amusing ourselves as usual. I have received letters from men occupying responsible positions in the country who consider that in view of what they term the international situation there should be no opera season next summer at Covent Garden. When I see closed all the theatres, music-halls, cinemas, football grounds, and cricket fields in the kingdom by reason of some veritable national emergency, then and then only shall I acknowledge a grain of sense in such an extraordinary suggestion.

"For something like two hundred years Covent Garden has been the home of international opera. The renown of this ancient theatre is such that every foreign as well as native artist aspires to appear there some time during his or her career. The superior character of its performances has contributed as much as anything else in our artistic life to establishing London in the pre-eminent position it occupies to-day in the international world of music.

"And yet it is seriously proposed that because we are suffering from a temporary access of jitters and jumps that would bring discredit upon a community of elderly nuns we should discontinue an event that is as regular a feature of our yearly calendar as the Royal Academy, the Military Tattoo, or the Eton and Harrow cricket match.

" Even during the really grim days of 1914–1918 London was never without an opera at some time or other of the year. I recall with especial gratification certain performances at Drury Lane which I conducted myself to the sound of German bombs exploding within a few feet of the theatre, to say nothing of our own anti-aircraft guns—when neither performers nor public paid the slightest heed to such distractions, but behaved in every respect as in normal times.

" The international situation ! What undesirable use is being made of this phrase to divert so many from the enjoyment of their own particular pleasures ! And among the objects it is deemed necessary to abandon it is generally something of an exalted kind, artistic or cultural, that is indicated first. Let us therefore, the subject being International, see how other countries are behaving during this period of stress and uncertainty.

" When the King and Queen visited Paris they attended a State performance at the *Opéra*—an institution, incidentally, which runs for ten months in the year. When the Prime Minister went to Rome, he was invited as a matter of course to the Opera, which paid him and his fellow-countrymen the happy compliment of playing *Falstaff*. In New York at this moment there is running an opera season of five months' duration, in which are to be heard all the great artists of the world—German, Italian, French, British, and Scandinavian. Such is the American attitude to music and opera, in spite of a political antipathy to Nazism and Fascism that exceeds even our own.

" In Germany it is hardly necessary to inform the reader that in upwards of seventy towns, opera is being given practically all the year round. As for the rest of the world, I have yet to hear that at Stockholm or Prague, at Budapest or Brussels, or any other capital has it even been suggested that the opera houses should be closed.

" Only in London is such a proposition capable of utterance. And when it is remembered that our season lasts no more than seven or eight weeks, it will be realised how fantastic it is that such a sacrifice should be offered to the altars of prejudice or poltroonery. What would the rest of the world have to say if we provided such a deplorable exhibition of timidity and narrow-mindedness ? Only a few weeks ago German artists were invited to the Paris *Opéra*, and the theatre was crowded to welcome them. Similarly,

French and English singers and musicians appear in Germany, and
are treated with respect and cordiality. Let us on our part show
that in matters of art and culture, and especially in music, which
is the common property of the entire world, we can rise above the
ephemeral conditions of purely political discord, and maintain our
old reputation for national sanity and understanding.

"There must, and shall be, a season at Covent Garden ; and I
shall be surprised if it does not begin as usual on May 1 next,
conducted on lines similar to those familiar to the world during
the past two centuries."

Unmoved by apprehension, Sir Thomas began his preliminary
work, and had just arranged a visit of the German Opera from
Prague when politics intervened. With the now familiar technique,
President Hacha of Czechoslovakia was ordered to Berlin on March
13th. On March 15th Hitler moved into Prague.

Covent Garden changed its plans and cancelled the official visit of
the Czech Opera, but a number of singers who escaped from Prague
found a place among the cast of the International Season during the
summer.

While the Continent was a prey to policital convulsions, the Royal
Opera House was the scene of a friendly demonstration of the first
order. On the occasion of the State visit of the French President and
Mme. Lebrun to England a command performance took place.
Sir Thomas had been asked in January to arrange a gala performance
at Covent Garden.

The old and dignified Opera House was decorated for the occasion
with the finest tapestries and French furniture to be found in England.
A fragment of tapestry had been found woven in honour of the
marriage of Charles I and Henrietta Maria of France in 1625, and it
bore the following words, so significant also for the present occasion :
"*Aimez vous, les Uns les Autres*". This tapestry was hung at the
entrance of the Royal anteroom and greeted the arriving guest of
honour.

The Court, the *Corps Diplomatique*, members of English society,
and many high dignitaries were assembled in the festive splendour
of the Opera House, which has seen so many memorable Gala
performances in the course of centuries.

As early as March 28th, London musical life again reflected political events. Pau Casals, that great lover of freedom, had offered to give a concert in the Albert Hall " to aid Spanish children ", who were suffering unspeakably as a result of the Spanish Civil War. Franco's victory seemed imminent, and official circles remained non-committal. On the day of the concert (March 28th), the Spanish Republic surrendered to Franco. A strangely tense atmosphere pervaded the Albert Hall, but I have never heard Casals play more beautifully.

When in 1942 the Nazis overran the rest of France, Casals was said to be one of a number of political prisoners turned over to Franco. This was, however, denied later.

I had written to him some time before, trying to find out how he was, and whether he would not be able to come to England and play with the London Philharmonic Orchestra. This was his reply :

" PRADES,
7 juillet 1942.

" MA CHÈRE AMIE,—Vous me faites un bien grand plaisir avec votre lettre. J'ai pensé tant à vous et à tous mes amis ainsi qu'à mon cher public de Londres et de toute l'Angleterre duquel j'ai reçu sympathie et fidélité depuis 43 ans ! Rien ne me ferait plus de plaisir que de revoir tant de personnes et de choses qui me sont chères dans ce pays. Malheureusement les difficiles circonstances du moment m'en empêchent et Dieu sait pour combien de temps encore.

" Toutes ces années mes activités artistiques ont été réduites à la Suisse et en France. Ici il ne s'agit pour moi que de me rendre utile à ce bon peuple Françai set à mes compatriotes exilés — le sentiment d'aider me soutient dans mes propres préoccupations. Dites à l'Orchestre combien j'apprécie leur cordiale salutation à laquelle je corresponds de tout mon cœur. A tous mes meilleurs vœux.

" A vous, chère amie, ma reconnaissance et affection.—Votre.
" PAU CASALS.
" VILLA COLETTE,
ROUTE DE RIA, PRADES,
PYRÉNÉES ORIENTALES."

Shortly afterwards the Anglo-Polish pact against aggression was concluded. Naïve indeed were those minds which were surprised at the fact that Mussolini selected Good Friday (April 6th) for his invasion

of Albania. Hardly had the sympathy for poor Albania and the
fleeing Zog family with their new baby died down, when it was
made known that Hitler had denounced the Anglo-German Naval
Agreement as well as the German-Polish Non-Aggression Pact.
This was on April 25, 1939.

Meanwhile, London prepared for the summer. As usual, there
was to be a rich and interesting musical programme. A huge
" London Music Festival " had been organised which was to embrace
all activities of the different musical organisations, opera houses,
ballets, etc., and was to last for five or six weeks.

For the non-initiated the months of May and June passed without
apparent political excitement. It seemed that the U.S.S.R. was the
critical counterweight in the balance of European power. Both
months were filled with the activities of the German-Soviet and
Franco-Anglo-Soviet negotiations.

The Covent Garden Season began on May 2nd with the *Bartered
Bride*. It was the last International Season before the war and—
perhaps—for a long time to come, and would never have taken
place without Sir Thomas's untiring energy. By great personal
sacrifice he undertook this precarious venture, and was its artistic
and organising director. This season was considerably prejudiced by
the darkening international horizon. Since some of the arrangements had to be made at the last moment, not all the casts were
satisfactory. As far as possible, Sir Thomas chose the *voices* he needed,
irrespective of politics. Thus, for the last time before the war, artists
from European and American opera houses assembled peacefully in
the happy atmosphere of Covent Garden.

The German opera, with the exception of the *Ring* and *Tristan*,
which Sir Thomas conducted himself, was entrusted to Weingartner,
who with youthful fire devoted himself to his task.

When I think of that last Opera Season I find that it embodies for
me a past epoch. . . . How delightful it was behind the scenes ;
how we enjoyed the rehearsals with their ups and downs—and how
we looked forward to the performances in the evenings ! Almost
every night, no matter how late it was, we met again at the Savoy
where there was hardly a seat to be found, and at every table there
were friends. . . . We enjoyed those weeks to the full, living as we
were on top of a volcano !

Immediately after the end of the Covent Garden Season I went to Paris for a week. Paris was sunny and warm, and I breathed its air with delight ; yet I felt the tension, and the first question put to me when I came to the Opera was : "*Croyez vous que nous aurons la guerre ?*"

Paris was then the Mecca of a strange genus of intermediary acting "unofficially" for official organisations—musical and otherwise. Italy, in particular, was feverishly seeking for great international artists, and I was approached by people putting out feelers to find out whether Sir Thomas would conduct at La Scala. At the same time—so I was told—they intended to invite Stokowsky and other conductors. Like the Germans earlier on, the Italians still used for their manipulations abroad those very people whom they would not acknowledge at home.

For all the "appeasement" of Munich, France was openly anti-German at that time. As I have already said, the usual German opera performances in Paris under Furtwängler had been cancelled by order of the French Government. For the last time I visited the Palais Royal and the officials of the Ministère des Beaux Arts, whom I had known for a long time, were strongly of the opinion that one could not possibly invite Furtwängler officially any longer. Apparently these tendencies were so strong that even the all-powerful Rouché could not overrule them.

However, the French dramatic soprano Germaine Lubin continued to sing at Bayreuth ! While I was in Paris we spent a quiet evening together. On that evening this sensitive and beautiful singer told me how much she owed artistically to Bayreuth, and how much she liked being there. She was just returning there, and I noticed, in her case as in that of many others, how remote artists are from politics—as long as they do not affect them personally.

The main object of my Paris trip was to see a performance of Berlioz's *Les Troyens*. Sir Thomas wished to present *Les Troyens* during the season of 1940, and hearing of the Paris production sent me to see it. This project was destined to be still-born.

The outstanding feature of the production was the *décor*. The burning wall of Troy was unforgettable. This performance was one of the last events of continental international opera life before the war. Artists from all over the world were present. Behind me

360

sat Koussevitzky from Boston with his friends ; and a little farther on were Hindemith and his wife who at that time lived in the Rhône Valley. After the opera, they had discussions with Massine about a new ballet. Dr. Graf, the former stage manager of Vienna and Salzburg, now at the New York Metropolitan Opera, was there. I went out with him after the performance. He saw the approach of war clearly and inevitably, and was restlessly waiting to go back to America to join his family.

Many from Paris went on to Lucerne to the Music Festival there, where Toscanini was the centre of attraction. I returned to London and have not left England since.

After my return from Paris, a friend of mine, a member of Parliament, invited me to have tea with him at the House. The House of Commons—like the whole of Westminster—has always had a special fascination for me—this dates from long before I came to live in England. I am sure that this must hold, too, for most English people. It all comes back to me : the kindly policeman at the entrance, the members in their pin-stripe trousers and black jackets walking about the corridors looking sure of themselves and at ease, the sunlight filtering through to the terrace of this historic building, where we all sat and had tea, united by the sense of belonging to a free and powerful country. Only in England can a foreigner be received at such a place so simply and without prejudice. I was much impressed by this.

While I was sitting there drinking in the atmosphere, I remembered an incident from the past.

It was shortly after the Nazis had received a majority in the *Reichstag*. The Germans did not then realise the far-reaching effects of this event. The Nazis at that time were regarded as a curious mutation or " sport " of *homo sapiens*. It was known that the National Socialist members used to meet in a restaurant near the old *Reichstag*, called *Zum schwarzen Ferkel* (" The Black Piglet "). A Dutch friend, just returned from Java, had visited me in Berlin, and he also thought the Nazis a strange offshoot of the human family. I suggested going to this restaurant. " Perhaps we'll see some of them," I said, " there is nothing to stop us." We went. The *Reichstag* was sitting, Nazi members were coming and going, sitting at tables and drinking beer.

Suddenly the door was flung open. A very fat man with a rosy face came in. Everybody jumped up from their seats and clicked their heels :

" Heil, Herr Präsident ! " they roared. It was Goering who had just become President of the *Reichstag*. As I drank my tea at Westminster I savoured the contrast.

Meanwhile, Sir Thomas had agreed to accept an invitation to Australia. It had also been planned that the London Philharmonic Orchestra should visit the United States and Canada under his direction. I started the preliminary work for this undertaking, which promised to be highly interesting and politically significant.

The fact that Sir Thomas was going to leave England for some time did not mean that he was less concerned with the fate of the London Philharmonic Orchestra. Only the initiated know what it means to keep an orchestra going—from purely private sources and without any subsidy—and Sir Thomas had borne this responsibility for many years. He still carried the burden in the summer of 1939, and thus he agreed to give a concert every Sunday, transmitted by Radio Luxembourg, at the beginning of which he introduced the programme.

In August I was at the seaside, staying at the house of an English friend. Under the blue summer sky on the coast, far away from the turmoil of busy London, I enjoyed the rest and the glorious weather. Meanwhile, the wheels rolled on. The next scene on the tragic European stage was the *entr'acte* in Tyrol. Seen against the fresco of the impending world catastrophe, the fate of the Tyrolese was but a miniature. Hitler, while making the welfare of Germans in the Sudetenland and in Memel a pretext for his policy of aggression, accepted the expulsion from their homes by the Italian Government of seven thousand German-speaking Tyrolese on August 7, 1939. Consistent inconsistency is a characteristic of Hitler's, and his cynicism reached a peak with the signing of the Russo-German Non-Aggression Pact on August 21st, ratified in Moscow on August 23rd. The photo of Stalin shaking hands with the grinning Ribbentrop was published by the world Press. Machiavelli out-Machiavellied !

How many people had been arrested, killed, or expelled for relations with the Soviet Union at the beginning of the Hitler régime ! How

many distinguished physicians and research workers had been persecuted and expelled from Germany because they had accepted the
Soviet Union's invitation to advise and medically examine Russia's
leaders ! How strongly was the anti-Soviet feeling whipped up
in the younger generation in Germany ! How it had been hammered
into people's minds that Russian meant Jew and Communist—the
deadly enemies of Fascism and " a danger to Europe " ! Now
suddenly, the U.S.S.R. became the ideal partner ! Those who
listened to the German wireless announcements and speeches at that
time will testify to the breathtaking and cynical impudence with
which this change of front was made palatable to the German people.

Events followed in such quick succession that it was difficult to
get a clear picture of the German reaction to this pact. The Danzig
problem, artificially puffed up by the Nazis, suddenly dominated
the political field. When Hitler concluded his Non-Aggression Pact
with Poland, neither the position of Danzig nor the Polish Corridor
had disturbed him. Now it was *their* turn on the programme.
White books and innumerable political pamphlets have recorded
every phase of these days, which were almost unbearable in their
tension.

From August 19th onwards I was the guest at the country house
in Dorsetshire of English friends, closely connected with the Foreign
Office. I had long found out that one of the main features of the
British character is a certain genius for silence, a reserve which refuses
to talk over things which Germans, for instance, would discuss at
length. However, in August 1939, the situation was so grave that
it ousted all tradition. One could not get away from the one and only
subject.

England was definitely unprepared for war, yet already certain
precautionary measures had been taken. Since an immediate air
attack on London might occur, the evacuation of children from the
Metropolis and its suburbs had been organised. The friends with
whom I was staying had offered a wing of their great house for this
purpose. Everything was ready for the reception of forty evacuees
aged one to three years and their nurses. As long as they were not
definitely announced there was still hope.

Meanwhile, the German-Polish frontiers were closed. Britons
and Frenchmen left Berlin. The British Fleet was mobilised. On

the same day we were told that the children were on their way. My heart sank. By such small incidents do we sometimes record great moments. I shall always remember my feeling when the buses with their loads of children stopped in front of the house. The children were crying with fatigue. We all helped to put them to bed. Their distress was for me the symbol of the despair which my country had brought on the world.

Chapter 43

MANY WHO listened with apprehension to the Prime Minister's words in which he declared England to be in a state of war with Germany realised that this was not only going to be a war between nations, it was to be a war of ideas, and its issue would mean life or death for those things that many of us have been brought up to cherish and to venerate.

After a period of suspense any clear decision brings relief. But, for me, the same questions arose as in 1938 : Where did I belong ? Where was I to be *allowed* to belong ? Would I be allowed to continue my work ? Would I be allowed to work at all ?

Sir Thomas put an end to my apprehensions. He asked me to return to London immediately as there were many things to do, especially in connection with the Opera House.

Naturally the movements of aliens had to be carefully checked, but even in these first turbulent days, all was done in a kind and human way. The local police rang up Bow Street and I was permitted to travel to London.

Meanwhile it had been decided that Covent Garden could not be used in wartime for its normal purposes. The London Philharmonic Orchestra's office had to be removed from the beloved Opera House and Sir Thomas Beecham's rooms at the top of the building had to be cleared. This task fell to me. It was a sad but inevitable exit, and I stored Sir Thomas's musical library and papers at Boosey & Hawkes' Denman Street premises, taking home with me only a few indispensable files.

The London Philharmonic Orchestra, however, had to face a far more complex situation than a mere transfer of their office. Not only were many musical engagements cancelled upon the outbreak of the war, but the company which had hitherto supported the Orchestra was unable to carry on, and the London Philharmonic Orchestra was threatened with disbandment.

The Orchestra did not wait for State or municipal help. They decided to take their fate in their own hands. With the full approval of Sir Thomas Beecham they appointed a committee of six playing members as directors, including Thomas Russell, a viola player in the Orchestra, who was elected Secretary and Business Manager by his colleagues. This function he has performed with unusual capability, combining an experience acquired as one of the rank and file with a highly developed faculty for unobtrusively but firmly piloting the ship of the Orchestra. The aim of the reconstituted management was to keep this splendid organisation alive, and to continue to serve the best traditions of music.

Gradually a few concerts were undertaken in the provinces, and on October 29th the Orchestra's first London concert directed by Sir Thomas Beecham in wartime was given in Queen's Hall.

As I have mentioned, Sir Thomas had intended to retire temporarily from musical life, but in view of the war and the situation of the Orchestra, he was willing to resume his activities.

The first London concert given by Sir Thomas and the reconstituted London Philharmonic Orchestra had a full house and an enthusiastic audience. After the concert he was congratulated on his decision by a member of the public who asked him what had persuaded him to reappear. " My dear fellow," replied Sir Thomas, " we were given to understand that the country was in a state of emergency, and so I emerged."

Soon the regular Sunday concerts were resumed at Queen's Hall, and the little platform alcove behind the curtain saw many old friends who, although dispersed all over the country in different war work, tried to snatch an hour of music on Sundays.

During this first winter of war, our life went on much as usual. One quickly got used to the blackout, and friends met in an informal way. The course of the war was eagerly followed, but as the theatre of action was still outside England events assumed the fatal remoteness which is characteristic when the trouble is not actually on one's doorstep.

[1 9 4 0]

The little ship of the London Philharmonic Orchestra steered bravely through the waves, yet in spite of all enthusiasm, it seemed inevitable that some sort of financial backing should be sought. The Orchestra had decided to issue a printed appeal in the programme of their Beecham Sunday Concert on January 14th, and Sir Thomas declared himself willing to support this appeal by a speech.

After the interval he mounted the platform. This is what he said :

"I have been asked by the committee of the Orchestra, which is now a self-governing body, to say a few words of explanation to you respecting the printed document to be found in your programmes.

"It is with great pleasure that I do this, but I think I shall speak more eloquently if I do not look at it, for although its meaning is sufficiently clear, it does not say one-quarter enough. As you see, it is an appeal to the public to support this Orchestra in a certain way.

"You, of course, are the élite of London musical society. Don't feel too encouraged—it is not much to be proud of. But if there is in this Metropolis a modicum of interest in the art of music—and there is very little—I think most of it is centred within these walls this afternoon.

"I do not know if many of you are aware how this Orchestra has been carried on since its foundation ; anyway, it is my pleasing duty to-day to instruct you. In every country in the world but this, musical institutions are of a permanent character. There are, of course, permanent institutions here, but they are hardly in my sense of the word musical. Do not think that I have any particular one in mind at this moment.

"There are colleges and academies, but I am speaking of grown-up institutions, not homes of education, and of these we have none supported by the State, the municipality, or by private patronage on any scale worth considering. There is nothing here corresponding to that which we see in New York, Philadelphia, Boston, Chicago, and—ahem !—Berlin or Vienna, and so on.

'How are these kept going? By the State, the municipality, or the private patron who provide large sums of money, because they think it worth while to maintain their existence for the instruction as well as the edification of the public. There, it is realised that the public should have the opportunity of hearing the best music at moderate prices. So you can in this town; but if you pay *very* moderate prices as you have done to-day, it hardly remunerates the orchestra, and the conductor not at all.

" This is the only country in the world where musicians are not expected to live like ordinary people. It is a tradition here that composers and most instrumentalists have always starved, and as we are a sentimental people we think that this tradition should be upheld.

" Now I would like you to know that this war is pressing very hard upon most artistic organisations. I am not referring to individuals, and I should like to make it clear that it is not in the single members of this Orchestra that I am primarily interested, except naturally in a personal way, for they are all very good fellows.

" What I am concerned about is the Orchestra as a co-operative body, which has achieved an almost unique position in the world through having played together almost daily for many years past. This condition of unbroken association is peculiar to this Orchestra and to it alone, for not one of its great rivals in the cities I have mentioned has found it possible to play together all the year round, even with a handsome subsidy. And they have not been allowed to play in theatres, music-halls, cafés, or even in the street; they have performed nothing but the finest music, be it in the concert hall or the opera house. And how has this been possible? Until a few months ago by the devotion of a few individuals and by them alone. But the decline of prosperity, the deterioration of the international position, and finally the outbreak of war, have put an end to this source of supply. To-day, the Orchestra is without one powerful friend or any means of support except that which the public which has listened to it for the past seven years may now choose to give it.

" Let us compare its position with that of other great orchestras which are kept together in spite of the hazards of war or even peace. In New York, for seven months' work a year, which is the term of its contract, the Orchestra costs its guarantors an annual sum of not less than £20,000, that is to say, the amount representing the difference between cost of maintenance and the public receipts at concerts. The same conditions prevail in Philadelphia, Boston,

Chicago, and the other great American cities ; and even in countries
of the second rank and in Continental towns no larger than an
English city of a moderate size, orchestras as well as opera houses
enjoy some measure of endowment and security of tenure.

"Ever since its foundation the Orchestra has been giving
concerts all over the country, concerts which have the highest
instructional value, but which necessarily have been uncommercial
and unremunerative. You will understand that to continue this
important branch of its work will be impossible if the Orchestra
be forced to rely upon its own resources. It would be a thousand
pities, especially at a moment like this when the available circle of
high-class entertainment has contracted woefully, if this crusading
side of its activities had to be abandoned, and it is for this cause
more than for any other that the present Appeal is being made.
You here are the faithful. Some of you may know someone who
has a little money left. I do not—nor am I ingenious at evading
Income Tax, or other inequitable claims made upon me by the
State. For what you and they then can give, both I and the
Orchestra will be deeply grateful."

In view of the public's spontaneous and generous response the
Orchestra felt that they owed their friends a more gracious form of
acknowledgement than merely a formal receipt for donations, and
thus the first number of the *London Philharmonic Post*, a bi-monthly
bulletin, informing the public of the activities and progress of the
Orchestra, was issued on March 1, 1940. Copies of the first and
second numbers are already rare, and sought after by collectors. In
two years this magazine, edited by Thomas Russell, could boast a
list of some five thousand subscribers, and 12,500 copies of each issue
were disposed of with the greatest ease. This represents a circulation
far larger than that of any other musical paper in the country. The
educational value of the *Philharmonic Post* was beyond doubt, and the
paper served as a useful link between the Orchestra and its public.

At the beginning of 1940 much interest was aroused by the Finnish
war. The wife of the Finnish Minister, Mme. de Gripenberg, was
indefatigable in her activities. She travelled, lectured, collected
money, and asked Sir Thomas to conduct a concert in aid of the
Finland Fund.

Sir Thomas, ever the ardent admirer of Sibelius, acceded, and on
April 4th, three weeks after the Finno-Soviet armistice, conducted

the London Philharmonic Orchestra at Queen's Hall in an all-Sibelius programme. The house was full.

With this concert we arrive at a moment of importance : it was the last given by Sir Thomas Beecham before his departure to Australia, and, as circumstances have developed, has proved to be his last appearance in England up to the time of writing.

The London Philharmonic Orchestra gave him a farewell dinner at Pagani's. Several speeches were made. The Chairman of the Orchestra, Charles Gregory, and Sir Thomas both spoke in a manner which showed that, whatever happened, between the Orchestra and Sir Thomas there would always be a bond of unshakable devotion.

Shortly afterwards, Sir Thomas left England. He parted from me with a hearty handshake. Although he had arranged that I was to join him in the autumn in America, I had a prophetic conviction that many things were to happen before we should meet again.

Chapter 44

ON APRIL 9th I received a letter from Oslo. It was from Furt-wängler. He said he was touring Norway and Sweden, and would be pleased to hear from me at Copenhagen where he was due to arrive on April 9th. The letter had taken a fortnight ; it would have been anyway too late for a written reply. As I stepped out of my house to inquire whether a telegram to Denmark was permitted, I saw big posters everywhere : " DENMARK AND NORWAY INVADED ". This was my reply.

Another phase of the war had begun.

So far the general public in England was in the position of an onlooker, and musical life was able to struggle along. A concert for the Polish Relief Fund took place on April 25th. All sorts of summer concerts were planned to be held in the Queen's Hall, and an Anglo-French Festival with the co-operation of prominent French artists was fixed for June and July by the Association of British Musicians, and the London Philharmonic Orchestra.

Hardly had the shock of the Scandinavian invasion been overcome than on May 10th, Holland, Belgium, and Luxembourg were overrun. On May 11th, the British Prime Minister, Mr. Neville Chamberlain, resigned, and the Right Honourable Winston Churchill, the " man of destiny ", became Prime Minister.

On May 17th the Germans entered Brussels ; on May 26th Calais fell, and Boulogne was occupied ; on May 28th Leopold of Belgium surrendered with his army. England began to tremble for its Expeditionary Force. On May 29th the defence of Dunkirk began. The B.E.F. was being evacuated. On June 4th the Germans entered Dunkirk.

On that day Churchill delivered a speech in the House of Commons. There was something in the voice of the man bearing that burden of crucial responsibility which told us that a supreme moment had been reached. It filled us all with heaviest presentiments, and yet with a holy courage to live for the great cause through whatever might come.

Parts of this speech, which stirred every listener to the depths of his soul have been often quoted, but they can never be remembered too often. They were a clarion call to mankind, and epitomise the spirit of England.

" We shall go on to the end ; we shall fight in France, we shall fight on the seas and oceans ; we shall fight with growing confidence and growing strength in the air ; we shall defend our island, whatever the cost may be ; we shall fight on the beaches ; we shall fight in the landing-grounds ; we shall fight in the fields and the streets ; we shall fight in the hills. We shall never surrender ! . . ."

On June 10th Italy entered the war while the Germans were at the doors of Paris. On June 14th Paris fell, and the Swastika fluttered from the Eiffel Tower. The German Army swept on and on ; on June 17th Marshal Pétain sued for peace, and the Franco-German armistice was signed on June 22nd.

The Anglo-French Music Festival collapsed with the fall of France. During the great upheaval caused by the occupation of the Western Continent, which changed—at least for a while—the map of Europe, the fate of millions of people became a problem. Many of the countries now occupied had given refuge to exiles emigrant from the Reich, who had settled there, often in poverty, but at least with the freedom to breathe. Many of them were trapped again, others moved South and West. Some were able to get to America, but many were caught in the net of the complicated passport, emigration, and immigration regulations. Not only the emigrants from the Nazi régime were on the move—the very people of the occupied countries fled ; but this is not the place to describe the terrible hardships suffered by them.

England had suddenly become a last citadel of free men. What was to be her fate ? Many arrived from the Continent, from France, Denmark, and Holland, from Norway and Belgium. Governments were set up and national offices were opened. Great Britain, the land of splendid isolation, suddenly became the most cosmopolitan place imaginable.

In the circumstances, what was more likely than that Hitler, after the fall of France, would immediately start his much-prophesied invasion of Great Britain ? England had to reckon with this menace. There seemed no time to lose. Every precaution had to be taken. Consequently the authorities had to take their measures, one of which was the almost wholesale internment of all male " enemy aliens ", among them inevitably many notable enemies of the Nazis. Even Nobel prize-winners, men of science, who had found a haven in England's universities, were rounded up and interned. They took it with great dignity, and a famous scientist told me that not for anything would he have missed his internment, so much had it brought out the sympathy " 'twixt man and man ".

There was a persistent rumour that women would soon share the same fate in view of their potential danger at this crucial time.

I am afraid that I resented the situation and was deeply depressed. Here was England, sworn to defend freedom and liberty. Was there no other way than the wholesale internment of black *and* white sheep ? A great weariness overcame me. I had no strength left to fight, and decided to await my fate. After all my ordeals, I felt that it was humiliating that this should happen.

A small incident may illustrate how little the situation of refugees from the Nazis was then really understood.

About this time I was invited to dinner at the house of an M.P. and found myself in a company which included officials from the Home Office. A discussion was started on the internment question, and I was interrogated about several of the Germans. Then one of the men said : " You don't mean to say that you Germans here are not thrilled by the German victory in France ! ' My country right or wrong,' you know ? " I tried to explain that the present Germany was not our country. It had expelled us, it did not want us. How could he imagine that we could hail a victory of the Nazis who had betrayed the real Germany, destroyed our life, and bereft us of our homeland ?

He was unable to follow me. He was a thorough Britisher. He could not imagine himself in my place, for in Britain the idea of a country disowning and rejecting some of its citizens seemed utterly incredible. This absolute inability to comprehend increased my despondency. The old desperate feeling, the relic of Nazi times again welled up in me, and after dinner I quietly slipped out of the house.

During that night I could not sleep. I thought about the Orchestra. Sir Thomas's absence had only strengthened my link with it. I had shared with its members their heroic struggle and went daily to their office. Now all the old complexes were dragged up again, and I suddenly felt that I might do harm to the Orchestra by being seen too much in their company. I therefore went next morning to the London Philharmonic Orchestra office in order to have it out. The Directors were just holding a meeting, and I burst in upon them : " Tell me frankly," I asked. " Do you prefer that I should avoid coming here for the time being ? After all, I am an enemy alien, and it might harm you." " Are you crazy ? " exclaimed Francis Bradley. " We aren't Nazis ! Whatever do you imagine ? " They did not say this out of politeness ; I felt immediately they meant what they said. They were just as straight in their attitude to me as they were to themselves. Had it been possible to increase my admiration and attachment to this splendid body of men, this occasion would have sufficed to do so. I have never forgotten it.

The internment fever soon died down. Only a relatively small number of women were rounded up and later the great majority were released.

It is no wonder that with the Western Continent overrun, and the Channel Ports in Nazi hands, not only musical life but the whole life of the British Isles existed only from one day to the next. There were hardly any concerts, and as the Orchestra had no capital they soon found themselves high and dry. One morning Felix Aprahamian, Thomas Russell's enthusiastic assistant, telephoned to me and said : " Doctor Geissmar, if no one comes to our help, we shall have to sell the office furniture." How dreadful this sounded ! I fully realised what it meant. Such moments occur in the history of most orchestras. The very structure of orchestral life—this interweaving of artistic and commercial venture—is doomed to precariousness if not wisely supported. The Vienna Philharmonic had adjusted their difficulties, the Berlin Philharmonic had become a Reichs Orchestra, but what was to be done for this indomitable band of men ? They were determined to hold together, to carry on in the spirit in which they had been founded. They had played through splendid Covent Garden seasons ; for the Royal Philharmonic and Royal Choral Societies ; they had given the London public their traditional Sunday concerts ; they had visited the provinces ; they had been pioneers of British orchestral playing on the Continent. They bore the name of London, the capital of the British Empire. *They* could not ring up London's Lord Mayor as I had rung the *Oberbürgermeister* of Berlin, who, in spite of all difficulties, had once come immediately to our aid with a cheque. Nor could they appeal to any other authority. Friends ? Yes, they had many— they had a large, though anonymous following ; but there was a war on, and who would be willing or able to throw money into music at that moment ?

I wrote a line to Mr. James Smith, one of the supporters and directors of Covent Garden seasons, and at the same time on the Board of the Royal Philharmonic Society. He had often helped generously, and I felt sure that even if he could not assist at the moment with money, he might give practical advice. He was just then serving in the Army, and was stationed at Chatham as a sergeant. A few days after I had written he rang me up : " I am in a call box ", he said. " I have just had your letter. Of course the London Philharmonic Orchestra must be saved. I do not know how much I have in my bank-account just now, but what there is I will give to the London Philharmonic Orchestra. I haven't much use for money myself in my present life." That same week the

Orchestra received from him a cheque for £1000. This gave them a start, and they were able to bridge their difficulties. Soon afterwards they gave a concert at Queen's Hall, which they called a " Musical Manifesto ", where J. B. Priestley made an appeal. The first result of this was a cheque of £1000 sent by an anonymous Scottish donor to Mr. Priestley, and other gifts small and large poured in freely from all sections of the public. Privates and schoolchildren sent their half-crowns, and richer men sent their share.

The Orchestra continued to give a few concerts, and then accepted the offer of Jack Hylton to tour England, playing a kind of weekly " Prom " in many provincial towns. The London County Council, too, invited the Mayors and Corporations of all boroughs in Greater London to a concert by the London Philharmonic Orchestra in the Central Hall, Westminster, a gesture of sympathy with the Orchestra in its moment of crisis which was greatly appreciated by them.

By such support, and by the *esprit de corps* of the players, who had decided to keep together even without regular pay, the London Philharmonic Orchestra was able to survive a period which might be called England's darkest hour in this war.

Chapter 45

ON JUNE 25th at one a.m. I was awakened by a most peculiar sound, wailing and persistent. A green and yellow light seemed to flicker within my eyes. It was London's first air-raid warning (the alarm which sounded at the declaration of war was a false alert). I remembered suddenly that early on during the war a little slip of paper had been pushed under my door by the air-raid warden saying that my old house, 36 Red Lion Square, was considered unsafe, and that in the case of a raid I was to go to the nearest shelter.

I dressed quickly and rushed my mother across the Square. It was pitch dark. Shuffling feet were heard from the people hurrying out of their shaky houses in all the little side-streets to the shelters, while the droning of an aeroplane was heard overhead. It was a strange night, later on to be followed by many alike, crammed together with a crowd of people and waiting for the " All Clear " which in the autumn was only to sound in the early morning hours.

This night of June 24th was the precursor of the blitz on London. At that stage, however, we had nothing more than occasional reconnaissances to contend with. It was a lovely summer, and one got into the habit of using one or other of the Parks as a summer resort. There were parts of Hyde Park where one could forget that one was in London. Of course, wartime Hyde Park was not quite the same. There were the notorious Hyde Park guns, which months later made such a terrific noise. There were, too, peaceful pasturing sheep, and there were loving couples. There were also a great number of people who took their work to the Park and spent their time sitting on the green grass. Incidentally, the beginning of this book was written there.

As soon as the day raids started, however, and the night raids developed more seriously, the Park became one of the least safe places in London. In the morning one used to see the craters of the bombs, and little boys ran about to collect the shrapnel. At first one settled nearer the borders to be able to get quickly to a shelter, but soon had to give up even this.

While, as I have mentioned, the London Philharmonic Orchestra was touring England under the auspices of Jack Hylton, the London Symphony Orchestra played for the Proms. The B.B.C. Orchestra, which in recent years had been the Prom Orchestra, was not available that year, and it had been decided that the London Symphony Orchestra was to play for Sir Henry Wood, the venerated Prom Conductor, whose forty-sixth season this was.

With the increasing raids, however, sirens and other sounds which were anything but musical were frequently heard during these concerts which were held at Queen's Hall and were intended to last until the end of September. In spite of the threatening blitz, the Proms, this peculiar feature of English musical life, were as much in demand as ever and as early as five p.m. the doorsteps of Queen's Hall were besieged by people who feared to be prevented later on by the blitz to get to the Hall. With the lengthening nights the alerts came earlier and earlier, and generally were heard in the middle of the concert ; but the audience remained, and the music went on and the public returned just as keen on their concert the following day. The police requested everybody to stay put during alerts and frequently people—an average of 1500—who had arrived at the Hall by five in the afternoon were still there at dawn. Of course they were hungry, and Mr. West, who was in charge of the refreshments at Queen's Hall, soon switched over to a new form of catering business. Hundreds of gallons of coffee were supplied, and sandwiches were made and consumed by the thousand—as a matter of fact Mr. West raided all the neighbourhood to feed the stranded flock, who were also tired, naturally, because they had no night's rest. This was especially so as with the growing blitz the "last trains" were temporarily stopped, and only left half an hour after the "All Clear", which never went before dawn. Thus it had become impossible to combine a Prom Concert with a night's sleep. But also in this emergency the Queen's Hall management was ingenious. People slept on the Prom floor, they slept in the comfortable seats upstairs, while the space under the circle was specially coveted by the cautious ones. When the "All Clear" had sounded the sleepers were, however, jostled out of the way with gruff humour by the attendants.

It was certainly an amazing and unique experience. Queen's Hall, the place of so many famous memories, has certainly never witnessed such scenes. The evening of August 26th has especially remained vividly in all our minds. The concert, which had been conducted by Sir Henry Wood, was over, and a heavy raid was still in progress. The police requested everybody to stay where they were. The resourcefulness and wit of English musicians is well known, but what they were to do in such a situation was still to be seen. Soon the Orchestra and members of the audience took in hand the task of amusing the public, from which some hitherto undiscovered talent also emerged, assisting the good cause. All sorts of features were presented.

Sir Henry has disappeared—has been listening no doubt from behind the curtain in the wings. But who is this tall smiling figure in evening-dress standing at the side of the platform? It is Sir Adrian Boult, come as from conducting a concert of his own. The Orchestra begins amusingly to reverse the principle of Haydn's Farewell Symphony, and arrive late, one by one. For the opening bars, a *tutti* passage, only a trombone and a clarinet are in their places, to play the fitful notes allotted to them in the harmony. Then Sir Adrian Boult strolls up to the percussion desk and adds embellishments with cymbals and triangle, till finally a real, if slightly unorthodox, *tutti* is achieved for the closing chord.

Again the Orchestra assembled. Ceremoniously the librarian distributed the parts for the *Figaro* Overture. Who was going to conduct ? A hush spread through the hall, while Sir Henry Wood peeped from behind the platform curtain to see what was going to happen. It was then pompously announced that " a famous British conductor now in Australia " was going to conduct the Overture to *Figaro*. The audience was amazed to see the living image of Sir Thomas Beecham with the well-trimmed beard walk, with the famous *maestoso* gait to the rostrum, and go through the ritual of— in the words of the *Star*—" the sundry familiar and well-beloved wrist-flicks, hisses, and the stressful stamps of the first conductor of Mozart in the world ". There is no need to say that the impersonator began by throwing away the score and disdainfully ordering the conductor's desk to be removed. Any uncertainty was dispelled when the audience was addressed before the performance, and reference was made to another orchestra " apparently up to some high jinks elsewhere with Mr. Hylton " and also to broadcasting. *And* the conductor found it necessary to shout " Shut up ! " in the middle. The stretched-out arms and the baton, down-pointed in the familiar way for the *Figaro* opening, began to evoke something astonishingly like the world-famous Beecham interpretation ! As the impersonator reached the wings after the performance, Sir Henry, who recognised him as one of his own violins, said with kindly surprise : " I did not know you were a conductor ". Still loftily in the part, " Sir Thomas " replied : " Ah, yes, Sir Henry, and I understand you, too, conduct sometimes ! "

A member of the audience then made a speech suggesting that everybody would agree that they were getting much more than their original money's worth, and that they ought to contribute to the Musicians' Pension Fund. Thereupon Sir Adrian was given a large wastepaper basket, lined with newspaper to keep the coins in, and was soon seen taking it round the hall.

I must reveal that the impersonator of " a famous British conductor now in Australia " was Mr. Ralph Nicholson, a young member of the

London Symphony's violin section, now in the Air Force. Since this incident, Mr. Nicholson has become known for his impersonations, and when I had the privilege of being present at one of his private shows, I only wondered that this exceptional talent of his was not more exploited. He told me that since the Queen's Hall episode many people asked him to " do Sir Thomas " and that he has a special outfit for this purpose, including the well-known grey linen jacket and the world-famous goatee. He gave me a photo of himself in the rôle of Sir Thomas, and I could not tell it from the original.

The raid sessions at Queen's Hall quickly became publicised and added to the attraction of the Proms. The following conversation actually took place at the Queen's Hall box-office. WOMAN : " Do you think there will be an air raid to-night ? " BOX OFFICE, politely : " Sorry, Madam, we can't tell you." WOMAN : " Well, I am only going to come if you think there *will* be a raid ! "

However, the increasing seriousness of the blitz made the continuation of concerts in London inadvisable, and on September 7th, this memorable Prom season of 1940 came to an end.

But not all musical blitz stories were so humorous as those of the Proms all-night sessions. One morning during this period when I arrived at the London Philharmonic Orchestra office I found everyone in consternation : " We do not know ", said Felix, " whether we can count on the Orchestra leaving for Glasgow with all the first violins. We have just had a telephone message from somebody living near Wynn Reeves to say that his house had a direct hit last night. It is just a rubble heap, and the rescue workers have not yet found anyone in the debris ". On Euston Station, however, Wynn Reeves turned up. Fortunately he and his wife had spent this particular night with friends. Such strange coincidences happened frequently, and made us realise that we were in the hands of fate.

Meanwhile the London Philharmonic Orchestra had more or less recovered financially. New plans were being made and fresh courage was taken. We were grateful to our friends, and decided to give a " thanksgiving " party at my house. We invited Mr. J. B. Priestley and other friends of the Orchestra, who had been kind and helpful to us. All five Directors of the Orchestra came and, of course, the inevitable Felix. We had a cold supper of sausages, potato salad, bretzel and beer, and soon were engrossed in great debates.

It was a lovely evening. We stood on the roof garden with its wonderful view of St. Paul's. From this lofty station we saw strange coloured lights, gleaming far away in the direction of the Thames estuary, and we could not quite make out what they were. With the growing darkness, the sirens sounded. The lights we had seen were the first flares over the East End. We spent the night listening to Priestley in his rôle of raconteur. The raid did not stop until early dawn. The noise was often so loud that we could not hear each other speak. When morning came and the " All Clear " went, the sky in the direction of St. Paul's was blood-red—London's docks were burning.

With the night warnings of June we thought air raids were coming, with the nuisance raids of August we felt they had arrived, but only now, without clearly realising what we were in for, we had come to that hardly believable experience—the blitz on London. It has been recorded in a thousand ways, and yet no one who has not witnessed it can have an idea of the greatness shown by the people of London : the calm resolution of all the Defence Services, the patience and kindliness of those gathered in the shelters (often insufficient in the beginning), the stubbornness in carrying on after sleepless nights and harassed days, the indomitable courage of everyone, and last but not least the ever present humour, the sympathy without sentimentality— the greatness of it all.

The London police, of course, had a hard task in these days as many can witness to. There was nothing they did not do. There were no " incidents " in which they did not play their part. But how encouraging and cheerful they always were.

Again and again I had the experience that this unique team of men had their own special way of dealing with mankind. Several times a tiny light had shown through the blackout curtains at Red Lion Square, and the constable on night duty had rung my bell to admonish me. One Saturday I went away for the week-end and in my absence my charwoman left the light burning through an enormous unshuttered window. When I came back I was told " the police have been here and will call again ". Terrified I waited for the avenger of Justice. I was fully aware that a bright light shining was a serious offence in those days. The policeman came, took down all particulars, and soon after I was summoned to appear before a police court. When I arrived at the appointed hour there were all sorts of people waiting about. Many constables were present to attend to " their " cases. Soon I received an encouraging nod from the one who had interviewed me. (Incidentally there was an air raid going on and the whole procedure was removed to the basement while this lasted.) After some time " my bobbie " came over to where I sat waiting in trepidation : " It is our turn now ", he told me, and took me into the Court, just as if we were to appear together before a marriage registrar. I was fined £1.

The continuous bombing of the centre of the town made it inadvisable to stay on in Red Lion Square in a rickety house, and so I arranged for my mother to live in Hampstead while I myself, on the point of joining Sir Thomas in America, continued to spend my nights in public shelters. Holborn, the City, and the East End were increasingly raided. Great gaps stared where houses had stood the previous day. Streets were torn open. Buildings were roped off on account of their liability to crash, and tops of houses were found burned out by the thousands of incendiaries showered over London at night. In these nights so many big fires were started that some of the small ones could not be adequately dealt with.

One morning when I came to my house, after a ten hours' raid (on September 24th), a sorry sight lay before my eyes. Water was pouring down the sides of the house, and the square was full of rubble, glass, and splinters. The top of the house had been burnt out.

Tears rushed to my eyes for a moment. I had again lost my home, built up after such trials, and with all that was left of my old family possessions. It was a shock, especially when I saw the remnants of my library scattered between charred timbers. But I quickly pulled myself together ; I honestly felt that no personal sacrifice was big enough if it contributed one iota to the battle for the freedom of the world.

This conviction sustained me through the next few hours, when I had to deal with what had been such an exquisite home. But we all are only human, and gradually I began to feel a sharp reaction. I left this scene of destruction and rushed to the London Philharmonic

380

Orchestra office, where I found Gregory, Russell, and Felix. Into their sympathetic ears I poured out my tale. Felix came back with me to Red Lion Square so that I did not have to go alone.

Even if it should appear sentimental, I feel I must say that this day created another link between myself and the London Philharmonic Orchestra, stronger than those which had been forged by the bright days of the past.

Meanwhile the blitz continued. While the days were an uninterrupted chain of warnings — by then called by the optimistic name of " Alerts "—followed by " All Clears ", the raiders came over, and explosions of guns and bombs mingled the long nights through.

I was waiting for my boat for New York when I received a cable from Sir Thomas telling me that he had extended his stay in Australia and I was not to leave until I heard further. I therefore decided to move to the house where my mother had gone, until I saw how things were going to develop.

My new address, 25 Lyncroft Gardens, Hampstead, was in a quiet little street off Finchley Road, where all the houses looked alike. Many of the inhabitants had lived there ever since the street was built. The owner of our new abode was the dignified and charming Mrs. Edith Biggs, one of those active and cheerful English women who seem to get things done without any fuss. She came from a seafaring family ; two of her brothers had been captains in the Merchant Navy, and one of them and her sister had been born at sea.

The other inhabitant of the house was her housekeeper, Annie Purcell, a direct descendant of the great composer ; she had been with the family for thirty-four years. A musical visitor says she recognises in Miss Purcell the same deep-set beautiful eyes which appear in the portrait of the composer, attributed to Kneller, which is in the National Portrait Gallery. Last, but not least there was a Sealyham called Bunty, who ruled the house inexorably.

It was a time of uninterrupted raids for fifty-two nights. Though no one really dared undress at this stage of things, one eventually got accustomed to the pandemonium. In the middle of my first night at Lyncroft Gardens, we suddenly heard Annie's voice crying : " There is a German aeroplane in the street ! " I rushed out. What a sight ! The sky was lit up by fires in the City. Our street was ablaze. It was not a German aeroplane, but several " Molotov bread-baskets " dropped all over the street, with their scores of smaller incendiaries. The top storeys of four houses were burning. Wardens rushed about offering their help. Firemen arrived. When I returned to my room there was a funny smell and a crackling sound. I looked up. An incendiary bomb was eating its way through the ceiling, and beginning to throw off sparks and suffocating fumes.

I could not help remembering our fire-fighting lesson in which the tall, rosy-faced, blue-eyed fireman had instructed us how to deal with incendiary bombs : " Some can be put out with a stirrup pump ", he had said, " but others explode after two minutes. In which case, of course, any further instructions are unnecessary ". I had no time for further meditations, and while Mrs. Biggs (aged seventy-six !) wielded the garden hose over the bomb, I calmly called out into the street : " Number 25 on fire ". The neighbours as one family, assembled before our door, offering their help. Meanwhile " our bomb " was put out, after having done quite a lot of damage, not to mention the soaking of the rest of my now more than modest possessions.

These adventures concluded in the early morning with a good cup of tea, the English panacea for all ills.

Lyncroft Gardens gradually assumed its blitz routine. After seeing that the raids seemed to have become a constant institution, Mrs. Biggs declared " she couldn't be bothered " (a favourite expression of hers) with the blitz. Every evening at seven p.m., alarm or not, Annie appeared with her white cap and apron, dinner was served, the table shone with glass and silver, and flowers were never missing.

It is a historic precept that there is a limit to everything, but apparently this does not apply to the British.

One evening a bomb was heard screaming over our heads. " What a whizzy ! " said Annie placidly. An enormous bang followed. Our little house swayed and cracks appeared in the walls. Involuntarily I crouched. " Don't you worry," said Mrs. Biggs. " It's over."

Churchill's words flashed through my mind : " We shall never surrender ". No, I felt sure of that now. They (may I say " we ") would not. A few minutes later we learned that a house a few yards away in our block had crashed down through a direct hit. It might so easily have been ours.

For many nights this state of things went on. None of us was ever really nervous, but somehow the lack of sleep made itself felt. One night about midnight the telephone rang. According to instructions we were in the basement of the house. I rushed upstairs ; the noise of the guns almost prevented me from understanding who it was : it was Thomas Beecham, junior. " When are you coming down to stay with us ? " he asked. " You cannot possibly stay on in London all the time."

Before I had time to recover my senses it had been decided that I was to join them in Warwickshire at the end of the week. A few days later, I found myself motoring through the lovely country on the way to Tidmington Manor, an Elizabethan house of grey stone, with its own chapel in its grounds. Two avenues of century-old oak trees lead to the house, and as far as the eye can see there are meadows with flocks of sheep and cows grazing peacefully. Old cottages hide among ancient trees.

When I undressed, for the first night in nearly two months, in my comfortable and beautifully panelled room, I could not believe that I was the same person who had left Paddington Station during an air raid hardly a few hours before.

This visit to Warwickshire was the first of many to come.

I have learned to love the English country, either at stately Tidmington or from the Manor Farm, Compton Scorpion, the home of Sir Thomas's elder son, Adrian, and his wife. I have been with them through winter, spring, and summer, and the charm of the country has been enhanced by our evenings of music, so indispensable to the Beecham family. I have gone with them on Sundays to their little church, where their tenants join them, and Adrian Beecham, as the squire, reads the lesson, while the vicar offers prayers for all of his flock now on active service. Never have I come back from these visits to the English countryside other than filled with renewed courage and fresh hope for the survival of some of the worth-while things in life.

With the end of November 1940, the blitz began to die down. Even Londoners had a night or two without alarms, and life began to be reorganised. The Sunday Concerts in the Queen's Hall were resumed with the London Philharmonic Orchestra and various conductors. The other musical institutions also resumed their activities and to the old ventures new ones were added. The National Gallery, where Myra Hess organised concerts, was more than filled to capacity. They created a special public, and many well-known people, otherwise engulfed in war activity, were found attending these concerts daily. When I once said to Myra Hess how wonderful I thought her achievement to be, she replied : " I was just lucky ". It was more than that. With her exquisite programmes, she had given a new public what it needed, and this public did not leave her even when the blitz compelled her to remove the concerts to the basement of the museum.

More and more enterprises of all kinds were started, and the theatres began to be sold out night after night.

There was a growing demand for orchestral music all through the country, and the few conductors available—who were partly occupied by permanent jobs—had their hands full to meet all the demands made on their time and services. The number of concerts these men have conducted per year in this war time music boom is absolutely astounding. Dr. Malcolm Sargent, for instance, told me that in the Season of 1942 he averaged more than one Symphony Concert a day.

The London Philharmonic Orchestra, after having at first played under Hylton's auspices, began to expand touring and other activities on its own, and since the war began, it has played in a hundred places or so never visited by an orchestra before . . . bringing music to the people's very doors.

In addition to the British-born conductors holding the fort, there was a newcomer—Richard Tauber ! Tauber had been for many years a frequent visitor to England, and had acquired British nationality shortly after the outbreak of war on his return from South Africa.

Even in the times when he travelled round the world as an opera star, a lieder singer, or with one of his own or Lehar's musical comedies, Tauber had always had a passion for conducting. From childhood on he acquired a thorough knowledge of the concert and opera repertoire, his father being for many years the Director of the *Stadttheater* at Chemnitz.

One day he approached the London Philharmonic Orchestra, proposing to do a concert with them for their benefit in which he was not only to sing but to conduct as well. Great astonishment, and I must confess, serious doubts, were expressed. Yet this concert proved a real success. Tauber was at once acknowledged to know his job, and this was the beginning of a musical friendship between the London Philharmonic Orchestra and the star tenor-conductor. They had always had an admiration for Tauber since their Covent Garden days, from which they remembered him as the only opera singer who succeeded in browbeating Sir Thomas, not by operatic temperament, but by sheer musicianship.

They remembered with amusement one stormy rehearsal at Covent Garden when Sir Thomas was conducting Smetana's *Bartered Bride* with a company recruited mostly from Prague, which included Tauber. At that time, Sir Thomas had his own views about this particular score, and was laying down the law to the baffled opera stars. Things were not going too well, and Sir Thomas's temper was rising as well as that of the singers', when Tauber came forward and, speaking on behalf of his colleagues, leant over the orchestral pit and said apologetically :

" Please, Sir Thomas, you must be more patient with us. Having sung this opera incorrectly for the past twenty-five years you cannot expect us to adapt ourselves to the correct way immediately." Sir Thomas, who always responds to wit and directness, saw the point at once !

Tauber's first provincial tour with the London Philharmonic Orchestra was a riotous success in more ways than one ; his Viennese humour, and his " Tauber cocktails " were most popular.

But there was a serious side to this activity. It is hard to realise the difficulties attendant on the provincial tours of the London Philharmonic Orchestra early in the war. Some of the most successful concerts seemed those when everything was most difficult, as at Burnley (in January 1940) when the small hall had been sold out on an obsolete seating plan, and Dr. Sargent's car was held up in a snowdrift on the moors. On that occasion, Thomas Matthews, then leader of the Orchestra, conducted at five minutes' notice a programme which included the first English performance of Aaron Copland's *Outdoor Overture*.

The following day, on their motor-coach trip to Barnsley, the entire party were fogbound, and missed the children's concert, arriving barely in time for the evening performance. At Preston, matters were worse—they arrived a whole day late, and at Wakefield the concert was cancelled because the van containing the instruments was lost by the railway company.

As the difficulty of travelling increased, so did that of finding adequate accommodation. In Stafford, for instance, most of the Orchestra spent their night wrapped in A.R.P. blankets on the dusty floor of the Town Hall in which they had given their concert.

Not the last to be afflicted by these orchestral Odysseys was the man in charge of the instruments. I wonder whether " connoisseurs of orchestra psychology " agree with me that the orchestra attendant —probably on account of his vast experience in dealing with unexpected situations—is frequently a resourceful man, full of character and originality. Where would the Berliners be without their Jastrau ? The Vienna Phil would loose all their charm without their Effenberger ; and—who could imagine the London Philharmonic Orchestra without Wally Knight, who has already been intimately connected with the Queen's Hall for over thirty years, and whose father preceded him there. Knight is always on the move from one end of the town to the other. In wartime London this is even more difficult for him than when he was continuously in demand at Covent Garden and at Queen's Hall simultaneously. He, too, has seen all sides of the war, and I remember a little bombed house in Soho being pointed out to me as the remains of what was once Wally's home. Thin and bony, with shrewd eyes, always wearing a cap, he firmly declares that if he doesn't get his daily double Scotch, he will not carry on. He is determinedly waiting for the day when the " Guv'nor " will be back. " You better write to him, that we want him here," he advised me. " He'll find me on the spot when he comes."

[1 9 4 1]

This is not the place to list all the important events which character-ised the year 1941 ; the Nazification of the Balkans and Greece, the loss of Crete, the war in Africa and the Middle East.

These were certainly the potent facts of that period, while the invasion of Russia on June 22nd by the Nazis and the attack on Hawaii, the Phillipines, Malaya, and Hong Kong by the Japanese in December are probably the most fateful events of that year.

In the beginning of 1941 although concert life had been resumed, occasional air raids occurred, and there was a need to feed air-raid wardens, rescue squads, firemen, demolition workers, and the bombed people themselves. All sorts of organisations, some of them American, as yet not active in the war, had presented mobile canteens working under the control of the Defence Services.

These canteens were served mainly by voluntary helpers, and the need of such canteens was more and more evident as time went by. Friends of the London Philharmonic Orchestra had the idea of pro-viding a mobile canteen, bearing the name of the Orchestra ; and Mr. James Smith and Mr. Keith Douglas, both on the Committee of the Royal Philharmonic Society, arranged for the provision of the " London Philharmonic Mobile Canteen ". This canteen was formally presented to the Mayor of St. Marylebone in front of Queen's Hall in the presence of Sir Henry Wood and the entire London Philharmonic Orchestra. On week-days it was on duty for defence workers, on Saturday afternoons and Sundays it was in action in front of Queen's Hall, decorated with posters advertising the concerts of the London Philharmonic Orchestra and London Symphony Orchestra. The canteen provided tea and biscuits for concert-goers, profits from which were given to the Lord Mayor of London's Air-Raid Distress Fund. Surprisingly large sums were collected in this way. Thus the London Philharmonic Orchestra contributed to the Lord Mayor's activities, rather than the Lord Mayor to those of the London Philharmonic Orchestra. Crowds gathered in the interval round the canteen, where popular Covent Garden singers were to be seen distributing tea or washing up the cups. The canteen went through bombs and air raids, and in emergency cases was often called out in the middle of the night to feed heavy rescue workers in the docks and East End, where terrible scenes were witnessed.

While in the first month of 1941 war life in England went on under a comparative lull, on the Continent a new phase of the war was in preparation ; and though on March 25th a moving and progressive celebration of the Greek Independence Day was held under the auspices of the Anglo-Hellenic League, only a fortnight later German armies invaded Yugo-Slavia and Greece, and the indestructible spirit of the brave Greek people was put to a hard test.

Neither did the lull for London last long ; the air attacks soon began again with renewed fury. We were in again for some rather serious weeks and on the unforgettable Wednesday and Saturday, April 16th and 19th, great damage was done to all parts of London. Red Lion Square was seriously hit again ; its lovely church was destroyed and many people were buried under its ruin in the shelter. The City was widely damaged.

On Saturday, May 10th, hundreds of planes raided the town ; the Chamber of the House of Commons, its Press Gallery, Strangers' and Ladies' Gallery were demolished. The heart of the British Empire's Government was hit. Westminster Abbey was seriously damaged and London's musical life received the severest blow which could befall it—Queen's Hall was destroyed.

Elgar's *Dream of Gerontius* had been given by the Royal Choral Society and the London Philharmonic Orchestra on the afternoon of Saturday, May 10th. There was to be a rehearsal next morning for the Sunday afternoon concert, and therefore nearly all the instruments had been left in the hall. When the Orchestra arrived on the Sunday morning the Queen's Hall was gone. It was completely gutted. Clouds of white smoke were seen pouring from the ruin ; hoses were winding in and out of the empty window frames and water was streaming everywhere. The charred remains of valuable instruments were being salvaged, a sad task in which the Orchestra joined. Double basses were being handed out in pieces and there were many instruments which could not be rescued at all.

When I arrived at the scene of destruction I found Mr. Charles Taylor, who had been manager of the Hall for many years. Mr. Taylor is always a busy man, but his quiet efficiency enables him to

run his affairs like a piece of smooth machinery and leaves him time
to spare to deal with exacting visitors. Consequently he was always
on the spot whenever anything was happening at or to Queen's
Hall. We shook hands, and though deeply moved, like a true
Britisher he did not reveal what this sight must have meant to him
personally. He just said : " It looks a bit untidy, doesn't it ? "
Mr. Alfred Matthews was also there—the head of the box-office,
who had worked at Queen's Hall for thirty-five years. He was
speechless. Many musicians and a great part of London's musical
public will agree with me that Mr. Matthews is more than a man—
he is an institution ! I had known him since my first visit to England
with Furtwängler. How often had I to appeal to him for his support
to get some friends into the sold-out hall for the Berlin Philharmonic's
Concerts ! How hard had we to fight with him to get some extra
chairs into the legendary corner behind the platform curtain, where
world-famous artists used often to sit instead of going into the hall !
Beloved corner, from which I saw the Berlin Philharmonic Orchestra
pass on to the platform, when I was still a guest in Great Britain, and
from which later on I received the nods and the " Hallo, Doctor " s'
from the London Philharmonic Orchestra players after a successful
concert ! Beloved corner, through which Sir Thomas passed before
stepping on the rostrum, giving me a last twinkle of the eye, and
from where, on his return I beamed at him and he responded in
silent understanding after the elation of a good performance !
Remembrances of all this shot through my mind as I stood there
with these two men, so intimately connected with the Queen's Hall.
Was all that really gone ? Inconceivable that Matthews should never
again be in the box-office, and that no more questions could be put
to him about the booking !

Sir Thomas never asked bluntly about the box-office receipts.
Not even to me would he have ever revealed that he was anxious
to know how a concert was going. What he did was to ring me up
in the early morning, discuss several other questions, and then casually
ask : " Have you seen Mr. Matthews ? " This was my cue. Matthews
was to Sir Thomas the infallible weathercock. Matthews, shortly
after the box-office had opened, knew exactly how a concert would
go. He was always frank, and I have never known him to be wrong.
Sir Thomas trusted him implicitly.

But the moment was badly chosen for such meditations. It was eleven o'clock in the morning. There was no hall and barely any instruments. The Orchestra held council and decided that they did not want to fail their public. The concert had to take place as announced.

By three o'clock in the afternoon the concert had been transferred to a substitute hall, and instruments had been borrowed at a moment's notice. The public, having no idea that Queen's Hall was no more, were arriving for the concert. It was necessary to extemporise a box-office, and the staff were to be seen going in and out of the ruins with handfuls of tickets and change under umbrellas, while water, hot enough to make tea with, was pouring through the ceiling. An emergency box-office was soon established on the pavement, and did a roaring trade transferring the tickets for the emergency hall. There was soon not a seat left. People were standing even right out on to the pavements, and hundreds were turned away—after having had a cup of tea from the London Philharmonic Orchestra's canteen which had been on duty for the Fire Brigade at Queen's Hall since early dawn, and had later on followed the Orchestra to the Duke's Hall of the Royal Academy of Music where this memorable concert took place. A member of the London Philharmonic Orchestra office staff, working voluntarily on the Sunday, recalls Thomas Russell coming into the office and saying fervently, " I left them playing like angels ".

The day passed with the elation which arises from a grave situation. The next morning, however, the grim reality had to be faced : the Orchestra, during the week, continuously played in the Provinces and in blitzed areas, but the Saturdays and Sundays were devoted to the London concerts which, owing to the growing demand for music had been booked at Queen's Hall throughout the summer. There was no doubt that these concerts would have to be carried through, though the Orchestra had lost its hall. Eventually all musical activities, including that year's Proms, in which the London Philharmonic Orchestra took part for the first time, were transferred to the Albert Hall, where, incidentally, both Mr. Taylor and Mr. Matthews now occupy their respective Queen's Hall positions.

Yet the most urgent need of the moment was the question of the instruments. The B.B.C. had kindly informed the public of the Orchestra's difficulties. From the moment of that appeal there was no peace. There was a continuous procession from every quarter. People queued up to the Orchestra's office laden with violins and violas. Cellos were deposited outside the doors. The Orchestra had meanwhile left with borrowed instruments for provincial concerts fixed up long before, and wherever they appeared, people turned up with instruments ! During their absence the three office telephones rang incessantly with people offering instruments, and a special person had to be engaged to deal with these calls alone. By every post hundreds of letters arrived about instruments only, and an emergency staff of voluntary helpers spent days and days in opening the letters.

From a purely human point of view it was a great privilege to read these letters. A wave of warm and spontaneous feeling poured out of them : a feeling of real sympathy and ready help which came from all sections of the public. Dignified letters arrived offering valuable old instruments, some of which were precious heirlooms. An old man wrote from a Yorkshire village ; he had no instrument to give, but he loved to mend them, and had unlimited time and patience for it. Could we accept his help in this way ? A bus-driver came all the way from Kent clasping a brown paper parcel under his arm. "It is a fiddle," he said. "I cannot bear to think that owing to the loss of his instrument, a player should be out of work. I know what that means."

There is no room to record in detail the moving generosity in which provincial orchestras joined with the general public. We filed about 3000 letters. We had about 1000 instruments, and with the consent of the owners were able to supply the needs of others.

During the same night in which Queen's Hall was destroyed, 36 Red Lion Square was hit for the third time. The house had long since been uninhabitable, but the residue of my furniture and other possessions had been stored in the basement. A direct hit from a high explosive razed the house and the adjoining buildings to the grounds. Nothing remained but rubble.

It would be an affectation to say that the loss of everything one possesses, of one's books, one's music, and one's treasured family heirlooms is other than a great sorrow. Although one shares such sorrow with millions of others, one can never quite recover from it.

Yet to have witnessed a disaster such as that of Queen's Hall, and to have experienced the deep feeling and human kindness that it evoked, gave one strength to bear one's own personal losses and made me proud to live among a brave and kind people.

Great emotions seemed to dwarf all others at the time, but before leaving this blitz period I must recollect a small incident which occurred at the time.

As I have mentioned, Sir Thomas Beecham's musical library, a collection of priceless scores and orchestral parts, had, after the exit from Covent Garden, been housed at Boosey & Hawkes' premises in Denman Street. This building had received a direct hit in a previous blitz which tore off the front of the house. But with the capriciousness of fate, no great damage had been done to the interior. The same night that Queen's Hall was destroyed, a heavy bomb fell in front of the Denman Street premises, tearing up the street, and wrecking the building. As soon as I heard of this, I rushed down. How would I find the treasures entrusted to my care for the use of London Philharmonic Orchestra ? I arrived on the scene ; demolition squads were busy, joined by Boosey & Hawkes' staff, in rescuing what they could from the ruins, which were announced to be unsafe. " What about the library ? " I shouted across the crater which barred my way. The demolition man raised his arm and pointed to a wall left standing gaunt against the open sky. There, preserved by a miracle, stood the library shelves. " Your stuff is safe, Miss," he said. Then he helped me across, and gave me his hand ; with him I climbed up the shaky building and with immense relief started to rescue this collection of music, the fruit of so many years of work.

[1 9 4 2]

Chapter 46

THE SOVIET resistance drew the Luftwaffe to the East, and Londonders thankfully recognised the milestone in English war life which was marked by the ending of the blitz period. More and more this " fortress life " adjusted itself to the conditions of a long war period. Life in London especially became increasingly interesting. The different National Governments and groups temporarily residing in England all gradually developed their political, social, and cultural activities. Concerts and lectures were given, and meetings were held attended by members of many nations. The organisation of the London Philharmonic Orchestra was well equipped to cope with a number of national manifestations. Among them may be mentioned a brilliant series of French concerts given at the instance of the French National Committee. These drew large and appreciative crowds. The Orchestra recorded some Polish music for the Polish Government, and at the request of the Society for Cultural Relations with U.S.S.R., organised a number of interesting orchestral concerts of Russian music, which included the first performance in England of Khatchaturian's now popular Piano Concerto, Shostakovich's Fifth Symphony, and other works. The centenary of Grieg's birth was fittingly marked by a concert at the Albert Hall at which the London Philharmonic Orchestra played.

I myself, being on the Committee of the International Women's Service Groups in Great Britain—a group comprising women from thirty-two nations united in Britain during the war—arranged a concert at the Wigmore Hall at which talent from seven of these nations was delightfully presented.

There is much more that could be told about life in wartime England, but this would go beyond the scope of this book. It is a strange life in many respects, but as is so frequently the case, unusual conditions are often the source of new energies and a new strength in everybody.

In October 1942 the London Philharmonic Orchestra celebrated its tenth anniversary. Ten years ! How short this period seems in comparison to the existence of the other orchestras with which I have been connected—with the hundred years' tradition of the Vienna Philharmonic, and the fifty years of the Berliners. And yet, what a gallant struggle is comprised in these ten years ; the struggle for acknowledgement, the struggle for artistic existence, and always the struggle for life in its plainest meaning. The Vienna Orchestra, whatever its difficulties might have been, had always had a backbone because they were at the same time the Opera Orchestra. The Berlin Philharmonic—a concert orchestra only—also had its struggles—though they were less crucial. Yet it had no choice but to rush into Hitler's arms and become *Reichsorchester* in order to save its existence and its carefully planned contracts with its members which, pledging them for a limited number of services per week, still left them enough time for practising, for playing chamber-music, and for the important task of teaching the rising generation, and which, last, but not least, guaranteed their pensions.

The London Philharmonic has had none of these facilities. The *esprit-de-corps* of its members had often to replace the material advantages other orchestras had to offer. In this way alone they have held the fort—often under conditions unworthy in view of their services to England's musical life. This was, in point of fact, known—and on their tenth anniversary they received messages and congratulations from all over the world—and there was a unanimous feeling of admiration for their achievement which was perhaps best expressed in a letter from Sir Thomas Beecham, their founder :

". . . I have been following your activities during the past two years with pride and admiration. That you would maintain your pre-eminent standard of excellence I have always taken for granted. But your sturdy independence and unflagging resolution to make yourselves an indispensable element in the life of the nation have raised you from the status of private enterprise to that of a public institution. I trust that this honorable achievement is adequately realised and valued by our fellow-citizens, especially those in whose power it is to make hard and winding paths of high endeavour easier and straighter for the intrepid traveller on them. . . .

England makes many plans for post-war developments and changes for the future. Perhaps a way may be found to preserve artistic " freedom and liberty " of action by a wise support, without the adverse consequences suffered by many famous orchestras on the Continent. Perhaps England will create a new way to support the arts, a way worthy of matching that which she fights for ; and which will avoid the evil of governmental dictatorship on the one hand, and financial want with its contingent commercial exigencies on the other.

And so, while the problems of wartime England pass before my eyes, I realise more than ever what is England's mission to the present world, and that in England a banner is hoisted which signals to the world in the making.

Those who, like myself, have experienced the agonies and anguish of persecution will join in my gratitude for living in a country free in spirit. Many a time I find myself noticing incidents that one takes for granted in England, and finding myself forced to the question : Why has the German people, who after all have great qualities, thrown all this away—and allowed themselves to be robbed of all that is finest in life ?

How ironical it is that a movement—describing itself as " National Socialism "—should give the German people an empty façade of dictatorial splendour but should destroy in them the warmth of humanity and the dignity of simplicity—all that is natural and free.

During the Christmas of 1942 I had an experience which symbolised for me the difference between life in Germany as I had witnessed it since 1933, and life in England. The traditional " Carol-concert " of the Royal Choral Society under the direction of Dr. Malcolm Sargent was sold out. I asked Dr. Sargent whether he could get me in, as I wished my mother to hear for once the full Albert Hall singing the lovely age-old Christmas carols. He sent me two seats in his box and I sat down with my mother. Suddenly the door opened, and a lady in grey asked whether this was Dr. Sargent's box. We immediately recognised Mrs. Churchill. She was with her daughter, who was in the uniform of the A.T.S., and smilingly tried to prevent us from giving her the front seats in the box.

With what a tremendous panoply and show Frau Goebbels or Frau Emmy Goering would have surrounded themselves on a similar occasion ! But here was the wife of the British Prime Minister, bearing a proud and historic name, quietly slipping in to share a box with two refugees. This was democracy : this was England.

And now my tale draws to a close. I am sitting in the sun at Adrian Beecham's farm in Warwickshire. The war is not yet over. From the blue sky the drone of bombers setting out for the Continent plays a sinister descant to the thorough-bass of the throb of the tractor drawing the plough. But the earth goes on in its eternal rhythm, the daffodils sway in the breeze, the birds build their nests, and the lambs nestle beside their mothers. Horses plod across the meadows, and the farmer sows his seed. Upstairs in the nursery a new generation is growing up.

May it grow into a world where what is great and noble in mankind can be as free as the daffodils in the wind.

" COMPTON SCORPION MANOR,   *April* 1943.
        WARWICKSHIRE."

Index

Berlin State Opera, 21–2, 87, 99, 104,
142–3, 160, 181, 207, 223, 224, 261–2,
263,283, 318, 333
Berchtesgaden, 102, 325, 326
Berlioz, H., 360
Bielefeld, 65
Biggs, Edith, 381–2
Bilse'sche Orchester, 27–8
Bismarck, Countess Beatrix, 338–9
Bismarck, Count O. von, 29, 282
Blomberg, Field-Marshal von, 237
Bockelmann, R., 138, 290
Bodanzky, A., 90, 133, 184
Boehm, K., 220
Bonnet, G., 344
Boosey & Hawkes, 364
Bose, F. von, 131
Boston Symphony Orchestra, 39
Boulogne, 370
Boult, Sir A., 317, 319, 376–7
Bradley, F., 372
Brahms Centenary, 69, 85, 86, 319
Brahms Festivals, 22, 85
Brahms, J., 8, 20, 27, 41–2, 304
Breslau, 40
British Broadcasting Corporation, 35, 228,
300–1, 317, 319, 390
Symphony Concerts of, 228
Television programmes, 289
British Council, the, 227, 253
Brockhaus, Max, 35, 237
Bruckner, A., 42, 303
Brussel, R., 48, 191
Buenos Aires, 352
Bülow, Cosima, 55
Bülow, H. von, 27, 28, 29, 31, 53–4, 62, 282
Bülow, Marie von, 30
Burney, C., 7
Busch, A., 76, 92, 111, 346
Busch, F., 92
Buxbaum, F., 303, 330

CALAIS, 370
Cambridge Theatre, the, 315
Cambridge University Library, 334
Capell, R., 334
Carl Rosa Company, the, 299
Caruso, 271
Casals, P., 69, 85, 91, 319, 358
Casella, A., 107
Cassadó, G., 107
Cebotari, Maria, 262
Cerruti, Elisabetha, 107, 130, 172–3
Cerruti, V., 107, 118, 130–1, 172–3
Chaliapin, F., 308
Chamberlain, Sir A., 226, 281
Chamberlain, Lady A., 226, 254, 256
Chamberlain, Eva, 54–5, 122, 206, 307

Chamberlain, Houston S., 55
Chamberlain, Rt. Hon. Neville, 277, 317,
344–5, 352, 354, 355, 370
Chaplin, Charlie, 51
Cheney, S., 272
Christie, J., 316, 327
Churchill, Clementine, 395
Churchill, Rt. Hon. W. S., 370
Ciano, Count G., 119–20
Ciano, Countess Edda, 120–1
Cincinatti Symphony Orchestra, 299
Clerk, Sir G., 281
Coleman, W., 267–8
Cologne, 40, 247, 248, 250
Colombo, Anita, 34, 50
Concertgebouw Orchestra, 20, 322
Copenhagen, 33
Cortot, A., 73, 91
Couvreux, Lucienne, 17 -2, 190
Covent Garden Opera, ς, 125–6, 163,
177–8, 186 *et seq.*
Coronation Season at, 195, 201, 207, 216,
218–20
English Society and, 266
International Season (1938), 335, 336,
353, 357
staff personalities, 265–79
Coventry, 328
Croxford, J., 272
Curtius, L., 18
Czech Opera, 357
Czech Philharmonic Orchestra, 315
Czechoslovakia, 336, 342–5, 357

Daily Telegraph, 316, 353
Daladier, E., 344
Danzig, 363
Decline of the West, 43
Denmark, 369
Destinn, Emmy, 271
Deutsche Allgemeine Zeitung, 141
Dibelius, Prof. M., 305
Die Meistersinger, 70
Dirksen, H. von, 333
Dlabac, F., 46, 330
Dodd, William E., 171
Doernberg, A. von, 303
Dollfuss, E., 85, 88, 133, 326
Assassination of, 313
Don Giovanni, 241
Douglas, K., 292, 387
Dresden, 40, 237, 264
Dresden State Opera, 228, 262
Dufour-Feronce, A., 35
Dunkirk, 370

EBENHAUSEN, 157, 161
Ebert, C., 125

A Mingled Chime

SIR THOMAS BEECHAM

This vivid, eccentric, and quirky memoir of his early life has all the characteristics of brilliance and passion that brought Sir Thomas Beecham to the forefront of British orchestral and opera conductors. His prolific output of recordings has ensured his reputation as conductor for posterity; this witty autobiography performs the same office for the man himself.

'The big tenor bell in *A Mingled Chime* is the art of music and it is rung by the artist who of all British executant musicians has established his claim internationally to the title of genius, perhaps the first Englishman to be ranked among the great conductors of the world. The smaller bells are education (public school, university, conservatoire), politics, business, literature and painting, rung by a man of the world, a connoisseur and a wit . . . A mingled chime indeed, containing a detailed and sober account of years of effort to give the British public the best opera and orchestral music . . . containing penetrating musical criticism and equally just criticism of men, shrewd and without malice. Like Papageno with his chime of magic bells he sets us dancing to his tune.'   **Times Literary Supplement**

'It would be useless to attempt a summary of the good stories that Beecham relates.'   **Listener**

'The author's innumerable anecdotes are told with characteristic wit. His comments on famous composers and performers are fascinating, often provocative, but always shrewd and worthy of being closely pondered. The whole book is of extraordinary interest.'   **Manchester Guardian**

'What he has given us in the way of autobiography whets our appetite for more. He writes quite as well as he speaks, and we all know what that means . . . the story of his own myriad musical activities is told without the least exaggeration.'
Sunday Times

Also in *The Lively Arts* series

Chaliapin

MAXIM GORKY

In the world of singing, and especially in opera, few names can cast a spell equal to that of Chaliapin, the great Russian bass who died fifty years ago in April 1938. There can be few autobiographies as enthralling or as perceptive as this one, for it was originally told to Chaliapin's close friend, Maxim Gorky, one of the most compelling novelists and dramatists of this century. Gorky eventually composed this narrative from those extensive conversations, and the result is an absorbing account of victory over early deprivation to final world-wide acclaim and recognition. It is still possible to hear Chaliapin's incomparable voice on recordings. Now we can read his words.

'Chaliapin was the motive force for my own career, and I have humbly walked in his shadow. This book explains both his art and his indomitable spirit. When I first sang in *Boris Godunov*, his interpretation of excerpts was always on my gramophone. With all superb artists, a wealth of experience must be brought to bear on all their creations. Here we discover where that golden voice was mined.'   **Boris Christoff**

'I believe that Chaliapin's last apperance in opera was at the Theatre Royal, Drury Lane, in June 1914, the eve of the First World War. Yet even those who never heard him in the flesh can recognize his unmatched authority and power from early acoustic recordings. This book is some compensation for a new generation, who are given memorable views of a personality that was both larger than life but could yet encompass the smallest nuance of emotion and humour.'
Sir John Barbirolli

'Chaliapin was my hero when I was young, and I only regret that he did not live for me to write anything for him. This book should be in the hands of any singer who takes his vocation seriously. I know of no other that so searchingly explores the making of great art, and no one who could have assembled the words as brilliantly as my friend, Maxim Gorky.'
Dimitri Shostakovitch

'A story that haunts the mind as powerfully as the voice reaches our soul.'   **Boris Pasternak**

Liszt

SIR SACHEVERELL SITWELL

Sacheverell Sitwell, who celebrated his 90th birthday in November 1987, is the modern writer most in tune with the Romantic age – as his many books on its art, its architecture and ballet have shown. His study of Liszt is the most sympathetic and engaging to have appeared this century, Sitwell making this dazzling and protean musician a living figure. Over the last three decades, the reputation and the repertoire of Liszt have been greatly enlarged through the interpretations of such pianists as Arrau, Brendel and Bolet, and conductors like Haitink. Liszt led a life that was in keeping with his fiery and tumultuous talent, and no one has been so adept as Sitwell in making coherent the conflicting strains of his temperament.

'Mr Sitwell's ability to recreate scenes from myth or history, his imaginative skill in restating the themes of music and painting in literary terms, his facility with the devices of nostalgia, are all formidable. His senses range widely, his knowledge and memory of all the arts are remarkable.'   **The Times**

'He is not a writer of any particular age or fashion or school. He is peculiarly and refreshingly alone.'
                                                    Pamela Hansford-Johnson

'There is no doubt that subsequent research, especially amongst Hungarian archives, will amend some of the facts of Liszt's life. But this biography will never be wholly superseded, for Sitwell brings to it so much insight, affection, and intuitive understanding of this chameleon man.'
                                                    Dame Myra Hess

'Liszt and I could not be more different men. But he was my greatest Hungarian forbear, and my mentor at the piano from childhood onwards. This book summarizes for me what Liszt meant to his own generation, and why we neglect him at our peril. He made the piano that I use the expressive instrument of the soul.'   **Bela Bartok**

Also in The Lively Arts series

A Life in the Theatre

TYRONE GUTHRIE

Tyrone Guthrie was one of the first British theatre directors to be as prominent as the actors in his plays – and they included Olivier, Gielgud, Richardson, Redgrave and Edith Evans. This autobiography, irreverent and opinionated, is justifiably considered the wittiest and most candid recollection of theatrical life in this country ever published by an insider.

'Tyrone Guthrie's book is a stimulating and delightful auto-biography, full of the characteristic energy and brilliance of the author.' **Sir John Gielgud**

'The most exciting and stimulating person in the theatre today, Guthrie's influence has extended from the British Isles to Australia, from Israel to Finland, from Canada to Texas. He is not only a great man of the theatre – an unpredictable and sometimes wayward genius and adventurer – but a great man in himself. His autobiography gives us a handsome slice of the man and his work. The omissions in it are typical of the man – his innumerable acts of kindness to young and old, his generosity, and the fact that so many of us owe him, largely, our careers.' **Sir Alec Guinness**

'One of the most important books on the Theatre that I have read for many a year. It is informative, witty and unpretentious, and I am sure it will be as fascinating and entertaining for the great public as it is for those of us who belong to the Theatre.' **Sir Noël Coward**

'Tyrone Guthrie is famous for his light touch when he handles a production in the theatre. Now he has produced a book of memoirs: coming from such authority they are of necessity interesting; they are also light, and easy to read.' **Sir Ralph Richardson**

'Dr Guthrie's book is hilarious, engrossing, shrewd, ironic, informative, disputatious and inspiring – a perfect mirror, in fact, of the man himself.' **New York Times**

Also in *The Lively Arts* series

Beerbohm Tree

HESKETH PEARSON

Before he found acclaim and recognition as the most entertaining biographer this century, Hesketh Pearson had been an actor, beginning his career under Beerbohm Tree. That combination of personal experience and theatrical insight makes this portrait unique — and it includes helpful material provided by Max Beerbohm, the actor's half-brother. Tree was a colossus of the theatre, as actor-manager, as kindly paterfamilias to his colleagues, and as absent-minded eccentric around whom anecdotes congregated.

'No actor has been accorded a finer memorial than this biography. It not only makes us aware of his great professional achievements, but it reveals a character who was both endearing and infuriating to his friends. He had no foes.'

James Agate

'An actor's fame tends to fade as the last curtain falls. So Hesketh Pearson has accomplished an invaluable task in ensuring that the applause for Beerbohm Tree lives on. His life was as rich, and varied, and individual as his appearances on stage, and it is captured in all its diversity here.'

Sir Neville Cardus

'One is tempted to pull out the plums of anecdote from this cornucopia of a book, and I am sure that many will be told as long as there are actors to tell them. Tree had the knack of putting his foot in it off stage, whilst keeping his stance steady on the boards. Hesketh Pearson captures him in all his grandeur and occasional absurdity.' **W. A. Darlington**

'The only thing missing from this splendidly entertaining book and my enjoyment of it is regret that I was not able to see the great man himself in full Shakespearian flight. But Pearson has a knack of suggesting what we have missed, and that is some compensation.' **Sir Ralph Richardson**

Kean

GILES PLAYFAIR

Edmund Kean, of all British actors, appeals most strongly to the imagination. What is known to be true, as this classic biography reveals, is so bizarre that no fiction could have a stranger hero. From a life of vagabondage, he became a strolling player until he reached London as Shylock at Drury Lane: his genius was immediately acclaimed. Hazlitt recorded the performance for posterity and Kean went on to the great Shakespearian roles, such as Macbeth and Iago. But his character was untamably wild, his life crammed with scandalous and uncouth exploits, and that, combined with a propensity for missing performances, turned the critics and playgoers who first idolized him into detractors. Kean lived a mere forty-three years, but his life has proved a rich subject for playwrights as distinct as Dumas and Sartre.

'The greatest artist is he who is greatest in the highest reaches of his art, even though he may lack the qualities necessary for the adequate execution of some minor details. It is not by his faults, but by his excellence, that we measure a great man. . . Thus estimated, Edmund Kean was incomparably the greatest actor I have ever seen.'
G. H. Lewes

'It was plain that a man of genius had lighted on the stage. To those who had the spirit and candour to hail the lucky omen, the recollection of that moment of startling, yet welcome surprise, will always be a proud and satisfactory one. . . Besides the excellence of the impassioned parts of Mr Kean's acting, there is a flexibility and indefiniteness of outline about it . . . of all Mr Kean's performances, we think this the most faultless and least *mannered*, always excepting his *Othello*, which is equally perfect and twenty times more powerful.'
William Hazlitt on Kean's Shylock

'Mr Kean's *Othello* is, we suppose, the finest piece of acting in the world. It is impossible either to describe or praise it adequately. . . In fact almost every scene or sentence in this extraordinary exhibition is a master-piece of natural passion.'
William Hazlitt on Kean's *Othello*

'He is almost the only actor who does not spoil Shakespeare.'
William Hazlitt on Kean's *Richard III*